DIGITAL DESIGN
AND COMPUTER
ORGANIZATION

DIGITAL DESIGN
AND COMPUTER
ORGANIZATION

HASSAN A. FARHAT

CRC PRESS

Boca Raton   London   New York   Washington, D.C.

Library of Congress Cataloging-in-Publication Data

Farhat, Hassan A.
   Digital design and computer organization / Hassan A. Farhat.
        p.   cm.
   Includes index.
   ISBN 0-8493-1191-8 (alk. paper)
      1. Digital electronics. 2. Logic circuits—Design and construction. 3. Computer
organization. I. Title.

   TK7868.D5F37 2004
   004.2'2—dc22   2003055805

This book contains information obtained from authentic and highly regarded sources. Reprinted material is quoted with permission, and sources are indicated. A wide variety of references are listed. Reasonable efforts have been made to publish reliable data and information, but the author and the publisher cannot assume responsibility for the validity of all materials or for the consequences of their use.

Visit the CRC Press Web site at www.crcpress.com

Dedication

TO MY FATHER

Acknowledgment

Sincere thanks go to the two acquiring editors from CRC Press: Nora Konopka as the main editor and Gerald Papke for his initial letter of encouragement and early correspondence. Nora's deadline extensions and kindness have made this task a reality. Many thanks for all their help go to the textbook's project editor, Gerry Jaffe, as well as to Jamie Sigal, Dawn Snider, and the other staff members who worked on the textbook.

Thanks to the staff of Electronics Workbench for supplying the software to be used with the text: in particular, Ian Suttie, vice president of sales, Joan Lewis-Milne, director of educational marketing, Scott Duncan, and the technical support staff that tested the circuits.

Thanks go to my students for their various inputs. Finally, sincere thanks and love go to my wife, son, and daughter for their encouragement, help, and understanding during the many hours it took to complete the textbook.

Preface

Digital Design and Computer Organization is an introduction to digital design with application to computer organization. The tools studied in the text are used in the design of digital systems. Many systems today are digital in nature. This includes digital cameras and digital computers, for example. The book is suitable for students majoring in Computer Science, Electrical Engineering, and Computer Engineering. The contributions of the text are as follows:

1. The emphasis of the textbook is on logic design with minimal reference to electrical properties. This is an advantage to computer science students that have had no previous training in electrical engineering. The text assumes no previous knowledge of electrical components (elementary coverage is included and is optional). Electrical engineering students can also benefit from the textbook since, if needed, the topics can be complemented with lab supplements that consider electrical constraints.

2. Outside the use of a schematic capture tool used to simulate designs from primitive gates, the textbook is written to be vendor independent. Minimal coverage of actual chips and functionality is considered. As a result, the discussion is presented in general terms that emphasize the principles of digital design.

3. Topics are covered in the context of computer organization. The last two chapters of the text introduce instruction set architecture and present a complete design of a simple AC-based CPU. In this context students relate the principles of digital design studied to the topic of computer organization.

4. To enhance topics coverage, the majority of the circuits presented in the text are found in the accompanying CD. These circuits were designed and tested using the Electronics Workbench package. Many of the circuits found in the text are screen captures from the package. The Electronics Workbench package was chosen due to its friendly graphical-user interface. With minimal previous knowledge, the student can start the design process from truth tables, for example, and progress through the textbook to more complex design. The included circuits provide students the ability to simulate the functionality of the circuits in a hands-on fashion.

5. Topics are introduced in a gradual fashion. The coverage starts with simple cases and builds on these cases to introduce general cases.

Chapter 1 covers numbers representations and arithmetic in different bases. The topics covered include positional number systems, data types and ranges, conversion between the different bases, arithmetic in different bases, coding, and floating-point number representation. Radix complements and diminished radix complements are introduced. Arithmetic using this representation, however, is deferred until Chapter 5.

Chapter 2 includes introduction to Boolean algebra and its properties, algebraic simplification of Boolean expressions, gate representations in terms of design and analysis. In addition, the chapter includes elementary electrical topics. The concepts of voltage, current, and resistance are introduced. These are then followed with Kirchhoff's laws, voltage division, RC circuits, and applications in CMOS gate design.

Chapter 3 begins with coverage of the canonical forms of Boolean functions and logical completeness. The design of circuits from canonical forms is considered; logical completeness is used to introduce additional gates and to introduce different two-level designs. Design automation tools and the Electronics Workbench are discussed.

Chapter 4 covers K-maps and the tabular method of minimizations for completely and incompletely specified functions. The chapter also includes multiple-output function minimization.

Chapter 5 deals with arithmetic and logic circuits. Topics covered include binary adders, look-ahead carry generators, magnitude comparators, binary subtractors, and multipliers. In addition, the chapter includes discussion of radix arithmetic, and allowable ranges are discussed in detail. The discussion includes the design of adders/subtractors based on the operands representation. The chapter concludes by designing an arithmetic logic unit in relation to computer organization. Bit-wise logic operations and multiplexers, as source selectors, are discussed in the context of the ALU (arithmetic logic unit) design.

Chapter 6 covers decoders, encoders, multiplexers, and demultiplexers. The design of Boolean functions, from decoder and multiplexers, and how to build larger units from smaller ones is covered. In addition, the chapter covers programmable logic devices (Read Only Memory [ROM], Programmable Logic Array [PLA], and Programmable Array Logic® [PAL®]). The design using diodes as a conceptual realization at lower levels is given in the chapter as well. Here students can use the Electronics Workbench to experiment. Switches are included to simulate the process of programming the devices.

Chapter 7 starts the discussion of sequential circuits. It covers latches, latches behavioral description (characteristic tables, equations, state diagrams, and timing diagrams), gated latches, master-slave flip-flops, ones catching, edge-triggered flip-flops, and introduces sequential circuit analysis.

Chapter 8 covers the design of sequential circuits by relating it to analysis as covered in the previous chapter. Here, the constraints on the design are relaxed. Design based on excitation equations is given, followed by design from characteristic equations and design from word problems. The chapter includes discussions of the two machine representations, Mealy and Moore, and how one converts from one machine to the other. In addition, state minimization is covered in the chapter.

Chapter 9 includes the design of registers, counters, and general-purpose registers/counters. The chapter introduces memory design by designing larger memory from smaller memory first. This is then followed with design of memory cells and the internal design of a static RAM. The chapter concludes with a discussion of register files and relates the discussion to CPU organization and the ALU designed in Chapter 5.

Chapter 10 is an introduction to instruction set architectures. Two different architectures (AC-based and general-purpose register-based) are discussed. Instructions formats in relation to both architectures are covered. Covered as well are translation of assembly instructions into machine instructions and the different addressing modes. Finally, the concept of macros as an alternative to hardware instructions is introduced. The homework section of this chapter includes discussion of stack-based instruction set architecture.

The book concludes with Chapter 11, where the design of a simple AC-based CPU is considered. To do this, we introduce the concept of a micro-operation and register-transfer languages. The design of register-transfer languages using direct connections and bus connections is then covered. This is followed with instruction set completeness, the instruction set of the AC-based CPU, the data-path and memory connections, and the control unit organization. The design of the CPU is then covered by considering the design of the combinational part of the control unit.

The instructor resources for the text include a solutions manual to the exercises given at the end of the chapters. This is in addition to a detailed set of lecture notes supplied in PowerPoint format.

The textbook is written to be suitable as 3-credit hour or 4-credit hour course. In a traditional 3-credit hour course, the minimal suggested topics coverage is

Chapter 1

Chapter 2 (Sections 2.6 through 2.11 are optional)

Chapter 3

Chapter 4

Chapter 5

Chapter 6 (Section 6.8 is optional)

Chapter 7

Chapter 8 (optional)

Chapter 9 (Sections 9.8 and 9.9 are optional)

The optional sections in Chapters 2 and 6 deal with the introductions to electrical circuits and designs of programmable logic devices using diodes. The intention is to give the reader with no electrical engineering background an elementary introduction to the topics. Chapter 8 deals with design of sequential circuits. Some instructors may cover the topic in a second digital course.

In a 4-credit hour course, the remaining chapters can be covered. This may be suitable in computer science curricula with two courses in the hardware area (digital design and computer architecture).

Author

Hassan A. Farhat received his Ph.D. in Computer Science and Engineering in 1988 from the University of Nebraska at Lincoln. His research interests are in very-large-scale integration (VLSI) testing and computer graphics. Among the publications in VLSI testing, Dr. Farhat received best paper contributor award at the IEEE International Conference in Computer Design (ICCD) in 1988. His teaching interests are in the hardware track (digital design, computer organization, and computer architecture); VLSI testing; and computer graphics.

Table of Contents

1

Numbers in Different Bases

1.1 Digital and Analog Data

This textbook is about the principle of digital computer design. The term "digital" is a characterization of data in a set. We say a set of data is digital if it contains a finite set of elements. Examples of digital data are the sets {0, 1}, {on, off}, {red, blue, green}, and {x: x is a decimal digit}. In each of the examples, the set of data is digital since the number of elements in the set is finite.

The set of data is analog if the set contains a continuous interval of data elements. As a result, the set of data contains infinite number of elements since continuous intervals contain infinite data elements. Examples of analog data are the set of real numbers, the set of all colors, and the set of real numbers between 0 and 10.

We often approximate analog data by converting the data into digital format. For example, time is analog. When communicating time, we usually give time in hours and minutes. An example is the time display on computer monitors.

Our discussion of digital design relates to digital computers. As the name implies, computers are digital, which means they process digital data. In addition, computers are programmable, i.e., the computer can be instructed to perform specific tasks according to a user, the programmer. The program is stored in the computer in digital format. The format is a sequence of 0 and 1 digits called bits.

1.2 Coding

Consider the schematic given in Figure 1.2.1 of a computer with a keyboard, a processing unit, and a monitor. When programming, the user may enter the program or data using the keyboard.

Note that the set that contains all keyboard data is digital since it contains a finite set of elements.

Since the computer processes binary data (data composed of 0s and 1s), the following three steps occur:

1. The keyboard data is encoded into a sequence of bits where letters, digits, and other symbols are assigned a binary code, code word. Encoding is a mapping that associates with each object in some set a unique element (code word) in some other set. In this case, the set of objects is the set of keyboard data. We would like to associate a binary code sequence with all keyboard data.

2. The second step in this process is for the computer to perform the needed task. This occurs in the central processing unit (CPU), which includes special electrical circuits that accomplish these tasks.

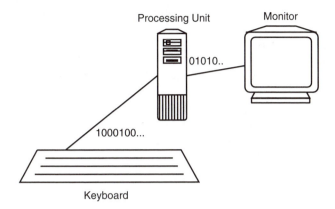

FIGURE 1.2.1
A Computer with a Keyboard, Processing Unit, and Monitor

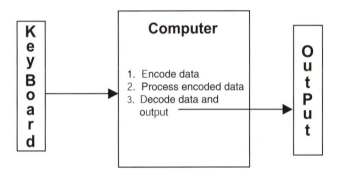

FIGURE 1.2.2
The Three Steps of Encoding, Processing, and Decoding

3. The last step is to convert the binary results back into user format, for example, in decimal digits and alphabets. This step is called decoding and is the reverse of encoding. Figure 1.2.2 shows the three steps.

Discussing the details of the three steps is the subject of this text. Since computers process binary data, this will be our starting point.

1.3 Positional Number System

In positional number systems, a number, N, is characterized by a base, b, also called a radix, and the coefficients $(0, 1, ..., (b - 1))$ that make up the number. In decimal numbers (base 10), the base is implicit and can be omitted if needed. When other bases are considered, the base is explicitly identified in the representation as $(N)_b$, or N_b, where b is the base.

For example, in base 10 the coefficients of N are 0, 1, ..., 9. Similarly, in base 5 the coefficients of the number are 0, 1, 2, 3, and 4, and for base 16 the coefficients of the number are the decimal digits 0 through 9 and the letters of the alphabet A, B, C, D, E, and F, representing the decimal numbers 10, 11, 12, 13, 14, and 15, respectively. The symbols are needed since the base of the number exceeds base 10. The first six letters of the alphabet are customarily used in addition to the ten decimal digits.

We consider two formats, numbers with no radix point and numbers with radix (decimal) points.

1.3.1   Numbers without Radix Point

For a given number $(N)_b = n_i n_{(i-1)}...n_0$ in some base, b, the expanded polynomial representation of the number is

$$(N)_b = n_i \times b^i + n_{(i-1)} \times b^{(i-1)} + n_{(i-2)} \times b^{(i-2)} + ... + n_0 \times b^0$$

The expanded representation is used to convert a number, in an arbitrary base, to the equivalent representation in base 10. The following three examples make use of the above equation.

Example 1.3.1

1. Write the decimal number 1023 in expanded form according to the format given above.
2. Find the base 10 values of
   i. $(1023)_5$
   ii. $(10111)_2$
   iii. $(23AF)_{16}$

Solution of part 1: The number is composed of four digits with $b = 10$ and $i = 3$. Hence, using the equation above, we have $n_3 = 1$, $n_2 = 0$, $n_1 = 2$, and $n_0 = 3$. The expanded number is obtained by substituting these values above to obtain $(1023)_{10} = 1 \times 10^3 + 0 \times 10^2 + 2 \times 10^1 + 3 \times 10^0$

Solution of part 2:

1. Here, we have $i = 3$ and $b = 5$. Hence

$$(1023)_5 = 1 \times 5^3 + 0 \times 5^2 + 2 \times 5^1 + 3 \times 5^0$$

$$= 125 + 0 + 10 + 3 = (138)_{10}$$

2. $(10111)_2 = 1 \times 2^4 + 0 \times 2^3 + 1 \times 2^2 + 1 \times 2^1 + 1 \times 2^0$

$$= 16 + 0 + 4 + 2 + 1 = (23)_{10}$$

3. $(23AF)_{16} = (2 \times 16^3) + (3 \times 16^2) + (A \times 16^1) + (F \times 16^0)$

$$= (2 \times 16^3) + (3 \times 16^2) + (10 \times 16^1) + (15 \times 16^0)$$

$$= 8192 + 768 + 160 + 15 = (9135)_{10}$$

1.3.2 Numbers with Radix Point

A number, $(N)b$, with a radix point (similar to the decimal point) is represented as

$$(N)_b = \left(n_i n_{(i-1)} \ldots n_0 \cdot n_{-1} n_{-2} \ldots n_{-m} \right)_b$$

with two parts: (1) the integer part $n_i n_{(i-1)} \ldots n_0$, and (2) the fractional part $n_{-1} n_{-2} \ldots n_{-m}$. The subscripts correspond to the location of a given digit relative to the radix point. The subscripts of the whole part start with 0, while the subscripts for the fractional part start with –1. For base 10, the radix point is called a decimal point. For base 2, the radix point is called a binary point.

For a given number in some arbitrary base, b, the equivalent decimal number is obtained by adding all the digits of the number after multiplying each by b^i, where i is the position of the digit.

Example 1.3.2
Find the equivalent decimal number for:

1. $(1023.21)_5$
2. $(10111.01)_2$

Solution: Using the procedure listed above for part 1, we obtain

$$(1023.21)_5 = 1 \times 5^3 + 0 \times 5^2 + 2 \times 5^1 + 3 \times 5^0 + 2 \times 5^{-1} + 1 \times 5^{-2}$$

$$= 125 + 0 + 10 + 3 + 2/5 + 1/25 = (138.44)_{10}$$

For part 2, we obtain

$$(10111.01)_2 = 1 \times 2^4 + 0 \times 2^3 + 1 \times 2^2 + 1 \times 2^1 + 1 \times 2^0 + 0 \times 2^{-1} + 1 \times 2^{-2}$$

$$= 16 + 0 + 4 + 2 + 1 + 0 + 1/4 = (23.25)_{10}$$

Commonly used bases in digital design and machine level programming are base 2, base 8, and base 16, referred to as binary, octal, and hexadecimal bases, respectively. We next discuss the conversion process between the three bases.

1.4   Octal and Hexadecimal Bases

Octal and hexadecimal bases are used to make the translation process between the user and the computer easier. Computers process binary information. In addition to data, programs that instruct the computer what to do are also represented in binary format. Early computer designers and programmers found that it is hard to recognize the meaning of instructions from their binary representations. In addition to the length of a binary pattern, it is hard to distinguish one binary pattern from another. Hence, it is difficult to distinguish one computer instruction from another when instructions are given in binary format. The use of the base 8 (octal base) and base 16 (hexadecimal base) simplifies this process. The process of conversion between the three different bases is discussed next. We first introduce some terminology.

The individual digits of a binary number are called bits. An *n*-bit number is a binary number that is composed of *n* bits. The most-significant digit (MSD) is the left-most digit (for binary numbers, it is called most-significant bit (MSB)). Similarly, the least-significant digit (LSD) is the right-most digit of the number (in the case of binary numbers, it is called least-significant bit (LSB)).

To convert a binary number to octal:

1. Group the binary numbers into sets of three bits. The reference point used is the binary point. For the integer part, in grouping the number we move from the binary point to the left; for the fractional part we move from the binary point to the right.
2. If needed, we append zeros on the left of the integer part (the MSB) and zeros on the right of the fractional part (the LSB), respectively. This is done to form complete groups of 3 bits.
3. Replace each group formed in 1 and 2 with its equivalent octal number.

Note that appending zeros on the left of the integer part and/or on the right of the fractional part does not change the value of the original number.

To convert a binary number to hexadecimal we follow the procedure listed above; however, the bits are grouped into groups of 4 bits.

To accomplish step 3 in the above procedure, we use Table 1.4.1(a) and (b). The following examples illustrate the use of the procedure outlined above.

TABLE 1.4.1(a)

Used to Convert 3-Bit Binary Number
to Equivalent Octal Digit

Binary	Octal Equivalent
000	0
001	1
010	2
011	3
100	4
101	5
110	6
111	7

TABLE 1.4.1(b)

Used to Convert 4-Bit Binary Number
to Equivalent Hexadecimal Digit

Binary Number	Decimal Equivalent	Hexadecimal Equivalent
0000	0	0
0001	1	1
0010	2	2
0011	3	3
0100	4	4
0101	5	5
0110	6	6
0111	7	7
1000	8	8
1001	9	9
1010	10	A
1011	11	B
1100	12	C
1101	13	D
1110	14	E
1111	15	F

Example 1.4.1
Convert the binary number 11010110.00111 into octal representation.

On grouping the binary digits into groups of three, we note that we need to append a zero on the left-hand side of the whole part and a zero on the right-hand side of the fractional part. The modified number, the grouping, and the equivalent octal number are given in Figure 1.4.1.

Example 1.4.2
Convert the binary number 111000110.001 into hexadecimal representation.

Similar to Example 1.4.1, on grouping the binary digits into groups of four, we note that we need to append three zeros on the left-hand side of the whole part and a zero on the right-hand side of the fractional part. The

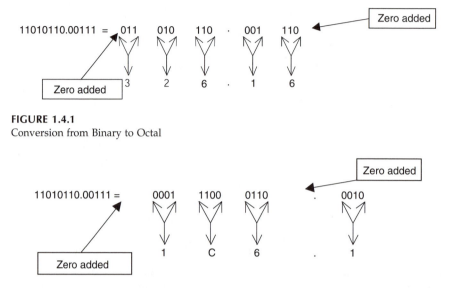

FIGURE 1.4.1
Conversion from Binary to Octal

FIGURE 1.4.2
Conversion from Binary to Hexadecimal

modified number, the grouping, and the equivalent hexadecimal number are given Figure 1.4.2.

Before we leave this section we note that the above process can be reversed, i.e., given a number in octal or hexadecimal form, one can find the binary equivalence by associating with each group the needed bit sequence. In addition, one can convert between the octal and hexadecimal bases by first converting the number into binary format; this can then be followed by the conversion as discussed above.

Example 1.4.3
Given the octal number $(127.25)_8$, find its hexadecimal equivalence.

Solution: We first convert the number into binary. The bits of the equivalent binary numbers are then grouped and the corresponding hexadecimal number is found accordingly:

$$(127.25)_8 \xrightarrow{\text{To Binary}} \underbrace{001}_{1}\underbrace{010}_{2}\underbrace{111}_{7}.\underbrace{010}_{2}\underbrace{101}_{5} \xrightarrow{\text{To Hex.}} \underbrace{0000}_{0}\underbrace{0101}_{5}\underbrace{0111}_{7}.\underbrace{0101}_{5}\underbrace{0100}_{4}$$

$$= (57.54)_{16}$$

1. 5 Operands Types and Their Range

We start our discussion by considering data types as related to programming languages and mathematics.

TABLE 1.5.1

Data Types

Computer Data Type	Mathematics Equivalent Type	Examples
Unsigned	Natural numbers	0, 5, 10
Signed	Integers	–5, 0, 1, 6
Fixed-point	Rational	1.2, 1.5
Floating-point	Rational	-2.1×10^5
Character	—	'A'

1.5.1   Data Types

In mathematics we characterize numbers in terms of their set of possible values. In particular, the characterization includes the sets of natural numbers, integer numbers, rational numbers, real numbers, and complex numbers. This characterization is carried into computer representation of numbers. This is done in programming languages, for example, under the variable declaration part. Here, the concept of a variable of a certain data type is important. In computer arithmetic we consider the representations shown in Table 1.5.1.

In computer arithmetic, with the exception of the last row, we deal with the data types listed in column 1. We assume unsigned integers to mean nonnegative integers (no sign is associated with the number); signed integers represent both positive and negative integers. The remaining two representations are used to approximate real numbers. Fixed-point representations include integers (signed or unsigned) with a radix point that separates two parts, the integer part and the fractional part. Floating-point representation is composed of two parts as well, a fixed-point part and a base-exponent part. For example, -2.1×10^5 contains two parts, –2.1 is the fixed-point part and 10^5 is the base-exponent part. We will say more about the representation later in the chapter.

1.5.2   Finite Range

Mathematics uses sets with infinite cardinality (the cardinality of a set is the number of elements in the set). Computers contain finite storage elements. As a result, computers process only subsets of such sets. When arithmetic is performed on operands (numbers), it is stored in registers having a finite number of storage elements. A register is characterized by the number of bits it contains. An n-bit register contains n storage elements; each element can store a bit for a total of n-bits. The finite number of bits limits the range of numbers that can be stored in the registers.

We relate our discussion to the odometer of a car in the case of storing decimal digits. The number of digits in the odometer is finite in size. As a

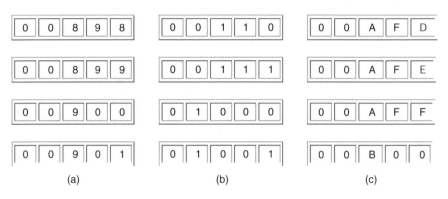

FIGURE 1.5.1
Counting in Different Bases

result, the range of values that can be stored (recorded) is finite as well. For the case of an odometer with 5 decimal digits, the range of numbers is from the smallest, 00000, to the largest, 99999 = 10^5 – 1. This yields a total of 10^5 numbers. The numbers stored are unsigned. In the odometer analogy, numbers in computers are stored in registers of finite size.

We relate the range of numbers in different bases to the process of counting in decimal. From this we conclude equations for the smallest and largest numbers of a given base.

In counting, the least-significant digit always changes. This digit is incremented until it reaches its maximum value (9). The maximum value is 1 less than the base, b. The next count causes the least-significant digit to change to 0. The next digit, however, is changed as well. In general, for a particular digit to change (be incremented or reset to 0), all preceding digits must assume their maximum value, $b - 1$. In base 10, this occurs when all previous digits assume the value 9. In binary this occurs when all preceding digits assume a value of 1, as seen in Figure 1.5.1(b), rows 2 and 3. And, in hexadecimal this occurs when all preceding digits assume a value of F, as shown in Figure 1.5.1(c), rows 3 and 4.

In Figure 1.5.1(a), the range of values that can be stored is 0 through 99999 (10^5 – 1) since the number of digits used is 5. Storing numbers outside this range causes an error called overflow if the number is larger than 99999. Similarly, if the number is smaller than 0, then an error called underflow occurs.

In general, the largest unsigned number that we could store in an n-bit register storing digits in base b is $b^n - 1$. For counting in binary using an n-bit register, the largest unsigned integer that can be stored is equal to $2^n - 1$. For example, for 3-, 4-, and 5-bit register one can store unsigned binary integers in the range $(000)_2$ to $(111)_2$ = 7, $(0000)_2$ to $(1111)_2$ = 15 and $(00000)_2$ to $(11111)_2$ = 31, respectively.

The range of the numbers changes if the number is stored in fixed-point format. For fixed-point format, we need to include the location of the radix point. The common locations of the radix point are at the right-most location of the register or at the left-most location, yielding an integer number and a fractional number, respectively. If the contents of an n-bit register represent a fraction, then the smallest range corresponds to 0 (all bits are 0). For the largest range we have

$$\left(a_{-1}a_{-2}a_{-3}a_{-4}\ldots a_{-m}\right)_2 = \left(\underbrace{.1111\ldots 1}_{m}\right)_2$$

$$= 2^{-1} + 2^{-2} + 2^{-3} + 2^{-4}\ldots 2^{-m}$$

$$= 2^{-m}\left(2^{(m-1)} + 2^{(m-2)} + 2^{(m-3)} + \ldots + 2^0\right)$$

$$= \frac{2^m - 1}{2^m}$$

$$= 1 - 2^{-m}$$

Hence, the 3-bit number, $(111)_2$, can be interpreted as the unsigned decimal number 7 or the fractional number 7/8.

Before we move to the next section, we list common units of binary measurements. Some of the common units of measurements used in the text are (1) 1 k (kilo) = 2^{10} = 1024 (approximately 1000); 1 M (mega) = 2^{20} and 1 G (giga) = 2^{30}. Finally, the size of a register can be given in terms of bytes, with a byte equaling 8 bits. Hence, a 4-byte register is a 32-bit register. The size of the register is sometimes referred to as word. Hence, a 32-bit register has a word size of 32 bits. The largest unsigned integer that can be stored in the register is $2^{32} - 1$, which is approximately 4 G.

1.6 Conversion of Decimal Numbers to Equivalent Numbers in Arbitrary Bases

Given the decimal number $(N)_{10} = (n_i n_{(i-1)} \ldots n_0.n_{-1}n_{-2} \ldots n_{-m})_{10}$; to find its equivalent number in a different base, we use two procedures applied to the integer and the fractional part of N.

1.6.1 Conversion of Integer Part

The process of converting a decimal number with no fractional part into an equivalent number in some base, b, is given in Algorithm 1.

Algorithm 1: Given a decimal number, N, with no fractional part, the equivalent number in some base, b, can be obtained by repeatedly dividing the original number and all subsequent quotients by the base b. The remainders are saved in the order they are formed. The process terminates

TABLE 1.6.1

Conversion from Base 10 to Arbitrary Bases

Remainders r_i	Original Number (N) and Successive Quotients (q_i)
	$N = 138$
$r_0 = 3$	$q_0 = 27$
$r_1 = 2$	$q_1 = 5$
$r_2 = 0$	$q_2 = 1$
$r_3 = 1$	$q_3 = 0$

when the final quotient obtained is 0. The equivalent number (in base b) is obtained by listing the remainders from least-significant digit to most-significant digit in the order they are formed.

The examples below illustrate the procedure outlined above.

Example 1.6.1
Convert the decimal number $(138)_{10}$ into an equivalent number in base 5.
  We apply the procedure outlined earlier, as shown in Table 1.6.1. In this example, the original number, 138, is shown in the upper right. The reminder of division of 138 by 5 is $r_0 = 3$. The quotient (q_0) is 27 as listed. Row 3 in the table is obtained by repeating the division process, but by using the quotient, 27, instead of the original number. Finally, the last row is obtained by dividing the quotient 1 ($q_2 = 1$) by 5 and saving the corresponding remainder and quotient in this row. Since the new quotient is 0, the process of conversion stops.
  The remainders obtained (listed in the order formed and from right to left) constitute the equivalent number in base 5; that is

$$(138)_{10} = (1023)_5$$

Example 1.6.2
Convert the decimal number 23 into an equivalent number in base 2. Using the procedure outlined in Algorithm 1, we obtain the results shown in Figure 1.6.1.

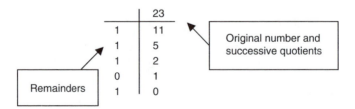

FIGURE 1.6.1
Conversion from Base 10 to Binary (Whole Part)

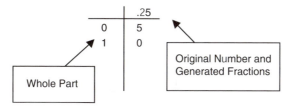

FIGURE 1.6.2
Conversion from Base 10 to Binary (Fractional Part)

The binary number representation of the decimal number 23 is then given as

$$(23)_{10} = (10111)_2$$

1.6.2 Converting the Fractional Part

The process of converting the fractional part of a decimal number into an equivalent number in some arbitrary base, b, is obtained using Algorithm 2.

> **Algorithm 2:** Repeatedly multiply the fractional part and all successively generated fractions by the base b with the integer result of each multiplication saved in the order it is formed. Continue until the fractional part value is 0. The fractional equivalent in base b is obtained by (1) listing the integer digits (in the order formed) from most significant (left) to least significant (right), and (2) appending a radix point on the left side of the number.

The examples below illustrate the use of Algorithm 2.

Example 1.6.3
Convert the decimal fraction 0.25 to an equivalent fraction in base 2.

Applying Algorithm 2, we obtain the results in Figure 1.6.2. The original fraction, 0.25, is given in row 1. Row 2 contains two columns; the combined columns are the result of 2 * (0.25). On multiplying the fraction 5 in row 2 by the number 2, we obtain the result shown in row 3. Since the updated fraction is 0, the algorithm terminates.

The equivalent fractional number in base 2 is obtained by (1) listing the whole parts from left to right in the order they are formed, and (2) appending a radix point to the left of the number. That is,

$$(0.25)_{10} = (0.01)_2$$

Example 1.6.4
Convert the fractional number $(0.44)_{10}$ to an equivalent fraction in base 5.

Following the procedure outlined in Algorithm 2, we obtain the results in Figure 1.6.3, i.e., $(0.44)_{10} = (0.21)_5$.

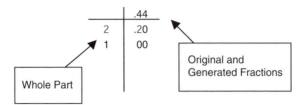

FIGURE 1.6.3
Converting $(0.44)_{10}$ to Base 5

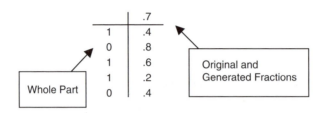

FIGURE 1.6.4
Converting $(0.7)_{10}$ to Binary

Example 1.6.5
Convert $(0.7)_{10}$ to an equivalent binary fraction.

Figure 1.6.4 shows the conversion process. As was discussed earlier, the result in row 3 (0.8) is obtained from multiplying the fractional part in the previous row (0.4) by 2. Now, referring to the last row, the fractional part under consideration is 0.4. As a result, on repeated multiplication of the generated fractions by 2, the sequence of whole digits obtained is (0110). This sequence is repeated indefinitely since the criteria for stopping the algorithm (a fraction of 0) cannot be satisfied.

The previous example points to an important fact about number conversions: some numbers are stored in the computer in an approximate and not-exact representation. (In mathematics, the equation $x * 1/x = 1$ is always true when x is not equal to 0. This is not the case when testing the condition in programming languages.)

To convert a fixed-point decimal number to an equivalent number in arbitrary base, process the integer part and fractional parts as described above and combine the two parts.

Example 1.6.6
Convert $(138.44)_{10}$ to the equivalent number in base 5.

From Examples 1.6.1 and 1.6.4, we have $(138)_{10} = (1023)_5$, and $(0.44)_{10} = (0.21)_5$. Combining the results yields $(138.44)_{10} = (1023.21)_5$.

1.7 Binary Arithmetic

In this section, we will discuss binary arithmetic with regard to the addition, subtraction, and multiplication operations as applied to unsigned integers and fixed-point numbers. We will first discuss decimal arithmetic. From this, we deduce arithmetic procedures on arbitrary.

1.7.1 Addition

In adding the decimal numbers A and B, we add the digits associated with the same location, including the carry that may be obtained from the previous location. The sum may require two digits to represent; this occurs if the sum exceeds 9 (1 less than the base value). The sum can be written as CS, with C the carry used into the next MSD of the sum. For example, the sum of the digits $7 + 5$ is 12. Hence, C is 1 and S is 2. The C and S terms satisfy:

$$S = (X + Y) \text{ MOD } b$$

$$C = (X + Y) \text{ DIV } b$$

where X and Y are the two digits to be added, and b is the base. The MOD operation returns the remainder of $(X + Y)/b$ while the DIV operation returns the quotient of the division.

In adding binary numbers, the individual digits used are 0 and 1. The result of adding two binary digits is given in Table 1.7.1. The table can be modified to include the addition of three binary digits. The modified table with a carry bit included is given in Table 1.7.2. In adding two binary numbers, we use the above table to compute the intermediate steps.

TABLE 1.7.1

Addition of Two Binary
Bits, Result Requires
Two Bits C and S

Original Digits	Sum	
$A + B$	C	S
$0 + 0$	0	0
$0 + 1$	0	1
$1 + 0$	0	1
$1 + 1$	1	0

TABLE 1.7.2

Addition of Three Binary Bits,
Result Requires Two Bits C and S

Original Digits	Sum	
Carry Digit + A + B	C	S
0 + 0 + 0	0	0
0 + 0 + 1	0	1
0 + 1 + 0	0	1
0 + 1 + 1	1	0
1 + 0 + 0	0	1
1 + 0 + 1	1	0
1 + 1 + 0	1	0
1 + 1 + 1	1	1

Example 1.7.1

Add the two binary numbers 11011 and 11001.

Using Table 1.7.2, we have the result shown in Figure 1.7.1.

The previous discussion can be applied to additions in arbitrary bases. The following example illustrates this for adding two numbers in base 5.

Example 1.7.2

Find $x + y$, where $x = (123.4)_5$ and $y = (241.1)_5$.

We illustrate the process by adding individual digits and recording the sum in decimal; the sum can then be converted into two digits (in the CS form discussed above) in base 5.

The addition proceeds from right to left. In determining the sum, carries are recorded as well. The sum is shown in Table 1.7.3. The first column contains the carry-in and the digits of the two numbers listed from least significant to most significant. The sum in decimal is obtained from corresponding row digits (this includes the carry-in digits). The initial carry-in digit is 0. The remaining carries are obtained from converting the decimal sum into base 5. For example, the first row produces a decimal sum of 5, which is converted to $(10)_5$. The carry of 1 is moved to the next row, and the process of addition is repeated on this row.

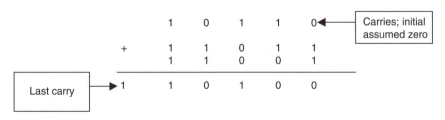

FIGURE 1.7.1

Addition of Two Binary Numbers 11011 + 110001, Upper Row Shows the Carries

TABLE 1.7.3

Base 5 Addition, 123.4 + 241.1

	Sum in	Sum in Base 5	
Carry + x + y	Decimal	C	S
0 + 4 + 1	5	1	0
1 + 3 + 1	5	1	0
1 + 2 + 4	7	1	2
1 + 1 + 2	4	0	4

TABLE 1.7.4

Base 16 Addition, 2397A.4 + 95CB.2

	Sum in	Sum in Base 16	
Carry + x + y	Decimal	C	S
0 + 4 + 2	6	0	6
0 + A + B	21	1	5
1 + 7 + C	20	1	4
1 + 9 + 5	15	0	F
0 + 3 + 9	12	0	C
0 + 2 + 0	2	0	2

The sum of the two numbers is obtained from the last column after including the radix point; the sum obtained is $(420.0)_5$.

Example 1.7.3

The sum $x + y$, where $x = (2397A.4)_{16}$ and $y = (95CB.2)_{16}$ is given in Table 1.7.4. From Table 1.7.4, $(2397A.4)_{16} + (95CB.2)_{16} = (2CF45.6)_{16}$. Note the added zero in the last row of the column with label y.

1.7.2   Subtraction

The process of subtraction in arbitrary base is derived from subtracting decimal numbers. We first illustrate by an example.

Example 1.7.4

Find $(1230015)_{10} - (1122124)_{10}$

Using common subtractions on decimal, we make the text box note shown in Figure 1.7.2.

On applying the above, we get the result shown in Figure 1.7.3 with the updated and original digits as shown. The result of subtraction is also given. As can be seen from the figure, there are no additional borrows needed.

Note that in forming $A - B$, A is called the minuend and B is called the subtrahend.

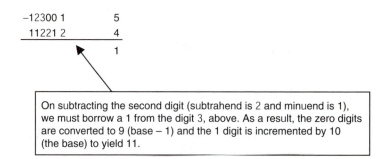

FIGURE 1.7.2
Decimal Subtraction

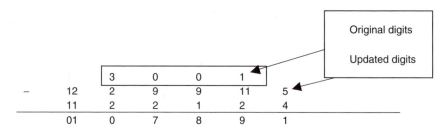

FIGURE 1.7.3
Decimal Subtraction

The above rule can be generalized to subtract numbers in a different base, b. For a borrow, the zero digits to the left are changed to $b - 1$, the digit that requires the borrow, a_i, is changed to $(a_i + b)$, and the digit that supplied the borrow, $a_{(i+j)}$, is decremented by 1.

We consider the following examples to illustrate.

Example 1.7.5
In this example we find $(12034)_5 - (11442)_5$.

The subtraction procedure is shown in Figure 1.7.4 using the steps outlined above.

Example 1.7.6
In this example, we find $(1100001)_2 - (1011101)_2$.

Using the procedure, we obtain Figure 1.7.5.

Example 1.7.7
Find $(1250A51)_{16} - (1170F31)_{16}$.

The result of the subtraction is shown in Figure 1.7.6.

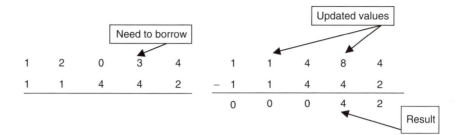

FIGURE 1.7.4
Base 5 Subtraction, 12034 – 11442

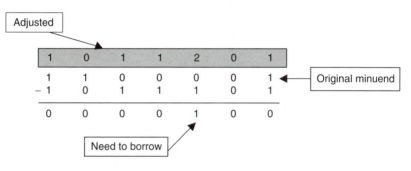

FIGURE 1.7.5
Base 2 Subtraction, 1100001 – 1011101

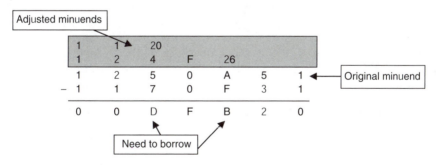

FIGURE 1.7.6
Base 16 Subtraction, 1250A51 – 1170F31

The adjusted minuends are shown in the shaded area in Figure 1.7.6. The first row is the result of the first initiated borrow; the row above it is the result of the second initiated borrow.

1.7.3 Multiplication

We restrict the process of multiplication to binary, and illustrate the process by an example.

Example 1.7.8
Form the product $(11001)_2 \times (1101)_2$.

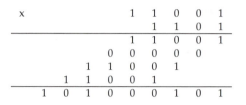

Note that the multiplicand (11001) is copied as is if the bit in the multiplier (1101) is 1. It is replaced by a row of zeros if the multiplier bit is 0. The process is similar to regular multiplication. In regular multiplication, we form the partial products as shown in the rows above. Each partial product is properly shifted one bit position to the left. To obtain the product, we add all partial products as shown in the last row.

1.8   Radix and Diminished Radix Complements

The previous discussion dealt with number representations that are nonnegative. In the next section, we discuss representation of negative numbers. First, however, we discuss two forms of complements that are used in signed arithmetic, the diminished radix and radix complement representations.

The diminished radix representation of a number is determined from three parameters: the base, b, the number of digits in the number, n, and the number itself, N. For a number N, the diminished radix representation of the number is

$$\left(b^n - 1\right) - N$$

The representation is referred to as $(b - 1)$'s complement. For example, in base 10, $b = 10$, the representation is referred to as 9's complement. Similarly, in base 2 the diminished radix representation is referred to as 1's complement.

Example 1.8.1
Form the 9's complement of the decimal number 123.
   Solution: Since $N = 123$, the number of digits, n, is 3 and

$$b^n - 1 = 10^3 - 1 = 999$$

Hence

$$\left(b^n - 1\right) - N = 999 - 123 = 876$$

What is $(b^n - 1)$? From the above example, we note that $(b^n - 1)$ is a number with n digits, with each digit equal to $b - 1$, i.e., to obtain the diminished radix complement of a number N, we subtract each digit in N from $(b - 1)$. The result is the desired diminished radix.

Example 1.8.2
In this example, we form the 1's complement of the binary number 10110.
   Using the previous observation, we have

$$11111 - 10110 = 01001$$

as the 1's complement of 10110.

   Note that the diminished radix complement of a number is obtained from its individual digits. The sum of the digit and the corresponding digit in the diminished radix complement must add to $(b - 1)$. For the 1's complement case, we obtain the complement by complementing each bit of the number. For each bit in the number, the sum of the bit and the corresponding bit in the 1's complement must add to $(b - 1 = 1)$. We apply the rule on a different base, using the example below.

Example 1.8.3
Find the 4's complement of $(1234)_5$.
   Using the above observation, the 4's complement is 3210 since

$$1 + 3 = 4, 2 + 2 = 4, 1 + 3 = 4, \text{ and } 0 + 4 = 4$$

   Similar to diminished radix complement, the radix complement representation is determined from three parameters: the base, b, the number of digits in the number, n, and the number itself, N. The representation is referred to as b's complement. It is called 10's complement in base 10 and 2's complement in base 2. For a number N, the radix complement representation of the number is

$$b\text{'s complement} = \begin{cases} b^n - N & \text{if } N \neq 0 \\ 0 & \text{if } N = 0 \end{cases}$$

   Note that $b^n - N = ((b^n - 1) - N) + 1$, i.e., for a given number N, we have b's complement of $N = (b - 1)$'s complement of $N + 1$.

Example 1.8.4
Form the 10's complement and 2's complement of the numbers 0821_{10} and 001011_2, respectively.
   For 0821_{10}, $n = 4$; the 10's complement is $10^4 - 0821 = 1 + 9999 - 0821 = 9179$. For 001011_2, $n = 6$; the 2's complement is $2^6 - 001011 = 1 + 111111 - 001011 = 110101$.

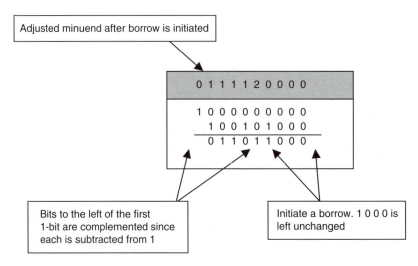

FIGURE 1.8.1
Forming 2's Complement. From the definition, no changes occur to the leftmost consecutive zeros in the number and first 1 bit that initiates the borrow. All remaining bits are complemented.

An alternative method of finding the 2's complement makes use of subtraction discussed earlier. Given a number, N, with m consecutive zeros followed by a 1 in the $m + 1$ position. As shown in Figure 1.8.1 with $N = 100101000$ for example, each of the first m bits remains unchanged ($0 - 0 = 0$) when forming the 2's complement of N. The ($m + 1$) bit is subtracted from 2, since this bit initiates a borrow, and as a result, remains unchanged ($2 - 1 = 1$). The remaining bits are subtracted from 1, i.e., each bit is complemented. The example below illustrates this.

Example 1.8.5
Form the 2's complement of the binary number 100101000.
We show the details of the above procedure in Figure 1.8.1. The 2's complement is shown as the last row of binary numbers.

1.9   Representation of Negative Numbers

In Section 1.5.2, we discussed overflow and underflow as conditions that are results of storing a number that is either too large or too small to fit in a predefined register size. Using unsigned integers, consider the case of forming $0011_2 - 0110_2$. The result is -3_{10}, which is too small to fit in a 4-bit register. In this section, we discuss presentation of negative numbers. Since computers use only binary data, negative numbers are represented using binary digits only.

Sign bits

FIGURE 1.9.1
Signed Magnitude Representation, Most-Significant Bit Used to Represent the Sign of the Number

1.9.1 The Three Representations

We consider three representations

1. Signed Magnitude
2. Diminished Radix Complement
3. Radix Complement

In the signed magnitude representation, the number is composed of a sign part and a magnitude part. This is similar to the way we represent negative numbers. For example, "–123" represents a negative number in decimal. Its sign part is "–"; its magnitude is "123."

When representing the number in binary, since the allowable digits are 0 and 1, we code one of the bits to represent the sign. The bit is the MSB with 0 to mean a nonnegative number and a 1 to mean a negative number. Hence, –6 and +6 can be represented as shown in Figure 1.9.1.

Negative numbers can also be represented using either complement representation discussed in the previous section. (The advantage of the representations will be presented in Chapter 5 when we discuss the design of arithmetic units.) In both representations, the MSB is used as a sign bit with a 1 indicating the number is negative and a 0 indicating the number is positive. When other bases are used to represent negative numbers, we use 0 and $(b-1)$, for positive and negative representation, respectively. To find the representation of a negative number, we form its corresponding radix, or diminished, radix complement.

Example 1.9.1

Assuming four-digit numbers, find the 10's complement and 2's complement representation of the numbers -23_{10} and -11_2, respectively.

Solution: From the definition, we have 10's complement of 23 = $10^4 - 23$ = 9999 – 23 + 1 = 9977, i.e., –23 in this representation is 9977. Note the 9 indicates the number is negative. For the 2's complement, applying the previous observation on 00112 we obtain 1101 as the 2's complement representation of 0011_2 (11_{10}), i.e., $(-11)_{10}$ in this representation is 1101.

Example 1.9.2

List the 10's complement representations over positive and negative decimal numbers with two digits.

TABLE 1.9.1

Two-Digit Negative Numbers and Corresponding Decimal Value

$N + b$'s compl. of $N = 100$	Decimal Value	$N + b$'s compl. of $N = 100$	Decimal Value
? + 90	−10	? + 95	−5
? + 91	−9	? + 96	−4
? + 92	−8	? + 97	−3
? + 93	−7	? + 98	−2
? + 94	−6	? + 99	−1

Note: In the table, 90 represents the negative number $(-10)_{10}$. Other entries are read similarly.

Solution: Since the most-significant digit is used for the sign, we have a total of ten nonnegative numbers (00, 01, 02, ..., 09). For the negative representation, the most-significant digit is 9. The negative representations are 90, 91, 92, ..., 99.

To find the negative number associated with each representation, we make use of the equation

$$N + b\text{'s complement of } N = b^n$$

where $b^n = 100$. Table 1.9.1 makes use of the above equation.

Note that the negative representation of −10 is 90, and that the largest positive number is +9, with representation 09 (0 for the sign indicating positive number and 9 is the magnitude). This is a property of b's complement where the smallest negative number has no corresponding positive representation.

1.9.2 Range of the Numbers

For signed magnitude representation and an n-bit signed integer, the total possible allowable binary combinations is 2^n. Since one of the bits is used as a sign bit, the total range of positive numbers is +0 through $2^{(n-1)} - 1$. Similarly, the total range of negative numbers is $-(2^{(n-1)} - 1)$ to −0. Note that there are two different representations of 0 (a positive and a negative 0). Finally, note that the results apply to numbers in arbitrary bases with the positive range 0 to $b^{(n-1)} - 1$ and the negative range of $-(b^{(n-1)} - 1)$ to −0.

For b's complement representation, we generalize the result in the previous subsection. For such numbers, the nonnegative range is 0 to $b^{(n-1)} - 1$, where n is the total number of digits and b is the base of the number. The negative range is $-b^{(n-1)}$ to −1.

Similar analysis can be used on finding the diminished radix complement. Table 1.9.2 summarizes the results for the three representations.

Table 1.9.3 shows the representation of a 3-bit binary number in the three forms. Note that the three representations for positive numbers are the same.

TABLE 1.9.2

The Three Representations with Form, Ranges, MSD, and Remarks

Representation	Form	Positive Range	Negative Range	Remarks	MSD
Signed magnitude	Sign (magnitude)	+0 to $(b^{(n-1)} - 1)$	$-(b^{(n-1)} - 1)$ to -0	Two zeros	$0, (b-1)$
Diminished radix	$(b^{(n-1)} - 1) - N$	+0 to $(b^{(n-1)} - 1)$	$-(b^{(n-1)} - 1)$ to -0	Two zeros	$0, (b-1)$
Radix	$b^n - N$	+0 to $(b^{(n-1)} - 1)$	$-b^{(n-1)}$ to -1	One zero	$0, (b-1)$

TABLE 1.9.3

The Three Representations over a 3-Bit Operand Range

Decimal Value	Signed Magnitude	1's Complement	2's Complement
+0	000	000	000
+1	001	001	001
+2	010	010	010
+3	011	011	011
−0	100	111	No representation
−1	101	110	111
−2	110	101	110
−3	111	100	101
−4	No representation	No representation	100

Note as well that there are two representations for zero in signed and 1's complement representation. Finally, note that 2's complement representation contains one negative number (−4) that has no corresponding positive number.

The complement representations are awkward from a user point of view. They, however, are well suited for use in computer processing, as we will discuss in Chapter 5. Today, computers represent signed integers in 2's complement where negative numbers are stored in this form.

1.10 Coding and Binary Codes

Consider Table 1.9.3 where we represented positive and negative integers in three different forms. Each of the representations, in general, is called a code.

A code is an assignment that associates with each element in a set of objects another element, called code word, in some other set of objects. For example, in the 2's complement representation we can think of the assignment 100 as the 2's complement code word of the decimal integer −4. Similarly, 101 is the code word for the decimal integer −3. The set of objects considered in the table are the decimal integers in the range of −4 to +3. Their 2's complement code is as shown. The process of determining the code associated with a given object is called encoding. From a given code word, the process of determining the original object is called decoding.

TABLE 1.10.1

BCD and Excess 3 for the 10 Decimal Digits

Decimal Digit	BCD Code	Excess-3 Code
0	0000	0011
1	0001	0100
2	0010	0101
3	0011	0110
4	0100	0111
5	0101	1000
6	0110	1001
7	0111	1010
8	1000	1011
9	1001	1100

In this section, we consider four types of codes: binary coded decimal (BCD) code, Excess-m code, Gray code, and character code. For notation we use $X(n)$ to represent the code word of the object n, when code X is applied. For example, BCD(5) represent the BCD code for object 5.

1.10.1   BCD Code

In this coding scheme, we associate with each decimal digit a binary code. Since the number of digits is 10 (0 through 9), the minimum number of binary digits (bits) needed in a code word is 4. The BCD code is derived from the polynomial representation of binary numbers, i.e., the encoding of the decimal numbers 0, 1, 2, and 9 is given, respectively, as 0000, 0001, and 1001. Columns 1 and 2 of Table 1.10.1 show the ten decimal digits and the corresponding BCD codes. The BCD encoding requires larger number of bits than the previous encoding schemes we discussed.

The code is called weighted code since the decoded decimal associated with a given code word is the weighted sum of the digits making up the code word. The weights are 8, 4, 2, and 1, corresponding to the MSB to the LSB, respectively. The code is also called 8421 code.

Example 1.10.1

Find the code word, BCD(127), of 127_{10}.

In the BCD code representation, the encoding is obtained by associating with each digit the corresponding BCD code. The BCD codes for each digit are then concatenated. As a result, we have

$$127 \xrightarrow{\textit{Encode Each Digit}} \underset{1}{\underbrace{0001}} \ \underset{2}{\underbrace{0010}} \ \underset{7}{\underbrace{0111}} \xrightarrow{\textit{Concatenate}} 000100100111$$

i.e., BCD(127) = 000100100111.

Example 1.10.2
Decode the BCD code 0000100100110001, i.e., find the original number.

In finding the decimal equivalent of the above code, we group its bits into groups of four. We then replace each code by the corresponding decimal. The decimals are finally concatenated to obtain the desired results as shown below.

$$0000100100110001. \xrightarrow{Group} \underset{0}{\underbrace{0000}} \ \underset{9}{\underbrace{1001}} \ \underset{3}{\underbrace{0011}} \ \underset{1}{\underbrace{0001}} \xrightarrow{Concatenate} 0931$$

As can be seen from the example above, converting a decimal number to the corresponding BCD code is (computationally) simpler than employing the previous algorithms of finding the equivalent binary representation. Information in a computer can be entered through the use of a keyboard. As a result, the following takes place:

1. The alphanumeric (digits and nonnumeric characters) information is encoded to form a binary string.
2. The computer processes the encoded information.
3. The computer decodes the results into alphanumeric code that can be displayed on an output device such as a monitor. These tasks were shown in Figure 1.2.1 or Figure 1.2.2.

For tasks that are input/output intensive, using a code similar to BCD will speed up the process since the majority of the computation is done in the steps 1 and 3 discussed above. As a result, some computers may have special hardware for performing BCD arithmetic. Such hardware is slower than the hardware that processes information based on the straight binary representation discussed earlier. The speed-ups, however, are due to the frequency of executing steps 1 and 3, as discussed above.

1.10.2 The Excess-m Code

The Excess-m code is obtained from a given code word, c, by adding the number m to the code. For example, the Excess-3 code for the BCD code is obtained by adding the number 3 to each code word. Columns 1 and 3 of Table 1.10.1 show the decimal digits and the equivalent Excess-3 code of the BCD representation.

The Excess-3 code is not a weighted code and is an example of self-complementing codes. A code is said to be self-complementing if, for any decimal digit (0 through 9), one can obtain the code for 9's complement of the digit by complementing the individual digits of the code word. For example, in Table 1.10.1, the Excess-3 code for the decimal digit 3 is

$$BCD(3) + 3 = 0011 + 0011 = 0110$$

The Excess-3 representation for its 9's complement (6) is obtained by complementing the individual bits of 0110 to obtain 1001. An inspection of the table confirms this.

1.10.3   Gray Code

The next code we discuss is called Gray code. It is a special type of code that is called cyclic. A code is said to be cyclic if, by applying a circular shift to any code word, one would obtain another code word. It has the property that the distance between any two consecutive code words is equal to 1. The distance between two code words is equal to the number of bits where the two words differ.

The Gray code is a member of a class of codes called reflected codes. In this code, an $(n + 1)$-bit code can be generated from n-bit code as follows. The total number of $(n + 1)$-bit code words is twice the total number of the n-bit code words. The first half of the $(n + 1)$-bit code words is obtained from the n-bit code words by appending a zero to the left of MSB code words (see Figure 1.10.1). The remaining code words are obtained by reflecting the first half of the code words about the axis, as shown in Figure 1.10.1, and by replacing the MSB 0 with 1.

Gray code is used in cases where it is important not to obtain intermediate incorrect results (values). Consider the two consecutive BCD code words for 7 and 8, for example. To change from 0111 to 1000, we require four changes in the bit positions. If these changes do not occur simultaneously, then some (unwanted) intermediate results occur; for example, first bit changes before all others results in the intermediate code word 0110. We will see later in the text how these intermediate changes could cause problems in digital design.

Before we leave this section, we discuss a final coding scheme that deals with coding characters.

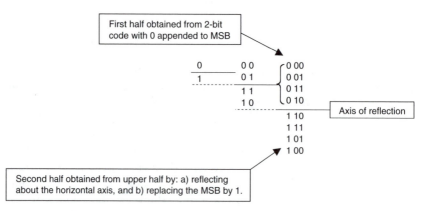

FIGURE 1.10.1
Forming Gray Code

1.10.4   Character Codes

In Figure 1.2.1, the computer receives encoded data for numbers and letters, as well as punctuations marks and other control characters. Our discussion of coding has been limited to numbers. We now consider alphanumeric binary codes. These are codes for digits, letters, and special characters, as well as control characters. Examples of special characters are ^, +, and $. Examples of control characters are the "space" key and the "delete" key on the keyboard.

Table 1.10.2 shows a common alphanumeric coding scheme, the American Standard Code for Information Interchange (ASCII, pronounced "ask-ee"). Another, less common, encoding scheme is the Extended Binary Coded Decimal Interchange Code (EBCIDIC).

TABLE 1.10.2

ASCII Character Set

(row in hex) $b_3b_2b_1b_0$	\multicolumn{8}{c}{$b_6b_5b_4$(column in octal)}
	0	1	2	3	4	5	6	7
0	NUL	DLE	SP	0	@	P	'	p
1	SOH	DC1	!	1	A	Q	a	q
2	STX	DC2	"	2	B	R	b	r
3	ETX	DC3	#	3	C	S	c	s
4	EOT	DC4	$	4	D	T	d	t
5	ENQ	NAK	%	5	E	U	e	u
6	ACK	SYN	&	6	F	V	f	v
7	BEL	ETB	'	7	G	W	g	w
8	BS	CAN	(	8	H	X	h	x
9	HT	EM	)	9	I	Y	i	y
A	LF	SUB	*	:	J	Z	j	z
B	VT	ESC	+	;	K	[	k	{
C	FF	RS	,	<	L	\	l	|
D	CR	GS	-	=	M	]	m	}
E	SO	RS	.	>	N	^	n	~
F	SI	US	/	?	O	_	o	DEL

Note: The control codes abbreviations are NUL, null; SOH, start of heading; STX, start of text; ETX, end of text; EOT, end of transmission; ENQ, enquiry; ACK, acknowledge; BEL, Bell; BS, backspace; HT, horizontal tab; LF, line feed; VT, vertical tab; FF, form feed; CR, carriage return; SO, shift out; SI, shift in; SP, space; DLE, data link escape; DC1, device control 1; DC2, device control 2; DC3, device control 3; DC4, device control 4; NAK, negative acknowledge; SYN, synchronize; ETB, end of transmission block; CAN, cancel; EM, end medium; SUB, substitute; ESC, escape; FS, file separator; GS, group separator; RS, record separator; US, unit separator; SP, space; DEL, delete or rub out.

1.11   Floating-Point Numbers

Real numbers are presented in the computer in either fixed-point or floating-point form. The floating-point format is used to represent very large (or very small) numbers needed in scientific applications. Consider the number 7×2^{64}, for example. Represented in binary, the number is $(111)_2$ followed by 64 zero bits. An alternative, more efficient representation is the floating-point form. Here, we store the binary representations of the exponent part (64) and the whole part (7); the base is implicit. The result is then

1 1 1	1 0 0 0 0 0 0
Integer part	Exponent part

In general, a floating-point number, F, is represented as

$$F = \mp M \times r^{E}$$

where M, the mantissa or significand, is a fixed-point number; E, the exponent (also called the characteristics), is an integer; and r is the base of the number.

   In general, a fixed-point number can be written in floating-point representation. The representation, however, is not unique.

Example 1.11.1
Represent the fixed-point decimal number 1.23 in floating-point format, using the exponents of 0, 1, and 2.
   The representations are, respectively,

$$1.23 = 1.23 \times 10^{0}$$

$$= 0.123 \times 10^{1}$$

$$= 0.0123 \times 10^{2}$$

We next look at the binary representation of floating-point numbers.

1.11.1   Binary Representation of Floating-Point

In binary representation of floating-point numbers, we have

$$F = (-1)^{s} M \times 2^{E}$$

where M and E are as stated above but with M representing a fractional part only; s is a single bit representing the sign of the number with $s = 0$ indicating a positive number and $s = 1$ indicating a negative number. The range of floating-point numbers depends on the number of bits allocated for each part of the significand and the exponent.

Example 1.11.2
Given the 7-bit code word, 1110101, decode the word assuming the code represents:

1. An unsigned integer
2. A signed integer in 2's complement
3. A character in ASCII code
4. A floating-point number of the form s, E, M, with M a 3-bit field

Solution:

1. As an unsigned integer, the code represents $2^6 + 2^5 + 2^4 + 2^2 + 2^0 = (117)_{10}$
2. As a signed number in 2's complement, the code represents $-(128 - 117) = (-11)_{10}$
3. As an ASCII character and from Table 1.10.2 , the code represents the letter "u"
4. Finally, as a floating point number we have

1	1 1 0	1 0 1
S: Sign Field	E: Exponent Field	M: Mantissa Field

or, the code represents

$$(-1)^s M \times 2^E = -(0.101)_2 \times 2^{(110)_2}$$

$$= -0.625 \times 2^6$$

In the previous example, we saw that the same code word could be used to represent different data objects. Note that the number of maximum allowable objects that can be encoded does not exceed the range imposed by the size of the code word (2^7). As a result, if the code represents unsigned integers, then the range is the integers 0 through 127. Similarly, if the code represents signed numbers in 2's complement, then this range is -64 to 63. Finally, if the code represents a floating-point number, then the largest possible number in the range corresponds to the code 0111111, which evaluates to $0.875 \times 128 = 112$. Similarly, the smallest number in the range would correspond to -112.

Since the floating-point representation is used to represent real numbers and since the maximum possible objects that can be encoded is 128, there are many real numbers between −112 and +112 that have no corresponding floating-point representation. As a result, increasing the range size decreases the number of possible representations within a given sub-range.

Example 1.11.3
From the previous example, find the range of floating-point numbers when the exponent field is increased by 1 and the mantissa field is decreased by 1. Repeat with the exponent field increased by 2 bits and the mantissa field is decreased by 2 bits, respectively.
Solution: With the new formats, the maximum positive range for the 1-bit change is

$$(-1)^s M \times 2^E = (0.11)_2 \times 2^{(1111)_2}$$

$$= 0.75 \times 2^{15}$$

$$= 24576$$

The maximum range for the 2-bit change is

$$(-1)^s M \times 2^E = (0.1)_2 \times 2^{(11111)_2}$$

$$= 0.5 \times 2^{31}$$

$$= 1073741824$$

The smallest negative range is obtained using the same representation with the sign bit, assuming a value of 1. We can represent only a maximum of 128 real numbers in the above ranges.

1.11.2   Normalized and Biased Floating-Point Representation

The previous representation may lead to different code words that represent the same encoded object. As an example, the two floating-point representations, $0.010 \times 2^{(101)_2}$ and $0.001 \times 2^{(110)_2}$ represent the same decimal number, $(8)_{10}$. To remove this ambiguity, floating-point numbers are represented in normalized form. A floating-point number is said to be in normalized form if the most-significant digit of the mantissa is not 0.

In addition to representing a number in normalized form, the exponents of a floating-point number is generally represented as a biased signed (Excess-m) integer. The bias is equal to $2^{(n-1)} - 1$, where n is the number of bits in the exponent field. This bias is added to the exponent to produce a biased exponent. We illustrate the above in two examples.

Example 1.11.4
Encode the fixed-point number $(110.10)_2$ into a biased normalized floating-point representation with the exponent and mantissa fields equal to 4 bits and 6 bits, respectively.

Solution: We first write 110.10 in normalized floating-point as

$$(110.10)_2 = (0.110100)_2 \times 2^3$$

We then add the bias 7 to the exponent to get a biased exponent $(10)_{10} = (1010)_2$.

The representation then is

0	1010	110100
S	E	M

Example 1.11.5
Given the normalized biased floating-point number shown below, find its decimal value.

0	110010	1010
S	E	M

Solution: The sign bit indicates the number is positive. Its mantissa is 0.1010, which is

$$\frac{1}{2} + \frac{1}{8} = 0.625$$

Its exponent is obtained by decrementing it by $2^{6-1} - 1 = 31$ to obtain 010011, which is $(19)_{10}$. Hence, the decimal value of the number is 0.625×2^{19}.

Chapter 1 Exercises

1.1 Find the base 10 values of
   (a) $(113)_5$
   (b) $(10110)_2$
   (c) $(23AAF)_{16}$

1.2 Find the equivalent decimal number for
   (a) $(102.211)_5$
   (b) $(1011.01)_2$
   (c) $(1111.11)_2$
   (d) $(AB.F1)_{16}$

1.3 Convert the binary number 110111110.00111 into octal representation.

1.4 Convert the binary number 10110111110.01 into octal representation.

1.5 Convert the binary number 1110111110.00111 into hexadecimal representation.

1.6 Convert the binary number 10111110.111 into hexadecimal representation.

1.7 Convert the octal number $(156.2)_8$ into hexadecimal representation.

1.8 Convert the base 10 number 127 into (a) binary, (b) octal, and (c) hexadecimal representation.

1.9 Repeat problem 1.8 on the base 10 number 508.101.

1.10 Given a binary number in fixed-point representation with n bits for the whole part and m bits for the fractional part. Give an equation in decimal form for the largest binary number.

1.11 Form the binary sum 10111011 + 01101011.

1.12 Repeat the previous problem on 110111.11 + 010110.01.

1.13 Form the base 5 sum of 1234 + 1441.

1.14 Form the base 5 sum of 1234.214 + 1024.341.

1.15 Form the octal sum of 1234.214 + 1024.341.

1.16 Repeat problem 1.15 on the sum 17.777 + 65.27.

1.17 Form the binary subtraction of 10111011 − 01101011.

1.18 Repeat problem 1.17 on 10101011.01 − 01101011.11.

1.19 Form the octal subtraction 127001 − 117231.

1.20 Compute the hexadecimal arithmetic expression 1A00F.1 − 0AFFF.7 + 123AA.2.

1.21 Form the 10's complement and 9's complement of the decimal number 123.

1.22 Form the 2's complement and 1's complement of the binary number 101100100.

1.23 Find the 8's complement and 7's complement of the octal number 1271001.

1.24 List all possible positive and negative numbers for an octal number with two digits and using the three representations of negative numbers signed, 7's complement, and 8's complement.

1.25 Given the binary code 1000100100110001. Determine the meaning of this code if the code represents

(a) A BCD code

(b) An unsigned integer

(c) A signed integer in signed magnitude

(d) A signed integer in 1's complement

(e) A signed integer in 2's complement

1.26 Represent the fixed-point decimal number 12.3 in floating point format using the exponents of 0, 1, and 2.

1.27 Encode the fixed-point number $(1010.10)_2$ into a biased normalized floating-point representation with the exponent and mantissa fields equal to 4 bits and 6 bits, respectively.

1.28 Given the normalized biased floating-point number shown below. Find its decimal value.

1	110011	1011

2

Boolean Algebra, and Gate
and Transistor Design

CONTENTS

In this chapter, we present Boolean algebra as a mechanism in the description, analysis, and design of digital systems. The algebra is fundamental to the field of digital design, which ranges from designs of simple circuits that perform addition in binary to the design of a complete functional microprocessor.

The design of circuits described by the algebra is considered at both the gate level and at the transistor level. In considering the transistor-level design, we introduce students with no electronics background to the fundamentals.

An understanding of the material in this chapter and the following chapter is fundamental to understanding the field of digital design.

2.1 Boolean or Switching Algebra

Computers process binary data. Switching (also called Boolean) algebra is defined over binary data. In particular, the algebra is defined over the set, S, of two binary values where $S = \{0, 1\}$. The set S constitutes the set of constants of the switching algebra. In addition to the set, the definition of the algebra involves the use of operations on the constants. In Boolean algebra, the operations defined are

1. "+"
2. "."
3. " ' "

Formally, the definition of a switching algebra is given below.

2.1.1 Definitions

Definition: A switching algebra is defined over the set $S = \{0, 1\}$, the binary operations "." and "+," and the unary operation " ' ", such that, for any two Boolean variables x and y in the set S, we have

1. $x + y = 0$, if $x = y = 0$; $x + y = 1$ otherwise.
2. $x.y = 1$, if $x = y = 1$; $x.y = 0$ otherwise.
3. $x' = 0$, if $x = 1$; $x' = 1$ if $x = 0$.

The operations "+", ".", and " ' " are called the logical OR, logical AND, and logical complement (or NOT) operators, respectively.

- The term "$x + y$" is read as "x or y."
- The term "$x . y$" is read as "x and y."

- x' is read as "not x" or "complement of x."
- x' can be written as $\bar{x}$.
- "+" and "." are sometimes called addition and multiplication.

In words, the operations "+" and "." require two operands. Each operand is a Boolean constant, 0 or 1. The "+" operation evaluates to 1 whenever one or both of the operands assume a value of 1. The "." operation assumes a value of 1 only when both operands assume a value of 1.

Note that we use xy to mean $x.y$, and $\bar{x}$ to replace x. Both are acceptable and interchangeable notations.

2.1.2 Boolean Expressions

The operations in the above definition, with Boolean variables included, are examples of Boolean expressions. Another example of a Boolean expression is "$x.y + z$," where x, y, and z are Boolean variables.

We distinguish between two forms of Boolean expression and call them simple and compound expressions. We assume that simple expressions are composed of a constant, a Boolean variable, or a combination of these with a single Boolean operator. The expressions given in the definition are examples of simple Boolean expressions. We assume that compound expressions contain at least two Boolean operators. Finally, we refer to both types of Boolean expression as expressions and identify their type when needed. The following are examples of simple Boolean expressions with x as a Boolean variable

1. 0
2. x
3. $x + 1$

The following are examples of compound Boolean expressions; x, y, and z are Boolean variables.

1. $x.y + z$
2. $x'.y' + z.z'$
3. $x.y.z + (x + y)'$

The compound expressions above can be evaluated for a given binary assignment to the Boolean variables x, y, and z. However, since each of the expressions includes more than one Boolean operator [expression (2), for example, contains six operators], we need to determine the order of using these operators. The order of computing each operator may yield a different result, as is the case in evaluating the arithmetic expression "$2 + 3 \times 4$." Here, the value of the expression is 14 if multiplication is done before addition; however, the value of the expression is 20 if addition is done before multiplication.

The rules that govern the order of computing operations are called precedence rules. For Boolean expressions, we use the following precedence rules in the order of highest to lowest precedence, as listed.

1. Parentheses (evaluated from innermost to outermost)
2. " ' " (the NOT Boolean operator)
3. "." (the AND Boolean operator)
4. "+" (the OR Boolean operator)

In the next section, we present algebraic properties of Boolean expressions. We show that the rules of commutativity and associativity are satisfied under the "+" and "." operations. For now, we assume that in computing expressions that involve operators with the same precedence rules the computation is done from left to right. The example below is used to illustrate the use of precedence rules.

Example 2.1.1
Compute the value of the expressions

1. $x.y + z$
2. $x'.y' + z.z'$
3. $x.y.z + (x + y)'$

For the assignment, $x = 1$, $y = 0$, and $z = 1$.
We compute the above expressions by substituting the values of the variables in the expressions and applying the precedence rules stated earlier. For the expression in part 1, we have

$$x.y + z = 1.0 + 1$$
$$= 0 + 1$$
$$= 1$$

For the expression in part 2, we have

$$x'.y' + z.z' = 1'.0' + 1.1'$$
$$= 0.0' + 1.1'$$
$$= 0.1 + 1.1'$$
$$= 0.1 + 1.0$$

$$= 0 + 1.0$$

$$= 0 + 0$$

$$= 0$$

For the expression in part 3, we have

$$x.y.z + (x + y)' = 1.0.1 + (1 + 0)'$$

$$= 1.0.1 + (0)'$$

$$= 0.1 + 1$$

$$= 0 + 1$$

$$= 1$$

2.1.3   Truth Tables

Assume in the previous subsection we were asked to find all possible variable assignments that cause the expressions given in the previous examples to evaluate to 1. One possible solution to the problem is to use truth tables. A truth table is composed of columns and rows. The columns in the table belong to two sub-tables. One of the sub-tables is a collection of columns with the number of columns equal to the number of different variables found in the expression. The other sub-table includes columns that are associated with the value of one or more expressions.

The number of rows in the table corresponds to the total number of possible assignments to the variables found in the expression. These variables are called input variables. This number is finite and is equal to 2^n, where n is the number of variables. For example: (1) for an expression over a singe variable, x, the number of rows is two ($x = 0$ and $x = 1$); and (2) for an expression over two variables x and y, the number of rows is four ($xy = 00$, 01, 10, and 11). And, in general, for an expression over n variables, the number of rows in the truth table is 2^n.

The truth table for the AND, OR, and NOT given in the definition above are given in Table 2.1.1. Row 1 of Table 2.1.1(a) is read as follows: For $x = y = 0$, the result of $x + y$ is 0. Other rows are read similarly.

We illustrate the construction of truth tables for the expressions given in the Example 2.1.1. In computing these expressions, we compute sub-expressions of each as needed. A sub-expression is an expression within the original larger expression. We then form the value of the expression from its component sub-expressions.

TABLE 2.1.1

The Three Boolean Operations

x	y	$x + y$	x	y	$x \cdot y$	x	x'
0	0	0	0	0	0	0	1
0	1	1	0	1	0	1	0
1	0	1	1	0	0		
1	1	1	1	1	1		
	(a)			(b)		(c)	

TABLE 2.1.2

Truth Table for the Boolean Expression $xy + z$

x	y	z	xy[a]	$xy + z$[b]
0	0	0	0	0
0	0	1	0	1
0	1	0	0	0
0	1	1	0	1
1	0	0	0	0
1	0	1	0	1
1	1	0	1	1
1	1	1	1	1

[a] Sub-expression xy.
[b] Expression value obtained from applying the logical OR operation on the columns with label z and xy.

Example 2.1.2

Form the truth tables associated with the three expressions given in Example 2.1.1.

The truth table for part (a) with the expression "$x.y + z$" is given in Table 2.1.2. The truth table for part (b) with the expression "$xy' + zz'''$" is given in Table 2.1.3. And the truth table for the last expression in part (c) is given in Table 2.1.4.

Definition: Two Boolean expressions over the same set of variables are said to be equal if and only if they are equal for all possible variable assignments in the domain, i.e., if the two expressions have identical truth tables.

Observations:

1. From Example 2.1.2, the sub-expression $(x + y)' = x'y'$ since the two expressions have identical truth tables.

2. The sub-expression zz' evaluates to zero independent of the value of x, y, and z.

3. $x'y' + zz' = x'y'$ since the two expressions have identical truth tables.

These observations are part of a list of properties of Boolean algebra. The list of properties is given next.

TABLE 2.1.3

Truth Table for the Boolean Expression $xy + zz'$

x	y	z	$x'y'$[a]	zz'	$xy + zz'$[b]
0	0	0	1	0	1
0	0	1	1	0	1
0	1	0	0	0	0
0	1	1	0	0	0
1	0	0	0	0	0
1	0	1	0	0	0
1	1	0	0	0	0
1	1	1	0	0	0

[a] Sub-expression x'.
[b] Expression value obtained from applying the logical OR operation on the columns with label zz' and $x'y'$.

TABLE 2.1.4

Truth Table for the Boolean Expression $xyz + (x + y)'$

x	y	z	$(x + y)'$	xyz	$xyz + (x + y)'$[a]
0	0	0	1	0	1
0	0	1	1	0	1
0	1	0	0	0	0
0	1	1	0	0	0
1	0	0	0	0	0
1	0	1	0	0	0
1	1	0	0	0	0
1	1	1	0	1	1

[a] Expression value obtained from applying the logical OR operation on the columns with label xyz and $(x + y)'$.

2.2 Properties of Boolean Algebra

2.2.1 Axioms

Boolean algebra has a set of properties that are called axioms or theorems. These properties are listed in Table 2.2.1. Associated with each property is the name of the property. We refer to them as theorems.

In proving that the equalities hold true, one needs to show that the two expressions on the opposite sides of the equality have identical truth tables. This method of proof is called perfect induction since we show equality over all possible values. The process of exhaustive proof is a result of the finite domain of possible values (for n variable, there are 2^n possible values in the domain).

TABLE 2.2.1

Boolean Algebra Properties

	Properties	Name of Property
1.	$x + 0 = x$	Identity
2.	$x + 1 = 1$	Null elements
3.	$x + y = y + x$	Commutative
4.	$(x + y) + z = x + (y + z)$	Associative
5.	$x + yz = (x + y)(x + z)$	Distributive
6.	$(x')' = x$	Involution
7.	$x + x = x$	Idempotance
8.	$x + x' = 1$	Complements
9.	$(x + y)' = x'.y'$	DeMorgan's

To prove the equality of each theorem, we form the truth table associated with both sides of the equalities. From the construction, we show that the expression values have identical columns. It is worth noting that some of the properties that hold in regular algebra hold as well in Boolean algebra. Some other theorems, however, do not hold true in regular algebra. Theorems 1, 3, and 4 hold true in both regular algebra and Boolean algebra.

Theorem 5 is the distributive property. In Boolean algebra, it is the case that addition (OR) distributes over multiplication (AND). Figure 2.2.1 includes some of the tables used to prove the equalities using perfect induction for the case of one and two variables.

Figure 2.2.2 contains the truth tables used to prove the theorems for the case of three variables.

2.2.2 Principle of Duality

The theorems above can be used to derive additional equalities using the principle of duality. In Boolean algebra, the dual of an expression is formed from the original expression as follows:

1. The constants in the expressions are changed; each occurrence of a 0 is replaced by an occurrence of a 1, and vice versa.
2. The operations in expressions are changed; each occurrence of a "." is replaced by an occurrence of "+", and vice versa.

In finding the duals of expressions, parentheses locations are preserved. It is important to note that some parentheses occurrence is implicit. As a result, in forming the dual, one may need to include the parentheses in the dual part of the expression. When the dual of the axioms listed above is formed, we obtain Table 2.2.2.

The dual property yields nine additional theorems. Some of these theorems, however, are the same as the original theorem, as noted in theorem

Identity						
x	$x + 0$				x	$x + x$
0	0				0	0
1	1				1	1

Identity

x	$x + 0$
0	0
1	1

Null Element

x	$x + 1$	1
0	1	1
1	1	1

Idempotancy

x	$x + x$
0	0
1	1

Involution

x	x'	$(x')'$
0	1	0
1	0	1

Commutativity

x y	$x + y$	$y + x$
0 0	0	0
0 1	1	1
1 0	1	1
1 1	1	1

Complements

x	$x + x'$
0	1
1	1

DeMorgan's Theorem

x y	x'	y'	x' y'	$(x + y)$	$(x + y)'$
0 0	1	1	1	0	1
0 1	1	0	0	1	0
1 0	0	1	0	1	0
1 1	0	0	0	1	0

FIGURE 2.2.1
Proof of Equalities of Boolean Properties Using Perfect Induction. Remaining equalities are shown in Figure 2.2.2

6b. In inspecting the theorems more closely, one can note that the dual of theorem 5b is the distributive property of addition over multiplication. This property is important in simplification of Boolean expressions.

The process of forming the dual of an expression can be applied to complex expressions as well. To do this, we break the original expression into smaller sub-expressions and repeatedly apply the dual operation on these expressions in a recursive fashion until the dual of the original expression is found. We illustrate this process in forming the dual of an expression in the following example.

Example 2.2.1
Form the dual of the expression

$$xyz + x'(y + z)$$

Distribitivity

x y z	yz	x + yz	(x + y)	(x + z)	(x + y) (x + z)
0 0 0	0	0	0	0	0
0 0 1	0	0	0	1	0
0 1 0	0	0	1	0	0
0 1 1	1	1	1	1	1
1 0 0	0	1	1	1	1
1 0 1	0	1	1	1	1
1 1 0	0	1	1	1	1
1 1 1	1	1	1	1	1

Associativity

x y z	(x + y)	(x + y) + z	(y + z)	x + (y + z)
0 0 0	0	0	0	0
0 0 1	0	1	1	1
0 1 0	1	1	1	1
0 1 1	1	1	1	1
1 0 0	1	1	0	1
1 0 1	1	1	1	1
1 1 0	1	1	1	1
1 1 1	1	1	1	1

FIGURE 2.2.2
Remaining Equalities

TABLE 2.2.2

Boolean Algebra Properties Expanded Using Dual of Expressions

	Original Property		Dual	Name
1a.	$x + 0 = x$	1b.	$x.1 = x$	Identity
2a.	$x + 1 = 1$	2b.	$x.0 = 0$	Null elements
3a.	$x + y = y + x$	3b.	$x.y = y.x$	Commutative
4a.	$(x + y) + z = x + (y + z)$	4b.	$(x.y).z = x.(y.z)$	Associative
5a.	$x + yz = (x + y)(x + z)$	5b.	$x.(y + z) = (x.y) + (x.z)$	Distributive
6a.	$(x')' = x$	6b.	$(x')' = x$	Involution
7a.	$x + x = x$	7b.	$x.x = x$	Idempotance
8a.	$x + x' = 1$	8b.	$x.x' = 0$	Complements
9a.	$(x + y)' = x'.y'$	9b.	$(x.y)' = x' + y'$	DeMorgan's

Solution: To find the dual of the expression, we break the above expression into smaller expressions and form the duals of each sub-expression.

$$e = \underbrace{xyz}_{e1} + \underbrace{x'(y+z)}_{e2}$$

Denote the dual of an expression e by e_d. With this notation, we have

$$e_d = e_{1d} \cdot e_{2d}$$

$$e_{1d} = (x + y + z)$$

$$e_{2d} = (x' + y \cdot z)$$

Replacing e_{1d} and e_{2d} with the corresponding value, in e_d above, we obtain

$$e_d = (x + y + z)(x' + y \cdot z)$$

Before we conclude this section, it is important to state that the above theorems apply as well when the Boolean variables are replaced by Boolean expressions. This is due to the fact that these expressions when evaluated will result in a value of 0 or 1 and, as a result, have the same effect on the overall equality as regular Boolean variables. We illustrate the above by two examples.

Example 2.2.2

Show that $xy + (xy)' = 1$, using the theorems found in Table 2.2.2; however, show that $xy + x' \cdot y'$ is not equal to 1.

Solution: By substituting $E = xy$ in the above expression, we obtain $E + E' = 1$. The equality holds true (theorem 8a) in Table 2.2.2.

The expression $xy + x'y'$ is not equal to 1. This can be verified using perfect induction, as shown in Table 2.2.3.

TABLE 2.2.3

Verifying $xy + x'y'$ Is Not Equal to 1

x	y	$xy + x'y'$
0	0	1
0	1	0
1	0	0
1	1	1

Example 2.2.3

Show that the expression $x'y' + xyz + x' + x$ evaluates to 1.

Solution: According to precedence rules, the last three operations performed are the three addition operations evaluated from left to right. As a result, the expression $x'y' + xyz + x' + x$ can be rewritten as

$$(x'y' + xyz) + x' + x = e_1 + (x' + x) \qquad (e_1 = x'y' + xyz)$$

$$= e_1 + 1 \qquad\qquad \text{(Table 2.2.2, theorem 8a)}$$

$$= 1 \qquad\qquad\qquad \text{(Table 2.2.2, theorem 2a)}$$

Example 2.2.4

Show that $(x + y + z)' = x'y'z'$.

Solution: We show the expression is true by referencing the theorems in Table 2.2.2.

$$(x + y + z)' = \left((x + y) + z\right)' \qquad \text{Associative theorem (4a)}$$

$$= (e + z)' \qquad\qquad \text{Let } e = x + y$$

$$= e' \cdot z' \qquad\qquad \text{DeMorgan's theorem (9a)}$$

$$= x' \cdot y' \cdot z' \qquad\qquad \text{DeMorgan's theorem (9a)}$$

The above example is an application of DeMorgan's rule to three variables; the rule can be generalized as

$$\overline{\left(A_1 . A_2 ...... A_n\right)} = \overline{A_1} + \overline{A_2} + ... + \overline{A_n}$$

and

$$\overline{\left(A_1 . A_2 ...... A_n\right)} = \overline{A_1} + \overline{A_2} + ... + \overline{A_n}$$

where $A_1, A_2, ..., A_n$ are Boolean variables or Boolean expressions.

Note that we have used alternative representation for complement.

We say more about simplification next.

2.3   Simplification of Boolean Expressions

Simplification of a Boolean function is the process of obtaining an equivalent Boolean function with less number of variables and/or operations. In the simplification, we make use of the theorems found in Table 2.2.2. This process of using the theorems to simplify functions is called deduction. We illustrate the process in several examples. The process was introduced in the previous section. We use the term *function* to mean expressions.

Example 2.3.1
Minimize the function $f(A,B) = A' + AB$.
  Using the theorems listed above, we have

$$f(A,B) = A' + AB$$
$$= (A' + A)(A' + B) \text{ (Axiom 5)}$$
$$= 1.(A' + B) \text{ (Axioms 3 and 8)}$$
$$= A' + B \text{ (Axioms 3 and 1)}$$

We listed axioms 3 and 8 above since $(A' + A) = A + A'$ according to axiom 3 and $A + A' = 1$ according to axiom 8. This is done for completeness as a first example. The use of these axioms is implicit in the following examples.

Example 2.3.2
Minimize the function $f(A,B) = A' + AB + B'$.

$$f(A,B) = A' + AB + B'$$
$$= (A' + A)(A' + B) + B' \text{ (Axiom 5)}$$
$$= 1.(A' + B) + B' \text{ (Axiom 8)}$$
$$= A' + B + B' \text{ (Axiom 1)}$$
$$= A' + 1 \text{ (Axiom 8)}$$
$$= 1 \text{ (Axiom 2)}$$

Example 2.3.3
Minimize the function $f(A,B,C) = A' + AB + B' + BC$.

$$f(A,B,C) = A' + AB + B' + BC$$
$$= (A' + A)(A' + B) + B' + BC \text{ (Axiom 5)}$$
$$= 1.(A' + B) + B' + BC \text{ (Axiom 8)}$$
$$= A' + B + B' + BC \text{ (Axiom 1)}$$
$$= A' + 1 + BC \text{ (Axiom 8)}$$
$$= 1 \text{ (Axiom 2)}$$

Axiom 2 is used above since $(A' + BC)$ can be used as x in "$1 + x = 1$."

Example 2.3.4

Minimize the function $F(A,B,C) = ABC + ABC' + AB'C + A'BC$.

In minimizing the function, we list the steps without reference to the properties number.

$$F(A,B,C) = \underline{ABC + ABC'} + AB'C + A'BC$$
$$\Downarrow$$
$$= \underline{AB + AB'C} + A'BC$$
$$\Downarrow$$
$$= A(B + B'C) + A'BC$$
$$= AB + \underline{AC + A'BC}$$
$$\Downarrow$$
$$= AB + AC + BC$$

An alternative method of minimization makes use of idempotance property "$x + x = x$." The property plays an important role in the K-map minimization discussed later in the text.

Example 2.3.5

Minimize the function $F(A, B, C) = ABC + ABC' + AB'C + A'BC$ by making repeated use of the rule $x + x = x$.

Solution: The rule above states that in an expression a product term can be repeated as many times as needed with the repetitions separated by "+." Using this rule on the term ABC in the equation, we obtain

$$F(A,B,C) = ABC + ABC + ABC + ABC' + AB'C + A'BC$$

$$= \underline{ABC + ABC'} + \underline{ABC + AB'C} + \underline{ABC + A'BC}$$
$$\Downarrow \qquad\qquad \Downarrow \qquad\qquad \Downarrow$$
$$= \quad AB + \qquad\quad AC + \qquad\qquad BC$$

In the next example, we minimize a property called the consensus theorem. In order to minimize the property, we need first to modify it. The modification expands the original expression.

Example 2.3.6

Minimize the function $F(A, B, C) = AB + A'C + BC$.

Solution: In order to minimize the function we first expand it as shown.

$$F(A,B,C) = AB + A'C + BC$$

$$= AB + A'C + BC(A + A')$$

$$= AB + A'C + ABC + A'BC$$

$$= AB + A'C + ABC + A'BC$$

$$= AB(1+C) + A'C(1+B)$$

$$= AB + A'C$$

Note that the function simplifies to its first two terms, and in addition, the first two terms contain the same variable (A) in complemented and uncomplemented form; the last term is the product obtained from variables in the first two terms with the A and A' variables excluded.

As the number of variables in a given function increases, the algebraic method of minimization becomes more tedious.

2.4 Boolean Function

The expressions defined earlier generate Boolean functions. Like arithmetic functions (for example, $f(x) = x^2 + x + 1$), Boolean functions are defined over Boolean variables we call arguments or inputs to the function. In the arithmetic expression above, the argument is the real number x.

2.4.1 Definitions

In arithmetic functions, many interesting functions are defined over a single argument. This is not the case in Boolean algebra due to the small finite domain. Examples of Boolean functions are

$$f_1(x,y) = x + y$$

$$f_2(x,y) = xy + x'y', \text{and}$$

$$f_3(A,B,C) = A'B'C + A(B+C)$$

The inputs to the function f_1 and f_2 are x and y, respectively. The inputs to f_3 are the Boolean variables A, B, and C. We evaluate functions for specific values of arguments. For example, $f_3(1,1,0) = 1$. We obtain this by substituting $A = 1$, $B = 1$, and $C = 0$ in the right side expression for f_3.

The functions are described in truth-tables format in a similar fashion to expressions descriptions.

Example 2.4.1

Consider the following voting scheme in a three-person committee. Each member votes yes or no on a given item; the result of the vote is the same

TABLE 2.4.1

Majority Function Truth Table

x	y	z	$f(x,y,z)$
0	0	0	0
0	0	1	0
0	1	0	0
0	1	1	1
1	0	0	0
1	0	1	1
1	1	0	1
1	1	1	1

as that of the majority of the committee votes. For example, if two or three committee members vote yes, then the result of the vote is communicated as yes. Model this problem as a truth table.

Solution: In modeling, we need to decide what the Boolean function represents and what its arguments are. The arguments of the function are committee members, x, y, and z. The votes are modeled in binary with a vote of yes modeled as 1 and a vote of no modeled as 0. The modeled Boolean function f is given in Table 2.4.1.

This function is called the majority function.

2.4.2 Representations (Realization)

If a Boolean function is described in truth table or algebraic form, then the description is called behavioral description. Designing or implementing a circuit that realizes a Boolean function is the process of generating a network of building blocks that realizes the behavioral description of the function. The design can be modeled at different levels of details. At the highest level, the design is modeled as a functional block that shows the arguments of the function as inputs to the block and the result of the function as an output of the block. The example of the majority function is shown in Figure 2.4.1.

Note that the details of the design are not shown; inputs are applied to the A, B, and C, and outputs are measured at F. The circuit is verified to be the majority function by applying all inputs and measuring the corresponding outputs. An application of an input means setting the value of the line to either 0 or 1. This will be discussed later.

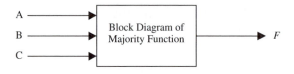

FIGURE 2.4.1
Block Diagram of the Majority Function. Only inputs and outputs are shown.

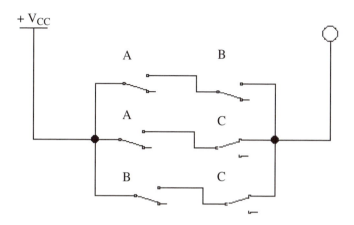

$+ V_{CC}$

A   B

A   C

B   C

FIGURE 2.4.2
Switch Realization of the Majority Function. The switch labels represent the Boolean variables

At another level, more details about the circuit are given. For example, at the switch level (shown in Figure 2.4.2), the building blocks of the circuit are switches that can be connected to a power source modeling the two binary values. The switches represent the input Boolean variables. A switch is open if the corresponding Boolean variable is 0. It is closed if the Boolean variable is 1. The output of the circuit is determined by the indicator lamp (shown as a circle). The lamp is on if it is connected to a voltage source (V_{CC}) through a closed path of switches.

As shown in Figure 2.4.2, a path from V_{CC} to the lamp is established (output = 1) if A is closed and B is closed (in Boolean algebra, if $AB = 1$), or if switches A and C are closed, or B and C are closed. Translated to a Boolean function we have $F(A,B,C) = AB + AC + BC$, with F measured at the lamp as a voltage of 0 (binary zero) or a voltage V_{CC} (binary 1).

In this text, we model the building blocks as logic gates. Logic gates are electrical circuits that model the behavior of simple logic operations (example, the AND, OR, and NOT logic operations). The circuit designed using logic gates is called a digital circuit. We will discuss logic gates in the next section. First, however, we note that digital circuits may have multiple outputs.

To illustrate, assume we would like to modify the majority function behavioral description so as to output the number of yes votes. This number is presented in binary, since digital circuits process binary data. Clearly, a single output is not sufficient since the maximum yes votes is $3_{10} = 11_2$. Table 2.4.2 shows the modified truth table. The truth table has the same set of inputs but it has two columns of output instead of one column. The columns are labeled F_1 and F_2.

For the input $xyz = 000$, the output is $F_1F_2 = 00$. For the input $xyz = 111$, the output is $F_1F_2 = (11)_2 = (3)_{10}$.

TABLE 2.4.2

Modified Voting (Majority
Function) Truth Table, F_1
and F_2 Columns Represent
Number of Yes Votes

x	y	z	F_1F_2
0	0	0	0 0
0	0	1	0 1
0	1	0	0 1
0	1	1	1 0
1	0	0	0 1
1	0	1	1 0
1	1	0	1 0
1	1	1	1 1

TABLE 2.4.3

An Example of a Function
and Its Complement

A	B	f	$\bar{f}$
0	0	1	0
0	1	0	1
1	0	0	1
1	1	1	0

2.4.3   Complement of Boolean Functions

The complement of a Boolean function, f, is defined as

$$\bar{f} = \begin{cases} 0 \text{ if } f = 1 \\ 1 \text{ if } f = 0 \end{cases}$$

By referring to the truth table of a function, the complement is obtained
by changing the entries corresponding to the function, f, in the table. The
entries with value 0 are replaced by entries with value 1, and vice versa. To
illustrate, we construct an example function and its complement in truth-
table format, as shown in Table 2.4.3.

The complement of the function can be found from the algebraic representation as well. To find the complement, we make repeated use of DeMorgan's
rule. We illustrate the method in the following two examples.

Example 2.4.2
Find the complement of $f(A,B,C) = A\bar{B}(C + \bar{A})$.

Solution: Using DeMorgan's rule, we have

$$\bar{f}(A,B,C) = \underbrace{\overline{\bar{A}\bar{B}}}_{e1\,e2}\underbrace{\overline{(C+\bar{A})}}_{e3}$$

$$= \overline{\bar{A}} + \overline{\bar{B}} + \overline{(C+\bar{A})}$$

$$= A + B + \bar{C}A$$

In the above example, one can think of the function as a product of sub-expressions (A, B', and (C +A')) as shown. DeMorgan's rule can then be applied to a function with three product terms to yield the sum of the terms with each term complemented.

Example 2.4.3
Given $f(A, B, C, D) = A\bar{B}(C + \bar{A}) + AD(\bar{B} + C)$, find the complement of f.
   The above function can be rewritten as $f(A, B, C, D) = e1 + e2$, with $e1 = A\bar{B}(C + \bar{A})$, and $e2 = AD(\bar{B} + C)$. As a result, we have

$$\bar{f}(A,B,C,D) = \overline{e1+e2} = \overline{e1}.\overline{e2}$$

with

$$\overline{e1} = \bar{A} + B + \bar{C}A$$

and

$$\overline{e2} = \bar{A} + \bar{D} + B\bar{C}$$

Substituting the above in the equation for $\bar{f}$, we get

$$\bar{f}(A,B,C,D) = (\bar{A}+B+\bar{C}A)(\bar{A}+\bar{D}+B\bar{C})$$

An alternative method to obtaining the complement of a function is first to find its dual. On the dual of the function, we replace all variables by the corresponding complements.
   To illustrate, consider the function $f(A, B, C) = A\bar{B}(C + \bar{A})$ given in the example above. The dual of the function, f_d, is

$$f_d(A,B,C) = A + \bar{B} + C\bar{A}$$

The complement is obtained from the dual by complementing the variables above to obtain

$$\bar{f}(A,B,C) = f_d(\bar{A},\bar{B},\bar{C}) = \bar{A} + B + \bar{C}A$$

2.5   Circuit Analysis and Gate Design

2.5.1   Circuit Analysis and Gate Representation

In digital circuit design, the problem of design is to convert a word problem to an actual circuit that realizes (implements) the solution. From the word problem, the process formalizes the problem as a set of Boolean functions and/or a set of truth tables. A digital circuit is then designed so as to realize the set of functions. Analysis is to determine the functionality of an already existing design. The circuit design we study is done at what is called the gate level.

The gate representation of the three Boolean operations (AND, OR, and NOT) is given in Figure 2.5.1.

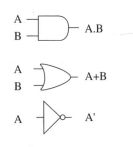

The gate level design can be thought of as one level above the transistor (switch) level. At this level, each gate is composed of a number of transistors. These transistors are connected to make the corresponding gate. The number of transistors is a function of the type of gate designed, as well as the type of switches used.

In the representation above, the variables A and B are treated as inputs to the gates. The output is determined according to the gate chosen. Our goal is to design the gate representations of functions from their word description. First, however, we cover the analysis process of a function designed at the gate level.

FIGURE 2.5.1
Gate Symbols of the Three Boolean Operations

We illustrate gate design and analysis by considering Figure 2.5.2. In the figure, the inputs to the circuit are A, B, and C. The output is the function $F(A,B,C)$. In order to connect crossing lines, we use a dot ".."; in the diagram, lines that are connected assume the same value. An example is given in Figure 2.5.3. In Figure 2.5.3(a), the four line segments assume the same value assigned to A. This is not the case for Figure 2.5.3(b).

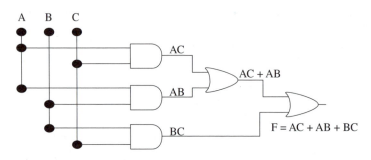

FIGURE 2.5.2
A Gate Design Example. Inputs are A, B, and C, and output is F.

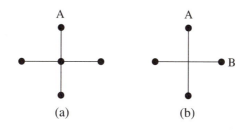

FIGURE 2.5.3
Wire Connections Notation. (a) Crossing lines are connected, (b) Crossing lines are not connected.

To determine the input/output relation of the circuit (analyze the circuit), we derive its truth table; or, alternatively, we derive the Boolean equation at the output of the circuit. In order to derive the function of the circuit, we proceed from inputs to outputs and assign the algebraic functions associated with each line in the circuit. The circuit shown in Figure 2.5.2 includes the algebraic assignments.

We formalize the analysis procedure as follows:

1. Associate with each line in the circuit a level number as follows:
    i. All inputs are assigned level 0.
    ii. For an output line of a gate, let all input levels be determined and let j = maximum level assigned to one or more of its inputs. The output line of the gate is assigned level $j + 1$.
    iii. Repeat step ii above until all line levels are determined.
2. Compute the algebraic representation of lines at level 1.
3. Assuming the algebraic representations of all lines at level i are computed, compute the algebraic representation of the lines at level $i + 1$.
4. Repeat step 3 until the algebraic representation of all the output lines is computed.

It is worth mentioning that due to the commutative rule for two variables A and B, the choice of assigning which input on an OR or AND gate is associated with a particular variable is not important. Similarly, due to associativity the two designs shown in Figure 2.5.4 are the same. This property does not hold true for some other gates that we will consider later.

2.5.2 Circuit Design

In this subsection, we present circuit design at the gate level. We illustrate with an example.

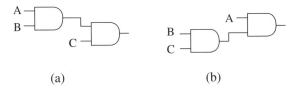

FIGURE 2.5.4
Associativity Property of AND Operation, (a) Circuit Realizes (AB)C, (b) Circuit Realizes A(BC)

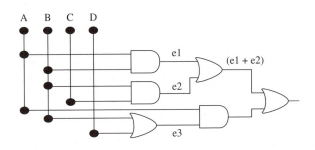

FIGURE 2.5.5
Design of $f(A, B, C, D) = AB + BC + A(B + D)$

Example 2.5.1
Design (realize or implement) the gate representation of the Boolean function

$$f(A,B,C,D) = AB + BC + A(B+D)$$

Solution: In order to design the function above we note that the OR (+) operations (excluding the OR operation inside the parentheses) are done last. Hence, f can be written as

$$f(A,B,C,D) = (e1 + e2) + e3$$

where $e1 = AB$, $e2 = BC$, and $e3 = A(B + D)$.

The design can proceed from the output back to the input of the circuit using the above equations. As a result, we could obtain the design shown in Figure 2.5.5 with $e1$, $e2$, and $e3$ as outputs of sub-circuits that are designed as well.

The design can be accomplished by proceeding from inputs as well. This is similar to performing the design according the precedence of operations within the expression. In the design, the $B + D$ term is first constructed. The output of the OR gate is then used as an input to the lower AND gate. The second input is the A term. The output of the AND gate is the term $A(B + D)$. The process of design is repeated on the remaining terms until the design for the expression is obtained.

(a)　　　　　　(b)

FIGURE 2.5.6
(a) Four Input AND Gate, (b) Four Input OR Gate

Note that the number of operations in the expression determines the number of gates needed in the design and that the location of the gates is arbitrary. For inputs we assume, in general, that inputs are to the left of the outputs.

2.5.3 Multiple Input Gates

Gate representations can be generalized to have more than two inputs. Figure 2.5.6 (a) shows a four-input AND gate. Similar to a regular AND gate, the output of this gate is 1 if all inputs assume the value of 1; the output is 0 otherwise. Figure 2.5.6(b) shows a four-input OR gate. The output of this gate is 1 whenever one or more inputs assume a value of 1. The output is 0 otherwise.

Actual gates are designed with different number of inputs. The number of inputs to a gate is called fan-in. The maximum allowable fan-in is a function of the actual design.

2.6 Electrical Circuits

In order to understand the discussion of transistors, we discuss the electrical properties of a circuit with voltage source and resistance first. From the discussion, we introduce voltage division and show how voltage division can be used to interpret electrical signals as logical 0 or 1 signals.

2.6.1 Voltage, Current, and Resistance

A voltage source with proper connections induces a current. Examples of voltage sources are the car battery, the laptop battery, and the flashlight batteries. Voltage sources have polarities. The polarities are given as "+" and "−." The voltage is measured in volts and can be a measure of difference in electric potential. The difference has to do with redistribution of electrons. Voltage sources are modeled as shown in Figure 2.6.1.

Current is the name given to electrons flowing through a reference area. It is related to the number of electrons that pass through a given area per

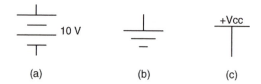

FIGURE 2.6.1
Three Different Representations of Voltage Sources

unit of time. An example of the area is a cross-section of a copper wire. Currents are measured in amperes (A).

Material can be classified as a conductor, a semiconductor, or as an insulator. A conductor is a medium that causes electrons to move freely within the material structure, producing a current if needed (copper and metal wires are examples). Semiconductors allow electrons to move, but less freely than conductors. Insulators are poor mediums for electron movement.

Resistance is associated with the material that limits the amount of free electron movement. Resistance is measured in ohms (Ω). Resistance is modeled as shown Figure 2.6.2.

An example of a familiar resistance is the filament found in a flashlight or a regular lamp. The filament has a resistance; the resistance is responsible for light emission. The lamp converts electric energy into light and heat energy.

FIGURE 2.6.2
Symbolic Representation of a Resistor

2.6.2   Ohm's Law

The voltage source, current, and resistance are related in an equation that is called Ohm's law. We illustrate the law in the diagram shown in Figure 2.6.3.

In the figure, the voltage source is given as 12 V. The resistance is labeled 1 k Ω (1000 Ohm). The flow of the current is shown to flow from the positive voltage node to the negative voltage node. For a current to flow there should be a closed path of wires between the positive end and the negative end of the voltage source.

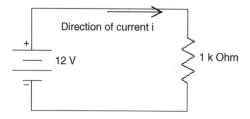

FIGURE 2.6.3
An Example Circuit to Illustrate Ohm's Law

The closed path is shown in the figure. The lines represent conducting wires, which are assumed to have zero resistance. An arrow represents the current, and indicates the direction of the current. By convention, the current flow is defined as opposite to the flow of electrons. In the circuit, electrons (negative charge) flow from the negative side of the voltage source to the positive side.

The amount of current that flows in the wires of the circuit is limited by the strength (value) of the resistance. Ohm's law relates the three values by the equation

$$V = IR$$

where V is the voltage source value in volts, I is the current through the wires in amperes, and R is the value of the resistance to the flow of current measured in ohms. The current value along the closed path is constant. The flow of electrons on the wires and in the resistance is the same throughout the loop. Example 2.6.1 illustrates the use of the equation.

Example 2.6.1

Compute the current value and its direction in the circuit given in Figure 2.6.3.

   Solution: Ohm's law yields $I = V/R = 12$ V$/1000 \, \Omega = 0.012$ A. The direction is as shown in the figure.

   A circuit may have multiple resistances. To find the current values in such a circuit we make use of Kirchhoff's voltage and current laws.

2.7   Kirchhoff's Laws and Voltage Division

Ohm's law can be combined with Kirchhoff's current and voltage laws to find the different voltages of points in a given circuit. Before discussing Kirchhoff's law, we will discuss voltage difference.

2.7.1   Voltage Difference

Different points in a given circuit assume different voltage values. Consider a circuit with a voltage source of 100 V that includes several resistances connected to form one or more closed loops with the voltage source. For such a circuit, one talks about a voltage difference between two different points in the circuit. For example, for the 100-V voltage source, the 100 V means that the difference in voltage between the positive side and the negative side of the circuit is 100 V; put another way, we say that the positive side of the voltage is at 100 volts higher than the negative side.

   For electrical circuits, points on conducting wires assume the same voltage value. However, when resistance is present in the circuit the points on the

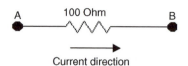

A   100 Ohm   B

Current direction

FIGURE 2.7.1
A Is at a Higher Voltage Than B

two sides of the resistance have different voltage values. As the current passes through the resistance, the resistance induces a voltage drop in the direction of the current. We illustrate using the diagram given in Figure 2.7.1. In the diagram, the voltage at point A is higher than the voltage at point B. The direction of the current and the resistance cause the drop in voltage. The drop is explained by Ohm's law. Given that the voltage at point A is V_A and that the current across the resistor is I, then the voltage at point B, V_B, is given as

$$V_B = V_A - IR$$

or, alternatively,

$$V_A - V_B = IR$$

2.7.2 Kirchhoff's Voltage Law

Kirchhoff's voltage law is used to find the different voltage drops in a circuit with several resistances or other elements that cause voltage drop. The rule states that the sum of voltage drops in a closed loop is equal to the sum of the voltage gains. As one travels along the loop in the direction of a current, a drop of IR occurs across a resistance with value R. A gain is obtained if we move from the negative to the positive nodes of a voltage source. In a circuit that is composed of a single voltage source of value V volts and several resistances, the voltage points in the circuit do not exceed the value V. We illustrate the use of Kirchhoff's law in the following example.

Example 2.7.1
For the circuit shown in Figure 2.7.2, find the current value through the circuit. What are the voltage values at the points a, b, and c?

According to Kirchhoff's voltage law, we have (current I flows in the direction shown)

$$100 = 100I + 400I$$

or

$$I = \frac{100}{500} = 0.2 \ A$$

As for the voltages, we know that point a in the circuit is at the same voltage as the voltage source since points on the same wire (with zero

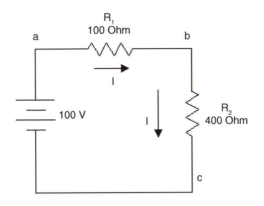

FIGURE 2.7.2
Circuit of Example 2.7.1

resistance) have the same voltage value. As a result, point *a* has the voltage $V_a = 100$ V. As to the voltage at point *b*, V_b is IR volts lower than point *a* since we move from *a* to *b* through the resistance and in the direction of the current. Hence,

$$V_b = V_a - 100I = 100 - 0.2(100) = 80 \text{ V}$$

Similarly,

$$V_c = V_b - 400I = 80 - 0.2(400) = 0 \text{ V}$$

Note that in the above circuit the voltage at point *c* was computed to 0 volts. As can be seen from the figure, the point *c* is at the same voltage as the point *d*, and as a result the negative point of the voltage source is assumed to have the voltage at 0 V. In electrical engineering terms, points at 0 V are said to be connected to ground.

The loop structure in the circuit example can be converted into a linear structure with the voltage source nodes (nodes *a* and *b*) separated, as shown in Figure 2.7.3. In this diagram, the 0 V reference has a special symbol. The symbol is that of ground reference voltage.

2.7.3 Voltage Division

If we refer to the example above and observe the voltage drops across the resistors, we note that the voltage source of 100 V was split between the two resistors. The amount of voltage drop across each resistor is a function of its value. The circuit is an example of a voltage division circuit. We assume voltage division works on two resistances as connected in the above example. The connection of resistances shown is called series connection. An example of a series connection is shown in Figure 2.7.4. In the diagram R_1, R_2, and R_3 are connected in series. The resistors are connected to form a single path and, as a result, the same current passes through all resistances.

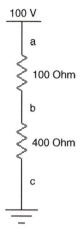

100 V

a

100 Ohm

b

400 Ohm

c

FIGURE 2.7.3
Removing Loop Representation as Shown in Figure 2.7.2. Note the 0 V (ground symbol).

R_1 R_2 R_3
100 Ohm   200 Ohm   500 Ohm

FIGURE 2.7.4
Series Connection of Resistors

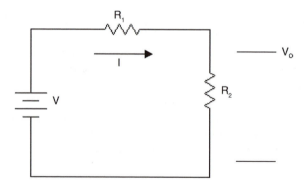

R_1

I

V_o

V

R_2

FIGURE 2.7.5
Voltage Division Circuit

We derive the voltage division equations by using the diagram shown in Figure 2.7.5. The diagram contains two arbitrary resistances, R_1 and R_2, which are connected in series.

From the previous discussion, we have

$$V = IR_1 + IR_2$$

that is,

$$I = \frac{V}{\left(R_1 + R_2\right)}$$

Using Ohm's voltage law, we have

$$V_o = V - IR_1$$

or, alternatively,

$$V_o = IR_2$$

The second alternative equation is due to the fact that V_o is IR_2 volts higher than 0 volts (ground) or $V_o = 0 + IR_2$.

Substituting the value of I in $V_o = IR_2$, we obtain

$$V_o = \left(\frac{R_2}{\left(R_1 + R_2\right)}\right) V$$

In the equation, the initial voltage was divided between the two resistances. We illustrate the use of voltage division on the three circuits in the example below.

Example 2.7.2
Find the current I and the voltage V_{out} for the three circuits shown in Figure 2.7.6. For the circuit in Figure 2.7.6(a), we obtain

$$V_{out} = \frac{R_2}{\left(R_1 + R_2\right)} * V$$

$$= \frac{500}{\left(500 + 500\right)} * 5 = 2.5 \text{ V}$$

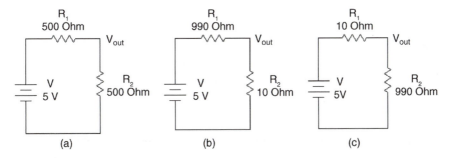

FIGURE 2.7.6
Circuits for Example 2.7.2

For the circuit in Figure 2.7.6(b), we have

$$V_{out} = \frac{R_2}{\left(R_1 + R_2\right)} * V$$

$$= \frac{10}{(990 + 10)} * 5 = 0.05 \text{ V}$$

For the circuit in Figure 2.7.6(c), we have

$$V_{out} = \frac{R_2}{\left(R_1 + R_2\right)} * V$$

$$= \frac{990}{(990 + 10)} * 5 = 4.95 \text{ V}$$

All circuits have the same current value

$$I = \frac{V}{\left(R_1 + R_2\right)} = \frac{5}{1000} = .005 \text{ A}$$

Note that, in the above example, if the two resistances are equal, then the voltage, V_{out}, is half that of the source voltage. For the other two cases, depending on the relative resistance values, V_{out} is either closer to the source voltage value or to the ground voltage value.

If the resistance value R_2 is such that $R_2 \gg R_1$, then V_{out} is approximately equal to the voltage source (5 V). However, if the resistance R_2 is chosen such that $R_1 \gg R_2$, then V_{out} is approximately equal to 0 V.

2.8   Kirchhoff's Current Law

Consider the example circuit shown in Figure 2.8.1. The circuit contains two voltage sources and two loops. To find the currents and voltage drops in such a circuit we make use of Kirchhoff's current law; it states that at any node in the circuit, the sum of currents entering the node is equal to the sum of currents leaving the node.

In finding the values of the currents in the loops, we make initial assumptions about the directions. Actual current directions are determined from the final answers. Positive values imply the initial assumed direction is correct. Negative values imply the current direction is opposite to the initial assumed

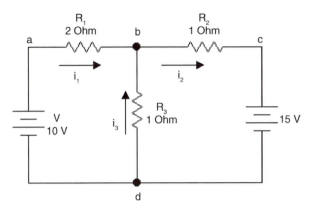

FIGURE 2.8.1
Circuit with Multiple Voltage Sources

direction. With each inner loop, we apply Kirchhoff's voltage law. In addition, with the proper nodes we make use of Kirchhoff's current law.

For a circuit with n current unknown values, one can always form a linear system with n linear equations. This system of linear equations can then be solved to find the current values in the circuit.

We illustrate this procedure in the two examples that follow.

Example 2.8.1
For the circuit shown in Figure 2.8.1 and for the initial current directions, apply Kirchhoff's voltage and current law to find the actual direction and value of the currents in the circuit.

Solution: We apply Kirchhoff's voltage laws on the inner two loops and form the voltage drops by visiting the nodes in clockwise fashion. For the left-most loop, from d to a, a gain of 10 volts is obtained (arbitrary start at d). A loss of I_1R_1 volts is obtained from point a to point b. Finally, to close the loop, a voltage gain of I_3R_3 is obtained from point b to point d. In equation form, we have

$$10 - 2i_1 + i_3 = 0$$

For the right-most loop, starting at point b and moving in clockwise fashion, we have three drops in voltage: (1) across R_2, (2) across the 15 volts, and (3) across the resistor R_3. In equation form, we have

$$-i_2 - 15 - i_3 = 0$$

The above equations are combined to form a system of linear equations (two equations and three unknowns, i_1, i_2, and i_3). To find a solution to the system, a third equation is needed. The equation is obtained using Kirchhoff's current law. At node b, we obtain

$$i_1 + i_3 - i_2 = 0$$

The above equations can be solved using Cramer's rule. Cramer's rule works on a linear system with n equations and n variables. For a system of linear equations of the form

$$a_{11}x_1 + a_{12}x_2 + a_{13}x_3 = b_1$$
$$a_{21}x_1 + a_{22}x_2 + a_{23}x_3 = b_2$$
$$a_{31}x_1 + a_{32}x_2 + a_{33}x_3 = b_3$$

the solution to the system is given as

$$x_i = \frac{|A_i|}{|A|}$$

where A is the coefficient matrix given as

$$A = \begin{pmatrix} a_{11} & a_{12} & a_{13} \\ a_{21} & a_{22} & a_{23} \\ a_{31} & a_{32} & a_{33} \end{pmatrix}$$

and $|A|$ is the determinant of the matrix A. A_i is a matrix obtained from A by replacing column i in A by the constant matrix, B, where

$$B = \begin{pmatrix} b_1 \\ b_2 \\ b_3 \end{pmatrix}$$

To solve the above system using Cramer's rule, we rewrite the system as

$$\begin{cases} -2i_1 + 0i_2 + i_3 = -10 \\ 0i_1 - i_2 - i_3 = 15 \\ i_1 - i_2 + i_3 = 0 \end{cases}$$

with

$$A = \begin{pmatrix} -2 & 0 & 1 \\ 0 & -1 & -1 \\ 1 & -1 & 1 \end{pmatrix}, \quad B = \begin{pmatrix} -10 \\ 15 \\ 0 \end{pmatrix}$$

For the determinant of A, we obtain

$$|A| = \begin{vmatrix} -2 & 0 & 1 \\ 0 & -1 & -1 \\ 1 & -1 & 1 \end{vmatrix} = -2\begin{vmatrix} -1 & -1 \\ -1 & 1 \end{vmatrix} - 0\begin{vmatrix} 0 & -1 \\ 1 & 1 \end{vmatrix} + 1\begin{vmatrix} 0 & -1 \\ 1 & -1 \end{vmatrix} = 5$$

and

$$|A_1| = \begin{vmatrix} -10 & 0 & 1 \\ 15 & -1 & -1 \\ 0 & -1 & 1 \end{vmatrix} = -10\begin{vmatrix} -1 & -1 \\ -1 & 1 \end{vmatrix} - 0\begin{vmatrix} 15 & -1 \\ 0 & 1 \end{vmatrix} + 1\begin{vmatrix} 15 & -1 \\ 0 & -1 \end{vmatrix} = 5$$

Similarly, for A_2 we have

$$|A_2| = \begin{vmatrix} -2 & 10 & 1 \\ 0 & 15 & -1 \\ 1 & 0 & 1 \end{vmatrix} = 35$$

and, for A_3 we have

$$|A_3| = \begin{vmatrix} -2 & 0 & -10 \\ 0 & -1 & 15 \\ 1 & -1 & 0 \end{vmatrix} = -40$$

From the above, we obtain

$$i_1 = 1, i_2 = 7, i_3 = -8$$

From the equations above, we conclude that the original assumptions about the currents for i_1 and i_2 are correct. The current for i_3, however, is opposite to the initial assumed direction.

The above procedure can be simplified by reducing the number of current variables in the system of linear equations. We illustrate the procedure by applying it to the circuit shown in Figure 2.8.2.

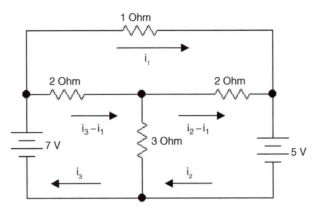

FIGURE 2.8.2
Circuit for Example 2.8.2

Example 2.8.2

In this example, we would like to find i_1, i_2, and i_3 in Figure 2.8.2.

In the above circuit, we use a more efficient procedure to find the currents in the circuit, as listed in the steps that follow.

1. The inner loops of the circuit are identified. With each loop we associate a current in clockwise fashion. In the diagram, there are three loops. On the outer branches of each we associate a current labeled i_1, i_2, and i_3 (an outer branch is a branch that is not shared by two or more loops).

2. For each branch we compute the current variables in terms of the variables generated in step 1. Here, we again assume a clockwise direction. Note that the direction chosen depends on the loop under consideration. For example, for either of the 2 Ω resistors, if we choose to form the direction of the corresponding current based on the upper loop, then the direction would be from right to left. If, however, we choose the direction based on the lower loops, then the directions of the currents would be from left to right. In the diagram, we chose the lower loops for the 2 Ω resistor and the lower right loop for the 3 Ω resistor, as seen in the diagram.

3. Once the currents are determined in the branches, the next step is to use Kirchhoff's voltage law for each loop. The equations for the three loops, top, lower right, and lower left, respectively, are

$$\begin{cases} -1i_1 + 2(i_2 - i_1) + 2(i_3 - i_1) = 0 \\ -2(i_2 - i_1) - 5 - 3(i_2 - i_3) = 0 \\ -2(i_3 - i_1) + 3(i_2 - i_3) + 7 = 0 \end{cases}$$

4. The above equations are written in as a system of linear equations. The left-hand side of each equation is composed of variables multiplied by the proper coefficients and arranged in the order i_1, i_2, and i_3. The right-hand side of each equation is a constant. The above equations rewritten are

$$\begin{cases} -5i_1 + 2i_2 + 2i_3 = 0 \\ 2i_1 - 5i_2 + 3i_3 = 5 \\ 2i_1 + 3i_2 - 5i_3 = -7 \end{cases}$$

5. The last step is to solve the system of linear equations to find the values of the currents i_1, i_2, and i_3, and verify the results as applied to Kirchhoff's current laws. Using Cramer's rule, we get

$$i_1 = 5\ A,\ i_2 = \frac{7}{4}\ A,\ i_3 = \frac{13}{4}\ A$$

2.9   RC Circuits

In this section, we present circuits with resistive and capacitive (RC) elements. Capacitors are components that store charge. The process of storing charge introduces a measurable element of delay in signal propagation. Gates designed using transistors, as will be discussed in the next section, include unintended RC elements called parasitic RC elements. Figure 2.9.1(a) shows an example of a capacitor composed of two plates separated as shown. The capacitor symbol is shown in Figure 2.9.1(b).

In Figure 2.9.1(a), the plates are elements that are capable of storing charge. Initially, there is no charge on the plates. However, when a voltage difference occurs between the two plates (the top and bottom plates are connected to

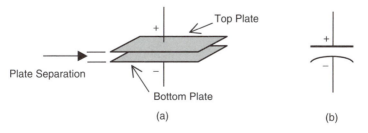

(a)   (b)

FIGURE 2.9.1

positive voltage and ground, or have a voltage difference with the top plate at higher voltage than the lower plate), positive charge is accumulated on the top plate. An equal amount of negative charge is accumulated on the lower plate. The charge (positive and negative) is protected from combining by the distance separating the two plates.

The amount of charge that can be stored on the plates is a function of the structure of the capacitor. The structure's capacitive measure is called capacitance. The capacitance unit of measurement is Farad (F). For the plate capacitor shown in the Figure 2.9.1, the capacitance is proportional to the area of the plate and, inversely, proportional to the distance separating the two plates.

For a given capacitor with a given capacitance, C, the amount of charge (Q) that is present on one of the plates of the capacitor is measured according to the relation

$$Q = CV_C$$

where C is the capacitance of the capacitor and V_c is the voltage difference between the top plate and the lower plate of the capacitor.

As mentioned earlier, current is a measure of electron (charge) flow per time. In equation form, since

$$Q = CV_C$$

we have

$$I = \frac{\Delta Q}{\Delta t} = \frac{\Delta V_C}{\Delta t}$$

where ΔQ is the change in charge over the time interval Δt.

The above equation states that as the voltage across a capacitor is applied, charge is accumulated on the plates of the capacitor. The charge is accumulated through the wires connecting the plates, resulting in a current through these wires.

We next show that the process of charging a capacitor in a circuit that contains resistive elements introduces a measurable element of delay.

Consider the circuit shown in Figure 2.9.2. According to Kirchhoff's voltage law, we have

$$V - IR - V_C = 0$$

with

$$i = \frac{dQ}{dt} = C\frac{dV_C}{dt}$$

We have

$$V - RC\frac{dV_C}{dt} - V_C = 0$$

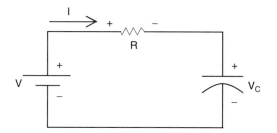

FIGURE 2.9.2
An Example of an RC Circuit

The previous equation can be rewritten as

$$\frac{dV_C}{V - V_C} = \left(\frac{1}{RC}\right) dt$$

Taking the integral of both sides, we have

$$\int \frac{dV_C}{V - V_C} = \frac{1}{RC} \int dt$$

or

$$-\ln(V - V_C) = \frac{t}{RC} + K$$

To find the value of K, we assume that at time $t = 0$, $V_c = 0$. Hence,

$$K = -\ln V$$

Substituting the value of K in the above, we have

$$-\ln(V - V_C) = \frac{t}{RC} + \ln V$$

which can be rewritten as

$$\ln(V - V_C) - \ln V = -\frac{t}{RC}$$

or

$$\ln\left(\frac{V - V_C}{V}\right) = -\frac{t}{RC}$$

with

$$-\frac{t}{RC} = \ln e^{-t/RC}$$

We have

$$\ln\left(\frac{V - V_C}{V}\right) = \ln e^{-t/RC}$$

or

$$\frac{V - V_C}{V} = e^{-t/RC}$$

which can be rewritten as

$$V_C(t) = V\left(1 - e^{\left(\frac{-t}{RC}\right)}\right)$$

The equation above measures the voltage difference across the capacitor as a function of time. Note that at time $t = 0$, $V_c(t) = 0$. Note in addition, as t increases toward infinity the exponent term in the above equation drops to 0, i.e., V_c becomes equal to V. The graph of V_c as a function of time is exponential. Its value at $t = 0$ is 0. As t approaches infinity, the value of V_c approaches V.

We make reference to the point t where $t = RC$. For this time, the exponent value is equal to –1. Hence,

$$V_C(RC) = V(1 - e^{-1}) \approx .63V$$

From the equation, for an RC value of 10^{-9}, for $t = 10^{-9}$ seconds (1 nanosecond), the voltage across the capacitor reaches approximately two thirds the value of the source voltage, V. The application of this in the design of digital circuits is as follows:

1. Gates are designed using transistors as the basic switching elements. Inherent in the design is the unintended creation of an RC element, as shown above. Since RC creation is unintended, the term used is parasitic RC.

2. The inputs to the gate are voltage sources, the V in the circuit above.

3. The output of the gate is measured at V_c. As a result, a change in the input (the voltage source) does not yield an immediate change in the output (V_c). Instead, the RC combination produces a delayed response. The length of the delay is proportional to the RC value; large RC values result in longer delays.

In the next section, we discuss transistors as switching elements and show how logic gates are designed using transistors.

2.10 Transistors and Logic Gates

The principle governing the design of large digital circuits today is the design of the primitive elements called transistors. Millions of these elements can be designed and compacted into a small area that does not exceed 0.25 in.² A transistor is an electrical component with three terminals. In the following, we restrict our discussion to what is commonly referred to as metal oxide semiconductor (MOS) transistors.

The term MOS is used due to an older method of generating a transistor by layering three components: metal, silicon dioxide, and semiconductors. Figure 2.10.1 is a schematic of a MOS transistor.

In Figure 2.10.1, the transistor acts as a switch. The switch is used to either connect or disconnect the source to the drain. This is done under the control of the gate, depending on the voltage applied to it.

The semiconductor layer is called a substrate. This layer is made out of silicon as a semiconductor. To enhance the conductability of silicon, impurities are added to it through a chemical process. These impurities can result in adding excess positive charge or excess negative charge. In the diagram, we see that excess negative charge is added in the proximity of both the source and the drain area. The rest of the substrate, however, has an excess positive charge.

A connection of the source to the drain is accomplished through a current, i.e., through the flow of electrons (negative charge) from the source to the

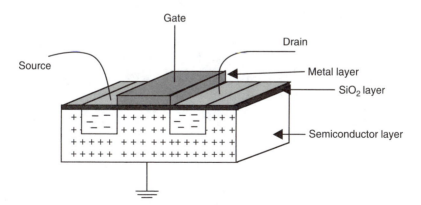

FIGURE 2.10.1
A Schematic of a MOS Transitor

drain. For this to happen, one needs to replace the positive charge between the source and drain with negative charge so as to establish a path. This is the area directly below the gate.

By observing the transistor schematic, we notice that the gate is separtated from the substrate below it by the SiO_2 layer. SiO_2 is glass that is placed between the substrate and the gate as an insulator. From our previous discussion, the combination of the gate, the SiO_2, and the substrate forms a capacitor.

The plates of the capacitor are the gates and the substrate. As a result, by applying a voltage at the gate input an accumalation of charge occurs at the gate plate. The charge applied is the cause of connecting the source to the drain (creating a path of electrons, and hence a current).

To see how this process works, consider the case where we apply positive voltage at the gate level. For this voltage, the net charge accumulated at the gate is positive. However, on the substrate side an equivalent amount of negative charge must be available close to the insulator. If one applies a large enough voltage at the gate level, the channel area under the gate will become negatively charged enough to create a path between the source and drain. Figure 2.10.2 shows the induced channel with negative charge.

Similarly, applying negative charge or leaving the voltage at zero ensures no path connects the source to the drain.

The gate then, in the context of transistor design, controls the switch location. For the transistor shown, a zero voltage applied to the gate simulates the behavior of a switch that is open. A positive voltage (5 V), on the other hand, causes a connection beween the source and drain to occur, in effect closing the switch between the source and the drain.

A final remark about the function of the voltage at the gate: by applying positive voltage at the gate level, the negative charge created in the channel

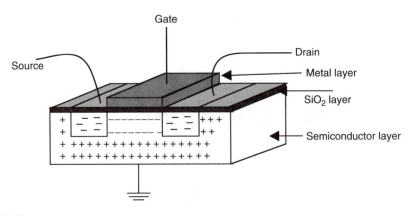

FIGURE 2.10.2
Induced Negative Charge Causes the Source and Drain to be Connected

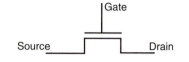

FIGURE 2.10.3
MOS Symbolic Representation

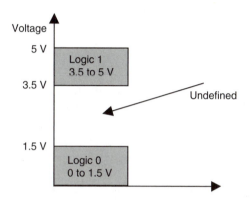

FIGURE 2.10.4
Mapping of voltages to Boolean constants

allows the current to flow through the channel with very little resistance. This is not the case, however, when a zero or negative voltage is applied. For this case, the absence of the negative charge in the channel creates a much larger resistance to the flow of the current. The gate voltage then is controlling the resistance within the switch itself. As a result, the transistor can be thought of as a voltage-controlled resistance. The gate voltage controls the resistance.

From the previous discussion, the transistor as a switch has two different resistances associated with it, depending on the gate voltage. The resistance is voltage controlled and may vary from 100 to over 10^{10} Ω. The presence of the capacitance and the lack of current flow from the gate to the source or from the gate to the drain is symbolized in Figure 2.10.3.

We next discuss the mapping of actual voltage signals to Boolean logic constants, as discussed earlier. The binary logic constants used in Boolean algebra are realized using voltages. Voltages, however, are analog signals. As a result, designers associate a range of voltage values with the logic signals 0 and 1. In general, the voltage ranges are between 0 and 5 V. Figure 2.10.4 shows an example, in which it is assumed that voltage values between 3.5 and 5 V are considered logic 1. Voltage values between 0 and 1.5 V are considered logic 0. The area between the two voltages produces an undefined logic value.

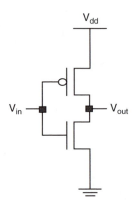

FIGURE 2.11.1
CMOS Design of an Inverter. The input is V_{in} and the output is V_{out}.

2.11 CMOS Gate Design

The above transistor design is abbreviated as nMOS. The n in the abbreviation is due to the fact that the areas close to the source and drain are negatively charged. An opposite scenario exists in transistor design. In the design, the areas around the drain and the source are positivly charged. The rest of the substrate, however, is negatively charged. To distinguish between both types of transistors, the term pMOS is used for this type of design.

For the pMOS transistor to connect the source to the drain, we need to induce positive charge in the channel area oppposite the gate. This can be done by applying a negative voltage at the gate level.

We next discuss the design of logic gates using both types of transistors, pMOS and nMOS. Gates designed using both types of transistors are called CMOS. The c in the term stands for complementary.

We start our discussion of CMOS transistors by analyzing the function of Figure 2.11.1.

As the names imply, V_{in} and V_{out} are the input and output voltages, respectively. The input voltage can assume values between 0 and 5 V. The voltage V_{dd} is assumed to be 5 V. From the figure, the source of the pMOS is connected to the high voltage V_{dd}. Similarly, the drain of the lower transistor is connected to 0 V (the ground). The pMOS transisitor is distinguished from the nMOS by the presence of the bubble at the gate input.

As can be seen, the input voltage (V_{in}) constitutes the gate voltage for both transistors. For this voltage, if the value it assumes is 0 V, then (according to the previous discussion) the pMOS transistor will be on and the nMOS transistor will be off. From the discussion as well, this input combination is

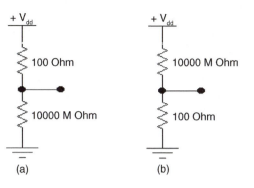

FIGURE 2.11.2
Switch Representaion of Figure 2.11.1, (a) $V_{in} = 0$, (b) $V_{in} = 5$

equivalent to creating a very large resistor for the lower transistor and a small resistance for the upper transistor (assume 10^{10} Ω vs. 100 Ω). An application of 5 V on V_{in} results in the opposite assignment of resistance values. Figure 2.11.2 shows the equivalent connections with the transistors replaced by resistances. Figure 2.11.2(a) is the equivalent circuit obtained for the case of $V_{in} = 0$ V. Similarly, Figure 2.11.2(b) is the equivalent circuit obtained for the case of $V_{in} = 5$ V. The M in the resistance measure units are 10^6.

Applying voltage division on both configurations for Figure 2.11.2(a), one obtains

$$V_{out} = \frac{10^{10}}{\left(100 + 10^{10}\right)} * 5 \approx 4.999 \text{ V}$$

and for Figure 2.11.2(b)

$$V_{out} = \frac{100}{\left(100 + 10^{10}\right)} * 5 \approx 0.00000005 \text{ V}$$

From the logic mapping discussed, the circuit functions as an inverter (NOT) gate. Actual CMOS inverters are fabricated so as to resemble the transistor design given in Figure 2.11.1.

To simplify the discussion, we assume a transistor that connects the source to the drain, an "on" transistor, is equivalent to a switch that is closed (the resistance is very small). An "off" transistor is equivalent to a switch that is open (the resistance is very high).

With the above simplification, the two cases disccused are shown in Figure 2.11.3. Notice in the figure, V_{out} is connected to +5 V or 0 V, but not both.

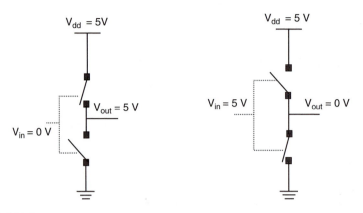

FIGURE 2.11.3
Resistor Representation Based on V_{in} Value in Figure 2.11.1, (a) $V_{in} = 0$, (b) $V_{in} = 5$

2.11.1   The AND CMOS Design

The AND CMOS design is shown in Figure 2.11.4. To illustrate, note that the inverter circuit just designed is part of the circuit as shown. In effect, the output of the inverter is the complement of the circuit that precedes it in the design. This output is labeled V_{out}. In addition, note that the AND design is composed of two parts, the nMOS part and the pMOS part. For the nMOS part, the switches corresponding to the input variables are connected in series fashion. For the pMOS part, however, the connection of the switches is done in parallel.

Finally, due to the fact that one of the switches is always off (causing very large resistance), the circuit allows minimal current from V_{dd} to ground. With the exception of transistors of output from 0 to 1 or vice versa, CMOS circuit uses very little current.

Before we leave this section, we show the design of a four-input AND gate in Figure 2.11.5.

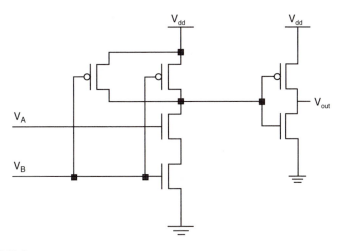

FIGURE 2.11.4
AND Gate CMOS Representation

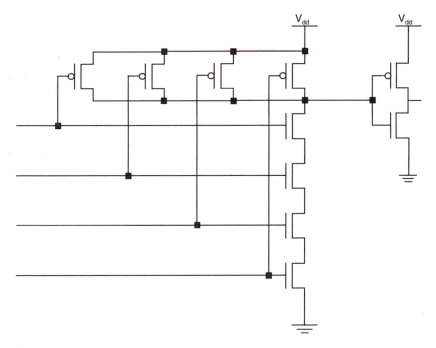

FIGURE 2.11.5
4-Input AND Gate CMOS Representation

Chapter 2 Exercises

2.1 Construct the truth table of the following expressions

(a) $x.y + z$

(b) $x'.y' + z.z'$

(c) $x.y.z + (x + y)'$

2.2 Construct the truth tables for the following expressions

(a) $(x.y)' + z$

(b) $x'.y' + z.w$

(c) $x.y.z + (x + y)' + 1$

2.3 Form the duals of the expressions

(a) $x.y + z(w + x'y')$

(b) $x'.y'.(1 + x)$

(c) $x.y.z + (x + y)'$

2.4 Form the dual of the expression $G'(AB(C' + D) + E(D' + F)(A + B)')$

2.5 Give an example of an expression that is equal to its dual.

2.6 Form the complements of the expressions

(a) $x.y + z(w + x'y')$

(b) $x'.y'.(1 + x)$

(c) $x.y.z + (x + y)'$

2.7 Form the complement of the expression in question 2.4 from its dual.

2.8 Form the complement of the expression in question 2.4 using De Morgan's rule.

2.9 Is it possible to find an expression where the expression is equal to its complement? Please explain.

2.10 Simplify the expressions

(a) $x.y + x'$

(b) $x'.y'.(1 + x)$

(c) $x + y + (x + y)'$

2.11 Simplify the expressions

(a) $xyz + x'yz + xy'z + xyz' + x'$

(b) $xyz + x'yz + y'$

(c) $xyz + x'(w + z') + yz(w + z')$

2.12 Simplify the following expressions by (1) forming the complements of the expressions, (2) by simplifying the complemented expression, and (3) by complementing the simplified expression.

(a) $(x + y + z)(x' + y + z)(x + y' + z)$

(b) $y'(y + z + x)z'$

(c) $(x + y)(x' + y)(z + x)(z' + x)$

2.13 Derive the algebraic equation of the circuit given in Figure E2.1. If possible, simplify the algebraic equation of the circuit.

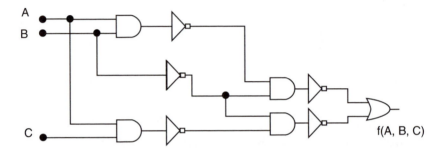

FIGURE E2.1

2.14 Show the gate design of the unsimplified and simplified Boolean equations given in problem 2.11.

2.15 For solution of problem 2.14, verify the circuit designs of the simplified and unsimplified expressions realize equal Boolean functions by constructing the corresponding truth tables.

2.16 Find the current values I_1, I_2, and I_3 in the circuit given in Figure E2.2. Assume the loop currents are in clockwise direction.

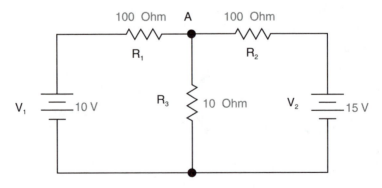

FIGURE E2.2
Current Directions Are Assumed to Be in Clockwise Direction

2.17 Find the voltage at node *A* in the circuit in Figure E2.2.

2.18 Find the currents I_1, I_2, and I_3 and the voltage V_A and V_B for the circuit given in Figure E.2.3.

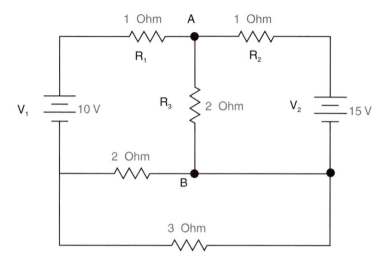

FIGURE E2.3
Current Directions Are Assumed to Be in Clockwise Direction

2.19 Repeat problem 2.18 on the circuit given in Figure E2.4.

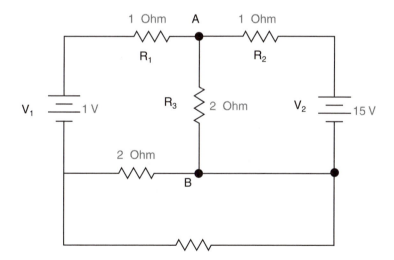

FIGURE E2.4
Current Directions Are Assumed to Be in Clockwise Direction

2.20 Show the CMOS design of a 2-input OR gate.

3

Canonical Forms and Logical Completeness

CONTENTS

3.1 Canonical Forms of Boolean Functions

Forming the canonical sum representation of a Boolean function is one of the standard forms of representing Boolean functions. Other forms are the sum of product form, the canonical product form, and the product of sum form. In this section, we discuss the canonical sum and canonical product form.

3.1.1 Canonical Sum Form

Definition: Over a set of variables, a minterm is a product term that includes all variables, with each variable presented in complemented or uncomplemented form.

Table 3.1.1 includes the minterms over one, two, and three variables. As can be seen from the table, the number of minterms associated with a given set of variables is equal to the number of different assignments the variables can assume. As a result, the number of minterms over n variables is equal to 2^n. We make the following remarks and notations about the above minterms:

1. To form a minterm associated with a given input assignment, a given variable in the minterm is represented in complemented form if it assumes a value of 0. It is represented in uncomplemented form if it assumes a value of 1. For example, over the variables A and B in Table 3.1.1(b) and the assignment $A = 0, B = 1$ the minterm associated with the input is $A'B$.

2. Minterms are associated with binary assignments to the input variables. For an input assignment interpreted as a binary number with

TABLE 3.1.1

(a), (b), and (c) Minterm Tables over 1, 2, and 3 Variables, Respectively

(a)		(b)				(c)				
A	Minterms	A	B	Minterms	A	B	C	Minterms	m_i	
0	A'	0	0	$A'B'$	0	0	0	$A'B'C'$	m_0	
1	A	0	1	$A'B$	0	0	1	$A'B'C$	m_1	
		1	0	AB'	0	1	0	$A'BC'$	m_2	
		1	1	AB	0	1	1	$A'BC$	m_3	
					1	0	0	$AB'C'$	m_4	
					1	0	1	$AB'C$	m_5	
					1	1	0	ABC'	m_6	
					1	1	1	ABC	m_7	

decimal value i, denote the corresponding minterm as m_i. The minterm notation for the case of three variables is shown in Table 3.1.1(c).

3. Since minterms are algebraic expressions, an assignment to the input variables causes these minterms to evaluate to a value of either 0 or 1. In fact, minterms can be thought of as functions; for example, over the three variables A, B, and C we have $m_0(A,B,C) = A'B'C'$, $m_1(A,B,C) = A'B'C$, etc.

4. A literal is a complemented or uncomplemented variable. From the definition of minterms, the algebraic representations of two minterms differ in at least one literal (there is at least one variable that is complemented in one minterm but uncomplemented in the other). As a result, the logical AND $m_i.m_j$ evaluates to 0 if i is not equal to j. That is, there is no input assignment that causes both minterms to assume a value of 1. For example, for the minterms $m_5 = AB'C$ and $m_4 = AB'C'$, we have $m_4.m_5 = (AB'C').(AB'C) = 0$.

5. Finally, for a given minterm, m_i the minterm assumes a value of 1 for only one input assignment (the input assignment with decimal value i). For example, for m_5 we have $m_5(1, 0, 1) = 1$. For this input, all other minterms assume a value of 0.

Definition: A Boolean function is said to be in canonical sum form if it is written as a sum of minterms.

Associated with each truth table is a unique Boolean function written in canonical sum form. To form the function, we include all minterms where the function assumes a value of 1. We illustrate why the canonical sum form works by the following example. Over two variables, assume the Boolean function is given, as shown in Table 3.1.2.

The corresponding canonical sum function is $f(A, B) = AB + A'B'$. Note that f_1 is equal to 1 if and only if $A = 1$ and $B = 1$ or if $A = 0$ and $B = 0$. This is the desired result, i.e., when we construct the truth table from the algebraic expression, we obtain the original truth table. The canonical sum representation is unique. For example, for this function there are four minterms to consider for

TABLE 3.1.2

Truth Table Used for Forming the
Canonical Sum of a Boolean Function

A	B	f
0	0	1
0	1	0
1	0	0
1	1	1

inclusion (or exclusion) in the canonical sum form. Removing any of the two minterms m_0 or m_1 will cause the function to assume a value of 0 for the inputs 00 and 11. As a result, one obtains the wrong truth table. Similarly, including any of the other two minterms will produce the wrong function since the function will assume a value of 1 when it should assume a value of 0.

In notation form and to simplify writing functions in canonical sum form, we adopt three different methods of writing functions:

1. The algebraic form discussed earlier; for example, the function $f(A,B) = AB + A'B'$.
2. As a sum of m_i, $f(A, B) = m_0 + m_1$.
3. Or, as an abbreviated sum form, $f(A, B) = \sum(0, 1)$.

One can convert from (1) to (2) by replacing each minterm by m_i, with i determined from the minterms in the equations. For example, the minterm AB is associated with the input $AB = 11$, which has decimal value 3. As a result, in (2) we add the term m_3. Similarly, one could convert the format in (2) to the format given in (1). The format given in (3) is an abbreviation. The Σ (sigma) term represents the logical OR of the minterms with indices as listed between parentheses. In the example, (0, 3) indicates the function in canonical form is obtained by OR-ing minterms m_0 and m_3, with each represented in the corresponding algebraic form. We illustrate the steps in two examples.

Example 3.1.1
In this example, we form the canonical sum representation of the majority function discussed in Chapter 2.

The first step in forming the canonical sum representation is to form the truth table as given in Table 3.1.3.

The second step is to form all minterms where the function assumes a value of 1. The final step is to OR these minterms to obtain the canonical sum form

$$f(A,B,C) = A'BC + AB'C + ABC' + ABC$$

$$= m_3 + m_5 + m_6 + m_7$$

$$= \sum(3,5,6,7)$$

TABLE 3.1.3

Example 3.1.1, Majority Function

A	B	C	$f(A,B,C)$
0	0	0	0
0	0	1	0
0	1	0	0
0	1	1	1
1	0	0	0
1	0	1	1
1	1	0	1
1	1	1	1

Note that we chose to write the function in the three different formats discussed earlier.

Example 3.1.2

In this example, we construct the canonical sum representation for a Boolean function that adds two binary numbers. Each binary number is composed of two bits as follows.

Let the two binary numbers be A and B with the bits of A and B represented as $A = A_2A_1$ and $B = B_2B_1$, respectively. The constructed function, F, requires multiple outputs. To determine the number of outputs that make up the function, we compute the maximum possible sum $(3 + 3 = 6)$. The sum in binary is 110 and, as a result, the function F requires three outputs. The truth table is given in Table 3.1.4.

TABLE 3.1.4

Example 3.1.2, Addition of 2 2-Bits Binary Numbers

A_2	A_1	B_2	B_1	C_3	S_2	S_1
0	0	0	0	0	0	0
0	0	0	1	0	0	1
0	0	1	0	0	1	0
0	0	1	1	0	1	1
0	1	0	0	0	0	1
0	1	0	1	0	1	0
0	1	1	0	0	1	1
0	1	1	1	1	0	0
1	0	0	0	0	1	0
1	0	0	1	0	1	1
1	0	1	0	1	0	0
1	0	1	1	1	0	1
1	1	0	0	0	1	1
1	1	0	1	1	0	0
1	1	1	0	1	0	1
1	1	1	1	1	1	0

In the table, the choice of the functions labels, C_3, S_2, and S_1, reflect the meaning of each. With each input $A_2A_1B_2B_1$, the sequence of functions $C_3S_2S_1$ (we call F) represents the sum $A_2A_1 + B_2B_1$. From the truth table, we obtain the canonical sum representation of three functions with

$$C_3 = A_2'A_1B_2B_1 + A_2A_1'B_2B_1' + A_2A_1'B_2B_1 + A_2A_1B_2'B_1 + A_2A_1B_2B_1' + A_2A_1B_2B_1$$

$$= m_7 + m_{10} + m_{11} + m_{13} + m_{14} + m_{15}$$

$$= \sum(7,10,11,13,14,15)$$

$$S_2 = A_2'A_1'B_2B_1' + A_2'A_1'B_2B_1 + A_2'A_1B_2'B_1 + A_2'A_1B_2B_1' + A_2A_1'B_2'B_1' + A_2A_1'B_2'B_1 +$$

$$\quad\quad A_2A_1B_2'B_1' + A_2A_1B_2B_1$$

$$= m_2 + m_3 + m_5 + m_6 + m_8 + m_9 + m_{12} + m_{15}$$

$$= \sum(2,3,5,6,8,9,12,15)$$

$$S_3 = A_2'A_1B_2'B_1 + A_2'A_1B_2B_1 + A_2'A_1B_2'B_1' + A_2'A_1B_2B_1' +$$

$$\quad\quad A_2A_1'B_2'B_1 + A_2A_1'B_2B_1 + A_2A_1B_2'B_1' + A_2A_1B_2B_1'$$

$$= m_1 + m_3 + m_4 + m_6 + m_9 + m_{11} + m_{12} + m_{14}$$

$$= \sum(1,3,4,6,9,11,12,14)$$

3.1.2   Canonical Product Form

The canonical product form is an alternative algebraic representation of a function. Formally, the representation is a product of maxterms as defined below.

Definition: A maxterm, over a set of variables, is a sum term of literals where each variable is presented in its complemented or uncomplemented form.

Maxterms are associated with binary assignments to the corresponding variables. For a given assignment, represent the corresponding variable in its complemented (uncomplemented) form if it assumes a value of 1 (0).

For example, over two variables, A and B, the maxterms $A + B$, $A + B'$, $A' + B$, and $A' + B'$, correspond to the input assignments 00, 01, 10, and 11, respectively. Similarly, for three variables one can generate eight maxterms, and in general, the number of maxterms associated with n variables is 2^n.

Definition: A Boolean function is said to be in canonical product form if the function is represented as a product of maxterms.

Notation: Let M_i denote the maxterm representing the binary input with an equivalent decimal value i. Table 3.1.5 shows the minterms and maxterms associated with the three variables A, B, and C.

TABLE 3.1.5

Minterms and Maxterms over Three Variables

A	B	C	Minterms	Maxterms
0	0	0	$m_0 = A'B'C'$	$M_0 = (A + B + C)$
0	0	1	$m_1 = A'B'C$	$M_1 = (A + B + C')$
0	1	0	$m_2 = A'BC'$	$M_2 = (A + B' + C)$
0	1	1	$m_3 = A'BC$	$M_3 = (A + B' + C')$
1	0	0	$m_4 = AB'C'$	$M_4 = (A' + B + C)$
1	0	1	$m_5 = AB'C$	$M_5 = (A' + B + C')$
1	1	0	$m_6 = ABC'$	$M_6 = (A' + B' + C)$
1	1	1	$m_7 = ABC$	$M_7 = (A' + B' + C')$

The canonical product representation of a function is obtained from the truth table as follows:

1. Form all the maxterms where the function assumes a value of 0.
2. AND all the maxterms formed in item 1 above.

Example 3.1.3
Form the canonical product representation of the function with the truth table given in Table 3.1.2.
Solution: The function assumes a value of 0 for the input combination $AB = 01$ and $AB = 10$. The corresponding maxterms are $(A + B')$ and $(A' + B)$, respectively. The canonical product representation of the function is

$$f(A,B) = (A + B')(A' + B)$$

Similar to the canonical sum form, we represent the canonical product in three forms:

1. In algebraic representation form; for example, $f(A, B) = (A + B')(A' + B)$.
2. In product of maxterms, M_i, form; for example, $f(A, B) = M_1.M_2$.
3. In abbreviated product (Π) form; for example, $f(A, B) = \Pi(1, 2)$ (or $f(A, B) = \Pi M_1.M_2$)).

The symbol Π (pi) represents the logical AND of the maxterms.
It is important to emphasize that the two representations of functions discussed (the canonical sum and canonical product) forms are (1) unique, meaning that for a given function described in truth-table form there exists one and only one function in canonical sum (or canonical product) form; and (2) equal, meaning that over the same truth table, although the two canonical representations have different algebraic representations, the functions are equal since they have the same truth table.
We discuss the relation between canonical sum and canonical product representation. Recall the complement of a given function f is defined as

TABLE 3.1.6

From Table 3.1.2 with Complement
Function Included

A	B	f	$\bar{f}$
0	0	1	0
0	1	0	1
1	0	0	1
1	1	1	0

$$\bar{f} = \begin{cases} 0 \text{ if } f = 1 \\ 1 \text{ if } f = 0 \end{cases}$$

By referring to truth tables, the complement of a function is obtained by changing the entries corresponding to the function, f, in the table. The entries with a value of 0 are replaced by entries with a value of 1, and vice versa. To illustrate, we reconstruct the function in Table 3.1.2 with the complement, as shown in Table 3.1.6.

By referring to Table 3.1.5 we note that minterms and maxterms are related by the equation

$$m_i = \overline{M_i}$$

The canonical product of a function can be obtained from the canonical sum representation of its complement. We illustrate by referring to the function in Table 3.1.6. The complement of the function is

$$\bar{f}(A,B) = \bar{A}B + A\bar{B}$$

$$= m_1 + m_2$$

Forming the complement of the above function yields the algebraic representation of f in canonical product form as shown

$$f(A,B) = \overline{\overline{f}}(A,B)$$

$$= \overline{\bar{A}B + A\bar{B}}$$

$$= (A + \bar{B})(\bar{A} + B)$$

$$= \overline{m_1 + m_2}$$

$$= M_1 \cdot M_2$$

$$\Pi(M_1, M_2)$$

The canonical product representation of the function above is the expected function as given earlier. Hence, one can obtain the canonical product representation of a function from its complement function in canonical sum form. When the canonical sum form is complemented, the result is another function in canonical product form.

Before we move to the next subsection, we conclude with the following: Given the canonical sum representation of a function in abbreviated form (Σ), one can generate the abbreviated canonical product representation (Π) form by including in the Π form all numbers not found in the Σ form. For example, for the majority function we have the abbreviated canonical sum representation $\Sigma(3, 5, 6, 7)$. As a result, the abbreviated product of sum representation is $\Pi(0, 1, 2, 4)$.

3.2   Sum of Product and Product of Sum Forms

The previous representations of Boolean functions in canonical forms are called standard forms. In this section we discuss two additional standard forms, the sum of products and the product of sums representations.

3.2.1   Sum of Product Form

The sum of product form is a general case of the canonical sum form. Similar to the canonical sum form, the algebraic representation is composed of sum of terms. The terms, however, need not be minterms; instead, each term is a product term. As a result, the canonical sum form is a special case of the sum of product form. We assume that a single literal is considered a product term.

Example 3.2.1
Over three variables, A, B, and C, the following are examples of functions in sum of product form:

1. $f(A,B,C) = AB + A'B'$
2. $f(A,B,C) = ABC$
3. $f(A,B) = A + B'$

In example 2, the function is in sum of product form. Here, however, there is no sum operation since the function includes a single product term. In addition, the function is in canonical sum form. The product term is a minterm. In example 3, the function is in sum of product form since it is a sum of two terms. Each term is a product term that includes a single literal.

Example 3.2.2

Over three variables, A, B, and C, the following are examples of functions not in sum of product form:

1. $f(A,B,C)=(AB)'+A'B'$
2. $f(A,B,C)=AB(A+C)$
3. $f(A,B,C)=(A+B')(C'+B)$

In example 1, the term $(AB)'$ is not a product term since it is not a product of literals.

3.2.2   Product of Sum Form

The product of sum form is a general case of the canonical product form. The terms used are sum terms of literals. Note that a single literal is considered a sum of literals (in this case, just one literal).

Example 3.2.3

Over three variables, A, B, and C, the following are examples of functions in product of sum form:

1. $f(A,B,C)=(A+B)(A'+B')$
2. $f(A,B,C)=(A+B+C)(A'+B'+C')$
3. $f(A,B)=A+B'+C$

In example 2, the function, in addition to being in product of sum form, is in canonical product form. In example 3, the function is in canonical product of sum form (the function contains one sum term $(A + B' + C)$). Is the function in canonical product form as well?

Example 3.2.4

Over three variables, A, B, and C, the following are examples of functions not in product of sum form:

1. $f(A,B,C)=(AB)'+A'B'$
2. $f(A,B,C)=AB(A+C)+A'$

3.2.3   Verification of Function Equality Using Canonical Forms

In Chapter 2, we defined equality of functions and stated that two functions over the same set of variables are equal if the two functions have the same truth table.

An alternative method of showing equality of functions given in algebraic forms is to expand each function algebraically and write the functions in canonical sum or canonical product form. Since the canonical sum or canonical product representation of a function is unique, the two functions are equal if they have identical canonical sum or canonical product representation. We illustrate this method of verification of equality in the two examples that follow.

Example 3.2.5
Show that $f_1(A, B, C) = AB + AB' + A'B'C'$ is equal to the function $f_2(A, B, C) = A + A'B'C'$ by expanding each function to the corresponding canonical sum representation.

Solution: In expanding the above function, we convert the terms in the function into minterms, as shown:

$$f_1(A,B,C) = AB + AB' + A'B'C'$$
$$= AB(C+C') + AB'(C+C') + A'B'C'$$
$$= ABC + ABC' + AB'C + AB'C' + A'B'C'$$
$$= \Sigma(0,4,5,6,7)$$

Similarly, for the function f_2 we have

$$f_2(A,B,C) = A + A'B'C'$$
$$= A(B+B') + A'B'C'$$
$$= AB + AB' + A'B'C'$$
$$= AB(C+C') + AB'(C+C') + A'B'C'$$
$$= ABC + ABC' + AB'C + AB'C' + A'B'C'$$
$$= \Sigma(0,4,5,6,7)$$

Since the two functions have identical canonical sum forms, they are equal.

Example 3.2.6
Algebraically expand the function $f(A, B, C) = A + B$ into canonical product form.

Solution: In the previous example, where needed, we introduced variables into products by multiplying by an expression that evaluates to 1. In the canonical product form, we add the needed variables to an expression using the rule $x + 0 = x$.

In the function $f(A, B, C) = A + B$, the variable C is missing from the function. As a result, the function can be rewritten and expanded as

$$f(A,B,C) = A + B$$
$$= A + B + CC'$$
$$= ((A + B) + C)((A + B) + C')$$
$$= (A + B + C)(A + B + C').$$

Note that in the above expansion we made use of the rule

$$x + y \cdot z = (x + y) \cdot (x + z)$$

3.3   Design of Functions in Standard Forms

In the design procedure discussed, we assume there is no restriction on the fan-in (the number of allowable inputs to a given gate) associated with gates.

3.3.1   Canonical Sum and Sum of Product Design

For the canonical sum form, the gate-level design is composed of two levels, an AND and an OR level (abbreviated as AND-OR). The second level is composed of a single OR gate. The first level contains AND gates. Each AND gate realizes one of the minterms found in the canonical sum.

For the sum of product, one follows a similar procedure as for the canonical sum case. The AND gates in the first level, however, realize the product terms found in the sum of product representation. For the cases where the product term is a single literal, the corresponding AND gate in the first level is removed. We illustrate the design procedure on the majority (voting) function described in Chapter 2. The canonical sum representation of the voting function written in the three forms discussed earlier are

1. $F(A,B,C) = A'BC + AB'C + ABC' + ABC$
2. $F(A,B,C) = m_3 + m_5 + m_6 + m_7$
3. $F(A,B,C) = \Sigma(m_3, m_5, m_6, m_7) = \Sigma(3,5,6,7)$

The design is accomplished using a two-level AND-OR. The first level is composed of four AND gates. Each AND gate realizes one of the minterms. The second level is a single OR gate. Its inputs are the outputs of the AND gates (the minterms) of level one. The design is shown in Figure 3.3.1.

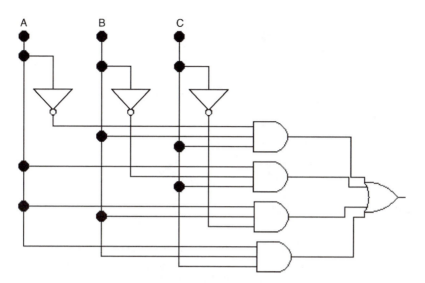

FIGURE 3.3.1
Design of $F(A,B,C) = A'BC + AB'C + ABC' + ABC$

We illustrate the design of functions written in sum of products by refer-ring to the majority function. From Chapter 2, Example 2.3.5, we found the minimized function is

$$F(A,B,C) = AB + BC + AC$$

The design of the function is similar to the above design; the AND gates in the first level, however, realize the product terms. As a result, the number of AND gates is three instead of four. In addition, each AND gate realizes a smaller product (2 vs. 3). The design is shown in Figure 3.3.2. To illustrate the saving, we show in a later section the design of the above circuits by mapping the design into a specific set of available gates. This process of design is called technology mapping.

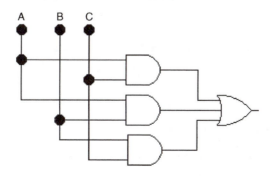

FIGURE 3.3.2
Design of $F(A,B,C) = AB + BC + AC$

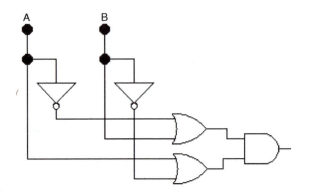

FIGURE 3.3.3
Design of $f(A,B) = (A' + B)(A + B')$

The design in Figure 3.3.2 represents the steps carried in the overall design process of a circuit when a two-level AND-OR design is desired. The first step in the design is to convert the word problem into a truth-table format. The second step is to generate the canonical sum representation of the function. The third step is to minimize the function. The fourth step is to design.

3.3.2   Canonical Product and Product of Sum Representation

The design of functions in canonical product, or product of sum representations, follows a similar procedure as the design of functions in canonical sum, or sum of products. A two-level gate design is used. Here, however, the first level is composed of OR gates. The second level is a single AND gate. For the case of canonical product, the first level of OR gates realizes the maxterms found in the canonical product. The number of OR gates is equal to the number of maxterms found in the function. For the case where the function is written in product of sum, the first level realizes the sum terms in the function. The number of gates is equal to the number of sum terms composed of two or more literals.

We illustrate the design procedure on the function with description given in Table 3.1.2. The canonical product form for the function is

$$f(A,B) = (A' + B)(A + B')$$

The design is shown in Figure 3.3.3.

3.4   Other Two Variable Functions

In this section, we consider additional two-variable functions. Some of the functions are associated with specific gates that realize them, as will be shown.

TABLE 3.4.1

All Possible Boolean Functions over Two Variables

A	B	F_0	F_1	F_2	F_3	F_4	F_5	F_6	F_7	F_8	F_9	F_{10}	F_{11}	F_{12}	F_{13}	F_{14}	F_{15}
0	0	0	0	0	0	0	0	0	0	1	1	1	1	1	1	1	1
0	1	0	0	0	0	1	1	1	1	0	0	0	0	1	1	1	1
1	0	0	0	1	1	0	0	1	1	0	0	1	1	0	0	1	1
1	1	0	1	0	1	0	1	0	1	0	1	0	1	0	1	0	1

TABLE 3.4.2

Additional Two Variable Operations

(a)			(b)			(c)			(d)		
A	B	NAND	A	B	NOR	A	B	XOR	A	B	Equivalence
0	0	1	0	0	0	0	0	0	0	0	1
0	1	1	0	1	0	0	1	1	0	1	0
1	0	1	1	0	0	1	0	1	1	0	0
1	1	0	1	1	0	1	1	0	1	1	1

3.4.1 Number of Boolean Functions over Two Variables

From the previous discussion, two functions over the same set of variables are different (not equal) if they have different truth tables. Table 3.4.1 includes all such possible functions over two variables. There are 16 different functions (the number of possible 4-bit combinations) The functions are labeled F_0 through F_{15} with F_0 and F_{15}, respectively, equal to 0 and 1, independent of the input assignments. Note the presence of the AND (F_1) and the OR (F_7) functions. Of the functions listed in the table, we discuss four functions of importance (in addition to the AND and the OR functions).

3.4.1.1 The NAND Function

This function is the complement of the AND function. Its value is equal to 0 if and only if both inputs assume the value of 1. The output is 0 otherwise. The truth table of the function is given in Table 3.4.2(a). The algebraic equation is

$$f_{NAND}(A,B) = (A \cdot B)' = A' + B'$$

The symbol for the NAND operation is $\uparrow$, i.e., $A \uparrow B = A' + B'$. The gate representation is shown in Figure 3.4.1(a).

3.4.1.2 The NOR Function

This function is the complement of the OR function. Its name is NOT OR, or NOR. Its truth table is given in Table 3.4.2(b). Its algebraic equation is

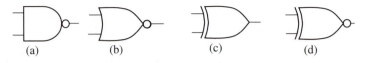

FIGURE 3.4.1
Gate Symbols (a) NAND, (b) NOR, (c) XOR, (d) EQUIVALENCE

$$f_{NOR}(A,B) = (A+B)' = A' \cdot B'$$

The symbol for the NOR operation is $\downarrow$, i.e., $A \downarrow B = A' \cdot B'$. The gate representation is shown in Figure 3.4.1(b).

3.4.1.3   The Exclusive OR Function

The Exclusive-OR (XOR) function evaluates to 1 when one of the inputs, but not both, evaluate to 1. The truth table of the function is given in Table 3.4.2(c). The algebraic representation is

$$f_{XOR}(A,B) = AB' + A'B = A \oplus B$$

As can be seen from the equation, the symbol for the XOR operation is $\oplus$. The gate representation is shown in Figure 3.4.1(c).

3.4.1.4   The Equivalence Function

The equivalence function, Exclusive NOR or XNOR, is the complement of the XOR function. Its truth table is given in Table 3.4.2(d). The algebraic equation is

$$f_{Equivalence}(A,B) = A'B' + AB$$

The symbol for the Equivalence operation is $\odot$. The gate representation of the function is given in Figure 3.4.1(d).

For the case of the AND and the OR gates, we could extend the gate design to include more than two inputs. This is due to the fact that the operations are both associative and commutative. The NAND and NOR operations, however, are not associative. As a result, one cannot extend the gate design from two inputs to multiple inputs. To illustrate, the failure of the associativity case for the NAND gate is referred to in Figure 3.4.2. As can be seen from the figure, the outputs are different and depend on the order of forming the NAND operations.

To extend the NAND gate to more than two inputs, we define the generalized NAND function as the complement of a multiple input AND gate. Similarly, we define the general NOR function as the complement of the

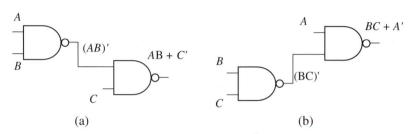

FIGURE 3.4.2
NAND Operation Is Not Associative

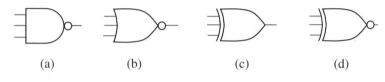

FIGURE 3.4.3
3-input Gates

general multiple input OR function. With these definitions, one can show the NAND and NOR operations are both associative and commutative. As a result, we can generate gate representations for these. The XOR and the XNOR operations are both associative and commutative. As a result, one can extend the gate representation to include more than two inputs. For the XOR function, one can show the output assumes a value of 1 when an odd number of the inputs assume a value of 1. Similarly for the equivalence function, one can show the output assumes a value of 1 when an even number of inputs assume a value of 1. Figure 3.4.3 shows examples of three-input gates for the four functions discussed.

The outputs for Figure 3.4.3(a) and Figure 3.4.3(b) are

$$f_{NAND}(A,B,C) = (A \cdot B \cdot C)' = A' + B' + C',$$

$$f_{NOR}(A,B,C) = (A + B + C)' = A'B'C'$$

The outputs for Figure 3.4.3(c) and Figure 3.4.3(d) are left as an exercise.

3.5 Logical Completeness

Logical completeness has to do with sets that include logic operations (functions) and constants, as given in the following definition.

3.5.1   Definition and Examples

Definition: A set, *S*, is said to be logically complete if and only if any Boolean function can be designed using only elements of the set *S*.

Example 3.5.1
We show the set *S* = {AND,OR,NOT} is logically complete as follows.

Any Boolean function is uniquely described in truth-table format. Earlier we associated with any truth table a unique function in canonical sum form. Since the canonical sum form includes only the three operations (AND, OR, and NOT), the function can be designed using a two-level AND-OR design with the inputs complemented using NOT gates if needed. As a result, any Boolean function can be designed using only elements from the set *S*.

The set *S* is our first logically complete set. To show that other sets are logically complete, we make use of this set. In general, one can show a given set, *S'*, is logically complete by showing all the operations found in already-known logically complete set, S, can be generated using elements from the set *S'* only.

Example 3.5.2
We show the two sets, *S'* = {OR,NOT} and *S"* = {AND,NOT}, are both logically complete sets.

For the set *S'*, in order to show the set is logically complete we need to show the operation in the already-known logically complete set *S* = {AND,OR,NOT} can be generated using the operations in the set *S'*. By observation, the only operation that one needs to generate is the AND operation. For this, we are restricted to using the operations OR and NOT from the set *S'*. Using DeMorgan's rule we have

$$A \cdot B = (A' + B')'$$

Note that the operations used in the right-hand side of the equality are those found in the set *S'*. Since we were able to generate the AND operation using the operations in *S'*, the set *S'* is logically complete.

One can also use gates to show logical completeness. Here, the function desired to generate is written in a block diagram fashion with the inputs and outputs specified. The details of the internal design of the block includes only gates (operations) from the set *S'* (NOT and OR gates). We illustrate this in Figure 3.5.1. The internal design of the AND gate is shown in Figure 3.5.2. Part (a) of the figure shows the three gates used. Figure 3.5.2(b) uses an abbreviated notation. The bubble at the input of the gate indicates the input variable is first inverted. Figure 3.5.2(c) shows the equivalent AND gate.

In a similar fashion, we show the set *S'* = {AND,NOT} is logically complete. The OR operation is missing from *S"*. To generate it, we use DeMorgan's rule as

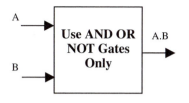

FIGURE 3.5.1
Block Diagram with Input/Output Labels and Operations Used in the Block

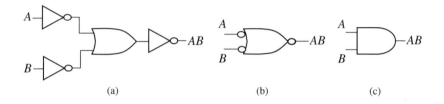

FIGURE 3.5.2
(a) Use of NOT and OR, (b) Equivalent Schematic, (c) Equivalent AND

$$A + B = (A' \cdot B')'$$

3.5.2 The NAND and NOR Gates as Logically Complete Gates

Each of the NAND and NOR gates are logically complete gates (operations). As a result, these gates are called universal gates. In the next section, we present methods of designing circuits using NAND circuits or NOR circuits only. Here we show the two gates are logically complete. To show the NAND is logically complete, we use the gate notation. We show that using NAND we could generate the set $S = \{AND, NOT\}$; and as a result, the NAND gate is logically complete. Figure 3.5.3(a) generates the NOT function. Using the gate above, we could generate the AND gate by inverting the output of a NAND gate, as shown in Figure 3.5.3(b).

We use a similar procedure to show the NOR gate is logically complete. Here, however, we generate the operations OR and NOT. Figure 3.5.4 generates the NOT and the OR gates.

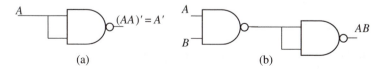

FIGURE 3.5.3
(a) Generation of NOT from NAND, (b) Generation of AND from NAND

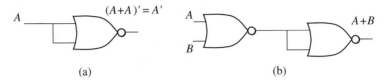

(a)   (b)

FIGURE 3.5.4
(a) Generation of NOT from NOR, (b) Generation of OR from NOR

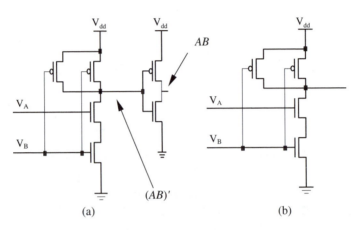

(a)   (b)

FIGURE 3.5.5
CMOS Design, (a) AND, (b) NAND

Before we conclude this section, we show the switch design of the AND and NAND gates at the CMOS transistor level. Figure 3.5.5(a) and Figure 3.5.5(b) show the design of the AND and NAND gates, respectively. We make two observations about the circuits:

1. The AND gate requires more transistor elements than the NAND gate
2. The delay in the NAND gate is shorter than that of the AND. For the AND gate, the output of the first set of switches (NAND gate) is complemented using the second level to produce the AND gate. This is similar to the design of AND from NAND, shown in Figure 3.5.3(b).

3.6   NAND and NOR Design of Combinational Circuits

Since both the NAND and NOR gates are logically complete, using either gate, one can design any combinational circuit. We show the design of two-level gates using both types of gates.

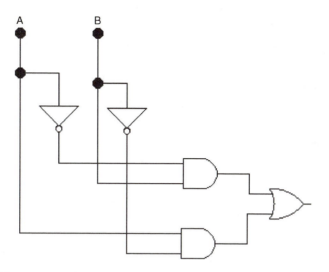

FIGURE 3.6.1
Example Circuit Used to Derive NAND-NAND Design

3.6.1 NAND Gate Design

For the NAND gate design, we discuss the procedure by the example circuit of a two-level AND-OR design, as shown in Figure 3.6.1. The gate design is that of the XOR gate design. On the circuit, we would like to replace the gates by the corresponding equivalent NAND gates. Using the previous discussion, we could replace both the NOT and AND gates by NAND gates. The newly transformed equivalent design is shown in Figure 3.6.2.

With the exception of the OR gate above, the circuit is composed of NAND gates. The OR gate, however, can be combined with the NAND gates at its inputs to form a NAND gate. Figure 3.6.3 shows the equivalence (both circuits have the same output). Replacing the NAND-OR gates in Figure 3.6.3(a) by the equivalent NAND gate in Figure 3.6.3(b), we obtain the circuit shown in Figure 3.6.4. Note that the new circuit obtained is similar to the original AND-OR circuit with one difference: the AND-OR gates are replaced by NAND gates. This can serve as a procedure to the design of functions using a two-level NAND-NAND gate. The procedure can be stated as follows:

1. From the word problem, construct the truth table behavioral description.
2. From the truth table, write the function in canonical sum form.
3. Minimize the canonical sum form obtained in (2) and write the minimum in sum of product form.
4. Design the function as a two-level AND-OR design but with all the gates (NOT, AND, and OR) replaced by NAND gates. (Single variables used as inputs into second level NAND gate are first inverted.)

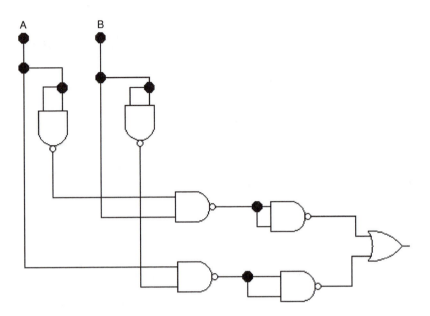

FIGURE 3.6.2
AND-OR Design, Inverters Are Replaced with NAND Gates

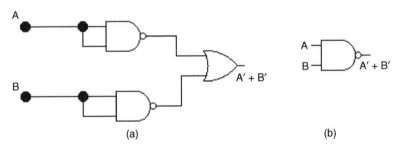

FIGURE 3.6.3
NAND Gate, (a) NAND-OR Design, (b) Equivalent NAND

3.6.2   NOR Gate Design

A similar procedure is used to design circuits using NOR gates only. In the previous example, we proceeded from a two-level AND-OR design to form a two-level NAND-NAND design. To illustrate the design using NOR gates, we start with the design of a two-level OR-AND. The design of the XOR function using a two level OR-AND is shown in Figure 3.6.5. Replacing the NOT and the OR gates with the equivalent NOR gate design we obtain the circuit shown in Figure 3.6.6. The combination of the NOR and AND gates shown in Figure 3.6.6 is equivalent to a NOR gate. We obtain Figure 3.6.7 by replacing this combination with the equivalent NOR gate. Similar to the

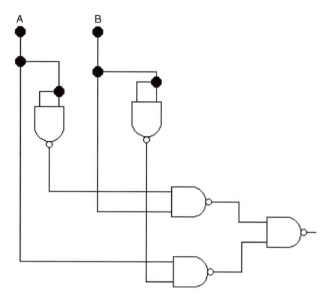

FIGURE 3.6.4
NAND-NAND Circuit of the XOR Function

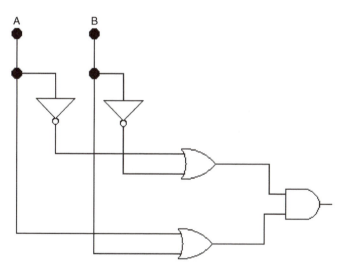

FIGURE 3.6.5
OR-AND Design of the XOR Function

NAND gate design, note that the new circuit obtained in Figure 3.6.7 is identical to the original OR-AND circuit with one difference: all the gates are replaced by NOR gates.

The previous can serve as a procedure to the design of functions using two-level NOR-NOR gates. The procedure is similar to the NAND-NAND

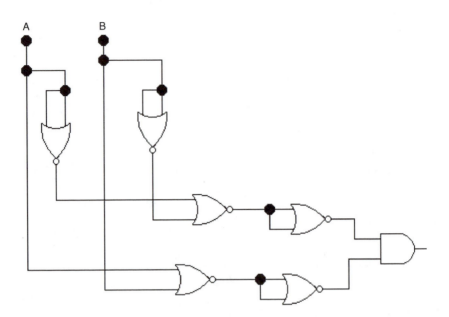

FIGURE 3.6.6
Figure Obtained from Figure 3.6.5, Replace Invertors and OR Gates by NOR Gates

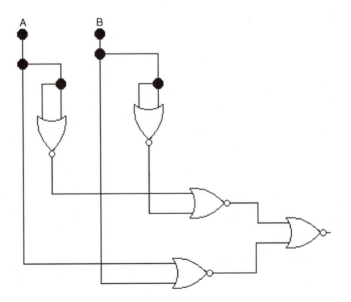

FIGURE 3.6.7
NOR-NOR Design of XOR Gate Obtained from Figure 3.6.6

gate design. Here, however, the function is designed using two-level OR-AND, i.e., the minimized function is written in sum of product form.

Before we conclude this section, we will discuss other design alternatives that we will be using in describing designs when programmable logic devices are covered in Chapter 6.

3.6.3   AND-OR-Invert and OR-AND-Invert Design

The design of circuits using three-level gates, AND-OR-Invert, can be accomplished in a fashion similar to the design using AND-OR design. Due to the presence of the inverter, however, the output of the circuit obtained is not the function, but its complement. To obtain the original function at the output, we simplify the complement of the function starting with its canonical sum representation. We then design the complement function using a procedure similar to the design using AND-OR, but with the inverter input attached to the output of the AND gate. The output of the inverter then produces the correct function.

For the case of the design using OR-AND-Invert, a similar procedure is used by starting with the complement of the function written in canonical product form.

We illustrate the procedure for the case of the XOR gate. The function and the complement equations in both the canonical sum and canonical product forms are given below.

$$f(A,B) = A'B + AB',$$

$$f(A,B) = (A' + B')(A + B),$$

$$\bar{f}(A,B) = A'B' + AB, \text{ and}$$

$$\bar{f}(A,B) = (A' + B)(A + B').$$

For the design of the function using OR-AND-Invert, we implement $\bar{f}$ written in canonical product. Figure 3.6.8(a) shows the design. Note the output of the circuit. The output is the function in canonical sum form. To obtain the output in canonical product form, we use AND-OR-Invert, i.e., we implement $\bar{f}$ as in canonical sum form.

3.7   Design Automation Tools and Levels of Abstraction

Today, CPU designs include millions of transistors placed in an area of approximately 0.25 in.^{2} To deal with the complexity of design, the design

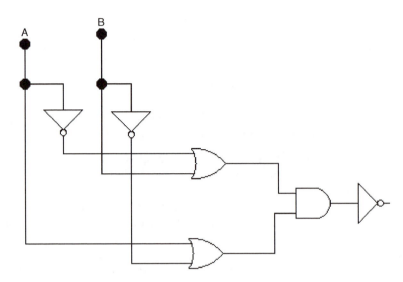

FIGURE3.6.8
AND-OR-INVERT Design of XOR

process is seen at different levels of abstractions (modular levels similar to programming). In addition, the design process is automated where computer-aided design tools are used extensively to reduce the complexity of design. These topics are discussed next.

3.7.1 Levels of Abstraction

In our study of topics thus far, we have encountered two levels of abstraction: the gate and the transistor levels. In the gate level, the gate is composed of several transistors. At this level, the detail of the internal transistor design is hidden. Figure 3.7.1 shows two additional levels of abstraction. The design at each level is an interconnection of components associated with the level. The components constitute the library of the level.

We consider first the highest level of abstraction, the processor level. At this level, the components used in the design are the central processing units (CPUs), memory, and input/output controllers, for example. These units form the building blocks at the processor level. The interconnection of these components yields the desired system.

At the register level, the internal design of the processor level is considered. Here, the internal design of the processor level library elements is shown in more detail. We consider the processor design as an example. Figure 3.7.2 shows a schematic at the two levels. The register level is partially shown. For example, the control unit diagrams are not included. In addition, the details of the arithmetic logic unit (ALU) are not shown.

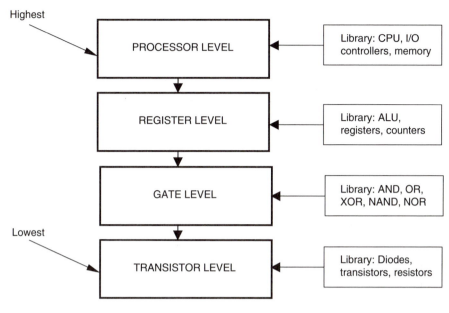

FIGURE 3.7.1
Levels of Abstraction

The purpose of the figure is to show that more details of the CPU internal design are seen at the register level. At this level, we use components such as adders, registers, and register files as the basic building blocks in the design. These components form the library elements of the register level.

The hierarchal view of design continues to lower levels with each lower level showing more details of the design. For example, more details about each of the building blocks used at the register level are studied at the gate level. Finally, at the transistor level, the details of the internal designs of gates are studied.

The levels of abstraction help in simplifying the design process. This is similar to modular programming where the program is broken into smaller sub-programs. This process is repeated until the sub-programs are simple to design. Our discussion in the text considers designs using the library components found at the gate and register levels.

3.7.2 Computer-Aided Design (CAD) Tools

Due to the complexity of digital system design, computers are used to aid in the overall design process through the use of special (tools) programs. We discuss these tools in relation to a simple-to-use package called MultiSim (previously known as the Electronics Workbench, EW). We relate the discussion of CAD tools used in design to the design process. The steps carried in design

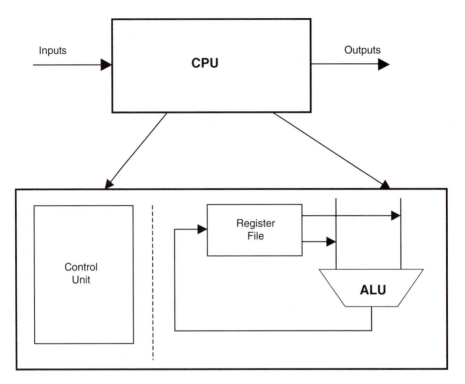

FIGURE 3.7.2
Register Level Abstraction

depend on the type of gates used. For example, if our objective is to design a given function using two-level AND-OR gates, then we follow these steps:

1. From the word problem, we develop the behavioral description in truth-table form.
2. From the truth table, construct the canonical sum representation of the function.
3. Simplify the canonical sum function into some of the product format.
4. Design the sum of product function using a two-level AND-OR gate.
5. Verify the design is correct by constructing the truth table from the circuit design.

The CAD tools (programs) used to realize the steps above are broken into classes. Each class contains a set of programs. Depending on the set of CAD tools used, the classes used may include programs that aid in design entry, synthesis, simulation, and placement and routing. We discuss the first three classes next.

3.7.2.1 Design Entry

These tools allow the user to enter the description of the circuit in many forms. These forms include behavioral description where the user enters the description in truth-table or algebraic equations format, for example. In addition, design entry tools include schematic capture tools. A schematic capture tool allows the user to enter a design using the graphical user interface (GUI) of the tool. Here, the design entry tool contains graphical symbols of the gates/units that one can use in the design. The set of allowable units forms the library the user can employ in the design. We will illustrate this process later. Other methods of design entry include entering the description in a Hardware Description Language (HDL). HDLs are similar to programming languages. The language has variable declarations, conditional statements, loop statements, and assignment statements, for example. Unlike programming languages, however, the purpose of the language is to describe circuit design.

3.7.2.2 Synthesis

After design entry of the circuit is completed, the next step is to synthesize the design. Synthesis usually involves several steps, including an optimization step. This step may, for example, optimize (minimize) the Boolean equations the user has entered. Following this optimization step, the next step in synthesis may involve generating the needed design. Here the target technology used in design is specified; for example, AND-OR, OR-AND, NAND-NAND, etc., synthesis may involve an already-existing design entered using schematic capture. The design can then be optimized and a new, more efficient design may be generated. The generated design may use a different set of gates.

3.7.2.3 Simulation

Simulation is similar to analysis where the purpose of simulation is to verify the synthesized circuit functions as intended. The simulation may involve the generation of the Boolean functions and/or truth tables from the circuit. For large circuits, the truth-table generation may not be feasible. Today, circuits may have 32 inputs requiring a truth table with 2^{32} entries, 4 G. As a result, designers check functionality by applying a predetermined set of inputs to the synthesized circuit. The circuit response to these inputs is then compared to a stored response. The process of generating the set of inputs is called test generation.

Test generation uses fault models. The model is chosen so as to resemble actual physical failures. An example of a fault model that is commonly used is called the single-stuck-at fault model. In this model, a single line in the circuit is assumed to be permanently stuck-at-zero or permanently stuck-at-one.

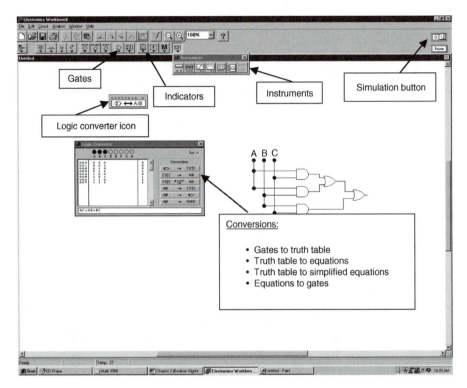

FIGURE 3.8.1
Graphical User Interface of the Electronics Workbench

3.8 Application to the Electronics Workbench (EW)

3.8.1 The Electronics Workbench

In this section, we introduce the Electronics Workbench package in the context of the discussion of the CAD tools discussed in the previous section. The CD provided with the text includes MultiSim (a modified version of the Electronics Workbench). A MultiSim tutorial is found in the accompanying CD. We look first at the GUI of the Electronics Workbench. We then look at the levels of abstraction of representing design details. Finally, we look at the three classes used in CAD tools (design entry, synthesis, and simulation).

The Electronics Workbench GUI is shown in Figure 3.8.1. The interface is used to communicate with the package in order to synthesize and simulate circuit design.

In the context of levels of abstraction, the interface allows us to perform the design at different levels of abstraction. In the figure, an arrow points to the gates button. When this button is pressed, a menu of available gates is

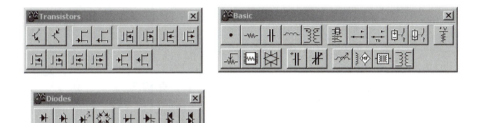

FIGURE 3.8.2
Gate-Level Library

FIGURE 3.8.3
As Shown in the Bin Labels, the Electronics Workbench provides Transistor, Resistor, and Diode
Libraries

shown. From this we could choose the gates discussed in this chapter to
perform the design. Figure 3.8.2 shows an example of the gates menu (bin).

At a lower level, one can perform design at the transistor and resistor level.
Figure 3.8.3 shows an example.

At a higher level, the interface allows the use of circuits that are composed
of many gates. Each of the circuits performs a specific task. For example,
Figure 3.8.4 shows an example of a circuit called 1-bit full adder. The details
of the circuit will be studied in Chapter 5. Part (a) of the figure includes the
bin containing the 1-bit full adder. Part (c) of the figure shows another circuit
labeled muxer. This circuit will be discussed in Chapter 5 as well.

3.8.2   Design Entry

We consider three methods of design entry as discussed earlier.

3.8.2.1   Design Entry through Truth Tables

Design entry through truth tables is accomplished by using the logic converter software tool found in the instruments bin. To use the converter, click
on instruments. Then click and drag the logic converter icon. Double-click
on the icon to open the converter. The process is shown in Figure 3.8.5.

The converter can be used as a design entry, synthesis, and simulate tool.
For design entry using the logic converter, one needs to translate the problem

(a)

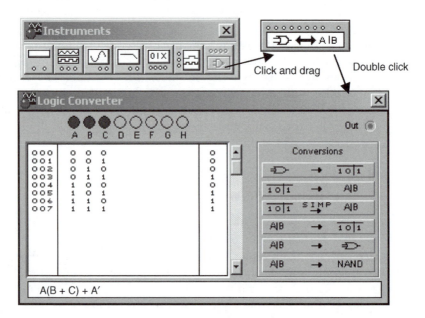

(b)   (c)

FIGURE 3.8.4
(a) Medium-Scale Integration Library; (b) Block Diagram of 1-Bit Full Adder; (c) Block Diagram Of A Generic Multiplexer

FIGURE 3.8.5
Text Box at Bottom of Converter Can Be Used to Type Boolean Equations in Design Entry

at hand to either a truth table or an algebraic form. The truth table is entered in the logic converter window by (1) selecting the number of input variables, and (2) setting the truth values of the function. To select the input variables, we click the circles with labels A, B, C, etc., as shown above. To enter the truth values of the function, we select the entries where the function assumes a value of 1 (use the mouse to select the entry) and by typing a 1 in these entries (initially, all values of the function are set to 0.)

3.8.2.2 Design Entry through Equations

The logic converter can be used to enter design description in Boolean equation format as well. This is done by typing the equations in the text box at the bottom of the converter (Figure 3.8.5). In the text box of the converter, we typed the Boolean equation $A(B + C) + A'$.

3.8.2.3 Design Entry Using Schematic Capture

In this method of design, the user can generate a schematic (a circuit) by choosing symbols from a set of graphics symbols supplied by the CAD tool. The symbols represent the available basic units called libraries supplied by the CAD tool. Figure 3.8.2, Figure 3.8.3, and Figure 3.8.4 show samples of the available library components.

In schematic capture design entry, we select our basic units based on the level of abstraction used. For example, at the gate level design, our basic units are the logic gates found in the logic gates library. To generate a design, we move the needed gates into the work area of the Electronics Workbench. We then apply the needed connections between the gates.

We illustrate the process of schematic capture by applying it to the design of a 1-bit magnitude comparator. The details of magnitude comparators are covered in Chapter 5.

The comparator we will design compares two 1-bit numbers, x and y, and as a result has two inputs only. It has three outputs, $f_<$, $f_=$, and $f_>$, corresponding to $x < y$, $x = y$ and $x > y$, respectively. The truth table of the circuit is shown in Table 3.8.1. An output of a function is set to 1 if the corresponding relation between the operands holds true. To design the circuit associated with the above truth table, we first construct the algebraic equation for each function. The algebraic equations are

TABLE 3.8.1

1-Bit Magnitude Comparator

x	y	$f_<$	$f_=$	$f_>$
0	0	0	1	0
0	1	1	0	0
1	0	0	0	1
0	1	0	1	0

$$f_<(x, y) = x'y$$

$$f_=(x, y) = x'y' + xy$$

$$f_>(x, y) = xy'$$

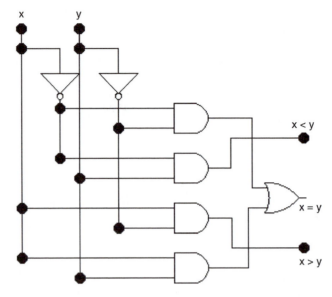

FIGURE 3.8.6
Design of the 1-Bit Magnitude Comparator

FIGURE 3.8.7
Gates Bin

We then design the three functions as shown in Figure 3.8.6. The circuit in the figure contains seven gates with connecting lines. The gates and the connections can be generated using the Electronics Workbench GUI. Similar to the logic converter, one clicks on the unit of interest and drags the unit to the working area. To generate the AND gates, we select these from the gates icon, as shown in Figure 3.8.7.

We use connectors to connect lines to the inputs and outputs of gates. The connectors are found in the "basic bin" shown in Figure 3.8.8. The connectors are used to create input and output lines and to cause multiple connections to the same signal. Each connector can have four connections, as shown in Figure 3.8.9. Connectors can have labels. To form a label associated with a connector, double-click on the connector. When this is done, one obtains the dialog box shown in Figure 3.8.10.

FIGURE 3.8.8
Basic Bin

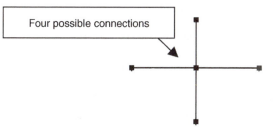

FIGURE 3.8.9
Connectors with Four Possible Connections

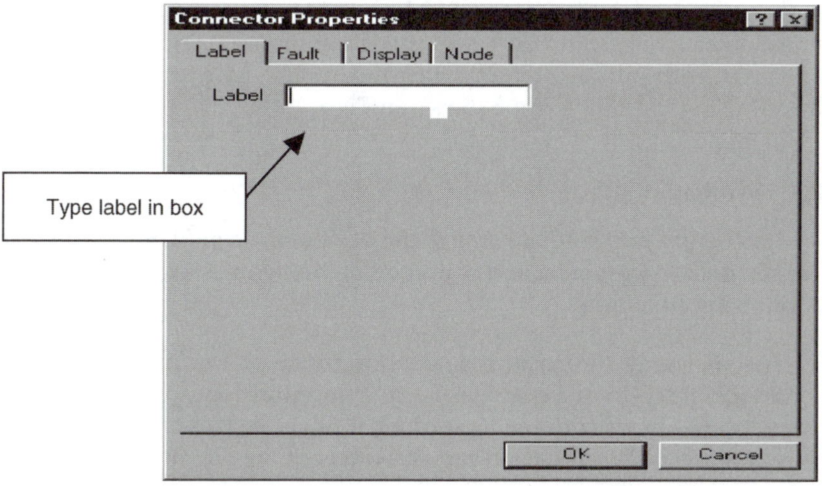

FIGURE 3.8.10
Connectors Dialogue

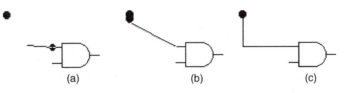

                    (a)   (b)   (c)

FIGURE 3.8.11
Establishing Connections between Connectors and Gates: (a) When the dot is displayed on the
input of the AND gate, click and drag the mouse button toward the connector as shown. (b) When
a dot is displayed, release the mouse button to establish connection. (c) Connection established.

FIGURE 3.8.12
Rotate Icons Used to Change Gate Orientation

In the circuit diagram, labels were given for the inputs x and y. The output
functions were labeled as $f_<$, $f_=$, and $f_>$, respectively. In making the connections
between the connectors and the gates, we move the mouse to the proximity
of the desired object until the mouse changes to a hand shape. In bringing
the mouse closer to the object, the mouse shape changes from a hand shape
to an arrow shape with a little black dot indicating a connection can be made.
The mouse can then be clicked and dragged to the next connection. An
example is shown in Figure 3.8.11.

One can repeat the connection process on the remaining lines in the circuit.
Note that lines can be connected. To connect a gate input to a line, we proceed
in a similar fashion by starting at the gate input/output. We then drag the
mouse to the line until a dot is displayed. The dot is an indicator that a
connection can be established by releasing the mouse. Figure 3.8.6 contains
an inverter with output pointing downward. The gate orientation can be
changed using the rotate icons shown in Figure 3.8.12.

3.8.3 Synthesis

The purpose of synthesis is to realize the design of a circuit entered through
the CAD tools. In the realization of the circuit, the synthesis tool may perform
the following two tasks.

1. The tool may be instructed to optimize the description given in
   design entry. In our case, we assume optimization is based on generating a circuit with the least number of gates. This can be done by
   minimizing the set of Boolean equations of the circuit.
2. The synthesis tool uses technology mapping to realize the design.
   Here the tool is instructed to use a specific set of units from the
   library. We illustrate the above using the Electronics Workbench.

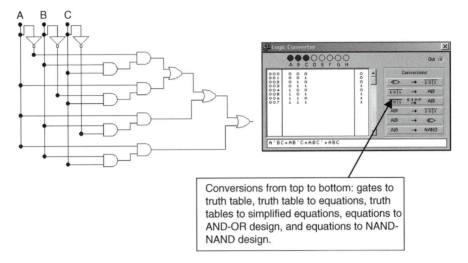

Conversions from top to bottom: gates to truth table, truth table to equations, truth tables to simplified equations, equations to AND-OR design, and equations to NAND-NAND design.

FIGURE 3.8.13

Synthesis Process: Click on the truth table to equations button and note equations in the bottom of the text box. Follow by clicking equations to the AND button to obtain the circuit on the right.

3.8.3.1 Synthesis from Truth Table

The logic converter used with design entry can be used to synthesize the circuit as well. The realization is based on two methods of technology mappings. One uses AND-OR gates; the other uses NAND gates. To accomplish the synthesis process from truth tables, we synthesize the majority function with a truth table generated during design entry. To synthesize, we first generate the Boolean functions by clicking the conversion button to convert it from the truth table to an equation. We then click on the button that maps the equation to the proper set of gates. Figure 3.8.13 shows this process. The figure includes a text box indicating the buttons with corresponding conversions. When this is done, the design of an unoptimized circuit is displayed on the screen. To generate an optimized design, we repeat the steps above with step 1 replaced by pressing the truth table to minimized equation button. When this is done, the circuit generated is a simplified circuit. Note that when the circuit is generated, one can move the entire circuit by clicking and dragging the circuit where needed. Finally, if we desire to synthesize the circuit using NAND gates, the last step is replaced by pressing the equations to the NAND gate button.

3.8.3.2 Synthesis from Equations

To synthesize from equations, we follow a similar procedure to synthesize from a truth table. First, however, we need to convert the equations to truth-table format. This is done in order to generate the minimal function.

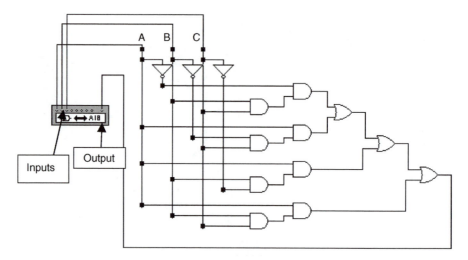

FIGURE 3.8.14
The Logic Converter

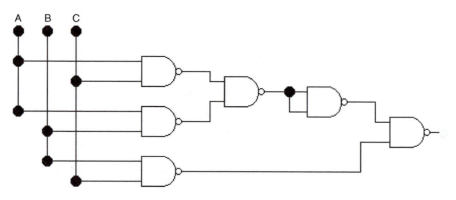

FIGURE 3.8.15
Optimized Gate Design of the Majority Function as Generated by EW

3.8.3.3   Synthesis from Schematic Capture

In this method of design, the circuit is already given (designed). The purpose of this step of synthesis is either to map the design to a different technology (for example, AND-OR to NAND-NAND) or to generate an optimized design. For a circuit with a single output, the logic converter can be used to provide an alternative synthesized circuit. To do this, we connect the inputs of the circuit to the inputs of the logic converter. Similarly, we connect the output part of the circuit to the output of the logic converter. This process is shown in Figure 3.8.14 on the majority circuit generated earlier.

To generate the alternative design, first double-click on the logic converter to open it. Follow that by clicking the gate to truth table button. From the truth table, we follow the synthesis steps discussed earlier. Figure 3.8.15 shows the alternative optimized NAND gate design. The design is obtained by clicking the truth table to optimized equations button and following that by clicking the equations to NAND button.

3.8.4 Simulation

The purpose of simulation is to verify that the synthesized design performs according to expectation. For a single output circuit and with the number of inputs not exceeding eight, one can use the logic converter to generate the truth table and/or canonical sum representation of a given design. The truth table or the functions can then be compared to the expected known response of the circuit. The connections of the circuit to the logic converter are similar to the connections used for synthesis from schematic capture discussed earlier. For circuits with multiple outputs, we use a set of switches and indicators. The switches are used to adjust the input values, and the indicators are used to record the output values. Figure 3.8.16 shows a schematic of the circuit with the needed connections added.

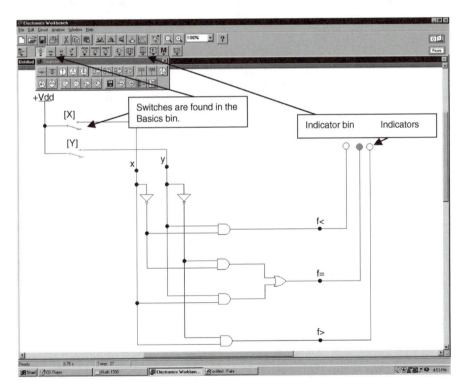

FIGURE 3.8.16
Simulation Using EW, Switches Represent Inputs, Indicators Represent Outputs

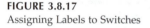

FIGURE 3.8.17
Assigning Labels to Switches

As seen in Figure 3.8.1.6, the voltage source is labeled V_{dd} and is found in the sources bin. The switches are found in the basic bin described earlier. The switches play the role of supplying a value of 0 or a value of 1 to the inputs of the circuit, depending on the location of the switch. A value of 1 is supplied to the input if V_{dd} is connected to the input via the switch. If no connection exists, then a value of 0 is supplied as an input. In the diagram above, both of the x and y input values are 0 since no connection is made between V_{dd} and any of the inputs. The switch labels (x and y) identify the letters on the keyboard that cause the switch to toggle between two different positions. In the case of the circuit above, pressing the x or y keys on the keyboard causes the switches to toggle. To assign letters to switches, double-click on the switch after selecting it to obtain the dialog box shown in Figure 3.8.17, type the desired letter in the text box with label key, and press the OK button.

The indicators are used to display the value of the function for a specific input assignment. The indicator color changes to red if the function output is 1. The indicators in the diagram are found in the indicator bin. After the circuit is designed, to simulate the function of the circuit one needs to click on the activate simulation switch found at the top right corner of the Electronic Workbench.

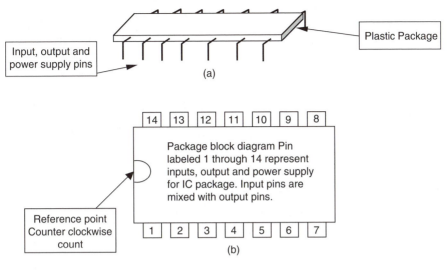

FIGURE 3.9.1
Schematic of an IC Chip, (a) Side View, (b) Top View

3.9 Integrated Circuits

In this section, we briefly discuss integrated circuits (ICs). Actual digital systems are built from integrated circuit chips. A chip interface to the outside world is through a set of pins connected to a rectangular (possibly plastic) box. The actual circuit is enclosed inside the plastic box and may occupy a very small fraction of the overall area of the chip. Figure 3.9.1 shows a schematic of an IC chip; part (a) of the figure shows a side view, part (b) shows a top view. The pins and the plastic box constitute the packaging part of the circuit. The packaging can be done using different procedures. The schematic shown is called dual in-line package (DIP). The pins of the chip correspond to the interface of the circuit with the outside world, including inputs, outputs, and power supply inputs.

The functional relation between the inputs and outputs is characterized by a pin-out diagram. An example pin-out diagram is shown in Figure 3.9.2. The figure includes different chips with numbers distinguishing each chip. The diagrams are pin-out diagrams of a popular logic family called TTL (transistor–transistor logic). In the figure, the size of the gates is intended to indicate the small area occupied by the actual circuit. We will give a design example using these chips shortly.

Depending on the number of gates in a chip, chips are characterized as small-scale integration (SSI), medium-scale integration (MSI), large-scale integration (LSI), and very-large-scale integration (VLSI). We will discuss

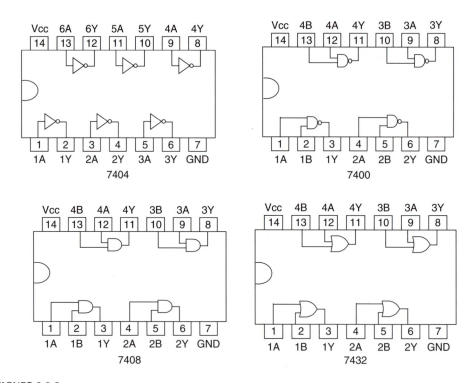

FIGURE 3.9.2
Sample SSI Chips

these next. In the discussion, we relate these to the levels of abstraction discussed earlier. In addition, we relate these characteristics to the topics covered in the text.

3.9.1   Small-Scale Integration (SSI)

SSI is a classification of chips with very few gates, usually less than ten. An example of such circuits is given in Figure 3.9.2. SSI chips fit into the gate abstraction level.

3.9.2   Medium-Scale Integration (MSI)

MSI are a class of chips with functional units such as adders and magnitude computers. Thus, MSI chips fit into the register level of abstraction. The number of gates on an MSI circuit is usually greater than ten, but smaller than one thousand.

3.9.3   Large-Scale Integration (LSI)

The number of gates found in an LSI chip is between 1,000 and 100,000 gates. The chips may include the design of a simple processor, the control unit of

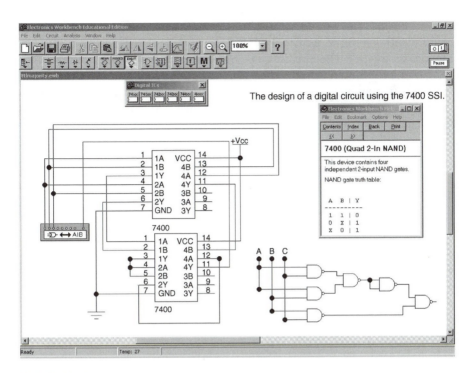

FIGURE 3.9.3
Sample Majority Circuit Design Using 7400 IC Chips

a processor, or other interface units. Discussion of the design of a simple processor is covered in Chapter 11.

3.9.4 Very-Large-Scale Integration (VLSI)

VLSI is the next level of integration. At this level, the circuit complexity is usually given in the number of transistors, with this number exceeding 10^6 transistors. The Pentium™ series of processors are part of this class. The first Pentium processor, for example, contained a little over 3 million transistors. The actual circuit occupied approximately 0.9 cm^2 (0.25 in.^{2}). VLSI and LSI chips fit into the processor level of abstraction.

Our study in this text deals with the principles of digital design and application of the principle to circuits found in the three levels, SSI, MSI, and LSI. The emphasis is on the principle of digital design with no reference to actual chips found in the market to accomplish the design. As a result, our library of circuits will be built from primitive logic gates. Before we conclude this topic, however, we give a sample example design using SSI chip circuits, as shown in Figure 3.9.3.

The screen capture in the figure is from the Electronics Workbench. It shows the design of the majority function using the 7400 chip, shown in Figure 3.9.2. The chip is found in the digital IC bin, as shown in the figure under "74xx." The power supply and ground connections are needed in order for the circuit to work. The inputs to the circuit are supplied through the logic converter. The NAND gate circuit shown is obtained from the logic converter by following the synthesis steps discussed earlier. Trace the circuit to verify it does realize the set of NAND gates shown in the figure. As homework, determine the number of 7400 chips needed to do the design of the majority function without simplifying it first!

Chapter 3 Exercises

3.1 Show that the logical AND of any two minterms over the same variables, $x_1, x_2, \ldots, x_n$ is equal to 0 if the two minterms are different.

3.2 Show that the logical OR of any two maxterms over the same variables, $x_1, x_2, \ldots, x_n$ is equal to 1 if the two maxterms are different.

3.3 Given the truth table shown in Figure E3.1, construct

   (a) The canonical sum representation of f

   (b) The canonical product representation of f

   (c) The canonical sum representation of f'

   (d) The canonical product representation of f'

A	B	C	$f(A,B,C)$
0	0	0	1
0	0	1	0
0	1	0	0
0	1	1	1
1	0	0	0
1	0	1	1
1	1	0	1
1	1	1	1

FIGURE E3.1

3.4 Write your answers in question 3.3 as a sum (or product) of m_i (or M_i) terms.

3.5 Write your answers in question 3.3 using the Σ or Π form.

3.6 Given the canonical sum $f(A, B, C) = \Sigma(0, 4, 5)$.

   (a) Form the canonical product representation of f in Π format.

   (b) Form the canonical product representation of f in algebraic format.

   (c) Form the canonical sum representation of f' in the Σ format.

3.7 Identify each function according to representation in sum of product, product of sum, canonical sum, or canonical product. Note that a function may be represented in more than one format.

   (a) $F(A, B, C) = AB + (AB)'$

   (b) $F(A, B, C) = AB + A'B'$

(c) $F(A, B, C) = ABC$

(d) $F(A, B, C) = A + B$

(e) $F(A, B, C) = A + B + C$

(f) $F(A, B, C) = AB + A'(B' + C)$

3.8 Algebraically, expand the function $F(A, B, C) = AB + A'B'$ into canonical sum form.

3.9 Repeat problem 3.8 on the function $F(A, B, C) = A + B$.

3.10 A set is said to be weak logically complete if the set includes Boolean constants. When Boolean constants are included in the set they can be used as inputs to any of the operations in the set. Show that the following sets are weak logically complete:

(a) $S = \{1, \oplus, AND\}$

(b) $S = \{F, 1\}$ with $F(A, B, C) = A'BC + AB'C + ABC'$

3.11 Given the function described in Figure E3.1:

(a) Minimize the function in sum of product form.

(b) Minimize the complement of the function in sum of product form.

(c) Design the function using a two-level

    i. AND-OR

    ii. OR-AND

    iii. NAND-NAND

    iv. NOR-NOR

(d) Design the function using

    i. AND-OR-INVERT

    ii. OR-AND-INVERT

3.12 Is it possible to design general functions using a two-level AND-NOR? Please explain.

3.13 Is it possible to design general functions using a two-level OR-NAND? Please explain.

3.14 Design the circuits generated in problem 3.11 using the Electronics Workbench. Verify your design is correct by using the logic converter to construct the truth tables from the circuit design. The process was discussed in the previous chapter.

4

Minimization of Boolean Functions

CONTENTS

4.1 Logical Adjacencies and K-Map Construction

The purpose of this chapter is to discuss Boolean functions' minimization. This topic was introduced in Chapter 2 where we used the properties of

Boolean algebra to minimize Boolean functions. We introduce alternative methods of minimization and relate the discussion to knowledge gained from minimization earlier. We start with a definition. The definition relates minterms based on their algebraic representations.

4.1.1 Logical Adjacency

Definition: Two minterms are said to be logically adjacent (over the same set of variables) if their algebraic representation differs in one location only where a variable is presented as is in one minterm and complemented in the other. For brevity, we call the minterms adjacent.

Example 4.1.1
Over the set of variables A, B, and C, the two minterms, m_0 and m_1, are logically adjacent since their algebraic representation differs only in the C variable $m_0 = A'B'C'$ and $m_1 = A'B'C$.

Over n variables, each minterm is adjacent to n other minterms. This is the case since with each variable we can associate an adjacent minterm. The adjacent minterm has the variable complemented if it is uncomplemented in the original minterm, and vice versa.

Example 4.1.2
Over the variables A, B, C, and D, the minterm m_4 is adjacent to four other adjacent minterms. The minterm $m_4 = A'BC'D'$. The adjacent minterms are $m_{12} = ABC'D'$, $m_0 = A'B'C'D'$, $m_6 = A'BCD'$, and $m_5 = A'BC'D$.

Logical adjacencies are used in the minimization process of Boolean functions as follows. A function written in canonical sum format that includes adjacent minterms can be minimized by combining the minterms into a single product term.

Example 4.1.3
Consider the two adjacent minterms m_0 and m_1 over the set of variables A, B, and C. If the minterms are part of the canonical sum representation of a given function, then their sum can be simplified to

$$m_0 + m_1 = A'B'C' + A'B'C$$

$$= A'B'$$

Note the product term includes one less variable than found in either minterm. Note as well the variable missing in the product is the variable where the two minterms differ.

The concept of adjacency can be used in minimization without first forming the algebraic representation of minterms. To illustrate, note that the input associated with the two minterms m_0 and m_1 is the same with the exception

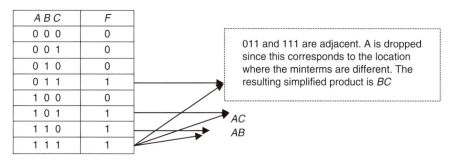

A B C	F
0 0 0	0
0 0 1	0
0 1 0	0
0 1 1	1
1 0 0	0
1 0 1	1
1 1 0	1
1 1 1	1

011 and 111 are adjacent. A is dropped since this corresponds to the location where the minterms are different. The resulting simplified product is *BC*

AC
AB

FIGURE 4.1.1
Adjacency Determination from Truth Table

of the C part. For this part, for one input the variable C assumes a value of 1, and in the other the variable assumes a value of 0. When forming the algebraic product, the product contains variables where the inputs are the same. The variable where the minterms are different is dropped. In forming the product, if an input assumes a value of 1, then the corresponding variable is presented as is. If the input assumes a value of 0, then the variable is presented in complemented form.

Example 4.1.4
Use the above observation to minimize the majority function without forming the algebraic representation first.
   Solution: We make use of the rule $x + x = x$. This rule is important as it allows us to reuse a minterm as many times as needed. It is also important when we discuss K-map minimization later. The truth table of the majority function is given in Figure 4.1.1. The table contains arrows used to group adjacent minterms (inputs). The corresponding simplified product term is shown as well. Note the minterm m_7 (input 111) is adjacent to the three other possible minterms. Note as well the logically adjacent minterms are not physically adjacent. By "physically adjacent" we mean minterms that are directly above or below the given minterm.

4.1.2 K-Map Construction

We consider two methods of minimization: the K-map method and the tabular method. Both methods make repeated use of logical adjacencies. The K-map method reconstructs the truth table entries in such a way to ensure that if two minterms are physically adjacent, then they are logically adjacent. This reconstruction makes it easier to identify logical adjacencies.
   The truth table construction is one-dimensional; the minterms as the inputs (minterms) are listed in rows. The K-map reconstructs the table as a two-dimensional table for functions over two to four variables. This is done to visually identify adjacencies, which we will discuss next.

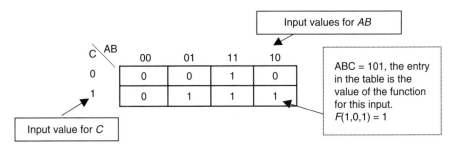

FIGURE 4.1.2
Majority Function Truth Table Reconstructed

4.1.2.1   The Inputs to the Table

The rows and columns of the table are labeled in binary. The binary combination of a specific row and column label represent an input in the truth table. The corresponding entry in the table represents the value of a given Boolean function. The value in the entry is 0 if the Boolean function assumes a value of 0 for the given input combination. The value of the entry is 1 otherwise. We illustrate by reconstructing the truth table for the majority function.

Example 4.1.5

In this example, we reconstruct the truth table of the majority function as a two-dimensional table. We arbitrarily choose the C variable as a row label of the table and the AB combined assignment as a label for the columns of the table. The number of rows in the table is two; one row is associated with the input $C = 0$ and another with the input $C = 1$. The number of columns in the table is four, corresponding to the four possible input values of AB. The reconstructed table is shown in Figure 4.1.2.

4.1.2.2   How Is the Table Read?

The row and column labels of the table are the input values of the variables A, B, and C. The column label contains the possible values of AB. Similarly, the row label lists the possible values of the variable C. The remaining entries in the table contain the function values associated with the corresponding inputs. For example, the value of the function for $AB = 10$ and $C = 1$ is the value of the entry with column label 10 and row label 1. This entry is assigned the value

$$F(1,0,1) = 1$$

By observing the table, we note the column labels do not follow the normal binary sequence 00, 01, 10, and 11. Instead the labels are listed so that if two minterms are physically adjacent, then they are logically adjacent as well. As stated earlier, minterms over three variables satisfy the property that each

TABLE 4.1.1

Adjacent Entries, "-- " Is Adjacent to Entries
with Labels "o"

CD \ AB	00	01	11	10
00			o	
01		x		
11				
10		o	--	o

minterm is logically adjacent to three others. In the above table, for minterms that are not located at a corner, the logically adjacent minterms are those that are physically adjacent (either on the same row or the same column). For corner minterms, the physically adjacent minterms in the same row or same column are adjacent to the corner minterm (there are two such minterms for each corner). The third adjacent minterm is obtained by noting that the last column and the first column differ in one location. Hence, the third adjacent minterm is found in the first or last column, depending on the corner minterm considered.

We illustrate this by constructing four-variable K-maps. The table format is shown in Table 4.1.1. To construct the table, choose input labels that differ in only one value as they are assigned in both the row and column order. This will ensure that physical adjacencies of minterms will yield logical adjacencies as well. In Table 4.1.1, the labels for the AB input differ in only one value as one moves from one column to an adjacent column. This is also the case for the row labels. With regard to logical adjacencies in this table, each minterm is adjacent to four other minterms. For example, the minterm corresponding to the input "$ABCD = 0101$" is logically adjacent to the four physically adjacent minterms. (Two of the adjacent minterms are the neighbor minterms found in the same row; the other two adjacent minterms are in the neighbors found in the same column.) Other adjacent minterms can be identified similarly, and by noting that the first row is adjacent to the last row, and the first column is adjacent to the last column. In the table, the cells with entry "o" are adjacent to the cell with entry "−−."

4.2 Subcube Formations

4.2.1 Filling the Table Entries

In the previous section, we constructed three- and four-variable K-maps. To enter the values of a Boolean function in a K-map, we form the truth table

TABLE 4.2.1
K-Map of Example 4.2.2, $f(A, B, C) = AB + AB' + A'B'C'$

C \\ AB	00	01	11	10
0	1		1	1
1			1	1

representation of the function or, equivalently, the canonical sum representation. We then enter the value of the function in the table, based on the labels as inputs.

Example 4.2.1
Form the K-map representation of the majority function.
   The table is formed from the truth table as shown in Figure 4.1.1 and Figure 4.1.2.

Example 4.2.2
Form the K-map table for the function $f(A,B,C) = AB + AB' + A'B'C'$.
   To form the table, we first expand the function to canonical sum form as follows:

$$f(A,B,C) = AB + AB' + A'B'C'$$
$$= AB(C + C') + AB'(C + C') + A'B'C'$$
$$= ABC + ABC' + AB'C + AB'C' + A'B'C'$$
$$= \Sigma(0,4,5,6,7)$$

The K-map for the above function is given in Table 4.2.1.

Example 4.2.3
Construct the K-map representation of the function $f(A,B,C,D) = \Sigma(0,1,5,7,8)$.
   The K-map representation is given in Table 4.2.2.
   A fast way to fill the table makes use of assigning decimal values with the table entries based on the decimal value of the minterm labels. The decimal values associated with the entries is shown in Table 4.2.3. We use this table in the following example.

Example 4.2.4
Construct the K-map representation of the function $f(A,B,C,D) = \Sigma(0,1,2,4,6,7,8,10,12,14)$.

TABLE 4.2.2
K-Map of Example 4.2.3, $f(A,B,C,D) =$
$\Sigma(0,1,5,7,8)$

CD \ AB	00	01	11	10
00	1			1
01	1	1	1	
11		1		
10				

TABLE 4.2.3
K-Map with Entries Labeled with Decimal
Values of Corresponding Minterms

CD \ AB	00	01	11	10
00	0	4	12	8
01	1	5	13	9
11	3	7	15	11
10	2	6	14	10

TABLE 4.2.4
K-Map of Example 4.2.4, $f(A,B,C,D) =$
$\Sigma(0,1,2,4,6,7,8,10,12,14)$

CD \ AB	00	01	11	10
00	1	1	1	1
01	1			
11		1		
10	1	1	1	1

The K-map representation based on the numbering in Table 4.2.3 yields
Table 4.2.4.

4.2.2 Subcubes and Minimization

The purpose of constructing K-maps is to aid in the simplification process
of Boolean functions. Earlier we mentioned the map makes repeated use of
logical adjacencies where two adjacent minterms in a Boolean function can

TABLE 4.2.5
K-Map of the Majority Function with "Boxes"
Enclosing 1-Entries in the Table

AB

C\	00	01	11	10
0	0	0	1	0
1	0	1	1	1

be reduced to a single product term with one less variable. Two adjacent minterms in a K-map form a subcube, which we will define later. On a map, subcubes are circled to indicate their relation.

We illustrate by applying the above to the K-map of the majority function. Table 4.2.5 shows the K-map of the majority function with the subcubes enclosed in boxes. Note that the boxes describe visually the process of minimization we discussed earlier where minterm m_7 is reused with each of the remaining minterms in the majority function. This can be done because of the rule $x + x = x$. Note also that the algebraic product associated with each pair of minterms can be derived from the table directly as follows.

The subcube with column label 11 represents the sum of minterms $m_6 + m_7$. In the table these two minterms have the same AB representation since both assume the same value over the two variables A and B. They differ in the C variable. As a result, when added the C variable is dropped from the product. The common product AB represents this subcube. Similar logic applies to the subcube containing m_3 and m_7. Here, the C variable remains part of the product since the two minterms assume the same value over this variable. In addition, in moving from one column to the next, one of the column labels, the A variable in this case, changes. As a result, the A variable is dropped from the algebraic representation and the remaining common product, BC, is the algebraic representation of the subcube. Similarly, we obtain the algebraic representation AC for the third subcube. The minimized sum is given by the equation that adds the algebraic representation of the three subcubes, i.e., $F(A,B,C) = AB + BC + AC$.

In forming subcubes we may need to form minterms at the edges/corners of the K-map. We illustrate by the following example.

Example 4.2.5
Using K-maps, find the minimum function $F(A,B,C) = \Sigma(0,3,4,7)$.

The K-map, subcubes, and algebraic representations are shown in Figure 4.2.1.

Note that the minterms at the upper left and upper right corners are adjacent. As a result, they are combined into a subcube, as shown. Since the minterms are in the same row, they share the same row label ($C = 0$). They

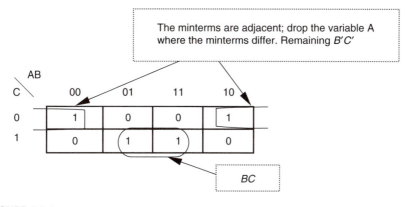

FIGURE 4.2.1
Subcube Formation and Corresponding Algebraic Representation

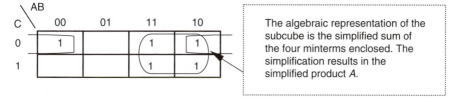

FIGURE 4.2.2
Subcube of Size 4 of Example 4.2.6

differ in one of the column variable labels, the A variable, as seen. When the A variable is removed, the remaining product contains two variables B and C, with both variables complemented since each assumes a value of 0. The product term $B'C'$ represents this subcube. When the product term representing the bottom subcube is formed, we obtain the minimized function $F(A,B,C) = BC + B'C'$.

The previous two examples involved forming subcubes that included two adjacent minterms. In the next example, we form subcubes that include four minterms. A formal definition of subcubes is given in the next section. Here, however, we mention that the subcube of interest contain 1-cells (entries in the table where the function assumes a value of 1), and the number of 1-cells in the subcube is always equal to 2^k for some integer k. For $k = 0$, 1, and 2, for example, the corresponding subcubes will contain 1, 2, and 4 1-cells, respectively. A subcube that contains a single 1-cell is identified by circling the single 1-cell in the subcube.

Example 4.2.6
Figure 4.2.2 shows a sample subcube of size 4 of the function given in Example 4.2.2.

The four minterms enclosed in the subcube of size 4 are minimized according to the rules given below to result in a single variable A:

$$AB'C' + AB'C + ABC' + ABC$$

$$= AB'(C' + C) + AB(C' + C)$$

$$= AB' + AB$$

$$= A$$

In the next section, we present methods of obtaining the algebraic representation associated with a subcube without using the algebraic simplification above.

4.3   K-Map Minimization

4.3.1   Subcubes and Prime Implicants

The following definitions are in relation to 1-cells in a given K-map.
   Definition: A subcube of 1-cells on a K-map satisfies the following conditions:

1. The number of 1-cells in the subcube is 2^k for some integer $K \geq 0$.
2. Each 1-cell in the subcube is adjacent to k other 1-cells in the subcube.

Example 4.3.1
The K-map considered previously is redrawn in Figure 4.3.1. The table shows sample subcubes of sizes 1, 2, and 4.
   All enclosed subcubes satisfy the first part of the definition, i.e., the sizes are a power of 2. In addition, all subcubes satisfy the second part of the definition as follows. The minterm with label 1 is adjacent to 0 other minterms in the subcube since its size is 2^0. For the two subcubes of size 2, each minterm must be adjacent to k other minterms in the subcube (in this case, $k = 1$). Finally, the subcubes of size 4 satisfies both conditions in the definition;

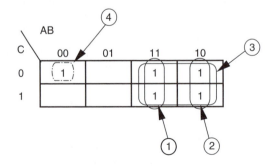

FIGURE 4.3.1
Sample Subcubes of Sizes 1, 2 and 4

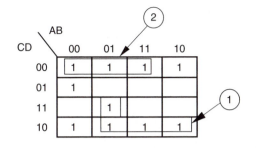

FIGURE 4.3.2
Examples of 1-Entries That Do Not Form Subcubes

for the second condition each minterm must be adjacent to two other minterms in the subcube ($k = 2$).

On the K-map, subcubes form a rectangular shape, given the fact that the last row and the first row are adjacent and the last column and first column are adjacent as well. The next example includes cases of 1 cells that do not form subcubes.

Example 4.3.2
The enclosed minterms in Figure 4.3.2 are not subcubes.

The enclosed box labeled 1 does not satisfy the adjacency condition (note the shape is not rectangular). The box labeled 2 does not satisfy the first condition.

In the next example, we form the largest possible subcubes not contained in any single larger subcube.

Example 4.3.3
Construct the K-map representation and form all subcubes not contained in any single larger subcube of the function

$$f(A,B,C,D) = \Sigma(0,1,5,7,8,13)$$

The K-map representation is given in Table 4.3.1. To form the largest subcubes not contained in any larger subcube, we start by attempting to form the largest subcube possible. In a K-map with 16 entries, the largest possible subcube is of size 16. For such a K-map, all entries must assume a value of 1. This is not the case in the above function. The next possible subcube is of size 8. Since the function does not contain eight 1s, we consider the next possible subcube of size 4. From the construction of the map, no subcubes of size 4 are possible. There are several subcubes of size 2, however, as shown in the diagram. None of these subcubes are contained in a larger subcube (there are no subcubes of size 4). Note that the subcube that contains the minterms m_1 and m_5 is not completely contained in a single subcube. It is included as a result.

TABLE 4.3.1
K-Map and Subcube Formation of
$f(A,B,C,D) = \Sigma(0,1,5,7,8,13)$

	AB			
CD	00	01	11	10
00	1			1
01	1	1	1	
11		1		
10				

The subcubes formed in the above example are called prime implicants, as stated in the following definition. Forming all possible prime implicants is the second step in the minimization process using K-maps. The first step is to form the K-map.

Definition: A prime implicant on a K-map satisfies the following conditions:

1. It is a subcube of 1-cells.
2. It cannot be contained completely in a single larger subcube, i.e., it is not a subset of a larger subcube.

Example 4.3.4
Of the four subcubes given in Figure 4.3.1, only subcube 3 forms a prime implicant. Subcubes 1 and 2 are contained in the larger subcube 3. As a result, none is a prime implicant. Subcube 4 is not a prime implicant since the figure is missing a subcube of size 2 containing the minterms in the upper-left and upper-right corners. Once this subcube is formed, the subcube with label 2 is completely contained in this larger subcube.

Example 4.3.5
Construct the K-map representation and identify all prime implicants of the function

$$f(A,B,C,D) = \sum (0,1,2,4,6,7,8,10,12,14)$$

The K-map representation and the corresponding prime implicants is given in Table 4.3.2. The K-map includes three prime implicants. Similar to the discussion in the previous example, we start by forming the largest possible prime implicants. In this case, we could form an implicant of size 8, as shown in the table. The prime implicant contains the four 1-cells in the first row and the four 1-cells in the last row. Note that since the rows are adjacent, the eight cells are enclosed in a rectangular shape.

The eight 1-cells contained in the prime implicant cannot be used to generate smaller prime implicants of sizes 4, 2, or 1 since these subcubes will

TABLE 4.3.2
K-Map and Subcube Formation of
$f(A,B,C,D) = \Sigma(0,1,2,4,6,7,8,10,12,14)$

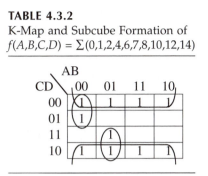

be completely contained in the larger prime implicants. The two 1-cells outside the prime implicant of size 8 are used to form two additional prime implicants, as shown in the table.

Example 4.3.6
Construct the K-map representation and identify all prime implicants of the function

$$f(A,B,C,D) = \sum (1,5,6,7,11,12,13,15)$$

Both the K-map representation and the prime implicants are given in Table 4.3.3. In the table, we first form the prime implicant of size 4 and follow that

TABLE 4.3.3
K-Map and Subcube Formation of
$f(A,B,C,D) = \Sigma(1,5,6,7,11,12,13,15)$

CD \ AB	00	01	11	10
00			1	
01	1	1	1	
11		1	1	1
10		1		

with the formation of the four prime implicants of size 2.

We next discuss the relationship between minimal functions, subcubes, and prime implicants.

4.3.2 K-Map Minimization

The minimization process of a K-map starts with first constructing the K-map from the truth table or from a word problem. The minimization is based on a relationship between prime implicants and the minimal function. The minimization is based on the function being represented in sum of product form. A function, f, is said to be minimal if

1. The function is written in sum of products form with the smallest number of product terms.
2. If another function, f_1, has the same number of product terms, then its product terms are not smaller (the product term contains fewer literals) than the function, f.

In Boolean algebra, it is possible for two functions to satisfy conditions 1 and 2. In this case, both functions are considered as an acceptable minimum. In mathematics, when there is more than one acceptable minimum (the minimum is not unique), the minimum function is referred to as a minimal function.

Example 4.3.7
In this example, we note the example function

$$F(A,B,C) = A + A'BC$$

is not minimal since the function can be simplified to

$$F(A,B,C) = A + BC$$

Both functions satisfy condition 1 of the definition (they contain the same number of product terms, two such terms). Only the second function, however, is minimal since its product terms contain fewer literals.

4.3.2.1 Relationship to Subcubes on a K-Map
Both the number and the size of product terms are related to subcubes in the K-map as follows:

1. With each subcube, we associate a product term. The product term is obtained by reducing the sum of the minterms found in the subcube to the corresponding algebraic representation. We consider Figure 4.3.1, for example. The product terms associated with the subcubes are listed in Table 4.3.4.
2. As seen from the table, larger subcubes contain minterms that can be added and reduced to a single product with fewer literals.

We apply the above two observations to the function in Example 4.3.1. The original function contained five product terms (the minterms), with each product composed of three literals. To reduce the function, we could write it as

TABLE 4.3.4

Subcubes and Corresponding Algebraic
Representation of the K-Map in Figure 4.3.1

Subcube	Algebraic Product
1	$AB = ABC' + ABC$
2	$AB' = AB'C' + AB'C$
3	$A = ABC + ABC' + AB'C + AB'C'$
4	$A'B'C$

$$f(A,B,C) = ABC + ABC' + AB'C + AB'C' + A'B'C'$$

$$= 1_{algebraic} + 2_{algebraic} + A'B'C'$$

$$= AB + AB' + A'B'C'$$

In the above, $1_{algebraic}$ and $2_{algebraic}$ are the algebraic representation of the sum of minterms found in subcubes 1 and 2. Alternatively, we could write the function as

$$f(A,B,C) = ABC + ABC' + AB'C + AB'C' + A'B'C'$$

$$= 3_{algebraic} + A'B'C'$$

$$= A + A'B'C'$$

As can be seen from the alternative reductions based on the choice of subcubes, the second alternative yields a better minimum. From the discussion we conclude:

1. Subcubes are algebraically associated with product terms. As a result, the number of subcubes chosen to include in the function is equal to the number of product terms.

2. Since our objective at a minimum is to obtain the smallest number of product terms, on a K-map we need to look for the least number of subcubes that contain all minterms of a function.

3. The size of the subcube affects the product term size. In Table 4.3.4, subcubes of size 2 are reduced to a single product term with one less variable than the original. For the case of subcube 3, the reduction in the number of variables is 2. In general, for a subcube of size 2^k, the product term representing the subcube contains k less variables.

4. Since our objective is to form product terms with the smallest number of variables, given a choice over more than one subcube that covers some minterms, we choose the largest possible subcube.

Thus, for a minimum we choose the smallest number of subcubes that cover the minterms of the function. This guarantees that the condition on the least number of product terms is met. In addition, we choose the largest possible subcubes. This guarantees the product terms chosen are the smallest. As a result, subcubes that are not prime implicants are disregarded and not considered since these subcubes can be contained in larger subcubes; the larger subcubes require smaller product terms. We formalize the minimization process next.

4.3.2.2   The Minimization Process
From the previous discussion, to minimize a function we

1. Construct the K-map representation of the function
2. Form all prime implicants of the function
3. Find the smallest number of prime implicants that cover (include) all the 1-cells of the function
4. Form the algebraic representation of each prime implicant found in item 3 and add these terms to form the minimal algebraic representation

We illustrate these concepts further. Assume a given function over four variables A, B, C, and D, and that during the minimization process we found that we need to use at least three subcubes to cover the 1-cells in the corresponding K-map of the function. Assume the coverage can be obtained in the following two ways:

1. The coverage is accomplished with three subcubes, each of size 2.
2. The coverage is accomplished with three subcubes. Two of the cubes are of size 4, the third is of size 2.

Then, the algebraic representation associated with each option results in a function with three product terms. For option 1, each of the product terms has three literals. This is not the case for option 2, however, as two of the product terms are of size 2 literals.

4.3.2.3   Essential Prime Implicants and Examples
We illustrate the minimization process on the example functions given earlier. For these examples, the first two steps in the minimizations, the formation of a K-map and prime implicants, were completed earlier. First, we introduce additional definitions. In observing the previous examples, we note that some 1-cells in the K-map are covered by only one prime implicant. Since in minimization the prime implicants chosen must cover all 1-cells, those implicants must be included in any selection.

Definition: A 1-cell in a K-map is said to be an essential 1-cell if, on forming all possible prime implicants, the 1-cell is contained (covered) by only one prime implicant.

Definition: An essential prime implicant is a prime implicant that contains one or more essential 1-cells.

Essential 1-cells in a K-map can be identified by placing an "*" in the cells. To form a minimum cover given all prime implicants, we follow the following steps:

1. Identify all essential 1-cells and, accordingly, all essential prime implicants. Add to the set of prime implicants the essential prime implicants identified.

2. In the K-map, replace the 1-cells covered by the essential prime implicants with "-" to signify the 1-cells are already covered.

3. On the remaining 1-cells, find the minimum number of prime implicants that cover the 1-cells and add to the set of prime implicants.

4. Form the minimal Boolean function by adding the algebraic representations of all the prime implicants found in step 3.

We illustrate the procedure on the previous examples.

Example 4.3.8

We consider the function given in example 4.3.3. The process is given in Figure 4.3.3.

Table 4.3.5 contains a list of prime implicants, the minterms they cover, whether the implicant is essential or not, and the algebraic representation. (We discuss how to obtain the algebraic representation later). From Figure 4.3.3(a), prime implicants PI_3, PI_4, and PI_5 are essential. As a result, they are included in any minimum cover. Figure 4.3.3(b) shows the reduced K-map with the 1-cells covered by the essential prime implicants replaced by "−".

Since all 1-cells must be covered, the remaining 1-cell can be covered by either of the two prime implicants PI_1 or PI_2. Since each prime implicant is

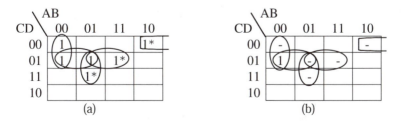

FIGURE 4.3.3
K-Map Minimization, (a) Essential Prime Implicants Identified, (b) New K-Map with Remaining Uncovered 1-Cells.

TABLE 4.3.5

Algebraic Representation of Prime Implicants of Figure 4.3.3

Prime Implicant (PI$_i$)[a]	Minterms Covered	Algebraic Representation
1	0, 1	$A'B'C'$
2	2, 5	$A'C'D$
3*	5, 7	$A'BD$
4*	0, 8	$B'C'D'$
5*	5, 13	$BC'D$

[a] An "*" in column 1 indicates an essential prime implicant.

TABLE 4.3.6

Number of Variables in a Product as a Function of the Size of the Corresponding Prime Implicant

Prime Implicant Size	Size of Product	Product Size over Four Variables
1	N	4
2	$N - 1$	3
4	$N - 2$	2
8	$N - 3$	1
16	$N - 4$	0 (the function equals 1)

of the same size, the function can be covered in two methods that yield two possible minimal functions.

The minimal functions obtained by including PI1 in the cover is

$$f(A,B,C,D) = A'BD + B'C'D' + BC'D + A'B'C'$$

The minimal function obtained by including PI$_2$ in the cover is

$$f(A,B,C,D) = A'BD + B'C'D' + BC'D + A'C'D$$

The algebraic representation associated with a prime implicant can be found as follows:

1. Over N variables, the number of variables in the product associated with an implicant is equal to

$$N - \log_2 m$$

    where m is the size of the implicant. Table 4.3.6 shows the size of the product term as a function of the prime implicant size.

2. To form the product associated with a given prime implicant, we follow the above rule to determine the size of the product term. To

TABLE 4.3.7

Implicants and Corresponding Algebraic Representation of Example 4.3.5

Prime Implicant $(PI_i)^a$	Minterms Covered	Algebraic Representation
1*	0,2,4,6,8,10,12,14	D'
2*	0,1	$A'B'C'$
3*	6,7	$A'BC$

^{a} An "*" in column 1 indicates an essential prime implicant.

determine the term, as we move across rows or columns, we keep variables that have the same binary assignments and discard variables with different binary assignment. For the product, the variable is presented as is, if it assumes a value of 1; it is complemented if it assumes a value of 0.

Example 4.3.8

When the procedure above is applied to Example 4.3.5, the three prime implicants formed are found to be essential prime implicants. These implicants cover all the 1-cells in the K-map. As a result, the minimal function is unique and is composed of the algebraic representation of the three essential implicants. Table 4.3.7 includes the implicants and the corresponding algebraic representations. The algebraic representation of the minimal function is

$$f(A,B,C,D) = D' + A'B'C' + A'BC$$

Example 4.3.9

For Example 4.3.6, after removing the 1-cells covered by the essential prime implicants, we obtain Table 4.3.8.

The essential prime implicants cover all the 1-cells. As a result, the function has a unique minimal representation. The prime implicants and corresponding algebraic representation is shown in Table 4.3.9. The minimal function is the sum of the algebraic representation of the first four prime implicants.

TABLE 4.3.8

K-Map of Example 4.3.6 with
Covered 1-Cells Removed

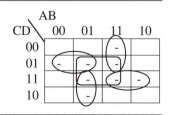

TABLE 4.3.9

Implicants and Corresponding Algebraic Representation of Example 4.3.6

Prime Implicant (PI$_i$)[a]	Minterms Covered	Algebraic Representation
1*	1,5	$A'C'D$
2*	6,7	$A'BC$
3*	12,13	ABC'
4*	11,15	ACD
5	5,7,13,15	BD

[a] An "*" in column 1 indicates an essential prime implicant.

4.4   Incompletely Specified Functions

We discuss incompletely specified functions in the context of the following problem.

The problem is to design a circuit with four inputs A, B, C, and D, and seven outputs a, b, c, d, e, f, and g. The input to the circuit is the binary representation of one of the ten decimal digits. Its output is chosen so as to display the equivalent decimal value using a seven-segment display. Figure 4.4.1 shows a schematic of the seven-segment display. The seven-segment display has seven light-emitting diodes (LEDs). By assigning a logical 1 to a given segment, the segment will emit light. The inputs to the display in Figure 4.4.1 are shown with labels "a" through "g". The display is found in some calculators with the LEDs replaced by liquid crystal displays (LCDs).

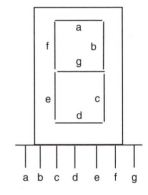

FIGURE 4.4.1
Schematic of Seven-Segment-Display

The circuit we want to design has seven outputs. The outputs serve as inputs to the seven-segment display, and as a result are labeled "a" through "g" as well. The block diagram given in Figure 4.4.2 below shows the inputs and outputs to the circuit to be designed. The circuit is called a BCD-to-seven-segment decoder.

The inputs to the circuit are the A, B, C, and D inputs. The inputs represent a decimal digit between 0 and 9. The output assigns values to "a" through "g" so as to display the corresponding decimal digit using Figure 4.4.1. For example, when the input $ABCD = 0000$ is applied, the decimal digit 0 is displayed using Figure 4.4.1. By inspection, this occurs when the "g" output is assigned a value of 0 and all remaining outputs are assigned a value of 1. The truth table associated with the BCD-to-seven-segment decoder circuit is shown in Table 4.4.1.

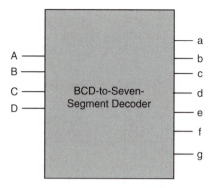

FIGURE 4.4.2
Block Diagram of a BCD-to-Seven Segment Display

TABLE 4.4.1

Truth Table of the BCD-Seven-Segment Display Decoder

A	B	C	D	a	b	c	d	e	f	g
0	0	0	0	1	1	1	1	1	1	0
0	0	0	1	0	1	1	0	0	0	0
0	0	1	0	1	1	0	1	1	0	1
0	0	1	1	1	1	1	1	0	0	1
0	1	0	0	0	1	1	0	0	1	1
0	1	0	1	1	0	1	1	0	1	1
0	1	1	0	1	0	1	1	1	1	1
0	1	1	1	1	1	1	0	0	0	0
1	0	0	0	1	1	1	1	1	1	1
1	0	0	1	1	1	1	1	0	1	1
1	0	1	0	X	X	X	X	X	X	X
1	0	1	1	X	X	X	X	X	X	X
1	1	0	0	X	X	X	X	X	X	X
1	1	0	1	X	X	X	X	X	X	X
1	1	1	0	X	X	X	X	X	X	X
1	1	1	1	X	X	X	X	X	X	X

Note that the table does not have output entries associated with binary combinations with decimal values exceeding 9. These combinations do not occur since the inputs are binary representations of one of the ten possible decimal digits. The designer does not define the functions over these inputs. Such functions are incompletely specified and are called partial functions in mathematics. For these functions we could make the assumption that over these input combinations, the function may assume any value (i.e., either a value of 0 or 1). The term used for the output in this case is a "don't-care" output, i.e., the output value is not important for the input combinations that exceed the, equivalent, decimal value 9.

How does the minimization procedure take into consideration the existence of don't-care conditions? Since a don't-care output can assume a value

TABLE 4.4.2

K-Map Minimization of Function a,
$a = A + C + BD + B'D'$

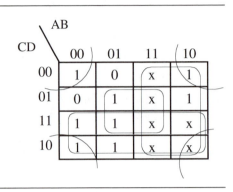

of 0 or 1 without affecting the part of the circuit where the function is specified, the function can be modified over these inputs so as to yield the best possible minimum. How? In the K-map procedure, we enter a don't-care value as "x" in the table; each x is then changed to a 1 or a 0 such that:

1. The choice of setting a 0 or 1 is so as to yield the smallest number of implicants to cover the original 1-cells
2. To result in the largest possible implicant sizes

Condition 1 reduces the number of product terms in the minimum. Condition 2 reduces the number of literals in the product terms.

We illustrate the minimization process for the first two functions. The minimization of the other functions is left as an exercise. For the function "*a*," we obtain the K-map with prime implicants as shown in Table 4.4.2. The algebraic representation of the minimal function is

$$a = A + C + BD + B'D'$$

For the function "*b*", we obtain the K-map shown in Table 4.4.3 The minimal algebraic representation is $b = B' + C'D' + CD$.

4.5 Product of Sum Minimization

The minimization of Boolean functions in product of sums can be accomplished in a similar fashion to the minimization in sum of product. The procedure is to first minimize the complement of the function. This is done

TABLE 4.4.3

K-Map Minimization of Function b,
$b = B' + C'D' + CD$

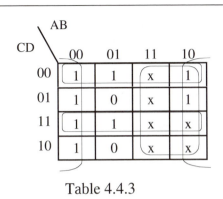

Table 4.4.3

TABLE 4.5.1

Finding Minimal Function in Product Of Sums,
Minimize about the 0 Entries

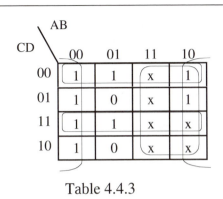

by forming prime implicants around the 0 values of a given function. The minimal algebraic value obtained is that of the complement of the function and is written in sum of product form. Using DeMorgan's rule and complementing the function will result in the product of sum algebraic representation of the function. We illustrate this for the case of the example function given in Table 4.5.1. The four prime implicants on the K-map above are essential prime implicant. The minimal complement is

$$\overline{f}(A,B,C,D) = AB'C'D' + A'BC + A'CD + BCD'$$

TABLE 4.5.2

Finding Minimal Function in Product of
Sums with X Entries, X Are Treated as 0s to
Form Largest Possible Subcubes

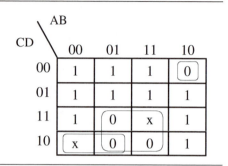

Using DeMorgan's rule we obtain

$$f(A,B,C,D) = \overline{\overline{f}}(A,B,C,D)$$

$$= \overline{(AB'C'D' + A'BC + A'CD + BCD')}$$

$$= (A' + B + C + D)(A + B' + C')(A + C' + D')(B' + C' + D)$$

For incompletly specified functions, we treat don't-cares as 0s so as to make the largest possible subcubes. This is illustrated in the example in Table 4.5.2. The minimized function is

$$\overline{f}(A,B,C,D) = AB'C'D' + BC$$

Note that the prime implicant corresponding to entries two and six was not included. The don't-care entry 2 is treated as 0 so as not to add an extra unneeded product term. The product of sum function can be obtained by complementing the above function.

4.6   The Quine-McCluskey or Tabular Method

The previous discussion of minimizing Boolean functions using K-map relied on visually identifying prime implicants and building the minimal set of prime implicants that cover all 1-cells. The procedure is not algorithmic. We next present an algorithmic procedure called the Quine-McCluskey or tabular method. As we discuss this procedure, we relate previous knowledge of minimization to the new procedure.

In the K-map method of minimization we partitioned the procedure into two parts. In the first part, we construct a table and identify all prime implicants. In the second part, we find a minimum set of prime implicants that cover all 1-cells of the function. Similarly, the Quine-McCluskey method is divided into two parts: in the first part, we construct all prime implicants; in the second part, we find the minimum set of prime implicants that cover all 1-cells.

4.6.1 Building Prime Implicants

In the K-map method, forming prime implicants was accomplished by, first, identifying the largest possible subcubes. In the tabular method, prime implicants are formed by starting with smallest possible subcubes (subcubes of size 1). From the initial set of subcubes, the algorithm proceeds in building larger ones. In forming larger subcubes we make use of logical adjacency. We illustrate this procedure in the example function given in Table 4.6.1.

When the K-map method is used on Table 4.6.1 we form prime implicants in the order indicated by the labels (First is the implicant with label 1 and last is the prime implicant with label 4). In the tabular method, the opposite occurs. Initially, each subcube of 1-cell is assumed to be a prime implicant. During this part, logical adjacency is used to combine subcubes of 1-cells. Those that are found to be logically adjacent are removed and tagged as not prime implicants since they are part of larger subcubes. We illustrate this for the example in Table 4.6.1.

Initially, all 1-cells are assumed potential prime implicants of size 1, i.e., the minterms corresponding to the inputs with decimal values 0, 5, 7, 10, 11, 13, and 15 are potential prime implicants. Next, logical adjacency is used to identify those subcubes that are not prime implicants. This can be done algorithmically by placing each minterm in a subgroup based on the number of 1s in the binary representation of the minterm. The subgroups are shown in Table 4.6.2.

TABLE 4.6.1

$f = \Sigma(0, 5, 7, 10, 11, 13, 15)$

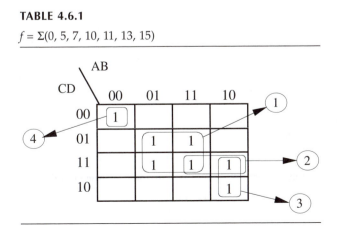

TABLE 4.6.2

Implicants Grouping Based on the Number 1's in the Binary Representation

Number of 1s[a]	Subgroup	Prime Implicant
0	$(0000) = (m_0)$	P_1
1	None exist	
2	$(0101,1010) = (m_5, m_6)$	
3	$(0111, 1011, 1101) = (m_7, m_{11}, m_{13})$	
4	$(1111) = (m_{15})$	

[a] The number of 1s in the binary representation of minterms.

Next, observe that if two minterms are adjacent then a necessary condition for the minterms is to be chosen from two adjacent subgroups (two subcubes chosen from subgroups that are not adjacent cannot be logically adjacent as the corresponding algebraic representation differ in more than one location). From Table 4.6.2, minterm m_0 is a prime implicant since it is not adjacent to any other minterm. In the table we label this prime implicant as P_1.

On inspecting the elements of subgroup 2 with the elements of subgroup 3, we find that minterm m_5 is adjacent to minterm m_7 and minterm m_{13}. As a result, none of this minterms is a prime implicant. The subcubes (m_5, m_7) and (m_5, m_{13}) are new possible prime implicants candidates of size 2. To represent these subcubes in binary format we note

$$m_5 + m_7 = A'BC'D + A'BCD = A'BD$$

In binary this can be represented as

$$01X1 \quad \text{or} \quad 01-1$$

with "−" or "X" indicating the variable C is removed. On applying the adjacency rule, we form two new subgroups of implicants based on the number of 1-cells in an implicant. Table 4.6.3 shows the two new subgroups of subcubes. In the table, we compare the elements of subgroup 2 to those in subgroup 3. We do this by comparing each element in subgroup 2 with all elements in subgroup 3. Our goal is to identify all prime implicants of size 2. Those that are found not to be prime implicants of size 2 are part of a larger subcube of size 4.

Two subcubes are part of a larger subcube if and only if (1) the relative location of the "−" is the same, and (2) if the remaining binary representation

TABLE 4.6.3

Subcubes of Size 2, Obtained from Table 4.6.2

Subgroups	Subcubes in Subgroup	Prime Implicant
2	$(0\ 1-1, -1\ 0\ 1, 1\ 0\ 1-)$	P_2: $1\ 0\ 1-$
3	$(-1\ 1\ 1, 1-1\ 1, 1\ 1-1)$	P_3: $1-1\ 1$

TABLE 4.6.4

Subcubes of Size 4, Obtained from Table 4.6.3

Subgroup	Subcubes in Subgroup	Prime Implicant
4	(–1–1)	P_4: –1–1

TABLE 4.6.5

Prime Implicant Table

Prime Implicants	Cells Covered
P_1: 0000	(0000)
P_2: 1 0 1 –	(1010, 1011)
P_3: 1 – 1 1	(1011, 1111)
P_4: – 1 – 1	(0101,0111,1101,1111)

differs in exactly one location. As a result, we note that the subcube 101– and 1–11 cannot be combined with any of the other subcubes. Hence, the two subcubes form prime implicants of size 2. This is shown in Table 4.6.3. In addition, we note that the subcubes 01–1 and 11–1 can be combined to produce a new subcube –1–1. Similarly, subcubes –101 and –111 can be combined to produce subcube –1–1 as well. Table 4.6.4 shows the new subcubes of size 4. Note that the two combinations result in the same subcube. As a result we choose only 1 combination in the table.

Since we are left with only one subgroup, this subgroup is a prime implicant and the process of forming prime implicants stops. Table 4.6.5 includes all prime implicants generated in this first phase. The table is similar, in terms of contents, to the list of prime implicants obtained by constructing them through the K-map method.

4.6.2 Finding Minimal Cover

In the second part of the tabular method, we find a minimal number of prime implicants that cover all the 1-cells. Similar to the K-map method, essential prime implicants are always included. The process of finding a minimal number of prime implicants can be done by representing Table 4.6.5 in the format shown in Table 4.6.6. The table includes additional columns (not found in Table 4.6.5). The columns are labeled with the minterms of the

TABLE 4.6.6

Prime Implicant Table, Reconstructed from Table 4.6.5

Prime Implicant	1-Cells Covered	m_0	m_5	m_7	m_{10}	m_{11}	m_{13}	m_{15}
P_1: 0000	(0000)	x						
P_2: 101–	(1010, 1011)				x	x		
P_3: 1–11	(1011, 1111)					x		x
P_4: –1–1	(0101,0111,1101,1111)		x	x			x	x

function. The rows are identified by the prime implicants generated in part one of the tabular method. With each prime implicant we identify the minterms it covers by placing an x in the corresponding column.

The table helps in identifying essential prime implicants as follows. For each column, if the column contains a single x, then the corresponding prime implicant on the row that contains the x is an essential prime implicant. This is similar to the K-map method; such a minterm is covered by only one prime implicant. This makes the minterm an essential minterm and the corresponding implicant an essential prime implicant. From the table, we find that minterms m_0, m_5, m_7, m_{10}, and m_{13} are essential minterms. This makes prime implicant P_1, P_2, and P_4 essential prime implicants.

Similar to the K-map method, we remove all minterms covered by essential prime implicants from further consideration (these minterms are covered). This will reduce the number of minterms to be considered. In the example function, once these minterm are removed, there are no further minterms to cover. As a result, step 2 of the method is completed.

Thus the minimal function is the sum of the algebraic representations of the prime implicants P_1, P_2, and P_4. From Table 4.6.6 P_1 is represented as 0000. As a result, its algebraic representation is

$$A'B'C'D'$$

Similarly, P_2 is represented as 101–. As a result, its algebraic representation is

$$AB'C$$

Similarly, for P_4 we obtain the algebraic product BD and hence the minimal function is

$$f(A,B,C,D) = A'B'C'D' + AB'C + BD$$

4.6.3   Algorithmic Procedure of the Tabular Method

We describe more formally the method of construction of prime implicants and the selection of a minimal cover. We present the method and apply the minimization procedure to the Boolean function $F(A,B,C,D,E) = \Sigma\ (0, 2, 5, 7, 10, 13, 14, 15, 18, 19, 21, 23, 29, 31)$. We first present the procedure for building prime implicants.

4.6.3.1   *Forming the Prime Implicants*

In this step, we start with an initial table of potential implicants. We then identify those that are actual implicants and generate a new table of potential implicants.

This process is repeated on the new table as an initial table until all implicants are identified as discussed next.

TABLE 4.6.7

Tabular Method, Construction of Prime Implicants, (a) Initial Table,
(b) Subcubes of Size 2 Obtained from (a)

Subcubes	Binary Representation					
0	0	0	0	0	0	√
2	0	0	0	1	0	√
5	0	0	1	0	1	√
10	0	1	0	1	0	√
18	1	0	0	1	0	√
7	0	0	1	1	1	√
13	0	1	1	0	1	√
14	0	1	1	1	0	√
19	1	0	0	1	1	√
21	1	0	1	0	1	√
15	0	1	1	1	1	√
23	1	0	1	1	1	√
29	1	1	1	0	1	√
31	1	1	1	1	1	√

(a)

Subcubes	Binary Representation					
(0, 2)	0	0	0	–	0	P1
(2, 10)	0	–	0	1	0	P2
(2, 18)	–	0	0	1	0	P3
(5, 7)	0	0	1	–	1	√
(5, 13)	0	–	1	0	1	√
(5, 21)	–	0	1	0	1	√
(10, 14)	0	1	–	1	0	P4
(18, 19)	1	0	0	1	–	P5
(7, 15)	0	–	1	1	1	√
(7, 23)	–	0	1	1	1	√
(13, 15)	0	1	1	–	1	√
(13, 29)	–	1	1	0	1	√
(14, 15)	0	1	1	1	–	P6
(19, 23)	1	0	–	1	1	P7
(21, 23)	1	0	1	–	1	√
(21, 29)	1	–	1	0	1	√
(15, 31)	–	1	1	1	1	√
(23, 31)	1	–	1	1	1	√
(29, 31)	1	1	1	–	1	√

(b)

Step 1: Initial table. Group the minterms according to the number of 1s found in the corresponding binary representation. Table 4.6.7 shows the minterms are divided into five groups based on the number of 1s found in the binary representations. Each of the minterms represents a subcube of size 1 as a potential prime implicant.

Step 2: Successive tables. Build a new table of subcubes (from the initial table) by checking for logical adjacencies. Logical adjacency is obtained if and only if the following two conditions are met.

1. The two subcubes belong to two adjacent groups (here we compare a given subcube with all subcubes in the group directly below it).

2. The subcubes' binary representation differs in exactly one location (a bit is 0 in one subcube and 1 in the other). All other locations, including the relative locations of the "–" (if it exists) must match.

Two subcubes that satisfy conditions 1 and 2 are marked "checked" in the initial table to indicate the subcubes are not prime implicants. They are combined into a larger subcube and are added to the new table (they are placed in the proper subgroup based on the number of 1s). The subcube binary representation is obtained from either subcube by replacing the bit position where they differ by a "–." Note that different combinations may lead to the same subcubes (subcubes that contain the same minterms). For these combinations, only one representative subcube is included in the new table.

Step 3: All unchecked subcubes in the initial table are prime implicants since these subcubes are not part of any larger subcube.

These implicants are assigned labels. The table generated in step 2 is now the initial table. If the initial table contains more than one group of subcubes then repeat step 2 above.

We illustrate the procedure by applying it to the example function. The initial table is shown in Table 4.6.7(a). The first column contains the minterms of the function with each minterm constituting a subcube of size 1. Table 4.6.7(b) is obtained by applying step 2 of the algorithm to Table 4.6.7(a). Consider the first subcube in Table 4.6.7(b), for example. The subcube is obtained by combining minterm 0 and minterm 2 into a larger subcube represented as (0, 2). Its binary representation is "000–0" as seen in the table. Similar comparisons yield Table 4.6.7(b).

In step 3, Table 4.6.7(b) becomes the initial table. Since it contains more than one group we repeat step 2 on this new initial table. From the table, subcube (0,2) cannot be combined with any of the elements in the adjacent group below it (the dashes locations do not match). Hence, (0,2) constitutes a prime implicant labeled as P_1 in the table. Based on matching the "–" location, subcube (2,10) can possibly be combined with subcube (5,13) only. The algebraic representations for these two subcubes, however, differ in more than one location (0–010 and 0–101). As a result, (2,10) becomes a prime implicant, P_2, as seen in the table. Similar analysis makes subcube (2,18) a prime implicant, P_3, as well.

We next move to the third group and compare its elements to group four. For subcube (5,7), we find that it can be combined with subcube (13,15) to yield a larger subcube. As a result, we check these two subcubes as part of a larger subcube. The new subcube formed is (5,7,13,15) with the binary representation 0-1-1. This subcube is added to a new table. To speed up the process, we search the table for other subcubes that form (5,7,13,15). We find (5,13) from group three and (7,15) from group four can be combined. These subcubes, as well as all other combinations found, are checked. In this case, no other combination exists. On completing step 2, we form the new table, Table 4.6.8.

TABLE 4.6.8

Subcubes of Size 4, Obtained from Table 4.6.7(b)

Subcubes	Binary Representation
(5,7,13,15)	0 – 1 – 1 √
(5,7,21,23)	– 0 1 – 1 √
(5,13,21,29)	– – 1 0 1 √
(7,15,23,31)	– – 1 1 1 √
(13,15,29,31)	– 1 1 – 1 √
(21,23,29,31)	1 – 1 – 1 √

TABLE 4.6.9

Subcubes of Size 8, Obtained from Table 4.6.8

(5,7,13,15,21,23,29,31)	$--1-1$	P8

TABLE 4.6.10

Table of Prime Implicants Used to Find Minimal Cover

Prime Implicants	0*	2	5*	7*	10	13*	14	15	18	19	21*	23	29*	31*
(5,7,13,15,21,23,29,31)*			x	x		x		x			x	x	x	x
(0,2)*	x	x												
(2,10)		x			x									
(2,18)		x							x					
(10,14)					x		x							
(14,15)							x	x						
(18,19)									x	x				
(19,23)										x		x		

* Indicates an essential prime implicant.

On applying step 3 and repeating step 2, we obtain Table 4.6.9. This completes the procedure of finding the set of prime implicants. After identifying the list of all prime implicants, we look for the minimal set that cover all 1-cells. This is the second major step in the algorithm.

4.6.3.2 Minimal Cover Procedure

The minimal cover procedure we follow is similar to the previously mentioned procedure. Table 4.6.10 shows the format used to find the minimal number of prime implicants. The number of rows in the table is equal to the number of prime implicants. The number of columns is equal to the number of minterms where the function assumes a value of 1. For a given prime implicant and a given minterm identifying an entry in the table, an x is placed in the entry if the corresponding minterm is covered by the given prime implicant. With each column in the table essential minterm are identified as well (these are columns that contain one x only). The corresponding prime implicant is an essential prime implicant. Both the essential minterms and the essential prime implicants are identified by an "*" in the table.

The reduced table is obtained by removing (1) all rows containing the essential prime implicant, and (2) all columns with minterms covered by the essential prime implicants. The new reduced table is shown in Table 4.6.11. By inspecting the table we note that of the remaining prime implicants no implicants are essential. To proceed in the minimization process we make use of the following definition.

Definition: Over the reduced table and with prime implicants of the same size we say two prime implicants are equal if they cover the same minterms; we say prime implicant x dominates prime implicant y if x is unequal to y and x covers all minterms covered by y. Alternatively, we say y is dominated by x.

TABLE 4.6.11

Reduced Table of Prime Implicant

Prime Implicants	Remaining Uncovered Minterms			
	10	14	18	19
(2,10)	x			
(2,18)			x	
(10,14)	x	x		
(14,15)		x		
(18,19)			x	x
(19,23)				x

TABLE 4.6.12

Final Reduced Table of Prime Implicants

Prime Implicants	10	14	18	19
(10,14)	x	x		
(18,19)			x	x

TABLE 4.6.13

Minimal Cover and Associated Algebraic Products

Prime Implicants	Binary Representation	Algebraic Product
(5,7,13,15,21,23,29,31)	$--1-1$	CE
(0,2)	$000-0$	A'B'C'E'
(10,14)	$01-10$	A'BDE'
(18,19)	$1001-$	AB'C'D

Using the concept of equality and dominance, Table 4.6.11 can be modified to create essential prime implicants by (1) with the exception of one implicant from each set of equal implicants, removing all other implicants in a given set; and (2) removing all dominated implicants.

On applying the above to Table 4.6.11, we note that implicants (2,10) is dominated by (10, 14). Similarly, we note that implicant (18,19) dominates (2,18). As a result, subcubes (2,10) and (2,18) are removed from the table. In addition, we remove implicants (14,15) and (19,23). The new reduced table is given in Table 4.6.12. From the table, prime implicants (10,14) and (18,19) are new essential prime implicants. In removing these implicants, and the corresponding columns, we have formed a minimal cover. Table 4.6.13 shows the minimal cover and the associated algebraic products. The minimal function is the sum of the algebraic products associated with the prime implicants chosen in the cover, i.e.,

$$F(A,B,C,D,E) = CE + A'B'C'E' + A'BDE' + AB'C'D$$

4.6.4 Decimal Method of Building Prime Implicants

We can accelerate the process of finding the list of prime implicants by working with decimal numbers instead of binary. To do this, we make the following observations.

Observation 1: Two minterms, x_1 and x_2, that belong to adjacent groups are logically adjacent if

1. The smaller number x_1 is in group i (number of 1s is equal to i) while the larger number is in the group that follows (group $i + 1$).
2. And, if $x_2 - x_1 = 2^k$ for some integer k.

Observation 2: If x_1 contains more 1s than x_2 and $x_1 < x_2$, then x_1 and x_2 are not logically adjacent.

Observation 1 states that the binary representations of the two numbers differ in one location only, i.e., the minterms are adjacent. We apply the observations to the above example. The table is constructed as before, minterms are placed in groups according to the number of 1s in their binary representations. However, the table is composed of decimal numbers instead of binary numbers as shown in Table 4.6.14. The steps of minimization are given below.

Step 1: Arrange minterms into groups depending on the number of 1s in binary representation. Present the minterms in decimal values. This step corresponds to Table 4.6.14(a).

Step 2: Use the procedure discussed to combine minterms into larger subcubes. This procedure yields a table with subcubes of size 2. The subcubes are presented as a pair of decimal numbers. In addition, the difference between the minterms is presented in parentheses. This step is shown in Table 4.6.14(b).

For example, minterms m_0 and m_2 are combined to form the entry "(0,2) (2)" since $2 - 0 = 2^1$. The difference, 2, helps in locating the bit position where the two minterms differ m_0 corresponds to the input 00000 and m_2 corresponds to the input 00010. The difference is in bit 2 of the numbers, i.e., (0,2) can be represented as 000-0. Check marks are added as done previously. Table 4.6.14(b) becomes the initial table as was done previously and the process is repeated.

In the comparisons to generate new tables, we compare smaller numbers in an upper group to larger numbers in the next, consecutive lower, group and combine the subcubes into larger subcubes. We restrict our comparison, however, to pairs with the same parenthesized difference. This is equivalent to comparing pairs with same relative location of the "–." For example, in the table we find group (0,2) cannot be combined with any of the groups (2,10) and (2,18) below it since (2) is associated with (0,2); (8) and (16) are associated with (2,10) and (2,18), respectively. As a result, (0,2) is marked as a prime implicant. Similar analysis results in identifying the subcubes (2,10) and (2,18) as prime implicants. This is true since (2,10) can be matched with

TABLE 4.6.14

Decimal Procedure for Identifying Prime Implicants

Minterms
0 √
2 √
5 √
10 √
18 √
7 √
13 √
14 √
19 √
21 √
15 √
23 √
29 √
31 √
(a)

Subcubes of size 2		
(0, 2)	(2)	P_1
(2, 10)	(8)	P_2
(2, 18)	(16)	P_3
(5,7)	(2)	√
(5, 13)	(18)	√
(5, 21)	(16)	√
(10, 14)	(4)	P_4
(18, 19)	(1)	P_5
(7, 15)	(8)	√
(7, 23)	(6)	√
(13, 15)	(2)	√
(13, 29)	(16)	√
(14, 15)	(1)	P_6
(19, 23)	(4)	P_7
(21, 23)	(2)	√
(21, 29)	(8)	√
(15, 31)	(16)	√
(23, 31)	(8)	√
(29, 31)	(2)	√
(b)		

$x_1 < x_2$ (2 < 10), and
$x_2 - x_1 = 10$ 2 = 2 = 8.
Hence combine 2 and 10
to get (2, 10)   (8)

only (5,13) in the table (due to 8 in parentheses). However, the difference $5 - 2$ is not equal to 2^k.

Similar to the tabular method when two pairs are merged we check these pairs and all other combinations that yield the same minterms in the new merged group (for examples, (5,7) and (13,5), (5,13) and (7,15)). In applying this to Table 4.6.14(b), we obtain Table 4.6.15.

On repeating step 2 in the above table, we combine rows 1 and 4 since

$$21 - 5 = 23 - 7 = 29 - 13 = 31 - 15 = 16$$

TABLE 4.6.15

Subcube of Size 4 Obtained from Table 4.6.14

(5,7,13,15)(2,8)√
(5,7,21,23)(2,16)√
(5,13,21,29)(8,16)
(7,15,23,31)(8,16)
(13,15,29,31)(2,16)√
(21,23,29,31)(2,8)√

Hence, the newly formed table contains the group "(5, 7, 13, 15, 21, 23, 29, 31) (2, 8, 16)"; the groups (5, 7, 13, 15) and (21, 23, 29, 31) are checked in Table 4.6.14. In addition, the remaining groups are checked, since in merging these groups one obtains the newly generated group (5, 7, 13, 15, 21, 23, 29, 31). Table 4.6.16 shows the result. The subcube in the table is the last prime implicant generated. To find its algebraic representation we form the binary representation of any of the minterms in the group with locations 1, 3, and 4 replaced by a dash corresponding to the exponents ($2^1 = 2$, $2^3 = 8$, and $2^4, = 16$).

The binary representation is then converted to algebraic representation by (1) placing the associated variable as is if it assumes a value of 1, (2) placing

TABLE 4.6.16

Subcubes of Size 8 Obtained from
Table 4.16.15

(5, 7, 13, 15, 21, 23, 29, 31) (2, 8, 16)	P_8

the associated variable in complemented form if it assumes a value of 0, and
(3) removing the variables that correspond to "−" in the binary representation. For example, for P_8 we have $(15)_{10} = (01111)_2$ with location 1, 3, and 4
replace by "−" the P_8 binary representation is "−−1−1." Hence the algebraic
representation of P_8 is *CE*. For the construction of the minimum cover, we
follow a procedure similar to the procedure discussed earlier.

4.7   Multiple-Output Function Minimization

The minimization procedure discussed so far treats functions over the same
set of inputs as independent functions with the minimization procedure
applied to each function separately. Consider the two-output circuit realizing
the functions

$$F_1 = \Sigma\ (0, 1, 8, 9, 10, 11) \text{ and } F_2 = \Sigma\ (0, 1, 10, 11, 12)$$

Treated as separate functions, we have the K-map representations as
shown in Table 4.7.1. The minimized functions are

$$F_1 = B'C' + AB'$$

$$F_2 = A'B'C' + ABC'D' + AB'C$$

TABLE 4.7.1

Multiple-Output Function Minimization, (a) $F_1 = \Sigma\ (0, 1, 8, 9, 10, 11)$,
(b) $F_2 = \Sigma\ (0, 1, 10, 11, 12)$

CD \ AB	00	01	11	10
00	1			1
01	1			1
11				1
10				1

(a)

CD \ AB	00	01	11	10
00	1		1	
01	1			
11				1
10				1

(b)

The design of the above functions requires the generations of separate product terms for each function. The product terms then are used as inputs into OR gates (one OR gate per function).

An alternative method to designing the functions is to do multiple output minimizations. In this context, we assume dependence between the two functions. Common product terms that belong to both functions can be generated only once. These terms are then routed to the proper OR gate accordingly. For example, by inspecting the above two tables, we note that the shaded region in the table for F_2 can be used to help in reducing the total number of product terms. How? When the functions are treated independently, the number of product terms needed is five. When we assume dependence, then F_1 and F_2 can be written as

$$F_1 = A'B'C' + AB'$$

$$F_2 = A'B'C' + ABC'D' + AB'C$$

The common product term is shown in bold. This reduced the number of product terms by one term. Note that independent of F_2, the algebraic representation of F_1 is not minimal. When we assume dependence, our task is no longer to find the minimum associated with a single given function. The task instead is to reduce the total number of product terms needed in the design of both functions. The design of the functions is shown in the Figure 4.7.1.

Note the use of the common product term $A'B'C'$ for both functions.

The minimization procedure of multiple output function is computationally expensive. It involves consideration of not only the given functions but all possible product functions as well. The product functions considered ranges from the product of two functions to products that include all functions. For a set of k functions, $F_1, F_2, \ldots, F_k$, the number of product functions

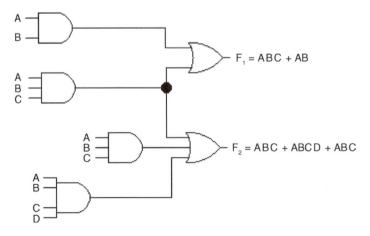

FIGURE 4.7.1
Circuit Realization of Functions in Table 4.7.1

that are considered in the minimization is equal to $2^k - (k + 1)$. This number includes all products of the form $F_i.F_j$, $F_i.F_j.F_k$, ..., $F_1.F_2 ... F_k$.

The number $2^k - (k + 1)$ is obtained from observing that the above products can be thought of as elements of the power set (set of all subsets of $\{F_1, F_2, ..., F_k\}$). The number of elements in the power set is 2^k. With the sets that contain a single element (there are k of those) and the empty set (there is one empty set) removed, we are left with the total possible products of $2^k - (k + 1)$. We explain the minimization procedure by applying it to the given three functions

1. $F_1 = \Sigma\ (0, 1, 2, 3, 6, 7, 14, 15)$
2. $F_2 = \Sigma\ (6, 8, 9, 10, 11, 14)$
3. $F_3 = \Sigma\ (4, 7, 12, 15)$

The first step is to form all the needed products: $F_1.F_2$, $F_1.F_3$, $F_2.F_3$, and $F_1.F_2.F_3$. By inspecting the above functions we find the only nonempty (nonzero product) corresponds to the two products $F_1.F_2$, and $F_1.F_3$ with $F_1.F_2 = \Sigma\ (6, 14)$ and $F_1.F_3 = \Sigma\ (7, 15)$. Note that the products formed are the common elements to the functions in the product term.

The second step is to form the prime implicant tables (using the tabular method) for each of the individual original functions and each of the corresponding product functions. For our case, we would need to form five prime implicant tables; three for the individual functions F_1, F_2, F_3; and two for the product functions $F_1.F_2$ and $F_1.F_3$. No implicant table is needed for the product $F_2.F_3$, and $F_1.F_2.F_3$ since these functions assume a value of 0 for all possible input combinations. In identifying the prime implicants we use K-maps since the number of input variables is small (4). Figure 4.7.2 shows the results.

The third step is to do simultaneous minimum prime-implicant cover. To accomplish this we create a common table as follows. The table columns are divided into groups. Each group lists all the minterms associated with each of the functions F_1, F_2, ..., F_k. In our case, there are three functions and hence we require three such groups. The rows of the table are labeled with the prime implicants found above. The rows form different groups as well depending on the function (product of functions) the prime implicant belongs to. As a result, the rows of the table are divided into five groups. Each group contains row labels of the function it belongs to (F_1, F_2, F_3; and two for the product functions $F_1.F_2$ and $F_1.F_3$). Table 4.7.2 shows the prime implicant table.

In the table, we included groups for the products $F_2.F_3$ and $F_1.F_2.F_3$ for completeness. Note, however, no prime implicants are associated with these functions. In addition, the entries of the table are filled according to the prime implicant characteristic. For prime implicants associated with each of the original functions, an x is placed in the column part of the corresponding function only. For example, for the function F_1 and its prime implicant, P_2, an x is placed in the column with label 6 for F_1 but not in the column labeled 6 of the function F_2. For other entries representing products of functions and a given prime implicant covering a given minterm, m_i, an x is placed in all

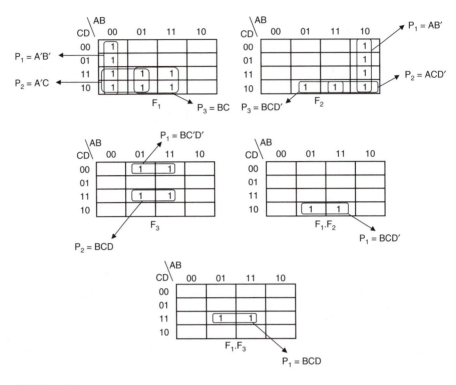

FIGURE 4.7.2
K-Maps for $F_1 = \Sigma\ (0, 1, 2, 3, 6, 7, 14, 15)$, $F_2 = \Sigma\ (6, 8, 9, 10, 11, 14)$, $F_3 = \Sigma\ (4, 7, 12, 15)$, and Corresponding Products

TABLE 4.7.2

Multiple-Output Prime-Implicant Table of Functions in Figure 4.7.2

		Minterms for F_1								Minterms for F_2						Minterms for F_3			
Implicants		0*	1	2	3	6	7	14	15	6	8*	9	10	11	14	4*	7	12	15
F_1	P_1*	x	x	x	x														
	P_2			x	x	x	x												
	P_3					x	x	x	x										
F_2	P_1*										x	x	x	x					
	P_2												x		x				
	P_3									x					x				
F_3	P_1*															x		x	
	P_2																x		x
F_1F_2	P_1					x		x		x				x					
F_1F_3	P_2				x		x										x		x
F_2F_3																			
$F_1F_2F_3$																			

* Indicates an essential prime implicant.

TABLE 4.7.3

Reduced Multiple-Output Prime Implicant Table Obtained from Table 4.7.2

Implicants		Minterms for F_1				Minterms for F_2		Minterms for F_3	
		6	7	14	15	6	14	7	15
F_1	P_2	x	x						
	P_3	x	x	x	x				
F_2	P_2						x		
	P_3					x	x		
F_3	P_2							x	x
$F_1.F_2$		x		x		x	x		
$F_1.F_3$			x		x			x	x

TABLE 4.7.4

Reduced Multiple-Output Prime Implicant Table Obtained from Table 4.7.3

Implicants		Minterms for F_1				Minterms for F_2		Minterms for F_3	
		6	7	14	15	6*	14*	7*	15*
F_1	P_2	x	x						
	P_3	x	x	x	x				
$F_1.F_2$*	P_1	x		x		x	x		
$F_1.F_3$*	P_1		x		x			x	x

* Indicates an essential prime implicant.

i columns of the functions included in the product. For example, for the prime implicant P_1 of the product $F_1.F_2$ an x is placed in column 6 of F_1 and column 6 of F_2.

Following the construction of the prime implicant table we find a minimum cover of all functions (F_1, F_2, and F_3). Here essential prime implicants are identified and removed from the table for single output function. From the table above, the essential prime implicants for each function are identified by an "*" next to the implicant. For each implicant the row of the table of the implicant is removed. In addition, the corresponding columns covered by the implicant are removed. Table 4.7.3 shows the reduced prime implicant table.

Applying the dominance definition to the above table we note that implicant P_2 of F_3 and F_2 can be removed. The reduced table is shown in Table 4.7.4. The reduced table shows the implicants P_1 of $F_1.F_2$ and P_1 of $F_1.F_3$ are essential implicants. When these implicants are included in the minimal function and the corresponding columns are removed the reduced prime implicant table obtained is empty.

The final step in the minimization process is to associate the products of the implicants with the three Boolean functions. The multiple-output minimized functions for F_1 is the sum of the algebraic representations for prime implicants P_1 of F_1, P_1 of $F_1.F_2$, and P_1 of $F_1.F_3$.

Similarly for F_2 the multiple-output minimized function is the sum P_1 of F_2, and P_1 of $F_1.F_2$. And, for the function F_3 the multiple-output minimized function is the sum of the algebraic representations for prime implicants P_1 of F_3, and P_1 of $F_1.F_3$.

The algebraic representations of the functions are

$$F_1 = A'B' + BCD' + BCD$$

$$F_2 = AB' + BCD'$$

$$F_3 = BC'D' + BCD$$

Note the algebraic representation for F_1 is not minimal if treated independently. Note as well the total number of product terms was reduced from eight to seven terms.

Chapter 4 Exercises

4.1 Given the function $f(A, B, C) = \Sigma(0, 1, 4, 5)$. Form the algebraic representation of the function and show that each minterm is adjacent to two other minterms.

4.2 Algebraically, simplify the function given in problem 4.1.

4.3 Given the function $f(A, B, C) = \Sigma(0, 1, 4, 5, 6)$.

   (a) Construct the K-map representation of f.

   (b) Form all subcubes of size 1 and give the corresponding algebraic representation.

   (c) Form all possible subcubes of size two of f and give the corresponding algebraic representation of each.

   (d) Is it possible to form subcubes of size 3? Explain.

   (e) Form all possible subcubes of size 4 of f.

   (f) Of the subcubes generated in the previous parts, identify those that are prime implicants and give the corresponding algebraic representation of each.

4.4 Given the function $f(A, B, C, D) = \Sigma(0, 2, 4, 5, 6, 8, 10, 13, 15)$. Form all prime implicants of size 4 and give the corresponding algebraic representation.

4.5 Given the function $f(A, B, C, D) = \Sigma(0, 2, 4, 6, 8, 10, 11, 12, 13, 14, 15)$. Form all prime implicants of size 8 and give the corresponding algebraic representations.

4.6 Form all prime implicants of the function given in problem 4.4 and give the algebraic representation of each.

4.7 Form all prime implicants of the function given in problem 4.5 and give the algebraic representation of each.

4.8 Identify all essential prime implicants of the function given in problem 4.4 and find all minimal functions.

4.9 Identify all essential prime implicants of the function given in problem 4.5 and find all minimal functions.

4.10 Given the function $f(A, B, C, D) = \Sigma(0, 1, 2, 6, 7, 8, 9, 13, 15) + d(3, 10)$.

   (a) Form the K-map representation of f.

   (b) Form all prime implicants of f.

   (c) Identify all essential prime implicants.

   (d) Find a minimal function of f.

4.11 Use K-maps to minimize the functions $c(A, B, C, D)$ of the seven-segment decoder discussed in section 4.4.

4.12 Use K-maps to minimize the functions $d(A, B, C, D)$ of the seven-segment decoder discussed in section 4.4. Note the d in the above represents a function and not the "don't-care" symbol.

4.13 Use K-maps to minimize the functions e through f of the seven-segment decoder discussed in section 4.4.

4.14 Given the function $f(A, B, C, D) = \Sigma(0, 2, 4, 5, 6, 8, 10, 13, 15)$. Form the minimal function in product of sums form.

4.15 Repeat problem 4.14 on the function $f(A, B, C, D) = \Sigma(0, 1, 2, 6, 7, 8, 9, 13, 15) + d(3, 10, 11)$.

4.16 Given the function $f(A, B, C, D) = \Sigma(0, 4, 5, 10, 11, 13, 15)$. Form all prime implicants of the table using the tabular method.

4.17 For the function given in problem 4.16 form all prime implicants using the tabular method with decimal entries representing min-terms.

4.18 Minimize the function given in problem 4.16 using the tabular method. Verify your answer is correct by minimizing the function using the K-map method.

4.19 Given the function $f(A, B, C, D) = \Sigma(0, 2, 4, 5, 6, 7, 10, 12, 13, 15, 16, 18, 20, 21, 22, 23, 26, 28, 29, 31)$. Minimize the function using the tabular method. Verify your minimization is correct by using the logic converter of the Electronics Workbench.

4.20 Given the functions $f_1(A, B, C, D) = (0, 5, 6, 8, 9, 11, 14, 15)$ and $f_2(A, B, C, D) = \Sigma(0, 1, 5, 6, 8, 11, 12, 14, 15)$. Minimize each function using the K-map method. Use the multiple-output minimization procedure to minimize both functions simultaneously.

5

Arithmetic Logic Circuits and Programmable Logic Devices

5.1   Binary Adders

5.1.1   Iterative Circuits

The previous discussion of digital circuit design converted a word problem into a truth table. The algebraic equations associated with the circuit were then derived (based on the implementation used (AND-OR, OR-AND, etc.)). The equations were then minimized and the implementation (design) was finally accomplished at the gate level.

Iterative design uses an alternative approach where the design is done in hierarchal fashion similar to programming. Here the larger problem is solved in terms of smaller problems. The smaller problems are then solved and used as a solution to the larger problem. We illustrate with an example of an n-bit binary adder. The adder inputs are two n-bit numbers A and B. Its output is the sum of the two binary numbers with an additional possible carry; i.e., the sum is an $(n + 1)$-bit number. The block diagram of the adder is shown in Figure 5.1.1. The solid lines shown with the dash indicate multiple inputs or outputs. The n indicates there are n such inputs. The dash can be removed from the figure.

The standard design procedure is not suitable in the design of a binary adder. Consider the case of adding two 16-bit numbers. The first step in the design is to generate the truth table for the above circuit. Since the number of inputs to the circuit is 32 bits (16 bits per number), one would need a truth table of size 2^{32} rows. As a result, this design procedure is not used.

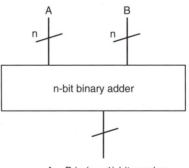

A + B is (n + 1)-bit number

FIGURE 5.1.1
Block Diagram of n-Bit Binary Adder

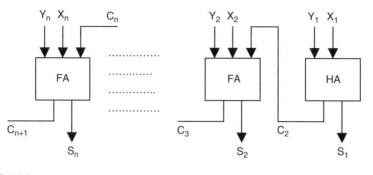

FIGURE 5.1.2
Ripple Carry Adder

An alternative design procedure is to make use of the properties of addition, as was done in Chapter 1, where addition was accomplished by adding two bits at a time with a previous carry included. We use a similar iterative approach in the design. Figure 5.1.2 shows an example of a binary adder that makes use of smaller 1-bit adders, called 1-bit full adders or 1-bit half adders. The circuit is called a ripple carry adder.

In the figure, each of the circuits adds the corresponding bits associated with two numbers, X and Y, with $X = X_n \ldots X_1$ and $Y = Y_n \ldots Y_1$. The first circuit from the right adds the first two bits of the number. There is no carry from previous stages. Such a circuit is called a half adder (HA). The remaining circuits add the corresponding bits and the additional carry generated by the previous bits. As a result, such a circuit has three inputs and is called a full adder. It generates a sum bit and an additional carry bit to use in the next consecutive stage. The adder is abbreviated as FA in the figure.

From the figure we note that the larger design problem has been reduced to a simpler design problem, mainly the design of the building blocks that are used in the figure.

5.1.2 Half and Full Adders

The design of the half and full adders follows the design procedure mentioned earlier, i.e., we first generate the truth tables of the circuits. From the truth tables, we then generate the needed equations and perform the design.

For the half-adder circuit, the circuit requires two inputs. It outputs the sum of its inputs in binary. Since this sum requires 2 bits, the circuit output is 2 bits as well. The truth table of the half adder is given in Table 5.1.1.

From the table, we note that the equations of the half adder are

$$C = AB$$

and

$$S = A \oplus B$$

TABLE 5.1.1

Truth Table of a Half Adder

AB	C	S
00	0	0
01	0	1
10	0	1
11	1	0

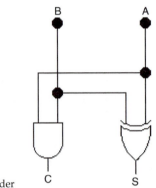

FIGURE 5.1.3
Design of a Half Adder

TABLE 5.1.2

Truth Table of a Full Adder

ABC_i	C_o	S
000	0	0
001	0	1
010	0	1
011	1	0
100	0	1
101	1	0
110	1	0
111	1	1

The design of the half adder is given in Figure 5.1.3. For the full adder circuit, we follow a similar procedure. Here, however, the circuit truth table requires three inputs, the two bits to be added and the previous carry. The truth table for the full adder is given in the Table 5.1.2.

To distinguish between the carry-in and carry-out, we used C_i to represent the carry-in from the previous stage. The carry-out into the next stage is represented as C_o. The design of the full adder can be accomplished by forming the Boolean equations and minimizing them. The sum equation, S, cannot be minimized, however, as can be verified by constructing the K-map. The C_o equation is that of the majority function and, as a result, requires a total of 4 gates (three AND and one OR gates). An alternative design procedure is to make use of half adders by rewriting the Boolean equations as

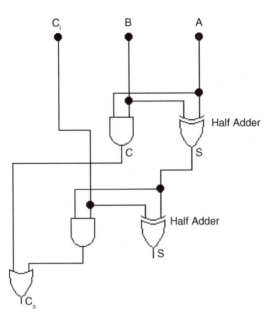

FIGURE 5.1.4
Design of a Full Adder from Two Half Adders

$$S = A'B'C_i + A'BC_i' + AB'C_i' + ABC_i$$

$$= A'(B'C_i + BC_i') + A(B'C_i' + BC_i)$$

$$= A'(B \oplus C) + A(B \oplus C)'$$

$$= A \oplus B \oplus C$$

For the carry equation, we have

$$C_o = ABC_i' + ABC_i + A'BC_i + AB'C_i$$

$$= AB(C_i + C_i') + C_i(A'B + AB')$$

$$= AB + C_i(A \oplus B)$$

The design of a full adder is shown in Figure 5.1.4.

The design of the *n*-bit adder from half adders and full adders, as shown in Figure 5.1.2, introduces delays in producing the sum. This delay is proportional to the size of the adder. The cause of the delay is related to the method by which the iterative circuit is designed. In this method, a carry ripples through the full adders to the next most-significant stages. The carry may have to propagate through all adders from the least-significant to most-significant digits; this can be seen in adding the two numbers 100000001 + 011111111. The correct sum is produced at the output after the initial carry produced by adding the two least-significant bits (LSB) is propagated through all adders of the circuit. The add operation is among the most commonly used arithmetic operations. As a result, it is useful to make such circuits faster. In the next section, we discuss carry look-ahead generator circuits. These circuits remove the ripple carry that causes the delay discussed earlier.

5.2   Look-Ahead Carry Generators

The delay introduced by the carry ripple adders is caused by the carry discussed at the end of the previous section. A carry look-ahead generator computes all carries in approximately the same amount of time (assuming no fan-in restrictions are imposed on the gates). We discuss how such a circuit functions and how it is designed by observing the carry equation generated earlier. We consider the *i*th bit full adder, as shown in Figure 5.2.1.

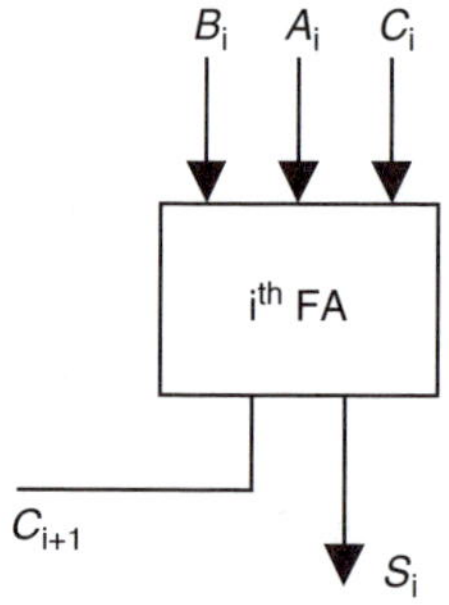

We assume the half adder (adding the least-significant bits) is replaced with a full adder with an input C_1 given as an initial carry (this carry will be used in signed arithmetic later in the chapter). For the above circuit, the carry-out, C_{i+1}, is written as

FIGURE 5.2.1
ith Bit Full Adder

$$C_{i+1} = A_i B_i + C_i \left(A_i \oplus B_i \right)$$

In the above equation, the cause of the delay is the term C_i. In order to generate the proper carry-out, C_{i+1}, the variable C_i must have the correct value. Since this term depends on previous terms, it is the source of the delay. In general, all bits of the two operands A and B as well as the initial carry C_1 are given at the inputs of the adder at the same time. As a result, if we could write the carry equations in a form that uses the operands and C_1, we could remove the source of the delay, as shown next.

We first introduce two equations, the carry-generate, G_i, and carry-propagate, P_i, equations

$$G_i = A_i B_i,$$

$$P_i = \left(A_i \oplus B_i \right), \text{ and as a result}$$

$$C_{i+1} = G_i + C_i P_i$$

In the above equations, the carry-generate and carry-propagate equations can be generated in parallel for all *i*. This can be obtained by applying the proper bits of the n-bit operands A and B to the inputs of n half adders. The look-ahead generator circuit is implemented by rewriting the carry equations in terms of the available G_i and P_i (independent of C_i). Since G_i and P_i are generated in parallel, the carries needed in the sum can be generated in parallel as well. We illustrate this next by rewriting the carry-out equations.

For the first carry from the least-significant added bits we have

$$C_2 = G_1 + C_1 P_1$$

The equation can be realized by a two-level AND-OR circuit. For the carry generated by the next added bits, our objective is to write the equations so as to include the carry-generate and carry-propagate equations only. We do this as

$$C_3 = G_2 + C_2 P_2$$
$$= G_2 + (G_1 + C_1 P_1) P_2$$
$$= G_2 + G_1 P_2 + C_1 P_1 P_2$$

The above equation can be realized by implementing a two-level AND-OR circuit as well.

As can be concluded from the above discussion, the process can be repeated on all carries to rewrite the equations independent of previous carries and as a function of the operand inputs only. These equations are written in sum of products form and, as a result, can be implemented using a two-level AND-OR realization. The above equations can be generalized for the case of computing C_5, for example, to obtain

$$C_5 = G_4 + G_3 P_4 + G_2 P_4 P_3 + G_1 P_4 P_3 P_2 + C_1 P_4 P_3 P_2 P_1$$

In general, we obtain

$$C_{i+1} = G_i + G_{i-1} P_i + G_{i-2} P_i P_{i-1} + G_{i-3} P_i P_{i-1} P_{i-2} + \ldots + C_1 P_i P_{i-1} P_{i-2} \ldots P_1$$

As can be seen from the equation, the number of product terms found in the sum is equal $(i + 1)$. The maximum number of variables in a product term is equal to $(i + 1)$ as well. As a result, the realizations of such equation for large values of i require multiple levels of gates due to the physical fan-in limitation. Before we conclude this section, we show the design of a 4-bit adder that uses a 4-bit carry generator as described by the equations given above. In the design, the carry-generate and -propagate inputs are realized using half adders first. The design of the adder with look-ahead carry generator circuit is shown in Figure 5.2.2.

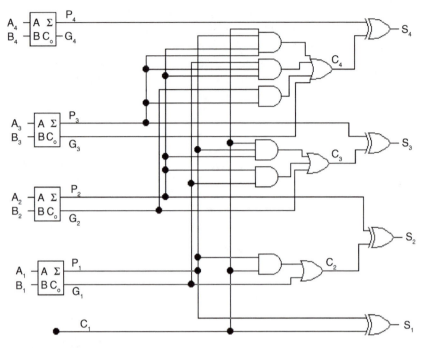

FIGURE 5.2.2
Design of a 4-Bit Adder with Lookahead Carry Generator Circuit Included

The circuit is composed of three parts. The first part generates the needed carry-propagate and carry-generate signals through the four half adders shown in the figure. The second part generates the needed carries through the set of AND-OR gates shown; this part is the look-ahead carry-generator circuit. Finally, the third part forms the sum through the XOR gates. This can be verified by making use of the sum equations since

$$S_i = A_i \oplus B_i \oplus C_i$$

$$= P_i \oplus C_i$$

The above circuit can be modified so as to include an additional carry-out (C_5) by implementing the equation for C_5 given above. In block diagram, the above circuit can be represented as shown in Figure 5.2.3.

The circuit can be then cascaded to generate an 8-bit full adder, as shown in Figure 5.2.4.

5.3 Magnitude Comparators

Magnitude comparators are circuits that compare the magnitudes of two binary operands. The circuits are hardware realizations of comparison operations that

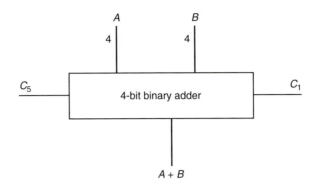

FIGURE 5.2.3
Block Diagram of a 4-Bit Binary Adder

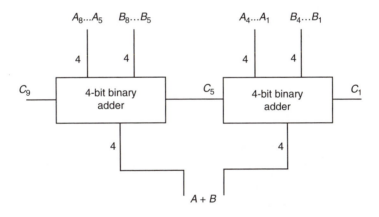

FIGURE 5.2.4
Constructing an 8-Bit Binary Adder from 4-Bit Adders

are done in programming languages. An n-bit magnitude comparator compares the magnitudes of two n-bit binary operands, A and B. The circuit in block diagram is shown in Figure 5.3.1. Each of the operands is n bits.

The circuit has three outputs, labeled $A < B$, $A = B$, and $A > B$. Only one of the outputs assumes a value of 1, depending on the relative magnitudes of the operands A and B. An output of 1 on the line with label $A < B$ indicates the magnitude of operand A is less than the magnitude of operand B. The outputs on the other lines are interpreted similarly.

Similar to the design of adders, the standard design procedure of constructing a truth table and forming the minimized function is not suitable in the design of magnitude comparators. Here, just as is the case for adders,

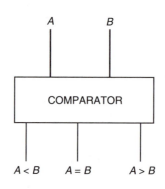

FIGURE 5.3.1
Block Diagram of a Magnitude Comparator

TABLE 5.3.1

Truth Table of a 1-Bit
Magnitude Comparator

AB	A < B	A = B	A > B
00	0	1	0
01	1	0	0
10	0	0	1
11	0	1	0

we could use an iterative approach in the design. First, we design a 1-bit magnitude comparator.

5.3.1 1-Bit Magnitude Comparator

A 1-bit magnitude comparator has a block diagram as shown in Figure 5.3.1, with each of the A and B operands of size 1 bit. The truth table of a 1-bit magnitude comparator is given in Table 5.3.1.

The design of the comparator is given in Figure 5.3.2. Note the equal output is designed using AND-OR-Invert so as to make use of the AND outputs.

The design of an n-bit magnitude comparator can be obtained from the design of a 1-bit magnitude comparator as discussed next.

5.3.2 Boolean Equations for the Equal Output

Let the two operands be

$$A = A_n A_{n-1} A_{n-2} \ldots A_1$$

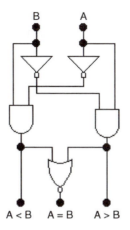

FIGURE 5.3.2
Design of a 1-Bit Magnitude Comparator

and

$$B = B_n B_{n-1} B_{n-2} \ldots B_1$$

Then, in order for A to be equal to B, each bit A_i in A must be equal to the corresponding bit B_i in B; i.e., for A to equal B we must have

$$\left(A_1 = B_1\right) \text{ and } \left(A_2 = B_2\right) \text{ and } \left(A_3 = B_3\right)\ldots \text{ and } \left(A_n = B_n\right)$$

When translated to Boolean equations, the Boolean equation for equality is

$$\left(\overline{A_1 \oplus B_1}\right)\left(\overline{A_2 \oplus B_2}\right)\left(\overline{A_3 \oplus B_3}\right)\ldots\left(\overline{A_n \oplus B_n}\right) = Y_1 Y_2 \ldots Y_n$$

In the above equation, we use

$$Y_i = \left(\overline{A_i \oplus B_i}\right)$$

The above equation is realized by (1) using a 1-bit magnitude comparator for each pair of bits in the operands A and B, and (2) by using the equal outputs of the comparators as inputs to a single AND gate. The output of the AND corresponds to the output for $A = B$.

5.3.3 Design of the $A > B$ Output

For the $A > B$ Boolean equation, we note that A is greater than B if the most-significant bit (MSB) of A, A_n, is greater than the MSB of B, B_n. This occurs if $A_n = 1$ and $B_n = 0$, which is represented as the Boolean product $A_n B_n'$. It could also occur if the two most-significant bits are equal and $A_n - 1 > B_{n-1}$. In Boolean equation form, the condition is written as

$$\left(\overline{A_n \oplus B_n} \right) A_{n-1} \overline{B}_{n-1} = Y_n A_{n-1} \overline{B}_{n-1}$$

The above analysis can be applied to the remaining bits to obtain the following Boolean function for the case of $A > B$:

$$A_n \overline{B}_n + Y_n A_{n-1} \overline{B}_{n-1} + Y_n Y_{n-1} A_{n-2} \overline{B}_{n-2} + \ldots + Y_n Y_{n-1} \ldots Y_2 A_1 \overline{B}_1$$

When applied to a 3-bit magnitude comparator, the above equation becomes

$$A_3 \overline{B}_3 + Y_3 A_2 \overline{B}_2 + Y_3 Y_2 A_1 \overline{B}_1$$

5.3.4   Boolean Equations for *A < B*

Similar analysis can be applied for the case of $B < A$ to obtain the Boolean equation

$$\overline{A}_n B_n + Y_n \overline{A}_{n-1} B_{n-1} + Y_n Y_{n-1} \overline{A}_{n-2} B_{n-2} + \ldots Y_n Y_{n-1} \ldots Y_2 \overline{A}_1 B_1$$

By inspecting the above Boolean equation, we note that the equations can be realized by processing the outputs of 1-bit magnitude comparators. We illustrate the design of a 3-bit magnitude comparator as shown in Figure 5.3.3. The design makes use of three 1-bit magnitude comparators. The outputs of the comparators are used as inputs to a two-level AND-OR gate to realize the needed equations.

5.3.5   Magnitude Comparators with Enable Lines

Magnitude comparators can be built with enable lines, which are inputs that cause a functional block to be in two modes: active (also called normal mode) or inactive. In the active mode, the comparator functions as intended. In the inactive mode, however, the comparator does not respond to inputs. This can be indicated by setting all output lines to zero. The enable line is a control line with input labeled E. For $E = 1$, the comparator functions in normal mode. For $E = 0$, all outputs are set to zero. Figure 5.3.4 shows a 1-bit magnitude comparator with a control enable input, E.

5.4   Binary Subtractors

In designing adders, we first considered the design of half adders. We then designed a 1-bit full adder and used the 1-bit full adder iteratively to design n-bit full adders. We use the same procedure in the design of n-bit subtractors.

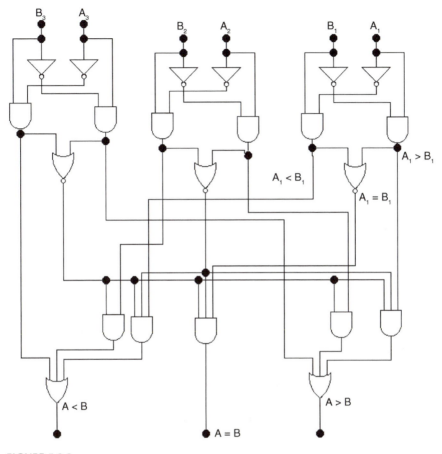

FIGURE 5.3.3
Design of a 3-Bit Magnitude Comparator from 1-Bit Magnitude Comparators

5.4.1 Half Subtractors

In forming $A - B$, both A and B are single bits. To compute the difference, we may need to borrow a 1 from a more-significant bit (example $0 - 1$). Half subtractors send the borrow request in the form of an output that will serve as an input to the next significant stage, as we will discuss later.

The truth table for the half subtractor is shown Table 5.4.1.

We discuss the second row of subtracting $0 - 1$. For this case, a borrow is needed from the next-significant stage. The subtractor informs the next-significant stage of the needed borrow (outputs a 1 on the borrow line) and then (assuming the borrow is satisfied) computes the difference. Since a borrow into A is made, the decimal value of the borrow is 2. As a result, the difference becomes $2 - 1 = 1$.

A 1-bit full subtractor is a circuit that has two outputs, as in the case of the half subtractor. We call these outputs B_n (borrow from next stage) and

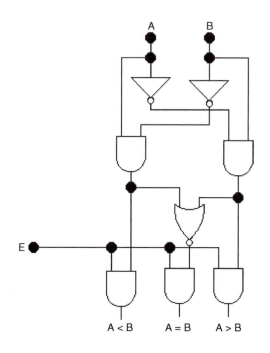

FIGURE 5.3.4
Design of a 1-Bit Magnitude Comparator with Enable Line

TABLE 5.4.1

Truth Table of a 1-Bit Half Subtractor

A	B	Borrow	Difference
0	0	0	0
0	1	1	1
1	0	0	1
1	1	0	0

D. For the inputs, in addition to the two bits to be subtracted, the subtractor has an input representing the borrow requests from the previous less-significant stage. We call the borrow B_p (borrow from previous stages). These three inputs are sufficient to compute the difference and to inform, through B_n, the next stage of a borrow if needed. The truth table of the 1-bit full subtractor is shown Figure 5.4.1. The figure includes discussion of forming the results of two rows of the truth table. The remaining row values can be completed using similar analysis.

The design of the half subtractor and 1-bit full subtractor follows similar procedures discussed for the case of 1-bit full adder, i.e., in order to design the 1-bit full subtractor, we use two half subtractors and a single OR gate. Figure 5.4.2 shows the design of a 1-bit full subtractor from two half subtractors. The Boolean equations for the borrow and difference outputs are computed in a fashion similar to those of a 1-bit full adder. The 1-bit full

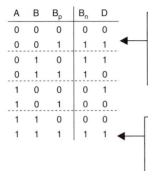

A	B	B_p	B_n	D
0	0	0	0	0
0	0	1	1	1
0	1	0	1	1
0	1	1	1	0
1	0	0	0	1
1	0	1	0	0
1	1	0	0	0
1	1	1	1	1

A borrow from the lower stage was requested $(B_p = 1)$. The borrow cannot be given by A since A = 0. As a result, this stage initiates a borrow request $(B_n = 1)$. Recall from Chapter 1 that this causes A to become equal to 1. Hence, computing the difference, we have $1 - 0 = 1$.

A borrow from the lower stage was requested $(B_p = 1)$. The borrow can be given by A since A = 1. Since the result now is to subtract $0 - 1$, this stage initiates a borrow request as well $(B_p = 1)$. The new result for A should be 2. The difference, then, is $2 - 1 = 1$ (D = 1).

FIGURE 5.4.1
Truth Table of a 1-Bit Full Subtractor

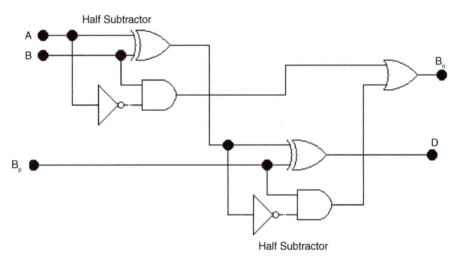

FIGURE 5.4.2
Design of a 1-Bit Full Subtractor from 1-Bit Half Subtractors

subtractor can then be used to construct 4-bit subtractors using the iterative approach used in the design of full adders. The subtractor can be used for signed operands. To subtract two numbers represented in signed magnitude, we use the following procedure:

1. The two numbers are compared using the magnitude comparator discussed in Section 5.3.

2. Depending on the relative magnitudes, we subtract the smaller magnitude from the larger one using the subtractor discussed in this section.

3. We append the proper sign to the result obtained in step 2.

These three steps are computationally expensive. A faster method of forming subtraction is by making use of radix complements, as we discuss in the next section.

5.5 Arithmetic Circuits Using Radix Complement

In the discussions that follow, we make use of two concepts we discussed earlier. The first is the case of overflow and underflow as side effects of finite storage. (Recall an overflow occurs if the result of arithmetic is too large to fit in the allocated storage and underflow indicates the result is too small.) The second concept has to do with coding and the interpretation of stored data. For example, if the same bit sequence, 1001, is interpreted as an unsigned number, its decimal value is 9. However, if the stored number is interpreted as a signed number in 2's complement, then its value is –7.

We first discuss subtraction of unsigned integers. The goal is to use addition to perform subtraction, i.e., the same unit (the adder) is used for both addition and subtraction. This leads to simpler designs.

5.5.1 Unsigned Addition and Subtraction

In unsigned addition and subtraction, both operands are stored as unsigned integers. As a result, an n-bit register is used to store integers in the range of 0 to $2^n - 1$. If the result of an arithmetic operation exceeds $2^n - 1$, we say an overflow occurred. Similarly, if the result is negative (smaller than 0), we say an underflow has occurred. Both conditions are possible when we apply addition and subtraction to unsigned numbers.

For addition, we realize the answer using the adder circuits discussed earlier. Here, an overflow occurs if the carry-out of the most-significant bit is equal to 1. For subtraction, we make use of radix complement (2's complement in the case of binary). The purpose is to simplify the hardware realization, as will be discussed later.

In forming $x - y$ (x is called the minuend and y is called the subtrahend), we

1. Add x to 2's complement of y, i.e., we form the arithmetic operation $x + (2^n - y)$.
2. If $x \geq y$, then the result in step 1 is $\geq 2^n$. By dropping the most-significant bit (value 2^n), the remaining bits form the correct result $(x - y)$.
3. If $x < y$, then the result is $< 2^n$. The actual result is negative, which cannot be represented as an unsigned number. As a result, an underflow occurs since the smallest possible number we could store is 0 unsigned.

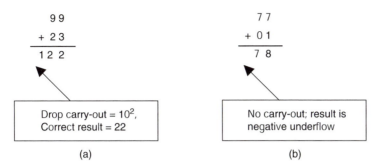

FIGURE 5.5.1
Example 5.5.1, Forming $(99)_{10} - (77)_{10}$ and $(77)_{10} - (99)_{10}$ Using 10's Complement

The above procedure applies to unsigned numbers in any base. We illustrate this process in two examples.

Example 5.5.1
Form $(99)_{10} - (77)_{10}$ and $(77)_{10} - (99)_{10}$ using the previous procedure. Assume both numbers are stored as unsigned integers.

Solution: Since we are considering unsigned number representation, each number is stored as a two-digit number. To subtract, we form the 10's complement of the subtrahend ($10^2 - 77 = 23$ in the first case and $10^2 - 99 = 01$ in the second case). We then add the result to the minuend to obtain the results shown in Figure 5.5.1(a) and (b), respectively.

As can be seen from the figure, when a carry-out of the most-significant digits occurs, the correct result is obtained when this carry is dropped from the result. The second case in the figure shows a carry-out of 0 out of the most-significant digits; this indicates a negative result, which causes an underflow.

Example 5.5.2
Compute $(11010)_2 - (01100)_2$ using 2's complement arithmetic. Assume the two operands are stored as unsigned operands.

Figure 5.5.2(a) shows the process of binary subtraction without applying the above procedure. The figure includes the subtraction done in decimal. Figure 5.5.2(b) shows the result when the above procedure is applied. In part (b) of the figure, we employ the addition operation to perform subtraction.

As can be seen from the figure, a carry-out of 1 from the most-significant bits does not indicate an overflow. The previous examples produced the correct result when the carry-out of the most-significant digits is not 0. The result obtained is not correct, however, if no carry-out of the most-significant bit is 0. This occurs only if $x < y$, leading to a negative result.

In summary, to perform $x - y$ of unsigned binary numbers using 2's complement:

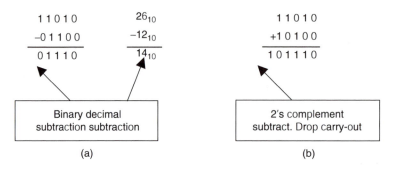

FIGURE 5.5.2
Example 5.5.2, Forming $(11010)_2 - (01100)_2$ Using 2's Complement Arithmetic

1. We add the 2's complement of y to x.
2. If the carry-out of the most-significant digit is equal to 1, the carry is ignored and the remaining bits constitute the correct result.
3. If the carry-out of the most-significant bit is 0, then this results in underflow since the result is negative, and hence is out of the allowable range.

5.5.2   Hardware Implementation of Unsigned Arithmetic

In the above procedure, we used the addition operation for both addition and subtraction operations, assuming the hardware of obtaining the 2's complement exists. In forming the 2's complement of the subtrahend, we form its 1's complement and add 1 to the result. Figure 5.5.3 shows the implementation of a circuit that is used for both addition and subtraction.

In Figure 5.5.3, the use of the XOR gate is as follows. The carry-in bit is used to select the circuit for either addition or subtraction. If the circuit is selected for addition, then the carry-in bit is set to 0. Setting this bit to 0 causes each XOR gate to output the B value as is. As a result, the circuit performs $A + B$. If the carry-in bit is 1, however, then the output of each XOR gate is the complement of its B input; as a result, the adder performs $A + B' + 1$. Using the above discussion, if a carry-out $= 1$ occurs, then the carry-out is ignored and the result in $S_3S_2S_1S_0$ is the correct subtraction result. An underflow occurs if the carry-out obtained is equal to 0.

Note that the choice of the arithmetic operation to perform is determined from a set of instructions that store the operation to be performed as well as the operands associated with the operation. We will discuss this later. We next extend the discussion to include signed operands. Our discussion deals specifically with 2's complement representations of negative numbers.

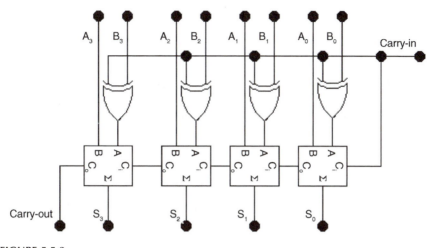

FIGURE 5.5.3
Circuit Design of 4-Bit Adder/Subtractor

5.5.3 Signed Number Arithmetic in Radix Complement

The previous discussion dealt with arithmetic on unsigned numbers and the use of radix complement to perform both addition and subtraction. In this section, we consider arithmetic on signed numbers presented in radix complement. Here, the interpretation of the operands differs. For example, in the previous section, the operand 11010 is interpreted as $(26)_{10}$. In 2's complement representation, this same operand represents the negative number $(-6)_{10}$. Before we discuss arithmetic on signed numbers, we present an alternative method of interpreting signed numbers in 2's complement.

5.5.3.1 An Alternative Method to Compute 2's Complement

Consider an n-bit signed binary number

$$x = a_{n-1}a_{n-2}\ldots a_0$$

represented in 2's complement form. Our objective is to find a polynomial representation that converts the number from its 2's complement representation to its decimal representation with the sign of the decimal number included. To do this, we note, if x is positive, then its decimal value is determined directly from the binary representation using the polynomial expanded form discussed in Chapter 1. If x is negative, however, we could find its decimal value by first finding its magnitude. From the magnitude we append a negative sign. For the magnitude of the number, we have

$$|x| = 2^n - x$$

$$= \left(2^n - a_{n-1}a_{n-2}\ldots a_0\right)$$

The above equation is obtained from the definition of 2's complement; the x term is written in binary. The $|x|$ term is the base 10 positive number. By appending a negative sign to the above equation and expanding the binary part into polynomial form, we obtain

$$-|x| = -\left(2^n - a_{n-1}a_{n-2}\ldots a_0\right)$$

$$= -2^n + 2^{n-1} + a_{n-2}2^{n-2} + \ldots + a_0 2^0$$

$$= -2^{n-1} + a_{n-2}2^{n-2} + \ldots + a_0 2^0$$

The above equation can be rewritten to account for the sign bit as follows:

Decimal value of x = $\begin{cases} = -2^{n-1}\underbrace{(0)}_{a_{(n-1)}} + a_{n-2}2^{n-2} + \ldots + a_0 2^0 & , x \geq 0 \\[2em] = -2^{n-1}\underbrace{(1)}_{a_{(n-1)}} + a_{n-2}2^{n-2} + \ldots + a_0 2^0 & , x \leq 0 \end{cases}$

The above equation holds true if it represents a positive number (upper equality) or negative number (lower equality). In all cases, the decimal value of x is found using the equation

$$\text{Decimal value of x} = \left(-a_{n-1}\right)2^{n-1} + a_{n-2}2^{n-2} + \ldots + a_0 2^0$$

Example 5.5.3
In this example we, use the above equation to compute the decimal values of the three signed numbers, 01110, 11011, and 1000, represented in 2's complement.
Solution: Using the above equations, we obtain

01110 in 2's complement = $(-0) \times (2^4) + (1 \times 2^3) + (1 \times 2^2) + (1 \times 2^1) + (0 \times 2^0)$

$$= (14)_{10}$$

11011 in 2's complement = $(-1) \times (2^4) + (1 \times 2^3) + (0 \times 2^2) + (1 \times 2^1) + (1 \times 2^0)$

$$= (-5)_{10}$$

10000 in 2's complement = $(-1) \times (2^4) + (0 \times 2^3) + (0 \times 2^2) + (0 \times 2^1) + (0 \times 2^0)$

$$= (-16)_{10}$$

5.5.3.2   Signed Arithmetic

Similar to unsigned arithmetic, signed arithmetic may lead to overflow or underflow, depending on the result of arithmetic. Here, however, the range includes positive as well as negative representation. For *n*-bit numbers, an overflow occurs if the result of the arithmetic is larger than the maximum positive number in the range $(2^{(n-1)} - 1)$. Similarly, an underflow occurs if the result is smaller than the smallest negative number $(-2^{(n-1)})$. We consider three cases. In the first case, no overflow or underflow is possible. In the second and third cases, it is possible that overflow and underflow occurs.

5.5.3.2.1   Case One (No Overflow or Underflow Is Possible)

When one performs arithmetic that results in the addition of a positive number to a negative number or vice versa, the sum can be represented as

$$result = -2^n + x + y$$

with both *x* and *y* being binary numbers with decimal value in the range $0 \le x \le 2^{(n-1)} - 1$ and $0 \le y \le 2^{(n-1)} - 1$. The above equation is deduced from the notation given in the preceding subsection, and the fact that each of the signed numbers is *n*-bits. Since one of the bits is used for the sign, the remaining *n* – 1 bits are used to represent each of the positive *x* and *y* values. To show no overflow or underflow occurs, we use the range of the *x* and *y* values to obtain

$$-2^{(n-1)} \le result \le -2^{(n-1)} + 2^{(n-1)} - 1 + 2^{(n-1)} - 1 = 2^{(n-1)} - 2$$

The result is always within the allowable range, between $-2^{(n-1)}$ and $2^{(n-1)} - 1$. Before we consider the next case, we make an observation about the sign bits. For the sign bits, since the operands are of opposite signs, their sum without the carry-in to the sign bit is 1. As a result, for all cases we have the carry-in to the sign bit is equal to the carry-out of the sign bits. This can be verified by considering both cases (a carry of 1 and a carry of 0 into the sign bits).

5.5.3.2.2   Case Two (Overflow Is Possible to Occur)

Here we consider signed arithmetic that yields the equivalence of adding positive operands. As a result, the arithmetic is equivalent to adding two $(n - 1)$-bit numbers *x* and *y* (the *n*th-most significant bit in both is equal to 0), with the sum *x* + *y* satisfying the condition

$$0 \le x + y \le \left(2^{(n-1)} - 1\right) + \left(2^{(n-1)} - 1\right) = 2^n - 2$$

As can be seen from the above equation, an overflow occurs if the sum exceeds the maximum allowable range $2^{(n-1)} - 1$. This occurs if the result causes a carry-in of 1 to the sign bits. Since both numbers are positive, the carry-out of the sign bit is 0. If the sum is less than $2^{(n-1)} - 1$, then the carry-in to the sign bits is equal to the carry-out of the sign bits. As a result, we note an overflow occurs if the two carries (into and out of the sign bits) are unequal. If the two carries are equal, then the sum is within the allowable range.

5.5.3.2.3   Case Three (Underflow Is Possible to Occur)

The final case considers the equivalent process of adding two negative operands, which is equivalent to adding the expression

$$-2^{(n-1)} + x - 2^{(n-1)} + y = -2^n + (x+y)$$

with the ranges of x and y as given earlier. In order for the sum to be within the acceptable range, we require

$$-2^{n-1} \leq -2^n + (x+y) \leq -1$$

The above inequality can be rewritten as

$$2^{n-1} \leq (x+y) \leq 2^n - 1$$

The lower bound on the sum indicates that a carry of 1 into the sign bit must take place in order to obtain a result within the specified range. If such a carry does take place, since the sign bit for each number is equal to 1, an equal carry of 1 out of the sign bit takes place as well. If the condition is not met, then underflow occurs. From the discussion, if the carry into the sign bit is equal to the carry-out of the sign bit, then the result is within the acceptable range. On the other hand, if the two carries are not equal, then an underflow has occurred.

Summary: From the three cases considered, we note the condition of detecting an underflow or overflow is the same. An overflow or underflow occurs (when performing signed addition or subtraction on operands represented in 2's complement) if and only if the carry-in to the sign bit is not equal to the carry-out of the sign bit. In performing subtraction using 2's complement, the 2's complement of the subtrahend is first formed. The test of overflow or underflow then depends on the nature of the operands (signed or unsigned), as discussed earlier.

We conclude this section with several examples. In all cases, we assume 5-bit binary number. As a result, the range of the negative numbers is –16 to –1. Similarly, the range of the positive numbers is 0 to 15. In the examples, we let C_i represent the carry-in to the sign bit. Similarly, we let C_o represent the carry-out of the sign bit. Figure 5.5.4 shows the arithmetic examples. The figure includes tests for overflow and underflow.

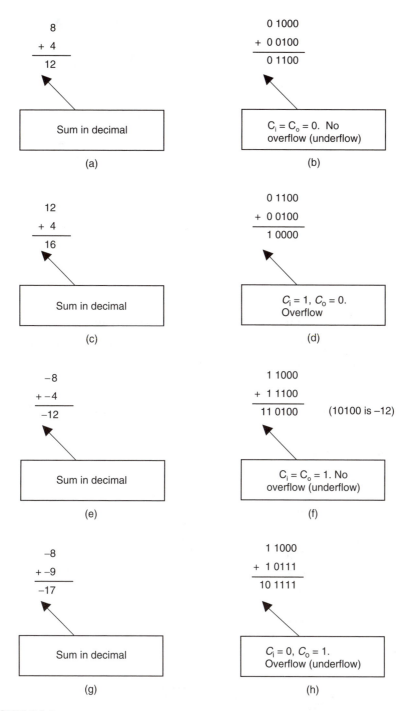

FIGURE 5.5.4
Arithmetic Using Signed 2's Complement Representation, Each Row Represents Decimal Arithmetic and Corresponding 2's Complement Arithmetic

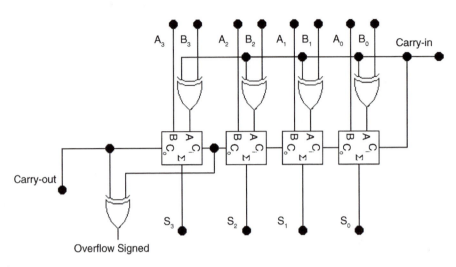

FIGURE 5.5.5
4-Bit Binary Adder/Subtractor of Signed Numbers in 2's Complement Representation

5.5.4 Hardware Implementation of Signed Arithmetic

The design of an arithmetic circuit that performs addition and subtraction of signed numbers represented in 2's complement is similar to the circuit shown in Figure 5.5.3. The circuit differs from Figure 5.5.3 in the added hardware to detect overflow and underflow. The circuit that detects unequal carries into and out of the sign bit is the XOR gate. Figure 5.5.5 shows the modified circuit.

5.6 Multiplier Circuits

Multiplication of binary numbers was considered in Chapter 1. In this section, we build circuits that realize binary multiplication. By referring to Chapter 1, we note that in forming $A \times B$, the bits of multiplicand A are multiplied by the bits of the multiplier B from least significant to most significant. The multiplicand is copied as is if the corresponding multiplier bit assumes a value of 1. It is replaced by a row of zeros if the corresponding multiplier bit assumes a value of 0. Our task is to convert the above process into a set of Boolean equations. From the Boolean equations, we could then implement the circuit.

Let $A = A_n A_{n-1} A_{n-2} \ldots A_1$ and $B = B_n B_{n-1} B_{n-2} \ldots B_1$. Then the result of multiplying A by bit B_1 of B can be written as the sequence of Boolean products

$$A_n B_1 \quad A_{n-1} B_1 \quad A_{n-2} B_1 \quad \ldots \quad A_1 B_1$$

with each $A_i B_j$ realized by an AND gate. For the case of 3-bit operands, $A \times B$ yields

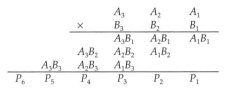

To form the product, we apply binary additions to the columns showing the partial products above (P_1 through P_6). The multiplication above can be accomplished using two binary adders as follows. First, we add the contents of row 1 to the contents of row 2. Second, the result is added to row 3 to obtain the correct product. Note that, when adding, one needs to account for the shifts used to form each row.

The design of a multiplier circuit that computes P_1 through P_6, is shown in the Figure 5.6.1.

The A_iB_j terms shown in the three rows are generated using rows of AND gates. The outputs of the AND gates are used as inputs to the first 3-bit full adder. Note the 0 used in the sum of the first 3-bit adder (MSB). Note as well, the first bit of the sum forms P_2 of the product P ($P = P_6P_5P_4P_3P_2P_1$). Finally, note that the carry-out of each adder is used in the next stage of the addition. A sample circuit design is shown in Figure 5.6.2.

The above procedure can be generalized to multiply two binary numbers of arbitrary sizes. To multiply two n-bit numbers, A and B, one would need $(n - 1)$ n-bit adders. The first adder is used for rows 1 and 2 (after proper shifting). The next adder adds row 3 to the outputs of the first adder (shifted

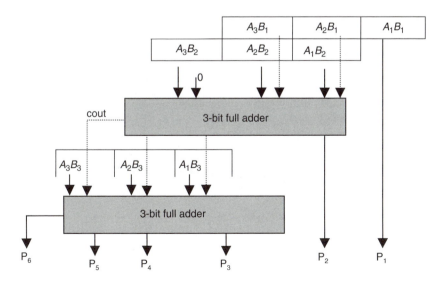

FIGURE 5.6.1
Multiplier Circuit, $(A = A_3A_2A_1) \times (B = B_3B_2B_1) = P_6\,P_5\,P_4\,P_3\,P_2\,P_1$

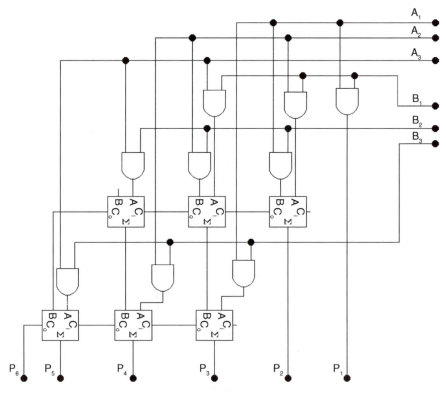

FIGURE 5.6.2
Multiplier Circuit Gate Design, $(A = A_3A_2A_1) \times (B = B_3B_2B_1) = P_6 \, P_5 \, P_4 \, P_3 \, P_2 \, P_1$

to the left). This process continues on the remaining rows. The last adder produces the remaining bits of the final product $(P_{2n}, ..., P_{(n-1)})$.

In the remainder of the chapter, we use the above circuits and concepts to study the logic design of an arithmetic logic unit. To design the unit, we make use of multiplexers circuits. The circuits are introduced in the next section and studied in more details in the next chapter.

5.7 Multiplexers

Consider the circuit shown in Figure 5.7.1. The circuit has a total of six inputs, $I_0, I_1, I_2, I_3, S_1,$ and S_0. The six inputs are split into two groups according to the input labels, as seen in the figure. The circuit has a single output F with the algebraic equation

$$F = S'_1 S'_0 I_0 + S_1 S'_0 I_1 + S'_1 S_0 I_0 + S_1 S_0 I_0$$

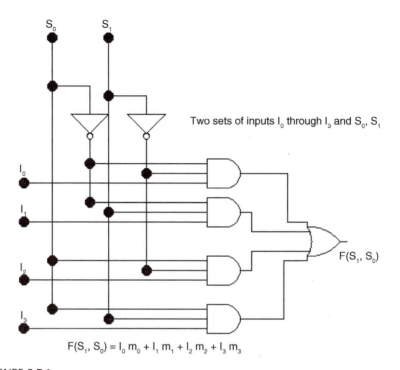

$$F(S_1, S_0) = I_0 m_0 + I_1 m_1 + I_2 m_2 + I_3 m_3$$

FIGURE 5.7.1
4-to-1 Multiplexer

TABLE 5.7.1

Abbreviated Truth Table
of 4-to-Multiplexer

S_1	S_0	Value of Function F
0	0	I_0
0	1	I_1
1	0	I_2
1	1	I_3

By assigning binary values to the inputs S_1 and S_0, we obtain the outputs shown in Table 5.7.1.

The truth table above is an abbreviated truth table as the data inputs are not shown as part of the table and the output is written as a function of the data inputs, instead of 0s and 1s. The data inputs can be included in the table. This, however, will increase the size of the table from 4 to 64 rows (2^6). The functionality of the circuit is better captured using the abbreviated table above.

The circuit is an example of a four-way switch. The switch connects one of the inputs to the single output *F*. The switch is controlled by the *S* inputs,

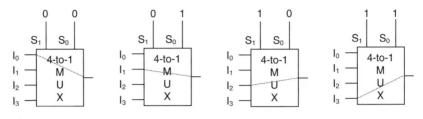

FIGURE 5.7.2
Switch Multiplexer Representation as a Function of the Select Inputs

called select or control inputs. By applying the proper binary assignment on
the select inputs, we can connect one of the four I inputs, called data inputs,
to the output F. The four possible switch locations as a function of the select
inputs are shown in Figure 5.7.2. The multiplexer given in the figure is called
a 4-to-1 multiplexer, sometimes abbreviated as 4-to-1 mux.

Since the function of the select lines is to determine which of the data lines
is connected to the output of the multiplexer, for m data lines one needs at
least $n = \lceil \log_2 m \rceil$ select lines, where $\lceil x \rceil$ is an integer value of the result rounded
up; the value is called the ceiling of x. In general, the number of select lines,
n, is related to the number of data lines, m, by the equation $m = 2^n$. Hence,
the multiplexers 2-to-1, 4-to-1, 8-to-1, and 16-to-1 have one, two, three, and
four select lines, respectively.

5.7.1   Design of Multiple Output Multiplexers

Multiplexers are used to connect several data sources to a common line of
communication (output). In such a case, the multiplexer acts as a large switch
that causes one source to place its contents on the common line. Each of the
sources, however, could be several bits (lines). Figure 5.7.3 is an example.

In Figure 5.7.3, each of the data inputs is 2 bits; the output is 2 bits as well.
The number of data sets in the figure is four (set 1 is I_{00} and I_{01}; similarly,
the other sets are I_{10} and I_{11}; I_{20} and I_{21}; and I_{30} and I_{31}). Since the number of
data sources is four, we need two select inputs to choose which of the data
sets is connected to the outputs.

The multiplexer in the figure is called a dual 4-to-1 multiplexer (four is
the number of data sets to be connected to the output). The term "dual"
means the circuit is composed of two 4-to-1 multiplexers, as can be observed
from the figure. In block diagram fashion, the dual 4-to-1 mux is shown in
Figure 5.7.4.

We use the block diagram shown in Figure 5.7.5 to represent an abbreviated
m n-to-1 multiplexer. The diagram represents m multiplexers; each multiplexer is n-to-1. The dash can be removed from the figure.

We will discuss multiplexers in more detail in the next chapter. In the next
section, we use multiplexers in the design of a small arithmetic logic unit.

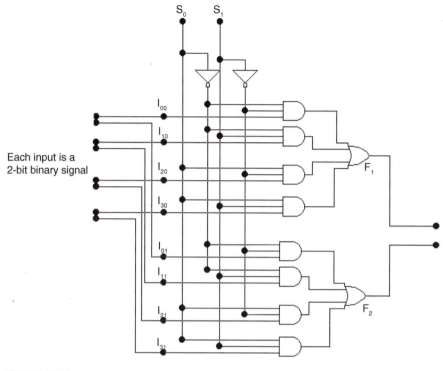

FIGURE 5.7.3
Dual 4-to-1 multiplexer design

5.8 Design of a Simple Arithmetic Logic Unit

The arithmetic logic unit (ALU) is found in the central processing unit of a computer. As the name implies, the unit performs both arithmetic and logic operations. We illustrate the design of a simple ALU using the design concepts discussed thus far. In our example, we assume:

1. The operands processed by the unit are 4 bits each.
2. The arithmetic operations performed are addition and subtraction.
3. The logic operations performed are the bit-wise AND, OR, and NOT. (We will give examples of bit-wise logic operations later).
4. In addition to the operations in 2 and 3, the unit could pass one of the operands to the output either as is, or shifted to the left by 1 bit.

The block diagram of the ALU is shown Figure 5.8.1. In the figure, the operands are two 4-bit numbers, A and B. The output is given at C; note that

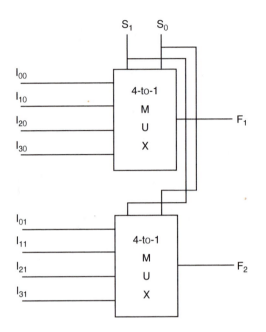

FIGURE 5.7.4
Design of dual 4-to-1 multiplexer from 4-to-1 multiplexers

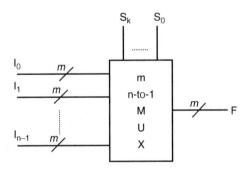

FIGURE 5.7.5
Block diagram representation of an *m* n-to-1 multiplexer

C is 5 bits. The *m* lines, labeled *S*, are used to choose the proper operation to be performed by the ALU. The shape of the ALU is a traditional shape used by convention. We next discuss the units used in the design.

5.8.1 Subtraction and the Arithmetic Unit

The arithmetic unit is composed of two parts — an addition part and a subtraction part. Both were discussed earlier in the chapter.

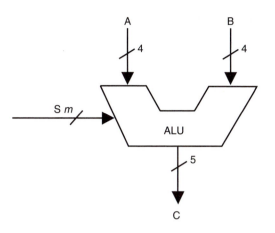

FIGURE 5.8.1
A block diagram of a 4-bit ALU

TABLE 5.8.1

Bit-Wise Logic Operations, (a) Bit-Wise AND,
(b) Bit-Wise OR

	(a) Bit-Wise AND					(b) Bit-Wise OR			
A =	1	1	0	1	A =	1	1	0	1
B =	1	1	0	0	B =	1	1	0	0
	1	1	0	0		1	1	0	1

5.8.2 Bit-Wise Logic Operations

Bit-wise logic operations are performed on operands with multiple bits. For our case, each of the operands is 4-bit wide. The example below illustrates the use each of the bit-wise logic operations.

Example 5.8.1
Form the bit-wise AND and OR operations on the operands $A = 1101$ and $B = 1100$; also form the bit-wise complement of the operand A.

Solution: In forming the bit-wise logic operations for the AND and the OR, we apply the logic operations on the individual bits of the operand A and the corresponding bits in the operand B. The results are shown in Table 5.8.1(a) and (b), respectively. For the complement operation, we complement the individual bits of A to obtain 0010. The design of the bit-wise operations can be accomplished using an array of AND, OR, or NOT gates.

5.8.3 Combinational Shift Left

The shift left operation can be used as a method of multiplying an unsigned binary number by 2. In shifting an operand left, the most-significant bit is shifted into an extra bit. The bit is used in computations that require additional bits such as the carry-out that may be produced from adding two 4-bit operands. The least-significant bit is set to 0. For example, when the binary operand 0101 (5_{10}) is shifted left, the new shifted value is 01010 (10_{10}). The shift left we design is combinational in nature. This is different than shift operations that are done by sequential circuits. We will discuss sequential circuits in later chapters.

Assuming the ALU outputs are $C_4C_3C_2C_1C_0$ with $A = A_3A_2A_1A_0$, the shift left operation results in

$$C_4 = A_3, C_3 = A_2, C_2 = A_1, C_1 = A_0, C_0 = 0$$

5.8.4 The Design of the ALU

By inspecting the ALU block diagram, we notice the multiple functions performed by the ALU appear at the set of common output lines. The ALU functions as follows. Depending on the specific request applied to the select lines of the ALU, the ALU responds by accomplishing the specific request and placing the result at its outputs. One method to accomplish the request is to have the multiple functional units compute the associated tasks and place the corresponding results on the data inputs of a multiplexer. The multiplexer in turn routes the correct result to its outputs, and hence the outputs of the ALU.

The multiplexer requires five outputs needed to place the results of the arithmetic and shift operations on the outputs of the ALU unit. For the data sets, the multiplexer inputs are the arithmetic results (two data sets for the addition and subtraction). Additional data sets needed are three sets for the logic operations, one to output operand A as is, and one additional input for the shift left operation. The number of the data inputs needed is seven. As a result, the multiplexer would require a minimum of three select lines ($\lceil \log_2 7 \rceil = 3$).

From the discussion, we conclude that five 8-to-1 multiplexers are needed in the design. The multiplexer requires three select lines, S_0, S_1, and S_2, used to route the proper result to the outputs of the ALU. The select lines assignment and corresponding associated functions are shown in Table 5.8.2. The choice of the assignments is arbitrary.

Note that the plus (+) symbol is used to represent regular binary addition as well as the bit-wise OR operation. The assignment $S_2S_1S_0 = 011$ is used to perform the logic OR and the assignment $S_2S_1S_0 = 101$ is used to perform the add operation. The block diagram of the ALU is shown in the Figure 5.8.2.

TABLE 5.8.2

ALU Function Table, Select Inputs
Determine the ALU Function

$S_2S_1S_0$	Function	$S_2S_1S_0$	Function
000	Shift left A	100	A'
001	A	101	$A + B$
010	A AND B	110	$A - B$
011	$A + B$	111	—

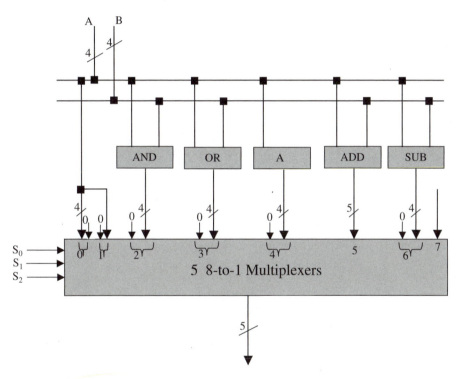

FIGURE 5.8.2
Block diagram design of the ALU

With the exception of the sum data input, note the application of zero as one of the inputs. Note as well, data set 7 is unused. We illustrate the function of the above circuit for the first case in Table 5.8.2. For this case, the bits of the A operand are shifted to the left by 1 bit by applying the input 000 on the select lines of the five multiplexers. Each multiplexer will route data line 0 to its output. As can be seen from the figure, the first bit of the output is set to 0 (the right-most multiplexer first data input is 0). The remaining multiplexers output the value of A. As a result, the effect of the circuit is to shift the contents of A to the left by 1 bit.

Chapter 5 Exercises

5.1 A 3-bit ripple adder can be drawn as shown in Figure E5.1. Assume the gate delays in the circuit are 2 ns, 2 ns, and 3 ns for the AND, OR and XOR gates, respectively. Compute the delay of C_2 and C_3 of the circuit.

$$X_3 \; Y_3 \;\; X_2 \; Y_2 \;\; X_1 \; Y_1 \; C_1$$

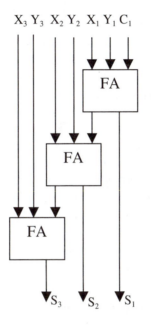

FIGURE E5.1

5.2 Generalize your results in question 1 for an arbitrary carry-out C_n. Write your answer in terms of n.

5.3 Compute C_6 of the carry lookahead generator equations.

5.4 Using the delays of gates as given in question 5.1 and a generalized design based on the lookahead carry generators equations, find the delay for each of the carry equations C_2, C_3, C_4, C_5, and C_6. Assume no additional delay is incurred by increasing the number of inputs to a gate. Generalize your answer to an arbitrary C_n.

5.5 Show the design of 2-bit adder with carry lookahead generator.

5.6 Assume A and B are two 5-bit unsigned operands. Compute the Boolean equations for $A > B$, $A < B$, and $A = B$.

5.7 Show the design of a 2-bit magnitude comparator.

5.8 An n-bit magnitude comparator can be designed from 1-bit magnitude comparators with enable lines. Show the design of a 5-bit magnitude comparator from 1-bit magnitude comparators with enable lines. Hint — the design can be accomplished with five 1-bit comparators and 2 additional gates.

5.9 Compute the maximum delays in the outputs of the 2-bit magnitude comparator given in question 5.7. Assume the delays through the gates are as given in question 5.1 and are not affected by the number of inputs to the gate. Assume as well the delay in the inverter or the NOR gate is 1 ns. Generalize your answer for an n-bit magnitude comparator.

5.10 For the same magnitude comparator sizes, is the delay in your design in question 5.8 larger than the maximum delay obtained in question 5.0? Please explain.

5.11 Design a 2-bit binary subtractor from 1-bit full subtractors. The subtractor inputs are $A = A_2A_1$, $B = B_2B_1$ and previous borrow Bp. Its outputs are $D = D_2D_1$ and Bn. The subtractor performs $A - B$.

5.12 Assign binary values to all lines in the design of the subtractor in question 5.11 based on the inputs $A = 10$ and $B = 01$ with $Bp = 0$ and $Bp = 1$. Verify the output is correct by constructing truth table entry for the input combinations given.

5.13 Repeat question 5.12 on $A = 10$ and $B = 11$.

5.14 Compute $1001011 - 0110101$ using 2's complement. Assume the operands are stored as unsigned binary numbers. State if an overflow or underflow has occurred.

5.15 Repeat problem 5.14 on $0101101 - 1000111$.

5.16 Using the polynomial representation of signed numbers represented in 2's complement (section 5.5.3) find the values of

(a) 00110111,

(b) 10010101,

(c) 10000000,

(d) 11111111, and

(e) 10000001

5.17 Assume one is to store the two 2's complement signed number $A = 0011$ and $B = 1011$ as 8-bit numbers. Determine how each should be represented as an 8-bit signed number in 2's complement. Generalize your answer to include arbitrary binary numbers.

5.18 Determine the maximum positive and minimum negative range of the following.

(a) An 8-bit binary number represented in signed 2's complement.

(b) A 5-digit decimal number represented in 10's complement.

(c) A 5-digit octal number represented in 7's complement.

5.19 Form the following arithmetic expressions based on signed number representation in radix complement as indicated with each expression.

(a) 10001010 − 10010100 (2's complement)

(b) 10001010 + 10010100 (2's complement)

(c) 90010 − 00501   (10's complement)

(d) 91501 + 02345   (10' complement)

5.20 Determine which of the previous arithmetic expressions resulted in overflow or underflow.

5.21 Assume one is to design a multiplier for $A \times B$ with A a 16-bit binary number and B an 8-bit binary number. Determine the number of adders used in the design and the size of each adder. In addition to the adders used in the design, what is the total number of AND gates? What is the total number of AND gates if A is an n-bit number and B is an m-bit number?

5.22 Show the design of a multiplier that performs $A \times B$ with $A = A_3A_2A_1A_0$ and $B = B_2B_1B_0$.

5.23 Form the bitwise AND, OR and NOT of the following:

(a) $A = 1111000$ and $B = 10101100$,

(b) $A = 0000000$ and $B = 10101111$,

(c) $A = (AF)_{16}$ and $B = (91)_{16}$

5.24 Show the complete design of a 2-bit ALU with function as described in Figure E5.2. $ALU.S_1$ and $ALU.S_2$ are used to select the proper operation to perform.

ALU.S$_1$	ALU.S$_0$	Function
0	0	Operand A is placed at the output of the ALU
0	1	Output = A + B (perform ADD)
1	0	Output bitwise AND of A and B
1	1	Output complement of A

FIGURE E5.2

6

Programmable Logic Devices

CONTENTS

6.1   Decoders

In Chapter 1, we discussed coding as a mapping between two sets of objects. In general, decoders are combinational circuits that are used as code converters. For example, the BCD-to-seven-segment decoder discussed in Section 4.4

is an example of such a decoder. In the circuit, a BCD code is presented at the input (the input is 4 bits). The output of the decoder is chosen to display the equivalent decimal value on a seven-segment display. As a result, the decoder acts as a code converter. It converts a BCD code into a decimal code.

6.1.1 Binary Decoders

There are several types of decoders. Of these, binary decoders are the most common type. An n-bit binary decoder has n inputs and a maximum of 2^n outputs. We consider two types of binary decoders. With each, for n inputs the decoder has 2^n outputs. The decoders are called n-to-2^n binary decoders. In an n-to-2^n binary decoder, the n inputs represent a binary code. For each binary input, exactly one of the 2^n outputs is activated (selected). From our previous discussions of minterms and maxterms, one method to select exactly one of the 2^n outputs (for each input combination) is to have the outputs realize the minterms associated with inputs. Here, each input causes exactly one output to assume a value of 1. All others assume a value of 0. For a given input, the output selected is the line that assumes a value of 1. Figure 6.1.1(a) and (b) show block diagrams of a 2-to-4 and a 3-to-8 decoder.

Note the minterm outputs of the decoders; due to these outputs an input on the decoder causes one output to assume a value of 1. All other outputs assume a value of 0. The gate design of the decoders is shown in Figure 6.1.2.

The truth table representation of a 3-to-8 binary decoder is given in Table 6.1.1.

In general, for an n-to-2^n decoder, the decoder design contains 2^n AND gates. The outputs of the AND gates are the minterms associated with the inputs. Another way to abbreviate decoders is to use the notation $n \times 2^n$ pronounced as n by 2^n.

An alternative method to selection can be accomplished by associating the outputs with maxterms instead of minterms. Since for each input combination

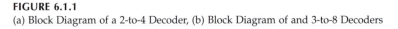

(a)   (b)

FIGURE 6.1.1
(a) Block Diagram of a 2-to-4 Decoder, (b) Block Diagram of and 3-to-8 Decoders

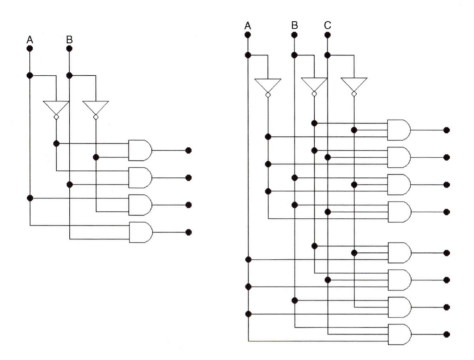

FIGURE 6.1.2
(a) Gate Design of a 2-to-4 Decoder, (b) Gate Design of a 3-to-8 Decoders

TABLE 6.1.1

Truth Table Representation of a 3-to-8 Binary Decoder with Minterms as Outputs

Inputs			Outputs							
A	B	C	D_0	D_1	D_2	D_3	D_4	D_5	D_6	D_7
0	0	0	1	0	0	0	0	0	0	0
0	0	1	0	1	0	0	0	0	0	0
0	1	0	0	0	1	0	0	0	0	0
0	1	1	0	0	0	1	0	0	0	0
1	0	0	0	0	0	0	1	0	0	0
1	0	1	0	0	0	0	0	1	0	0
1	1	0	0	0	0	0	0	0	1	0
1	1	1	0	0	0	0	0	0	0	1

exactly one output assumes a value of 0, the selected output is the one that assumes a value of 0. Figure 6.1.3 shows a block diagram of a 2-to-4 and a 3-to-8 decoder, with maxterms as the outputs. The gate design of a 3-to-8 decoder with maxterms as outputs is shown in Figure 6.1.4. The truth table representation is shown in Table 6.1.2.

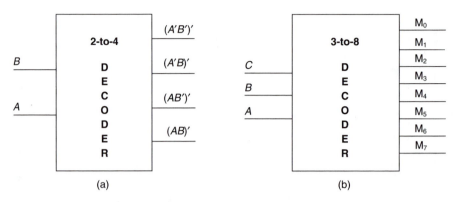

FIGURE 6.1.3
Block Diagrams of 2-to-4 and 3-to-8 Decoders with Maxterms as Outputs

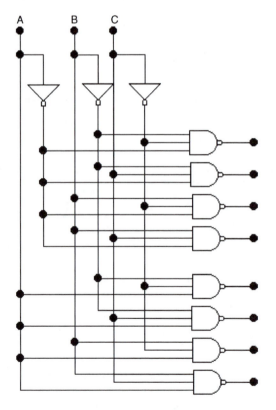

FIGURE 6.1.4
Gate Design of a 3-to-8 Decoder with Maxterms as Outputs

TABLE 6.1.2

Truth Table Representation of a 3-to-8 Binary Decoder
with Maxterms as Outputs

Inputs			Outputs							
A	B	C	D_0	D_1	D_2	D_3	D_4	D_5	D_6	D_7
0	0	0	0	1	1	1	1	1	1	1
0	0	1	1	0	1	1	1	1	1	1
0	1	0	1	1	0	1	1	1	1	1
0	1	1	1	1	1	0	1	1	1	1
1	0	0	1	1	1	1	0	1	1	1
1	0	1	1	1	1	1	1	0	1	1
1	1	0	1	1	1	1	1	1	0	1
1	1	1	1	1	1	1	1	1	1	0

6.1.2 Function Design Using Decoders

In Chapter 3, we presented a procedure to design functions from canonical sum representations. The design procedure uses two-level AND-OR gates, with the AND gates in the first level forming all the needed minterms. The minterms generated correspond to the inputs where the function assumes a value of 1. Since one type of the binary decoders considered outputs all possible minterms associated with a set of inputs, the AND gates in the decoder can serve as the first level in the two-level AND-OR design process. As a result, one can design combinational circuits by using a decoder of the proper size and an OR gate.

The design procedure is similar to the design of functions in canonical sum representation. The decoder supplies all the possible minterms. The needed minterms in the design are selected and used as inputs to an OR gate.

Example 6.1.1
Design the majority function using a decoder and a single OR gate.

Solution: Since the majority function has three inputs (A, B, and C), the decoder chosen must have three inputs as well. The majority function assumes a value of 1 for the inputs with decimal values 3, 5, 6, and 7. As a result, the inputs to the OR gate are the minterms m_3, m_5, m_6, and m_7. The minterms are found as the outputs D_3, D_5, D_6, and D_7 of the decoder. Figure 6.1.5 shows the design of the majority function.

By observing the circuit design in the previous example, one notices that the total number of gates used in the design exceeds what is needed. (The total number of gates is nine; the design of the simplified function requires the use of four gates and the design of the nonsimplified function requires the use of five gates.) The advantages of using decoders in the design process are attributed to two factors. First, the process can be automated, as discussed later in the text when we discuss programmable logic devices. Second, the

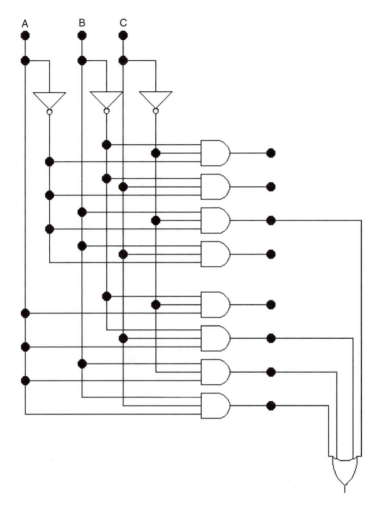

FIGURE 6.1.5
Design of the Majority Function Using 3-to-8 Binary Decoder

design may be more efficient when one considers the design of multiple-output functions over the same set of variables.

In multiple-output circuits over the same set of variables, the same decoder can be used as the minterm generator circuit for all functions considered. With each output we associate an OR gate. The gate is used to OR (sum the needed minterms). We illustrate this in the design of the circuit that evaluates $f(x) = x^2 + 1$, as discussed next.

Example 6.1.2
Use a single decoder and the needed OR gates to design the circuit that computes the function $f(x) = x^2 + 1$. Assume both x and $f(x)$ are represented in binary with the decimal value of x ranging from 0 to 3 inclusive.

TABLE 6.1.3

Truth Table of $f(x) = x^2 + 1$
Given in Example 6.1.2

A	B	F_4	F_3	F_2	F_1
0	0	0	0	0	1
0	1	0	0	1	0
1	0	0	1	0	1
1	1	1	0	1	0

The first step in the design is to generate the truth table of the function. The number of inputs in the table is determined from the argument x of the function. Since x assumes the decimal value 0, 1, 2, and 3, the input is 2 bits, which we will call A and B. Similarly, the number of outputs in the table depends on the maximum decimal value of the function $f(x)$. This occurs for the input $x = 3$ with $f(x) = 10$. When this maximum value is converted to binary, the number of bits needed is four. As a result, the number of outputs is four as well. We will call these outputs F_4, F_3, F_2, and F_1. The truth table is shown in Table 6.1.3. The design of the above function uses a single 2-to-4 decoder with 2 OR gates. The circuit has four outputs as shown in Figure 6.1.6.

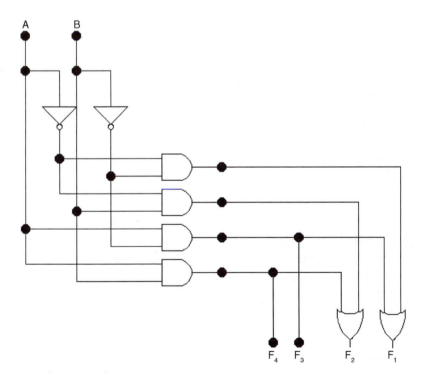

FIGURE 6.1.6
Design of $f(x) = x^2 + 1$. Using a 2-to-4 Decoder with Minterms as Outputs

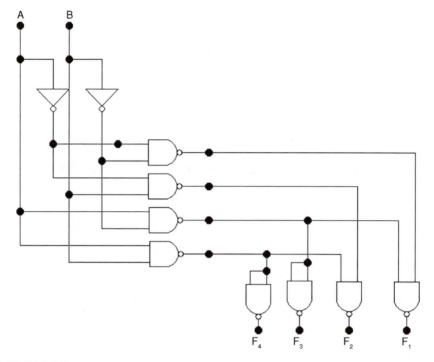

FIGURE 6.1.7
Design of $f(x) = x^2 + 1$. Using a 2-to-4 Decoder with Maxterms as Outputs

The design of functions using decoders with maxterms as outputs can be accomplished using a similar procedure as above. Here, however, one uses NAND gates instead of OR gates. The procedure is similar to the design using two-level NAND-NAND, as outlined in Chapter 3. Figure 6.1.7 shows the design of the function using a 2-to-4 binary decoder with maxterms as outputs. (Note the need of the NAND gates to act as inverters so as to generate the minterms).

6.1.3 Building Larger Decoders from Smaller Ones

It is possible to build larger decoders from smaller decoders. To accomplish this, we use decoders with enable lines. Enable lines are inputs that cause a functional block such as a decoder to be in one of two modes: active or inactive (this was discussed in Chapter 5.) In the active mode, the decoder functions as intended. In the inactive mode, however, the decoder does not respond to inputs. For the case of decoders with minterms as outputs with a single enable line input, E, we assume that for $E = 1$ the decoder is in the active mode. For $E = 0$, however, the decoder is in the inactive mode with all outputs assuming a value of 0 independent of the value on the inputs. Figures 6.1.8(a) and (b) show, respectively, the design of a 1-to-2 and a 2-to-4

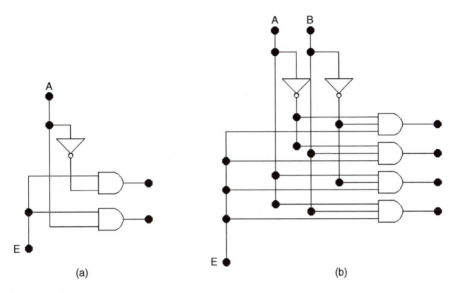

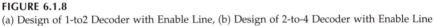

FIGURE 6.1.8
(a) Design of 1-to2 Decoder with Enable Line, (b) Design of 2-to-4 Decoder with Enable Line

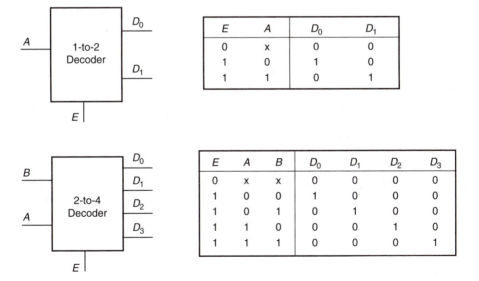

E	A	D_0	D_1
0	x	0	0
1	0	1	0
1	1	0	1

E	A	B	D_0	D_1	D_2	D_3
0	x	x	0	0	0	0
1	0	0	1	0	0	0
1	0	1	0	1	0	0
1	1	0	0	0	1	0
1	1	1	0	0	0	1

FIGURE 6.1.9
Truth Tables and Block Diagram Symbols of 1-to-2 and 2-to-4 Decoders with Enable Lines

decoder with enable line. The truth tables and block diagram symbols are shown in Figure 6.1.9.

To construct larger decoders from smaller ones, we make use of the enable line inputs. For example, using two 2-to-4 decoders and one 1-to-2 decoder

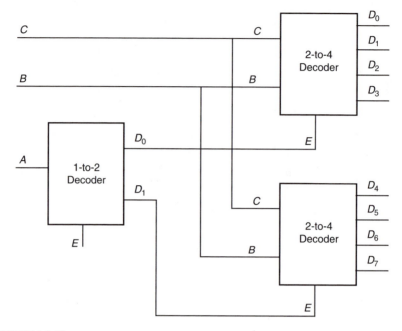

FIGURE 6.1.10
Design of a 3-to-8 Decoder from 1-to-2 and 2-to-4 Decoders with Enable Lines

with enable lines, we could construct a 3-to-8 decoder, as shown in Figure
6.1.10. Note the use of the most-significant input, A, as an input into the 1-to-
2 decoder. The input value, A, determines which of the two decoders is
enabled. For $A = 0$, the upper decoder is enabled. For $A = 1$, however, the
lower decoder is enabled. This can be related to the value of A in a three-
input truth table. For the upper half of the table, A assumes a value of 0. For
the lower half, A assumes a value of 1.

Within each part of the table (upper half or lower half), the values on the
variables B and C determine the relative minterm location within the half.
As a result, the two 2-to-4 decoders receive the same inputs B and C. Finally,
the enable line to the equivalent 3-to-8 circuit is the enable line for the 1-to-2
decoder.

6.2   Encoders

Encoder and decoder circuits are code converter circuits. Encoders assign a
code to objects (inputs). In decoders, the set of inputs is usually much smaller
than the set of outputs. In encoders, the opposite is true. Consider the process
of interactively entering information into the computer through the keyboard. Since information stored is in binary, an encoding process converts

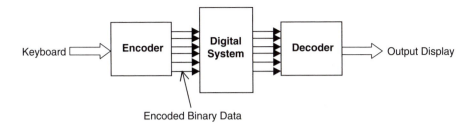

FIGURE 6.2.1
Encoding and Decoding of Data in Block Diagram

TABLE 6.2.1

Abbreviated Truth Table of a 4-to-2 Encoder

I_3	I_2	I_1	I_0	Y_1	Y_0
0	0	0	1	0	0
0	0	1	0	0	1
0	1	0	0	1	0
1	0	0	0	1	1

each key on the keyboard to a unique binary representation. This can be modeled as shown in Figure 6.2.1.

6.2.1 Binary Encoders

In the previous section on decoders, we considered n-to-m binary decoders. For these decoders, the input is a binary number with n bits. The output activated is D_i, where i is the decimal value of the binary input. A binary encoder works in an opposite fashion; for a given input representing a decimal value, the corresponding binary combination is produced at the output. In binary encoders, we assume that only one input is activated at a specific instant of time. This is similar to pressing a single key on a keyboard. The key pressed constitutes the input.

Similar to binary decoders, the number of inputs is related to the number of outputs. For n outputs, the number of inputs, m, does not exceed 2^n (the encoder is called m-to-n binary encoder). Table 6.2.1 shows an abbreviated truth table of a 4-to-2 encoder. The table contains four rows since it is assumed that exactly one input assumes a value of 1. The corresponding binary code associated with the input is displayed at the outputs.

The design of a 4-to-2 binary encoder is given in Figure 6.2.2(a). Due to the above assumption, the design is a set of OR gates since we have

$$Y_1 = I_3 + I_2$$

and

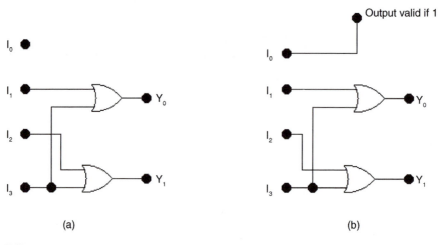

FIGURE 6.2.2
Designs of 4-to-2 Binary Encoder

$$Y_0 = I_3 + I_1$$

In Figure 6.2.2(a), the output of the encoder is the same if no input is activated (all inputs are 0) or if the input activated is the I_0 input ($I_0 = 1$). This causes ambiguity. To remove the ambiguity, an additional output that indicates a valid encoder output can be added. The output assumes a value of 1 when I_0 is equal to 1. The modified circuit is shown in Figure 6.2.2(b).

6.2.2   Priority Encoders

Priority encoders are used when more than one input may be activated at the same time. An analogy can be made when multiple requests are made to print documents on a common printer. In priority encoders, the input with highest priority gets processed first. Table 6.2.2 shows the function of a 4-to-2 priority encoder with the priority assigned according to the subscript of the input. Inputs with higher subscripts have higher priorities.

TABLE 6.2.2

Abbreviated Function of a 4-to-2 Priority
Encoder with the Priority Assigned
According to the Subscript of the Input

I_3	I_2	I_1	I_0	Y_1	Y_0
0	0	0	0	0	0
0	0	0	1	0	0
0	0	1	–	0	1
0	1	–	–	1	0
1	–	–	–	1	1

The above table is an abbreviated version of the 16 rows in the equivalent truth table. The "-" in the table are treated in a similar fashion as the tabular method. For example, the entry "01--" represents a subcube of 1 cells, where the variables I_3 and I_2 assume the values of 0 and 1, respectively. The algebraic expression for this subcube is $I_3'I_2$. We illustrate how the above table is obtained by first referring to the last row. For this row, an assignment of 1 to I_3 results in $Y_1Y_0 = 11$, independent of the binary assignments for the remaining input variables. For row 4 of the table, an output of 10 occurs only if the I_3 input assumes a value of 0, and the I_2 input assumes a value of 1. Similar analysis is applied to the rows 3 and 2.

The minimized algebraic equation for the two outputs Y_1 and Y_0 can be obtained by constructing the K-map for each function and following the minimization procedure discussed in Chapter 3. In the construction, the entry "01--" in the truth table corresponds to the four entries 0100, 0101, 0110, and 0111 in the K-map. The function value assigned to these entries is the same assignment given to the entry "01--." Alternatively, from the original table we could write the equation for Y_1 as

$$Y_1 = I_3 + I_3'I_2$$

The first term is the algebraic representation of the subcube "1---" while the second term is the algebraic representation for the subcube "01--." On using algebraic simplification, we have

$$Y_1 = I_3 + I_3'I_2$$
$$= \left(I_3 + I_3'\right) + \left(I_3 + I_2\right)$$
$$= I_3 + I_2$$

For the output Y_0, we have

$$Y_0 = I_3 + I_3'I_2'I_1$$
$$= I_3 + I_2'I_1$$

The design of the priority encoder is shown in Figure 6.2.3.

6.3 Multiplexers

Multiplexer circuits were discussed in the previous chapter in the context of being data selectors. The circuits act as switches connecting a set of data

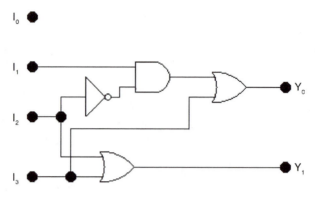

FIGURE 6.2.3
Design of the 4-to-2 Priority Encoder

inputs to a common data output using the control inputs. In this section, we expand on the use of multiplexers as function implementers and discuss constructing larger multiplexers from smaller ones. First, we consider the general design of multiplexers.

6.3.1 Design and Equations

From Chapter 5, the algebraic equation of a 4-to-1 multiplexer can be written as a sum of product terms. Each product term has the form $I_j m_j$, with m_j representing the minterm of the select inputs with decimal value j, and I_j is the corresponding data line. A similar procedure can be applied to obtain the algebraic equation of a larger multiplexer. For example, the algebraic equation of an 8-to-1 multiplexer is

$$F = I_0 m_0 + I_1 m_1 + I_2 m_2 + I_3 m_3 + I_4 m_4 + I_5 m_5 + I_6 m_6 + I_7 m_7$$

$$= \sum_{i=0}^{i=7} I_i m_i$$

The circuit design of an 8-to-1 multiplexer is shown in Figure 6.3.1. Note that the circuit has a certain commonality with a 3-to-8 decoder as follows: (1) the number of AND gates are equal, and (2) each AND gate produces the minterms as part of the product. They differ in the added data inputs and in the additional OR gate, as shown. In general, for a 2^n-to-1 multiplexer, the number of control inputs is equal to n. The algebraic equation of the multiplexer is given as

$$F = I_0 m_0 + I_1 m_1 + \ldots + I_{2^n - 1} m_{2^n - 1}$$

$$= \sum_{i=0}^{i=2^n - 1} I_i m_i$$

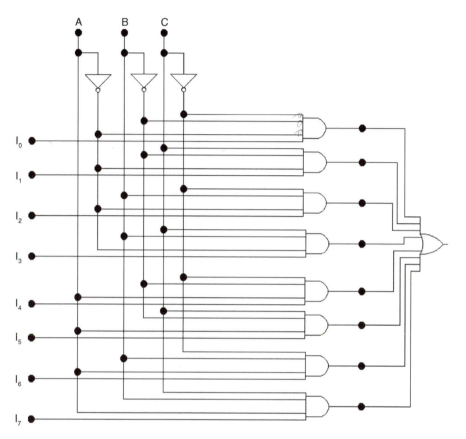

FIGURE 6.3.1
Design of an 8-to-1 Multiplexer

Assuming there is no fan-in restrictions on the design, such a circuit will have a total of 2^n $(n + 1)$-input AND gates and a single 2^n-input OR gate.

6.3.2 Design of Larger Multiplexers from Smaller Ones

Larger multiplexers can be constructed from smaller multiplexers. We illustrate this by designing an 8-to-1 multiplexer from 4-to-1 and 2-to-1 multiplexers. The circuit will require three control inputs, S_2, S_1, and S_0. Similar to decoders, the most-significant bit (S_2) assumes a value of 0 for the upper half of the data lines and a value of 1 or the lower half of the data lines. The most-significant bit of the control inputs, S_2, is used to select from two sets of data. If $S_2 = 0$, then one of the data inputs in the set $\{I_0, I_1, I_2, I_3\}$ is connected to the output. If $S_2 = 1$, then one of the data inputs in the set $\{I_4, I_5, I_6, I_7\}$ is connected to the output. Finally, the remaining control lines are used to select the relative data location within a set to connect to the output.

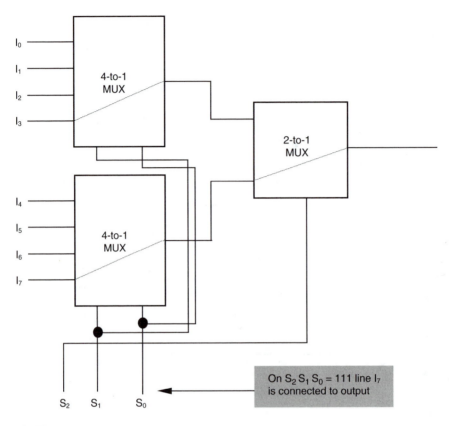

FIGURE 6.3.2
Design of an 8-to-1 Multiplexer from Smaller Multiplexers

Using the above observations, we obtain the circuit shown in Figure 6.3.2. In the figure, we show the connection from the data inputs to the output on the select inputs $S_2 S_1 S_0 = 111$.

6.3.3 Design of Boolean Functions Using Multiplexers

In Chapter 3, we showed that there are 16 Boolean functions over two variables and, in general, there are 2^{2^n} functions over n variables. A multiplexer with n control lines can be used to implement any of the 2^{2^n} functions. This is done by assigning Boolean constants to the select inputs of a multiplexer. Figure 6.3.3 shows the design of the XOR and OR functions.

Note that the inputs to the circuit (function) are applied at the select (control) part of the multiplexer. The output of the circuit is the multiplexer output.

The design is accomplished by setting the data lines of the multiplexer to the truth values of the function found in the truth table. We illustrate the design in the context of the input to the function, which acts as the select

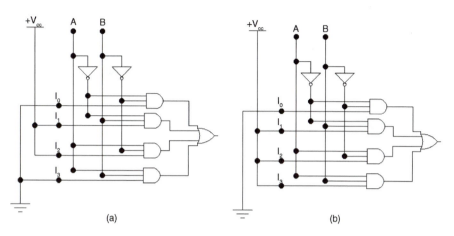

FIGURE 6.3.3
Design of the XOR, and OR Functions from 4-to-1 Multiplexers

input to the multiplexer. In particular, we use the input $AB = 00$, for example. For this input, the function outputs the value 0 for the XOR circuit design. Since this input selects the first data line of the multiplexer and places it at the output, we set this data line value to 0. Similar logic applies to the other entries of the multiplexer.

In using multiplexers in the design of functions, we choose multiplexers with the number of control inputs equal to the number of inputs in the function to be designed. The design is completed by setting the data inputs to the truth values of the Boolean function found in its truth table. The design can be accomplished with multiplexers with one less control input (n-1 select lines). In the design, one of the variables and/or its complement is used as an input to the data lines instead of the select lines. We illustrate this in the following example.

Example 6.3.1
Design the majority function using a multiplexer with two select lines.

Solution: Two of the inputs of the majority function are the inputs to the select lines of the multiplexer. Arbitrarily, we choose A and B while the inputs to the function are A, B, and C. The remaining input, C, its complement, and the constants 0 and 1 are used as inputs to the data lines as determined in the truth table given in Figure 6.3.4.

As noted in the figure, when $AB = 00$ the output of the function is zero independent of C, i.e., the data input I_0 is set to zero. On $AB = 01$, however, the output is dependent on the value of C. From the table, we have the value of the majority function is $F = C$, as observed. Similar analysis produces the reduced table given in Figure 6.3.5(a). The value of the function is given in terms of the Boolean constants as well as the literal C. The design is shown in Figure 6.3.5(b). Note the outer box containing the circuit design with the inputs and outputs. The design of the multiplexer is given in block diagram form.

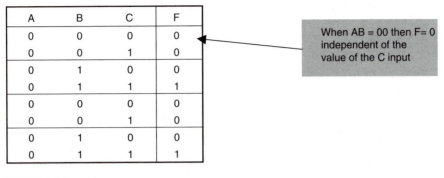

A	B	C	F
0	0	0	0
0	0	1	0
0	1	0	0
0	1	1	1
0	0	0	0
0	0	1	0
0	1	0	0
0	1	1	1

When AB = 00 then F= 0 independent of the value of the C input

FIGURE 6.3.4
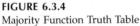
Majority Function Truth Table

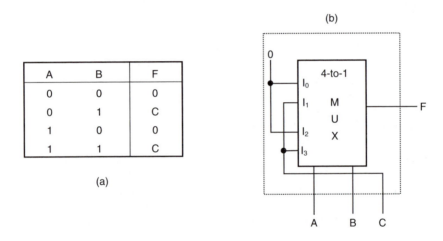

(b)

A	B	F
0	0	0
0	1	C
1	0	0
1	1	C

(a)

FIGURE 6.3.5
(a) Abbreviated Majority Function, (b) Design using 4-to-1 Multiplexer

We illustrate the function of the circuit for the input $ABC = 010$ and $ABC = 011$. Since the A and B values are the same ($AB = 01$) for both inputs, the multiplexer data input, I_1, is connected to the output. Since I_1 is connected to the input C, the value seen at the output is C, i.e., the output is 0 for the input $ABC = 010$, and 1 for the input $ABC = 011$. These values agree with the truth table. Similar analysis can be applied to other entries. Alternative designs can be obtained by using other variables as inputs to the select lines. To use BC as inputs, for example, we reconstruct the truth table as shown in Figure 6.3.6(a). The data input values to the multiplexer are shown in Figure 6.3.6(b). The design is given in Figure 6.3.6(c)

Field programmable gate arrays (FPGA) are devices that can be programmed to realize different functions. The term "programmed" will be discussed later. The circuits contain multiplexers that allow for the design of arbitrary functions. This is accomplished by setting the data inputs of the

(b)

B	C	F
0	0	0
0	1	A
1	0	0
1	1	A

B	C	A	F
0	0	0	0
0	0	1	0
0	1	0	0
0	1	1	1
0	0	0	0
0	0	1	0
0	1	0	0
0	1	1	1

(a)

(c)

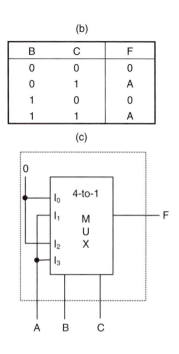

FIGURE 6.3.6
(a) Reconstructed Majority Function Truth Table, (b) Abbreviated Table, (c) Design Using 4-to-1 Multiplexer

multiplexer to specific values. The data inputs are memory elements that can store 0 and 1 values and, as a result, allow for realization of arbitrary functions without the need to do any wiring. In addition, multiplexers can be used as crossbar switches to establish different connections between several lines. The circuit design itself is, again, not changed. Instead, the multiplexer select and data values are set to specific values.

We illustrate the design of a 2×2 (pronounced "2-by-2") crossbar switch. An example of the function of a 2×2 crossbar switch in block diagram form is shown in Figure 6.3.7. The switch has two input sources, a and b, and two destinations, F_1 and F_2. Depending on the select inputs, the input sources can be connected to the outputs, as shown. The design of the crossbar switch can be accomplished using multiplexers as shown in Figure 6.3.8. Figure 6.3.8(a) shows the design using two 4-to-1 multiplexers. Figure 6.3.8(b) shows the outputs as a function of the select lines.

6.4 Demultiplexers

Similar to the relation between encoders and decoders, demultiplexers are related to multiplexers. In a multiplexer, one of n sources can be connected

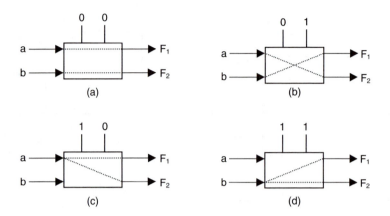

FIGURE 6.3.7
An Example of a 2 x 2 Crossbar Switch in Block Diagram

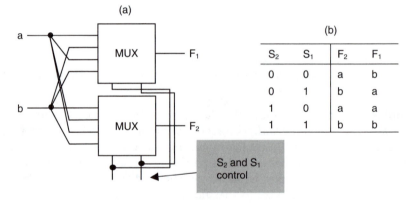

FIGURE 6.3.8
Design of a 2 x 2 crossbar switch using multiplexers

to a single output. In demultiplexers, one source can be connected to any of *n* outputs. For both circuits, a set of control inputs (select inputs) is used to select the line to be connected to the output. The schematic of a demultiplexer is shown in Figure 6.4.1(a). In the figure, a single input can be routed to any of four outputs. To select the correct output, the circuit contains two control (select) inputs. Figure 6.4.1(b) shows an example of routing the data input *D* to the top output, based on the select input *AB* = 00. The design of a demultiplexer can be realized using a decoder with an enable line. The enable line acts as the data input to the demultiplexer. The inputs to the decoder act as the control inputs to the demultiplexer. Figure 6.4.2 shows an example. Note the enable line to the decoder was moved, as shown, to indicate the enable line is the data line.

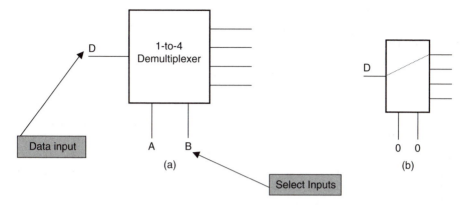

FIGURE 6.4.1
(a) 1-to-4 Demultiplexer in Block Diagram, (b) Switch Notation as a Function of the Select inputs

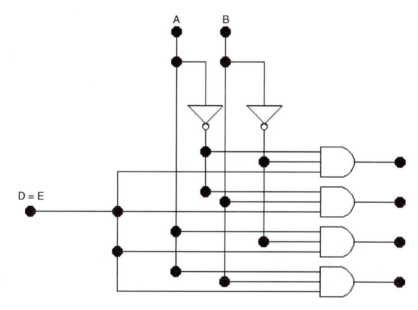

FIGURE 6.4.2
Design of a 1-to-4 Demultiplexer from a Decoder with Enable Line

6.5 Programmable Logic Arrays

6.5.1 Programmable Logic Devices (PLDs)

In the previous sections, we presented procedures for designing Boolean functions using decoders and multiplexers. In this section, we introduce programmable logic devices (PLDs). These devices are used in design automation where different designs are mapped to the same circuit architecture. The implementation of different functions is accomplished by programming the device. The term "programming" refers to altering the connections of the device using special tools.

We discuss programmable logic arrays (PLA), programmable array logic (PAL®), and Read-Only Memory (ROM). The three devices are constructed so as to implement functions in sum of product form and, as a result, include a level of AND gates (called AND array) and an additional level of OR gates (called OR array). The second level of the OR gate is used for the design of multiple output functions. By properly programming the device, one can implement different Boolean functions. We next discuss the three types of PLDs and show how they are used in the design of Boolean functions. In the discussion, we use simple examples that illustrate the definitions of each. Actual programmable logic devices may contain thousands of gates.

6.5.2 Programmable Logic Arrays

A sample schematic of a programmable logic array (PLA) is shown in Figure 6.5.1. The PLA is composed of two programmable arrays: an AND array and an OR array. Each of the cross-hatches (×) in Figure 6.5.1 represents a programmable connection. Initially, all the inputs (including the corresponding complements) are connected as inputs to each of the AND gates. This constitutes the AND array part of the PLA. Similarly, the OR array of the PLA is composed of inputs to three OR gates. The inputs to each OR gate are the AND outputs in the first level. Programming the PLA to realize a specific function is the process of establishing which connections to leave intact and which connections to take out. We illustrate this in the following example.

Example 6.5.1

Program the PLA given in Figure 6.5.1 to realize the majority function.

Solution: The truth table of the majority function is given in Table 6.5.1.

In designing the circuit using the PLA given in Figure 6.5.1, the PLA needs to meet the following three conditions:

1. The number of inputs to the PLA should not be less than the number of the inputs to the function. In the example, the number of inputs to the PLA is equal to the number of inputs to the function (three inputs).

2. The algebraic representation of the function must be in sum of product form and the number of products in the function should not exceed the number of AND gates in the PLA. For our example, the function in canonical sum form contains four product terms. The function in simplified form is composed of three product terms.

3. The number of outputs in the function should be less than or equal to the number of outputs of the PLA. This condition is met as well

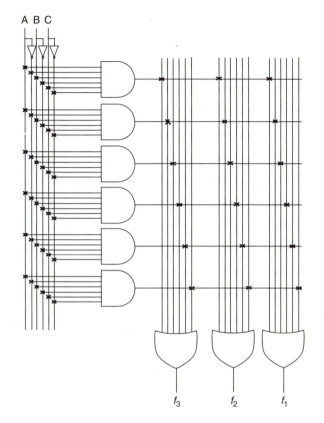

FIGURE 6.5.1
Sample schematic of a programmable Logic Array (PLA)

TABLE 6.5.1

Majority Function

A	B	C	f_1
0	0	0	0
0	0	1	0
0	1	0	0
0	1	1	1
1	0	0	0
1	0	1	1
1	1	0	1
1	1	1	1

since the PLA contains three outputs and the majority function is a single output function. The schematic of the programmed PLA is shown in Figure 6.5.2. Note that the PLA realizes the function in canonical sum form and not minimized form. This was done since the remaining AND gates were not used. The upper AND gate

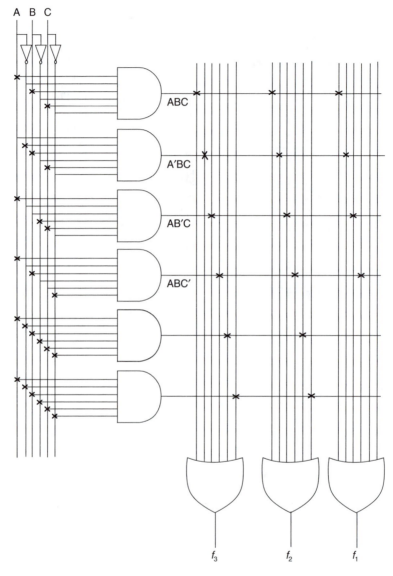

FIGURE 6.5.2
Design of majority function using a PLA

realizes *ABC*; the remaining AND gates realize the other three minterms. The output of the majority function is measured at the f_1
output of the PLA. Note that the outputs of each of the remaining
AND gates is 0.

To simplify presentations, the PLA given above is presented in a different
form and is based on the notation given in Figure 6.5.3; part (b) of the figure

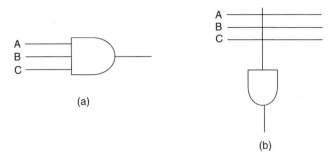

(a)

(b)

FIGURE 6.5.3
(a) 3-Input AND Gate, (b) Alternative Representation

is an alternative representation of part (a). In this representation, the AND gate is represented with a single input. A crossing of an input line with the AND gate input represents an input to the AND gate if an × (represents a programmable connection) or an • (represents a permanent connection, see Figure 6.6.1) is placed at the intersection. To illustrate, the PLA given in Figure 6.5.1 is presented as shown in Figure 6.5.4.

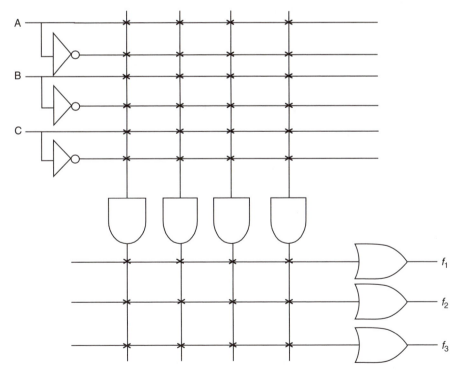

FIGURE 6.5.4
Reconstructed PLA of That Given in Figure 6.5.2

In the diagram, the columns represent the AND array. An × placed on intersecting lines represents a programmed connection. Initially, all inputs are connected to the inputs of each AND gate. For the OR array, all AND outputs are connected to each of the OR arrays.

Example 6.5.2
Show the design of a 1-bit full adder with inputs A, B, and C, using a PLA with seven AND gates in the AND array and three OR gates in the OR array.
Solution: The equations for the full adder are

$$Co(A,B,C) = \Sigma(m_3, m_5, m_6, m_7) = \Sigma(3,5,6,7)$$

and

$$S(A,B,C) = \Sigma(m_1, m_2, m_4, m_7) = \Sigma(1,2,4,7)$$

As can be seen from the equations, in the AND array we need to generate the seven product terms. Of these, minterm m_7 is common to both functions. Once these terms are generated, the next step is to generate the needed connections in the OR array. The design is shown Figure 6.5.5.

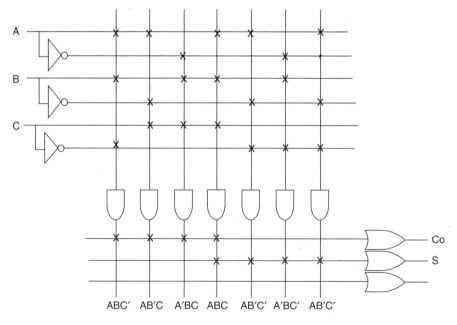

FIGURE 6.5.5
Design of a Full Adder Using PLAs

TABLE 6.5.2

Programming Table for the Full Adder
with Minimized Carry Equation

Product Terms	Inputs			Outputs
	A	B	C_i	CoS
AB	1	1	–	10
BC_i	1	–	1	10
AC_i	–	1	1	10
$A'B'C_i$	0	0	1	01
$A'BC_i'$	0	1	0	01
$AB'C_i$	1	0	0	01
ABC_i	1	1	1	01

An alternative design is to first minimize the functions at hand. Here, however, the alternative design does not yield a better design as the number of terms needed remains the same. (The sum equation cannot be minimized and the carry equation can be minimized to $C(A,B,C_i) = BC_i + AC_i + AB$). In both cases, the number of product terms needed is seven.

When using PLAs, it is less important to minimize the number of literals in a product term than it is to reduce the number of product terms. Reducing the number of product terms results in the use of less AND gates to design a function. Reducing the number of literals does not contribute to the overall saving since all AND gates are designed (programmed) to be connected to all possible inputs.

6.5.3   Tabular Description

The description of the design can be supplied in tabular form (programming table). The programming table for the full adder with minimized carry equation is given in Table 6.5.2. The table is formed as follows:

1. The number of rows in the table is equal to the number of product terms found in the sum of product representation of the functions to be designed. The product terms found in different functions are listed once in the table since these terms can be shared.

2. With each product term, we associate a string of symbols from the set {0, 1, -}. The string length is equal to the number of variables. For a given product term, the corresponding symbols of the string are set to 1, 0, or -. If a variable is absent from the product, then the corresponding location in the string is set to "-"; otherwise, the location is set to 0 or 1, depending on the variable in the product being complemented or uncomplemented, respectively. In the above

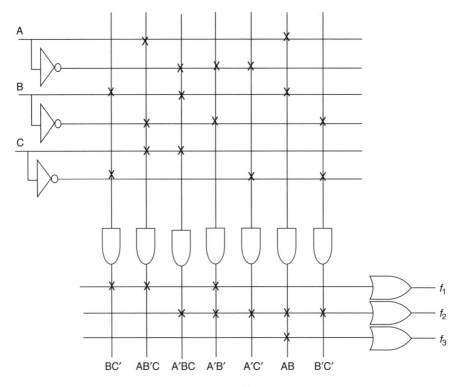

FIGURE 6.5.6
PLA Used in Example 6.5.3

table, columns 1 and 2 contain the product terms and the corresponding strings for the minimized 1-bit full adder equations.

3. The final column in the table contains a string of 0s and 1s. The
number of bits in the string is equal to the number of output functions of the PLA, with each bit corresponding to a specific function.
The bit assignment is 0 if the corresponding product term is not used
by the function; otherwise, the bit assignment is 1.

Example 6.5.3
Form the PLA programming table for the circuit given in Figure 6.5.6.
  Solution: The table contains seven rows (one row per product term or
AND gate). Column 1 of the table includes all product terms. The terms can
be read from the diagram as BC', $AB'C$, $A'BC$, $A'B'$, $A'C'$, AB, and $B'C'$.
Column 2 contains the binary assignment associated with each product term,
as shown in Table 6.5.3. Finally, column 3 contains three bit strings corresponding to the three functions. Note that this column can be read from the
circuit as well. For example, row 1 of this column is read as 001, corresponding to the output of the left-most AND gate (an × on the output of the gate

TABLE 6.5.3

Programming Table for Example 6.5.3

	Inputs			Outputs	
Product Terms	A	B	C	f_3	f_2f_1
BC'	–	1	0	0	01
AB'C	1	0	1	0	01
A'BC	0	1	1	0	10
A'B'	0	0	–	0	11
A'C'	0	–	0	0	10
AB	1	1	–	1	10
B'C'	–	0	0	0	10

and the line connected to the OR gate of f_1 is presented as 1). Similarly, the last row is assigned 010.

6.5.4 AND-OR-NOT Design

For functions that assume values of 1 over a large portion of the set of inputs, the canonical sum representation of the complement of the function contains less product terms. For these functions, one can save on the number of AND gates if the complement of the function is designed in the AND-OR array. To get the correct output, however, one needs to complement the output of the PLA. As a result, some PLDs contain additional circuitry used to complement the outputs from the AND-OR array. For this, the circuits contain XOR gates at the outputs of the OR array. One of the inputs of each of the XOR array is an output of an OR gate output, Y. The second input, X, is a programmed input. If the input X is 0, then the XOR gate output is that of Y. If the programmed input is 1, however, then the XOR outputs the complement of Y. We illustrate the design process in the next example.

Example 6.5.4

Use a PLA to realize the design of a circuit with four inputs, A_2, A_1, B_2, B_1, and with two outputs, F_1 and F_2. The inputs correspond to the two 2-bit numbers $A = A_2A_1$ and $B = B_2B_1$. F_1 assumes a value of 1 if and only if A is equal to B. F_2 assumes a value of 1 if and only if the sum $A + B$ is greater than or equal to 2.

Solution: The truth table for the above functions is given in Table 6.5.4.

Without minimization, the smallest possible number of product terms needed is obtained by designing F_1 and the complement function of F_2. The OR gate for F_2 is then complemented to produce the correct output. The PLA chosen needs to (1) have at least four inputs, (2) have at least six product terms, and (3) have at least one XOR gate associated with one of the outputs. The design is shown in Figure 6.5.7. Note the use of the XOR gates in the design.

TABLE 6.5.4

Truth Table of Example 6.5.4

A_2	A_1	B_2	B_1	F_1	F_2
0	0	0	0	1	0
0	0	0	1	0	0
0	0	1	0	0	1
0	0	1	1	0	1
0	1	0	0	0	0
0	1	0	1	1	1
0	1	1	0	0	1
0	1	1	1	0	1
1	0	0	0	0	1
1	0	0	1	0	1
1	0	1	0	1	1
1	0	1	1	0	1
1	1	0	0	0	1
1	1	0	1	0	1
1	1	1	0	0	1
1	1	1	1	1	1

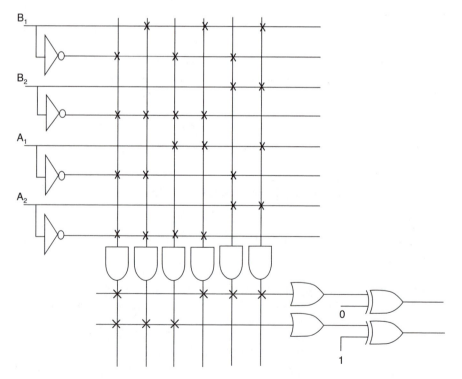

FIGURE 6.5.7
PLA Design of Example 6.5.4

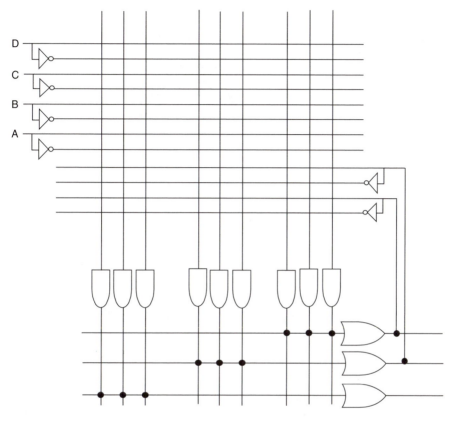

FIGURE 6.6.1
An Example of a PAL Circuit

6.6 Programmable Array Logic Devices

The cost of programmable logic devices is due to two factors: the cost of the programmable switching elements and the cost of the gates in the device. Programmable array logic (PAL®) devices are PLDs with the connections in the OR array fixed (nonprogrammable). In addition, each AND gate is used as input to a single OR gate, i.e., OR gates do not share product terms. This property allows the minimization of Boolean functions independent of each other. Figure 6.6.1 shows an example of a PAL. The connections to the OR array in the figure are fixed (presented as solid circles). In addition, the OR gates do not share common product terms. For some PALs, the OR gate's output is fed back as input terms to the AND gates. This is shown in the figure as well. The table representation of a PAL is similar to that of a PLA with the OR array part removed.

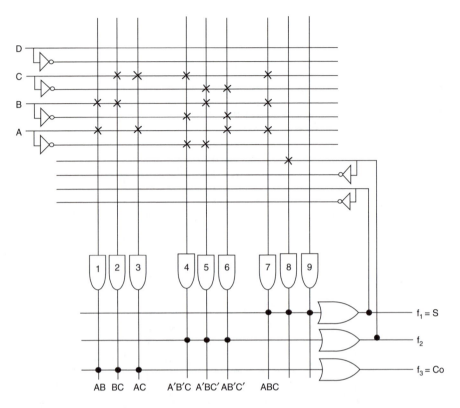

FIGURE 6.6.2
Design of a 1-Bit Adder Using the PAL circuit given in Figure 6.6.1

We illustrate the design and table formation on the 1-bit adder equations. From earlier discussion the canonical sum representation:

$$Co(A,B,C) = \Sigma(m_3, m_5, m_6, m_7) = \Sigma(3,5,6,7)$$

$$S(A,B,C) = \Sigma(m_1, m_2, m_4, m_7) = \Sigma(1,2,4,7)$$

With the carry equation reduced to $Co(A,B,C) = AB + BC + AC$, the PAL design is shown in Figure 6.6.2. Note the need to use one of the OR gates to form the sum equations as the sum requires four product terms. In particular, we use the second OR gate to form the expression $A'B'C + A'BC' + AB'C'$. This sum then is fed back to the AND array. The expression and the product term ABC are then OR-ed together to form the sum equation, $S = A'B'C + A'BC' + AB'C' + ABC$, as the output of the top OR gate.

The table associated with the above design is given in Table 6.6.1. In the table, we associated numbers with the product terms and separated them into groups based on the corresponding OR gates' inputs. In addition, since

TABLE 6.6.1

Programming Table of PAL Design in Figure 6.6.2

Gate, Product		AND Inputs					OR Outputs
		A	B	C	f_2	f_3	
1	AB	1	1	–	–	–	
2	BC	–	1	1	–	–	$f_3 = AB + BC + AC$
3	AC	1	–	1	–	–	
4	A'B'C	0	0	1	–	–	
5	A'BC'	0	1	0	–	–	$f_2 = \Sigma(m_1, m_2, m_4) = \Sigma(1,2,4)$
6	AB'C'	1	0	0	–	–	
7	ABC	1	1	1	–	–	$f_1 = \Sigma(m_1, m_2, m_4, m_7) = \Sigma(1,2,4,7)$
8	f_2	–	–	–	1	–	

some of the OR outputs are used as inputs in the AND array F, these functions are included as part of the product terms. We illustrate by referring to the first row of the table. For this row, the gate that forms the product is gate 1 (column 1 of the table). The product term is AB and the AND inputs are given as (11 - - -). The OR output is the logical OR of the three product terms, as shown in the figure.

6.7 Read-Only Memory

Read-only memory (ROM) circuits are among the oldest programmable logic devices. In PLA design, both the AND and the OR arrays are programmable. In PAL, the OR array connections were fixed but the AND array was programmable. In ROM, the AND array connections are fixed and the OR array connections are programmable. Furthermore, the AND array connections output all minterms associated with the inputs, i.e., the AND array is a decoder. Finally, in general there is no feedback from the OR array to the AND array and there are no inversion circuits at the outputs. From the description of ROM devices, one can model the design as shown in Figure 6.7.1. An example schematic of a ROM with three inputs and six OR gates in the OR array is given in Figure 6.7.2. As can be seen from the figure, the top part of the figure is a 3-to-8 decoder with permanent connections. The OR array is programmable.

To design functions using a ROM device, the function is represented in canonical sum form. This is equivalent to generating the needed truth tables of the functions. From the truth table, one can establish the needed connections in the OR array. As a result, no minimization procedure is needed to complete the design. This is an advantage; the disadvantage, however, is the number of AND gates found in ROM circuits.

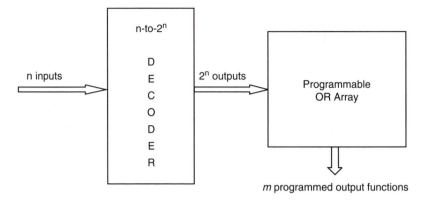

FIGURE 6.7.1
ROM Block Diagram

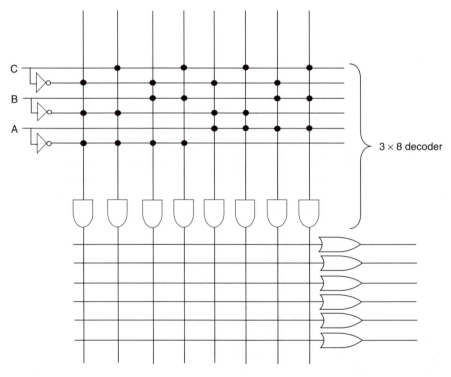

FIGURE 6.7.2
ROM Gate Representation

As an example, we illustrate the design procedure using the the functions as an example:

$$f_1(A_3, A_2, A_1) = A_3 A_1 + \overline{A}_2 A_1$$

$$f_2(A_3, A_2, A_1) = A_3 A_2$$

$$f_3(A_3, A_2, A_1) = \sum(0,1,2,7)$$

In order to design the above functions using a ROM device, we first write the equations in canonical sum form to get

$$f_1(A_3, A_2, A_1) = A_3 A_1 + \overline{A}_2 A_1$$

$$= A_3 A_1 (\overline{A}_2 + A_2) + \overline{A}_2 A_1 (\overline{A}_3 + A_3)$$

$$= \sum(1,5,7)$$

$$f_2(A_3, A_2, A_1) = A_3 A_2$$

$$= A_3 A_2 (\overline{A}_1 + A_1)$$

$$= \sum(6,7)$$

$$f_3(A_3, A_2, A_1) = \sum(0,1,2,7)$$

We next design the circuit for the above functions by selectively connecting the needed minterms associated with each function as shown in Figure 6.7.3.

Note that the design requires a ROM with a 3-to-8 binary decoder. In addition, the OR array requires at least three OR gates. Finally, note that there is no need to minimize a given function to design it using ROM. In fact, the function should be expanded to its canonical sum form.

6.8 Diodes and Programmable Logic Devices

This section is intended to illustrate how programmable logic devices can be designed at the transistor level. For simplicity, we discuss the design using diodes and present the discussion in a conceptual fashion. We first consider diode design.

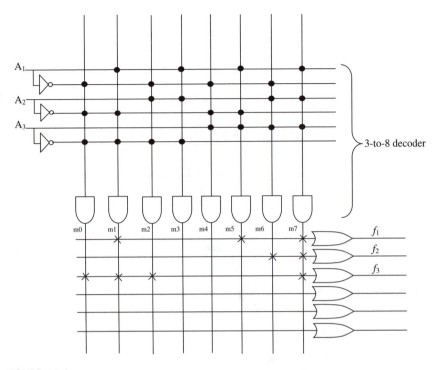

FIGURE 6.7.3
Design of $f_1(A_3, A_2, A_1) = A_3A_1 + \overline{A}_2A_1$, $f_2 = A_3A_2$, and $f_3 = \Sigma(0,1,2,7)$. Using ROM Circuits

6.8.1   Diodes

Similar to transistors, diodes are electrical elements whose design is based on semiconductors. Programmable logic devices can be designed using transistor switches as well as diodes.

The schematic of a diode is shown in Figure 6.8.1. As can be seen from Figure 6.8.1(a), the diode is composed of two types of semiconductors: a P type and an N type. By properly connecting the two sides of the diodes to voltage sources, the diode can function in one of two different modes. In one mode, the P side is attached to a positive voltage as compared to the negative side, N. In this mode, the diode conducts electricity and is said to be forward-biased. The voltage drop across the diode is minimal and can be approximated as 0 V. In the second mode, the negative side (N) is connected to a higher voltage than the positive side. In this mode, the diode is said to be reverse-biased and does not conduct electricity but behaves as an open switch. The graphic symbol of a diode is shown in Figure 6.8.1(b).

We illustrate the use of diodes in the design of the three logic operations (NOT, AND, and OR). Consider the three circuits shown in Figure 6.8.2. The

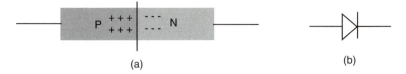

FIGURE 6.8.1
(a) Schematic of a Diode, (b) Graphic Symbol

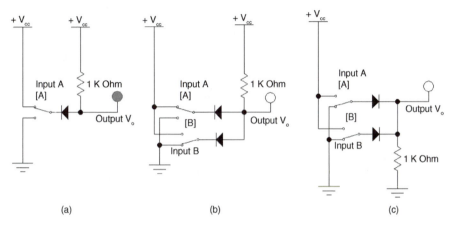

FIGURE 6.8.2
Diode Design of Logic Operations, (a) NOT Gate, (b) AND Gate, (c) OR Gate

inputs to the circuits in the figure are controlled by a switch and labeled *A* and *B*; depending on the position of the switch, the input is connected to logic 1 (V_{cc}) or logic 0 (ground). The output to the circuit is measured by the indicator as shown and is labeled V_o.

If *A* is connected to V_{cc} (logic 1) in Figure 6.8.2(a), then the diode is in reverse-bias. As a result, there is no current flowing in the 1-k Ω resistor and the output assumes a value of 1. Similarly, if the input is connected to logic 0 (ground), then the diode is in forward bias, i.e., the diode is in the conducting mode and the voltage drop across the diode is approximately 0. In other words the output is at logic value 0 V. From the discussion, the circuit in Figure 6.8.2(a) is a diode design of an inverter.

If both *A* and *B* are connected to V_{cc} in Figure 6.8.2(b), then both diodes are in reverse-bias and no current passes through the 1-k Ω resistor, i.e., the output is equal to V_{cc}. If either input is connected to ground, however, then the corresponding diode is in the forward-bias mode, causing a voltage drop of 0 across the diode, i.e., the output voltage is 0. The circuit in Figure 6.8.2(b) therefore is that of an AND gate.

Similar analysis can be applied to the circuit in Figure 6.8.2(c); the design is that of an OR gate.

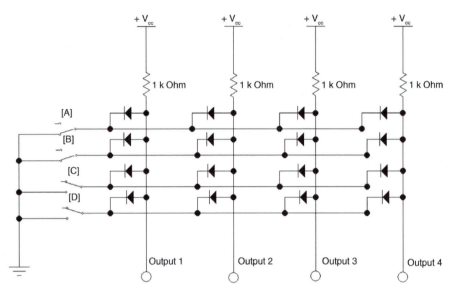

FIGURE 6.8.3
Design of an AND Array, Each Output Is the AND of the Four Input Variables

6.8.2 Programmable Logic Devices

We discuss the diode implementation of programmable logic devices by referring to Figure 6.8.3. We look at the column labeled Output 1. What does this part of the circuit do? In answering this question, we note that the output is connected to V_{cc} through the 1-k Ω resistor. We also note that along the path of V_{cc} to the output we have four diodes with one end of each diode connected to the path and the other end connected to one of the inputs. If none of the inputs is connected to logic 0 (i.e., the value of each input is 1), then none of the diodes is in forward-bias mode. As a result, there is no current that flows through the path and Output 1 assumes the value of V_{cc}. If any of the inputs assume a value of 0, however, then the corresponding diode is in forward bias. As a result, the voltage across the conducting diode assumes a value of 0, and as a result, the output assumes a value of 0. The above discussion indicates that Output 1 is the logical AND of the four input variables. Similar analysis results in each of the remaining outputs acting as the logical AND of the four input variables as well.

Now, consider the modified circuit shown in Figure 6.8.4. What does this circuit do? In answering this question, we note that it is similar to the circuit presented earlier. The difference with regard to Output 1 is as follows. The connection of the diode to input *D* is removed. As a result, input *D* does not affect the value of Output 1 and Output 1 is now a realization of the product *ABC*. By observation, similar notes can be made about Output 2, Output 3, and Output 4.

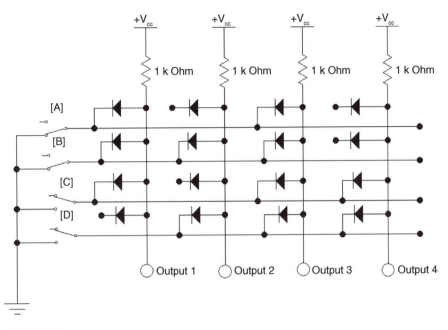

FIGURE 6.8.4
Programmable AND Array

   The above discussion illustrates the concept of programmable devices. The device to be programmed is the original device with all diode connections made. Programming the device means translating the specification of a circuit to be designed into a binary pattern that can be used to remove (program) diode connections. Since the structure is a realization of AND gates and since it is organized in an array fashion, the circuit structure is called an AND array.

   Devices such as AND arrays can be manufactured in mass quantities independent of a specific design. The same generic device can then be programmed to satisfy the realization of a specific Boolean function. The programming can be done by the manufacturer on the generic design or it can be done by the end user. In the latter case, the device is called field-programmable. In either case, special tools are used to break the established diode connections. Finally, some field-programmable devices are designs that allow the device to be reprogrammed. Here, special tools are used to establish new connections and/or remove old connections.

6.8.3   Diode Design of Programmable Logic Arrays

The simplified presentations of PLAs, used earlier, can be related to the diode design shown in Figure 6.8.5. The diagram contains two arrays: the AND array as discussed earlier and the OR array, composed of a single set of diodes connected in row order, as shown in the diagram. The output of each

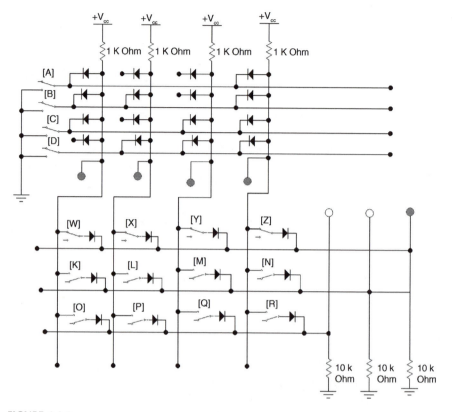

FIGURE 6.8.5
Diode Design of a PLA

row constitutes the output of one of the OR gates. As a result of the discussion, the number of columns in the diagram constitutes the number of AND gates. In the diagram, the AND array contains four AND gates. Similarly, the number of rows is equal to the number of OR gates. Note that this array of OR gates contains switches that can be programmed using the Electronics Workbench.

Chapter 6 Exercises

6.1 Given the function $f(A, B, C) = \Sigma(0, 1, 4, 5)$. Design the function using a 3-to-8 binary decoder with minterms as the decoder's outputs.

6.2 Design the function given above using a 3-to-8 decoder with maxterms as the decoder outputs.

6.3 Design the function $f(A, B, C) = A + BC$ using a 3-to-8 decoder.

6.4 Show the design of the function $f(x) = x^2 + x + 1$ where x is a decimal number between 0 and 7 inclusive. Use a design procedure similar to the procedure given in Example 6.1.2.

6.5 Show the design of a 2-bit binary adder using a 4-to-16 decoder.

6.6 Show the design of a 2-bit magnitude comparator using a 4-to-16 decoder.

6.7 Design a 4-to-16 decoder using 2-to-4 decoders with enable lines.

6.8 Show the design of the function in problem 6.1 using an 8-to-1 multiplexer.

6.9 Show the design of the function in problem 6.1 using a 4-to-1 multiplexer.

6.10 Design a 1-bit full adder using 8-to-1 multiplexers.

6.11 Design a 1-bit full subtractor using a 4-to-1 multiplexer.

6.12 Construct the truth table for a 2-bit binary subtractor and show the design of the function using a PLA of the proper size. If needed, minimize the function to reduce the total number of product terms. Construct the tabular representation (programming table) of the design.

6.13 Show the design of a 2-bit full adder using a PLA with AND-OR-NOT construct. Form the programming table of the design.

6.14 Show the design of a 1-bit full subtractor using a PAL of the proper size.

6.15 Show the design of a 2-bit magnitude comparator of a PAL with the proper size.

6.16 Form the design of a 2-bit magnitude comparator using a PAL with the three inputs to each of the OR gates in the OR plane. Form the number of feedbacks required to accomplish the design. Before the design, if possible, minimize the number of product terms first.

6.17 Show the design of the 2-bit magnitude comparator using a ROM of the proper size.

6.18 Assume a committee of four members, A, B, C, and D, votes on a specific task. The vote of each member is weighted by the number of stocks he/she owns. Assume a vote of yes by member A has a weight of 4. Similarly, assume the weights associated with a yes vote for each of B, C and D is 3, 2, and 1, respectively.

(a) Model the above as a truth table. The inputs to the table are the yes or no votes of the members. The output is the sum of the weights of the yes votes represented in binary.

(b) Design the function using a PLA of the proper size.

(c) Design the function using a PLA with AND-OR-NOT structure.

(d) Design the circuit with a PAL of the proper size.

(e) Design the function using a PAL with 3-input OR gates. Form the needed feedback from the OR array to the AND array.

6.19 Form the programming table of each part of problem 6.18.

7

Flip-Flops and Analysis of Sequential Circuits

CONTENTS

The previous chapters dealt with modeling and design of combinational circuits. Digital logic circuits can be characterized broadly as combinational or as sequential. In combinational circuits, the output of the circuit is a function of its current inputs only, irrespective of the previous inputs applied to the circuit. The behavior of combinational circuits can be described using truth tables or Boolean functions, for example. The description using either form shows the circuit response is a function of the current inputs only.

Not all digital circuits are combinational in nature as the behavior of some circuits depends not only on the current input, but also on previous inputs to the circuit. These circuits are called sequential circuits. Consider the case of a soda vending machine. The machine contains a digital circuit responsible for keeping track of the amount of money entered for a each transaction (a transaction is the input applied to obtain a can of soda). The circuit contains a single input (coin deposit input). Its output (ignoring the change output) is a signal to release/unrelease a can of soda. The circuit is sequential as the output depends on the coin entered currently as well as previous inputs. For example, on the same input of 25 cents the machine may release a can or wait for additional coins, depending on the previous inputs.

In this chapter, we discuss the primitive building blocks of sequential circuits and methods to describe (analyze) these circuits. The remaining chapters use the primitive sequential circuits as building blocks in the design and analysis of circuits found in digital computers. We start our discussion with latches.

7.1 Latches

7.1.1 Feedback Loops

In digital design, memory can be obtained using feedback loops where outputs of gates are fed back as inputs. To illustrate, consider the cross-coupled circuit diagram shown in Figure 7.1.1 (by cross-coupled we mean that the output of each gate is used as an input to the other gate). The circuit has no inputs but illustrates the fact that a binary value (placed in the circuit in some fashion) will be stored in the circuit indefinitely (as long as the power is on).

For example, if the output at Q is equal to 1, then due to the bottom inverter this output is converted to 0 on the output of the bottom inverter, which in

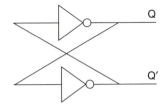

FIGURE 7.1.1
Cross-Coupled Circuit

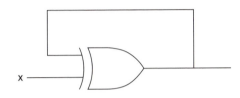

FIGURE 7.1.2
An Example of a Simple Sequential Circuit

turn is converted back to 1 by the upper inverter. This situation is repeated indefinitely. Note the use of the output labels Q and Q' to reflect the fact that one output is the complement of the other.

As another example, consider the circuit of an XOR gate with the output fed back as one of the inputs to the XOR gate, as shown in Figure 7.1.2. The circuit has a single external input and a single output. The circuit functions as a sequential circuit, since on the application of the same input ($x = 1$), the next output alternates between 0 and 1, or vice versa. In other words, the next output is a function of both the external input and current output.

We next discuss cross-coupled latches and see how the initial value to be stored in the cross-coupled network can be supplied in different ways leading to different types of latches.

7.1.2   SR Latches

A latch is a memory element that is used to store one bit of information. Latches in sequential circuits are analogous to the primitive gates in combinational circuits (AND, OR, NOT, etc.). We consider four types of latch memory elements SR, D, JK, and T latches. All four latches have two outputs where a binary bit and its complement are stored. The outputs are called Q and Q'. The number of inputs to each latch is either one or two inputs (depending on the nature of the latch) as indicated in Table 7.1.1. Columns 1, 2, 3, and 4 of the table represent, respectively, the latch type, the number of inputs, the label of each input, and the meaning of each input. Each of the four latches has two outputs, Q, and its complement, Q'.

In the table, the terms "set" and "reset" mean to set an input/output to 1 or reset it to 0. In this case, the value to be set (reset) is Q, the latch output.

TABLE 7.1.1

The Four Types of Latches Considered Are SR, D, JK, and T

Latch	Number of Inputs	Labels of Inputs	Meaning
SR	2	S, R	S = Set, R = Reset
D	1	D	D = Delay
JK	2	J, K	—
T	1	T	T = Toggle

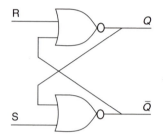

FIGURE 7.1.3
An SR Latch Circuit

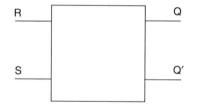

FIGURE 7.1.4
Block Diagram of an SR Latch

We show the design and function of each of the four latches by presenting a detailed discussion of the SR latch first. Other latches are built from modifications to the design of the SR latch

Consider the circuit shown in Figure 7.1.3. The circuit is an SR latch representing a 1-bit memory element. The contents of the memory element are the lines with label Q and its complement Q'. By applying the proper inputs we could store a 1 or 0 at the output Q. We will say more about what we mean by "store" later.

To distinguish between the current and next value at the output Q, we use the notation Q and $Q+$, respectively. Q and $Q+$ are measured at the same output but at different times. In relative terms, Q is measured before $Q+$. Hence, if Q is the current output, then $Q+$ is the next output. Similarly, if Q represents previous output, then $Q+$ represents the current output.

In block diagram the circuit above is shown in Figure 7.1.4. Its inputs are S and R; its outputs are Q and Q', with Q' the complement of Q. The function

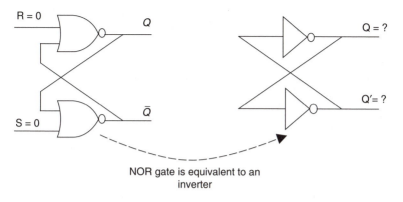

NOR gate is equivalent to an inverter

FIGURE 7.1.5
Effect of Assigning 0s to S and R

of the circuit can be determined from analysis of the gate representation above. In the analysis we make use of the following observations:

1. For the NOR gates connected in a cross-coupled fashion, by applying a 1 to one of the NOR inputs, the output is forced to 0, irrespective of the values assumed by other inputs.

2. An application of 0 to one of the inputs of the NOR gates causes the gate to behave as an inverter; its output is the complement of the other input.

3. We assume the propagation delays of the NOR gates are equal.

Initially, we assume the current values of Q and Q' are not known. With an input $S = R = 0$, the latch circuit reduces to the equivalent cross-coupled inverter circuit shown in Figure 7.1.5 with the outputs Q and Q' labeled "?" (not known). As a result, if the current output Q' is the complement of Q, the stored value at Q is unchanged, i.e., $Q+ = Q$. The output remains unchanged as long as the input values are unchanged. If, somehow, Q and Q' assume the same value, then the output $Q+$ will be the complement of Q. Similar logic applies to Q'. As a result, the outputs at Q and Q' continue to oscillate between 0 and 1 indefinitely (assuming $S = R = 0$). The oscillation is called critical race.

For an input of $S = R = 1$, both next output values ($Q+$ and $Q'+$) are forced to 0, irrespective of the current Q and Q' values. Latches require that the output at Q' is the complement of the output at Q. As a result, for the SR latch we say that the input $S = R = 1$ is not allowed since it contradicts the condition of having the latch outputs as complements of each other. In fact, if this input occurs followed by an input of $S = R = 0$, the latch will enter oscillation as discussed above.

There are two other cases to consider: (1) $S = 1$ and $R = 0$ and (2) $S = 0$ and $R = 1$. We consider the case of $S = 1$ and $R = 0$, which corresponds to setting the latch output. By "setting" we mean the output is 1 (store 1). On placing a 1 on S, the output at Q' ($Q'+$) is forced to 0, irrespective of its current value (if the current value is 0, then no change occurs). With R assuming a value of 0, the upper NOR gate acts as an inverter. It inverts the value on Q' and, as a result, $Q+ = 1$. As can be concluded, the next value stored at Q is 1, the latch is set. The S and R inputs are an abbreviation of set and reset, respectively.

For the case of $S = 0$ and $R = 1$, a similar analysis results in the next state, $Q+$, assuming a value of 0.

7.2 Behavioral Description

7.2.1 Characteristic Table

The behavior of an SR latch can be captured in a tabular form similar to the truth table representation called a characteristic table, as shown in Table 7.2.1(a) and (b). Note the difference as Q the current state (output) is used as part of the input. The last two entries in Table 7.2.1(a) assign "?" to $Q+$, indicating the input $S = R = 1$ is not allowed. To illustrate how the table is read, consider the entry $SRQ = 011$. For this entry, the current state is $Q = 1$ and the inputs are $S = 0$ and $R = 1$. From the table, the next state $Q+ = 0$. In generating the table we note that the state Q represents the output of the circuit before the application of the inputs S and R. The sequence of steps to generate the table is first to obtain the needed Q output, and then apply the inputs S and R. The observed output constitutes $Q+$.

An abbreviated characteristic table can be obtained by using S and R in the input columns as shown in Table 7.2.1(b). In the context of our earlier discussion of memory elements, to leave the contents of memory unchanged ($Q+ = Q$) we keep the values of S and R at 0. To store a 1, we assign 1 to S

TABLE 7.2.1

Characteristic Tables
of an SR Latch

(a)		(b)	
S R Q	Q+	S R	Q+
0 0 0	0	0 0	Q
0 0 1	1	0 1	0
0 1 0	0	1 0	1
0 1 1	0	1 1	?
1 0 0	1		
1 0 1	1		
1 1 0	?		
1 1 1	?		

and keep R at 0. Once a 1 is stored, S can be reset to 0. Finally, to store a 0, we assign a 1 to R and keep S at 0. We use the term "store" in the discussion since on the input $S = R = 0$ the output at Q remains unchanged, i.e., this value is stored at Q. Note that this condition is not possible in combinational circuits. In combinational circuits, on the same input $S = R = 0$ the output at Q will be either always 0 or always 1!

To summarize, from Table 7.2.1(b), during normal mode, the inputs S and R assume a value of 0. To store a 1 in the latch, we temporarily change the inputs from the normal mode values by setting S to 1 and resetting it back to the normal mode of 0. Similarly, to store a 0 we repeat the two steps with input R temporarily set to 1 instead.

7.2.2 Characteristic Equations

The characteristic equations of a sequential circuit are similar to Boolean functions in combinational circuits. The characteristic equations, however, are a function not only of external inputs but of current states as well. The characteristic equation for an SR latch can be derived from the characteristic table in a similar fashion to deriving Boolean functions from truth tables. For example, the canonical sum representation of the SR next state equation is determined from the table to be

$$Q+ = m_1 + m_4 + m_5$$
$$= S'R'Q + SR'Q' + SR'Q$$

The above equation gives the next, $Q+$, state value in terms of the current state, Q, and the current inputs, S and R. The characteristic equation can be treated as a Boolean function that can be minimized using standard procedures such as K-maps or the tabular method, for example. Using K-maps, the equation can be minimized to

$$Q+ = S + R'Q$$

In the minimization, the entries corresponding to $S = R = 1$ are treated as "don't-care" conditions. Note that given the characteristic equation above, one can construct the characteristic table in a straightforward fashion by assigning all possible values to the inputs and current states and, accordingly, determining the next state value. For example, for $S = 1$, $R = 0$ and $Q = 0$, we obtain

$$Q+ = S + R'Q$$
$$= 1 + 1.0 = 1$$

This corresponds to the fifth entry in Table 7.2.1.

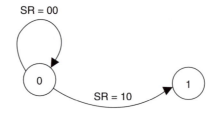

FIGURE 7.2.1
Partial State Diagram of an SR Latch

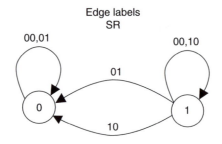

FIGURE 7.2.2
State Diagram of an SR Latch

7.2.3 State Diagrams

We will discuss state diagram construction in the context of sequential circuit analysis later in this chapter. For the SR latch and other latches, the state diagram is composed of labeled nodes (circles). The label indicates the current/next output of the latch Q. The nodes are connected with labeled directed edges. The edges are labeled as well. Each edge is labeled with one of the latch input combinations. We illustrate the construction of the diagram by considering Figure 7.2.1. In the figure, the node labels are 0 and 1, corresponding to the output of the latch. The edge labeled 10 corresponds to an input of $SR = 10$ with the current output 0 (the current output is the label of the node where the edge starts). As can be seen from the figure, the edge destination is the node with label 1, indicating the next output is 1. Similarly, the node with label 0 and input 00 corresponds to the current Q value of 0 and the current SR input of 00. On this input, the next output is 0 $(Q+ = Q)$. As a result, the edge in the diagram starts at node 0 and loops back to 0.

When we apply the above to all possible inputs of an SR latch, the state diagram will have two nodes (labels 0 and 1). From each node we process three edges starting at each node. The labels of the edges are $SR = 00, 01,$ and 10. Note that no edge with label 11 is processed since this input is not permitted on an SR latch. Figure 7.2.2 shows the complete state diagram.

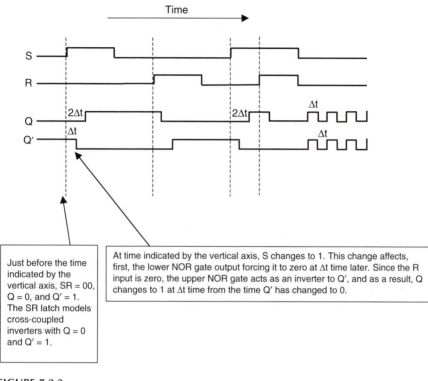

FIGURE 7.2.3
An Example Block Diagram

7.2.4 Timing Diagrams

We have used characteristic tables, characteristic equations, and state diagrams to describe the behavior of the SR latch. The behavior of the latch can be described using timing diagrams as well. In these diagrams, the horizontal axis represents time. The vertical axis contains the timing waveforms of inputs and outputs. We illustrate the timing diagram for an SR latch with NOR gates of equal delays. Figure 7.2.3 shows an example timing diagram. In the diagram, the inputs S and R assume one of two possible values, 0 or 1, as indicated by the top two waveforms. The low part of the form indicates an assignment of 0. Similarly, the high part of the waveform indicates an assignment of 1. In the diagram, each of the NOR gates has a generic propagation delay Δt, as shown. The delay Δt is measured from the time a change in the input occurs until the time the corresponding gate responds at its output. The illustration of the timing diagram is captured in the text boxes of the figure. Note the oscillation as a result of the application of the sequence $SR = 11$ followed by $SR = 00$.

We will revisit the above diagram in the discussion related to delays toward the end of this chapter. Until then, we adopt a simpler timing diagram

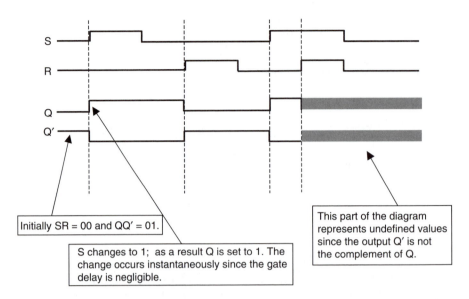

FIGURE 7.2.4
Timing Diagram of an SR Latch with the Delay Δt Approaches Zero

that assumes the delay Δt approaches 0. With this assumption, the response to the inputs by the designated gates is assumed to be instantaneous. The modified timing diagram is given in Figure 7.2.4. The description of the diagram is captured in the text boxes as well.

7.3   Other Primitive Latches

We consider three additional types of latches (later we present a modification of the latches design and call them flip-flops). Latches have two outputs, which are called Q and its complement Q'. The number of inputs to the latches varies from one to two inputs. The SR latch considered had two inputs, S (set) and R (reset). The additional latches considered are (1) the D (Delay) latch, (2) the JK latch, and (3) the T (toggle) latch. The number of inputs to each of the D and T latches is one; the number of inputs to the JK latch is two. The labels to the inputs follow the names of each latch; for example, the inputs to the JK latch are labeled J and K. Figure 7.3.1 is a block diagram (also called logic symbol) of each of the latches.

We first discuss the behavior of the three latches using the three forms: (1) characteristic tables, (2) characteristic equations, and (3) state diagrams. We then follow the discussion by analysis of the design of each.

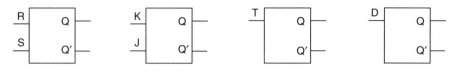

FIGURE 7.3.1
Block Diagram (Also Called Logic Symbol) of Each of the Latches

TABLE 7.3.1

Characteristic Tables of SR
and JK Latches

S R Q	Q+	J K Q	Q+
0 0 0	0	0 0 0	0
0 0 1	1	0 0 1	1
0 1 0	0	0 1 0	0
0 1 1	0	0 1 1	0
1 0 0	1	1 0 0	1
1 0 1	1	1 0 1	1
1 1 0	?	1 1 0	1
1 1 1	?	1 1 1	0

TABLE 7.3.2

Characteristic Tables
of T and D Latches

(a)		(b)	
T Q	Q+	D Q	Q+
0 0	0	0 0	0
0 1	1	0 1	0
1 0	1	1 0	1
1 1	0	1 1	1

7.3.1 Characteristic Tables of the Three Latches

In the previous section and the analysis of the SR latch, we found that the SR latch does not function properly on the input $S = R = 1$ ($Q+$ and $Q'+$ are equal, which contradicts the condition that the outputs of the latch are the complements of each other). The JK latch is obtained from an SR latch, with J playing the role of S and R playing the role of K. For the JK latch, an input of $J = K = 1$ is allowed. The characteristic tables for both SR and JK are shown in Table 7.3.1. Note the similarity of both latches for the inputs 000 through 101. For the last two rows, on the input $J = K = 1$, the next state $Q+$ is the complement of the current state Q.

The characteristic tables for the T and D latches are given in Table 7.3.2(a) and (b), respectively. By inspecting the table entries, we note the following.

- For the T latch: An input of 0 leaves the contents of the latch unchanged ($Q+ = Q$); an input of 1, however, causes the next state to be the complement of the current state.
- For the D latch: The next state ($Q+$) is equal to the input at D.

7.3.2 The Characteristic Equations

The characteristic equation of the three latches can be derived from their characteristic tables using algebraic simplification or the K-map method, for example. For the JK latch, the characteristic equation is found to be

$$Q+ = m_1 + m_4 + m_5 + m_6$$

$$= JQ' + K'Q$$

For the D latch, we obtain

$$Q+ = D$$

And, for the T latch, we obtain

$$Q+ = T \oplus Q$$

7.3.3 The State Diagrams

The state diagrams for the three latches JK, D, and T are shown in Figure 7.3.2.

7.4 The Latches Gate Design

The gate design for each of the four latches can be derived from the design of the SR latch.

7.4.1 D Latch Design

From the characteristic table for the D latch, we see that the output $Q+$ is the same as the input D. The circuit shown in Figure 7.4.1 uses an SR latch to implement a D latch. The D input is used as an input into the S part of the SR latch. Its complement is used as input into the R input of the SR latch.

For this circuit, an input of $D = 1$ produces an $S = 1$ and an $R = 0$. This input combination on the SR latch causes $Q+$ to be set to 1, irrespective of

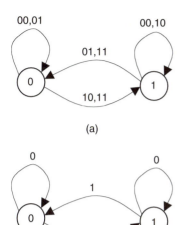

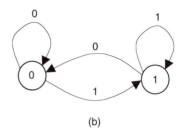

(a)

(b)

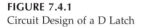

(c)

FIGURE 7.3.2
State Diagrams for the Three Latches JK, D, and T Are, Respectively, Shown in Parts (a), (b) and (c)

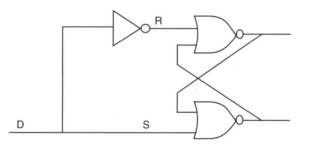

FIGURE 7.4.1
Circuit Design of a D Latch

the previous value of Q. Similarly, an input of $D = 0$ results in the assignment $S = 0$ and $R = 1$, which in turn causes $Q+ = 0$, irrespective of the previous value Q. The design is a D latch since the table generated from the design is that of a D latch. In block diagram, the design of a D latch from an SR latch is shown in Figure 7.4.2.

7.4.2 The JK Latch

The characteristic tables for the JK and SR latches are similar except for the last two rows, as seen in Table 7.3.1. For these two inputs, SR = 11 is not allowed for the SR latch, and for the JK latch the output $Q+$ is equal to Q'.

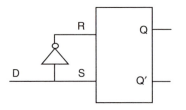

FIGURE 7.4.2
Block Diagram Design of a Δ Latch from an SR Latch.

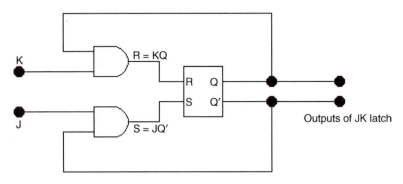

FIGURE 7.4.3
Design of a JK Latch from an SR Latch

The design of the JK latch makes use of this fact, as shown in Figure 7.4.3. As shown in the figure the design uses an SR latch in its block diagram form.

In verifying the circuit above is that of a JK latch, we make use of the characteristic table of the SR latch. We assign binary values to the J and K inputs and propagate the inputs through the AND gates. The outputs of the AND gates constitute the S and R inputs, which in turn determine the next output $Q+$. To determine $Q+$, we refer to the SR latch table. The verification in tabular form is given in Table 7.4.1. In the table, the $Q+$ output corresponds to the output of the SR latch, which is also the JK latch output, as shown in the figure. We consider the last row of the table for illustration. For this row, the external inputs J and K are set to 1. In addition, the current output Q is set to 1. For these conditions, the corresponding inputs to the SR latch are

$$S = JQ' = 0$$

and

$$R = KQ = 1$$

Since the inputs to the SR latch are SR = 01, the output of the latch is $Q+$ = 0 (this follows from the characteristic table of the SR latch). Since this output

TABLE 7.4.1

Table Used in Determining Next Outputs
of Figure 7.4.3

Inputs	Resulting S and R values			Output
J K Q	S = JQ′	R = KQ	Q	Q+
0 0 0	0	0	0	0
0 0 1	0	0	1	1
0 1 0	0	0	0	0
0 1 1	0	1	1	0
1 0 0	1	0	0	1
1 0 1	0	0	1	1
1 1 0	1	0	0	1
1 1 1	0	1	1	0

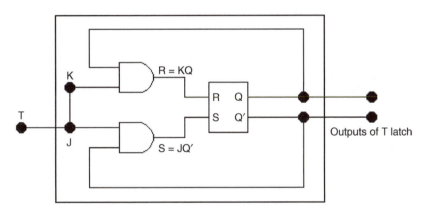

FIGURE 7.4.4
Circuit Design of a T Latch from a JK Latch

is that of JK, we have $Q+$ for the equivalent JK latch is 0. Other rows in the
table are interpreted in a similar fashion. The procedure in determining $Q+$
of a JK latch is an analysis procedure. We will formalize the procedure in
the analysis part of sequential circuits later in the chapter.

7.4.3 The T Latch

The T latch is obtained from the JK latch by connecting the input T to both
of the *J* and *K* inputs, as shown in Figure 7.4.4. An input $T = 0$ will result in
both inputs *J* and *K* assuming a value of 0, and hence the output $Q+$ assumes
the same value of the previous output Q ($Q+ = Q$). An input of $T = 1$, however,
results in $JK = 11$ and, as a result, $Q+ = Q'$. In block diagram, the design of
a T latch from a JK latch is shown in Figure 7.4.5.

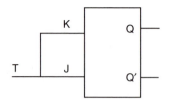

FIGURE 7.4.5
Block Diagram of a JK Latch with T Latch Design

7.5   Gated Latches

In the design of the latches shown earlier, the outputs to the latches could change any time the inputs change, after accounting for delays through the gates. When inputs to a latch directly affect the outputs, the outputs are called transparent. In many cases, we would like the latch to respond to inputs during specific intervals of time. During these intervals, the inputs are sampled by the latch in order to possibly change the output. This is done so as to synchronize the changes in a sequential circuit with many memory elements.

One method to cause changes during specific instances of time is through an additional input to create a gated latch or level sensitive latch. Figure 7.5.1 shows a gated SR latch. The additional input labeled C is used as follows: If $C = 0$, then changes in the input on S and R do not affect the outputs; if $C = 1$, however, the latch becomes transparent where changes in the input affect the output. In effect, C can be thought of as the enable input to the latch.

In the normal mode (when no changes to the outputs are desired), the control input C is set to 0.

The characteristic table for the gated SR latch above is given in Table 7.5.1. In the table, when $C = 0$ then the values on S and R do not play a role in determining the output and are effectively blocked from changing Q. In the table they are represented by "x" as don't-care conditions. The remaining three gated latches can be constructed in a similar fashion, as shown in Figure 7.5.2. The block diagram (logic symbol) representation of the gated latches is given in Figure 7.5.3.

TABLE 7.5.1

Characteristic Table of a Gated SR Latch

C S R	Q+
0 x x	Q
1 0 0	Q
1 0 1	0
1 1 0	1
1 1 1	?

In general, the gated input, C, to the latch is called a clock. A clock is a periodic square signal that changes between the logical values of 0 and 1 as a function of time. In periodic signals, one associates

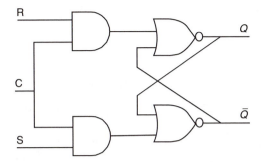

FIGURE 7.5.1
Circuit Design of a Gated SR Latch

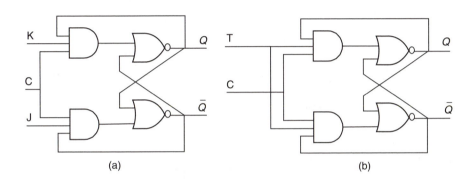

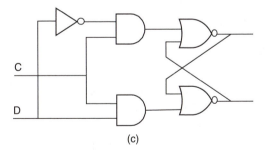

FIGURE 7.5.2
Gated Latches, (a) JK, (b) T, (c) D

the following. The period of the clock, T, is time of one cycle of the clock. The frequency, f, is the number of clock cycles per second with $f = 1/T$. The units of T is time, the units of f is Hertz (Hz) with 1 Hz = 1 cycle per second. Figure 7.5.4 shows the schematic of a clock.

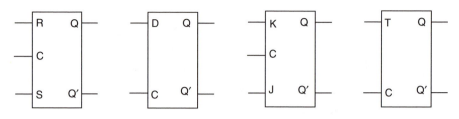

FIGURE 7.5.3
Block Diagram (Logic Symbol) Representation of the Gated Latches

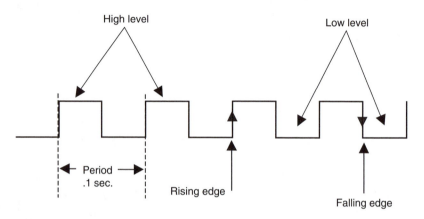

FIGURE 7.5.4
A Schematic of a Clock

In digital design, we make use of the following:

- Rising edge of the clock is the edge where the clock changes value from 0 to 1
- Falling edge of the clock is the edge where the clock changes value from 1 to 0
- High level is the period of time the clock assumes a value of 1
- Low level of the clock is the period where the clock assumes a value of 0
- Duty cycle is the percentage of clock cycle time the clock assumes a value of 1

Figure 7.5.4 shows a schematic with these terms identified in the diagram. From the figure, the period of the clock is 1/10 second and the frequency is 10 Hz. The duty cycle is 50%. A schematic of the timing diagram of a gated SR latch is shown in Figure 7.5.5.

In Figure 7.5.5, the clock controls the time interval the latch could respond to changes in the input. During the low level parts of the clock, changes in the inputs do no affect changes in the outputs. During the high level part of

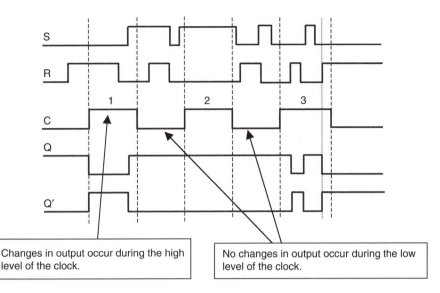

FIGURE 7.5.5
A Schematic of the Timing Diagram of a Gated SR Latch

the clock, input changes affect outputs. For the high level labeled 1 in the diagram, the output changes two times. During the high level labeled 2 no changes take place since the inputs keep the outputs the same. Finally, during the high level labeled 3 the outputs change three times.

7.6   Flip-Flops

7.6.1   Asynchronous and Synchronous Circuits

The previous discussion of gated latches imposes restrictions on when the outputs can respond to inputs. As a result, many of the memory elements in a sequential circuit can be activated during the same time intervals as dictated by a master clock of the circuit. When the latch inputs are allowed to affect outputs during specific instants of time, we say it is a synchronous latch. The latches in the system are synchronized by the master clock. Non-gated latches are called asynchronous latches since the outputs of the latch are transparent (any changes in the inputs could cause changes in the outputs). The synchronous gated latches discussed are level-sensitive latches as the changes in the output can occur during the high level of the clock (see Figure 7.5.5).

In synchronous circuits, it is desirable that, at most, one change in the output of a latch occurs during a clock cycle. The clock is used to cause the selected latches to make one change during the corresponding cycle. One

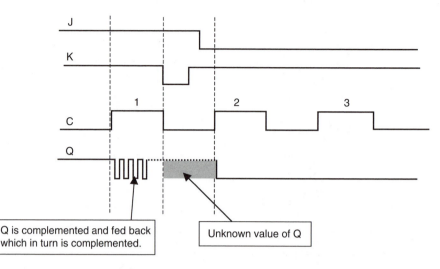

Q is complemented and fed back which in turn is complemented.

Unknown value of Q

FIGURE 7.6.1
A Timing Diagram Showing Many Changes in JK During 1 Clock Cycle

method to achieve this for the SR latch is to keep its inputs unchanged during the time the clock assumes a value of 1. This is the case for Figure 7.5.5 and for the cycle with label 2. It is not the case for the cycles with labels 1 and 3, however. For the level-sensitive latches with changes occurring during the high level of the clock, many changes are possible during the high level with the final change in state (output) occurring near the falling edge of the clock.

The property of causing no more than one change to occur during a clock cycle can be satisfied for the SR and D latches. This is done by keeping the inputs unchanged (allow one change) during the high level of the clock, as discussed. The property fails, however, when gated JK or T latches are used. To illustrate, consider Figure 7.6.1.

From the design of the JK latch discussed earlier, the outputs Q and Q' are fed back as inputs to the JK latch design (refer to JK latch design). Assume the time delay from inputs to the outputs (at Q) is Δt time units. On the input $J = K = 1$ (in the figure this occurs during the high level of clock cycle 1), the following takes place. It takes Δt time for the output at Q to change (to be complemented). Since the clock is still at 1 and since J and K assume a value of 1, the new value of Q is fed back and processed through the JK latch. At Δt time later, the Q value at the output is complemented again. This pattern continues as long as the input conditions do not change and the clock input is 1. This pattern of oscillation occurs during the first cycle of the clock. Its period is $2\Delta t$.

One method to solve the above problem is to use two latches to break the feedback that causes the oscillation. The combination of the two latches used in the design is called master–slave flip-flop. We will discuss master-slave flip-flops next.

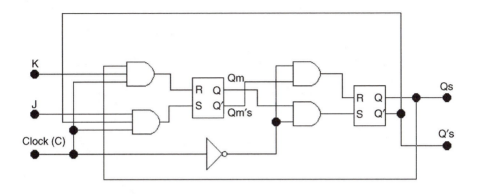

FIGURE 7.6.2
A Circuit Design of a Master–Slave Flip-Flop

7.6.2 Master–Slave Flip-Flops

The design of a master–slave flip-flop is composed of two latches. The outputs of the first latch (called the master) are connected to the inputs of the second latch (called the slave). The slave latch acts a D latch. Its function is to pass the master output when activated by the clock. To break the feedback loop from outputs to inputs, only one of the latches is activated at any instant of time. We illustrate the design of a JK master–slave flip-flop, as shown in Figure 7.6.2.

In Figure 7.6.2, the first SR latch acts as the master latch. The second latch acts as the slave. As seen from the figure, the slave latch acts as a D latch (its inputs are Qm and its complement Qm' as shown in the figure). Both are gated latches, with the slave latch activated during the low level of the clock and the master latch activated during the high level of the clock. Inputs are applied to the master latch and outputs are measured at the slave latch. The outputs of the master and inputs of the slave are internal to the design. One of the two latches is on at any time. In the figure, when clock = 1, the master is on and the slave is off. Similarly, when clock = 0, the master is off and the slave is on. We will discuss the function of the above circuit in the context of the timing diagram shown in Figure 7.6.3.

The diagram is an extension of Figure 7.6.2 with the new outputs for the master latch, Qm, and the slave latch, Qs, shown. The observed output is the output of the slave latch Qs. As can be seen from the figure, the correct output of the slave latch is made available at (or shortly after) the falling edge of the clock. The oscillation problem is removed since at any instant of time only one of the latches is on (for details, please refer to the text boxes of the figure). The master–slave latch is pulse-triggered, since on the first transition of the clock (the leading edge) the master latch is turned on. On the second transition of the clock (the falling edge), the slave is turned on.

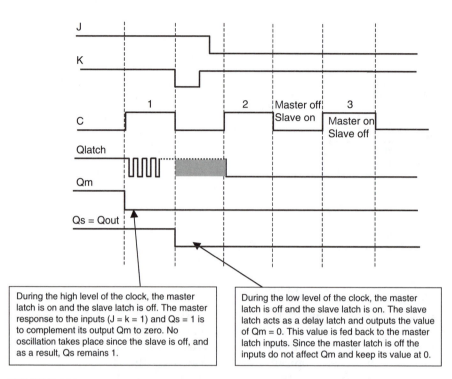

During the high level of the clock, the master latch is on and the slave latch is off. The master response to the inputs (J = k = 1) and Qs = 1 is to complement its output Qm to zero. No oscillation takes place since the slave is off, and as a result, Qs remains 1.

During the low level of the clock, the master latch is off and the slave latch is on. The slave latch acts as a delay latch and outputs the value of Qm = 0. This value is fed back to the master latch inputs. Since the master latch is off the inputs do not affect Qm and keep its value at 0.

FIGURE 7.6.3
Timing Diagram of a Master-Slave Flip-Flop

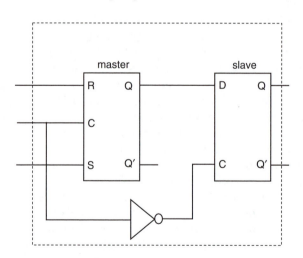

FIGURE 7.6.4
Design of a Master Slave SR Latch in Block Diagram

Similar to the design of a JK master–slave flip-flop, an SR, a D, and a T master–slave flip-flop design requires the use of two latches. The design of a master–slave SR latch in block diagram is shown in Figure 7.6.4 When forming timing diagrams of a master–slave flip-flop, we consider changes in the diagram at or shortly after the falling edge of the clock. No changes in the output take place until the next falling edge of the clock, i.e., the timing diagram remains the same over a clock cycle with the exception of a short interval that starts with the falling edge of the clock.

7.7 Glitches and Ones-Catching

The construction of master–slave flip-flops solved the problem of oscillation discussed earlier. The design, however, is incomplete due to a property called ones-catching. We discuss ones-catching by discussing glitches.

A glitch is a pulse that is not part of the correct function of the circuit and is caused by the design. A circuit is said to have a hazard if its design may result in glitches. Glitches are side effects of physical designs that are not part the logical behavior (truth table description) of a Boolean function. We illustrate glitches by considering an arbitrary function

$$f = f_1 + f_2$$

The function is a logical OR of two Boolean functions f_1 and f_2. In terms of design, the outputs of the circuits that realize the functions f_1 and f_2 can be used as inputs to a single OR gate to realize the function f. This is shown in Figure 7.7.1. Assume the circuits of f_1 and f_2 have propagation delays d_1 and d_2 with $d_1 < d_2$. An input assignment that causes f_1 to change from 1 to 0, and f_2 to change from 0 to 1 should keep the value of f unchanged. However, since f_1 changes to 0 faster than f_2 changes to 1, the inputs to the OR gates assume a value of 0 for a short duration of time and, as a result, the output is incorrectly set to 0 during this period of time.

Figure 7.7.2 shows a timing diagram that illustrates this. In the figure, the common input to both circuits occurs at time t. The difference in propagation delays is shown in the figure as well. Note the temporary wrong output of 0; the circuit is said to have static-zero hazard (a temporary unwanted glitch of 0 occurs). A circuit is said to have static-one hazard when a temporary

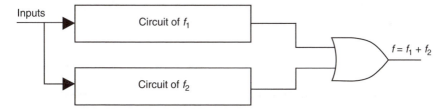

FIGURE 7.7.1
Circuits for f_1 and f_2 Have Different Delays d_1 and d_2 with $d_1 < d_2$

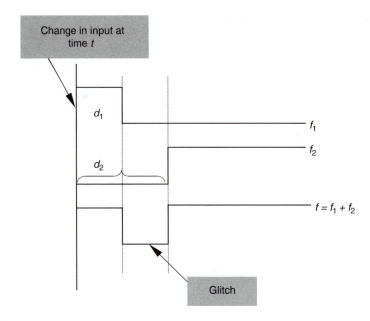

FIGURE 7.7.2
A Timing Schematic of a Glitch

unwanted glitch of 1 occurs due to change in the input assignment. The complement of the function f, f' with the above restrictions produces a static-one hazard.

Glitches may cause problems when using JK master–slave flip-flops. Assume the output of f' is used as the J input of a master–slave flip-flop; we use timing diagrams to show the effect of the above-described glitch. The timing diagram is given in Figure 7.7.3.

In the figure, the short pulses on the J signal represent glitches caused by the hardware, i.e., the actual input should be $J = 0$ and $K = 0$. The output should not change and remain at 0, as shown in the figure. Due to the glitches, however, the output incorrectly stores a value of 1. From the diagram, the first glitch occurs during the high level of the clock where the master is turned on. During this time, the master reads a 1 on J and a 0 on K. As a result, its output is set to 1. Following the glitch, this value is not changed since both J and K assume a value of 0. Shortly after the falling edge of the clock, this value is moved to the slave, i.e., $Qs = 1$! Note that the second glitch does not affect the circuit since it occurs while the master latch is off.

7.8   Edge-Triggered Flip-Flops

The above property is not present in edge-triggered flip-flops. In edge-triggered flip-flops the changes in output occur during the falling (or the

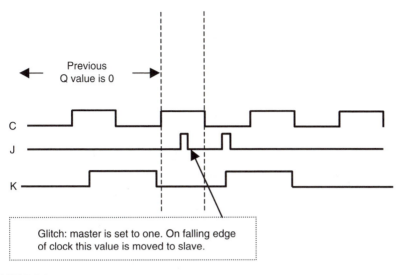

FIGURE 7.7.3
Timing Diagram Showing Ones Catching Property

rising) edge of the clock. In the design, there is no master latch that is turned on for half of a clock cycle. The diagram in Figure 7.8.1 is used to describe edge-triggered flip-flops. We will consider the concept of asynchronous preset first.

7.8.1 Asynchronous Preset

The diagram is composed of three SR latches. The output of the edge-triggered flip-flop is that of latch 3, as shown. The input line with label preset is used to force the output of the flip-flop to the value of 1 (output of gate 5) independent of the clock and other input values. To illustrate, on the input of preset = 1, the outputs of the NOR gates with preset as one of the inputs are forced to 0. Hence, the inputs to latch 3 from latch 1 and latch 2 assume a value of 0 (outputs of gates 2 and 3 are forced to 0). In addition, the lower NOR gate (6) of latch 3 is forced to 0 since preset is used as an input to this NOR gate as well. The inputs and outputs to latch 3 are shown in Figure 7.8.2.

The values in the figure are obtained independent of the values on other lines of the circuit. From the diagram, the output at Q assumes a value of 1 since the inputs to the upper NOR gate are both 0. As a result, the output of the circuit is set asynchronously to 1. The first row in Table 7.8.1 corresponds to the above discussion. In the table, an x entry means the value of the variable does not play a role in determining the output, i.e., x can be set to either 0 or 1.

During the normal operation of the circuit, the preset input is assigned the value of 0. With the preset input assigned a value of 0, the function of the NOR gates depends on the remaining inputs only since $(x + y + 0)' = x'y'$.

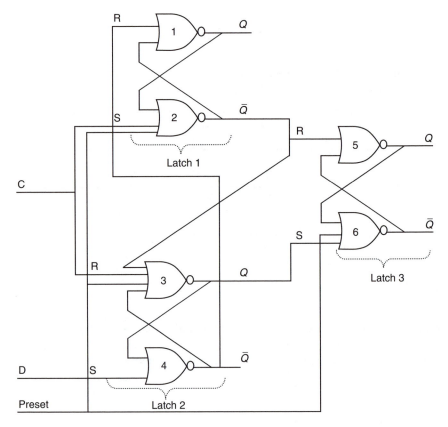

FIGURE 7.8.1
Schematic of an Edge-Triggered D Flip-Flop

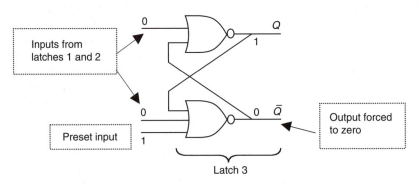

FIGURE 7.8.2
Input Assignment to Latch 3 from Figure 7.8.1 on Asynchronous Preset

As a result, for the remaining part of the analysis, we ignore the preset input since its value is set to 0. We will discuss asynchronous preset, however, later in this chapter and in the next chapter.

TABLE 7.8.1

Early Triggered Flip-
Flop of Figure 7.8.1

Preset	D	C	Q+
1	x	x	1
0	x	1	Q
0	0	↓	0
0	1	↓	1
0	x	0	Q
0	x	↑	Q

↓ represents falling edge;
↑ represents rising edge.

We analyze the circuit while the clock input assumes a value of 1, a value of 0, and on transitions from 1 to 0 or 0 to 1.

7.8.2   Clock Value Equal to 1

When the clock input C is equal to 1, the inputs to latch 3 are forced to 0 as discussed above for the case of the preset input. Since latch 3 is an SR latch, $SR = 00$ leaves the contents of the latch unchanged. This is shown in row 2 of the table. In addition, the lower NOR gate of latch 2 (gate 4 in Figure 7.8.1) is set to the complement of the input D, D' (recall since one of the inputs to the lower gate is 0, the gate complements the other input). By tracing this output, we note that it is used as an input to the top NOR gate (gate 1) of latch 1. The other input to the gate assumes a value of 0. As a result, the output of the top NOR gate is D.

7.8.3   Clock Makes a Transition from 1 to 0

With the above conditions, as the clock makes a transition from 1 to 0, the lower NOR gate (gate 2) in latch 1 behaves as an inverter of the top NOR gate. Hence, its output is D'. Thus the inputs to the upper NOR gate of latch 2 (gate 3) are D', D', and 0, which makes the output of this NOR gate equal to D. These values are used as inputs to latch 3, which results in $Q+ = D$. In rows 3 and 4 of Table 7.8.1, i.e., on the falling edge of the clock, the input value D is stored in the flip-flop. The symbol ↓ represents the falling edge of the clock.

7.8.4   Clock Value Is 0

When the clock value is 0, the above condition stated during the falling edge of the clock remains, i.e., the outputs of the NOR gates for latch 1 and latch 2 from top to bottom remain D, D', D, and D', respectively. If during this phase the input D changes, then the new value D is different from the old

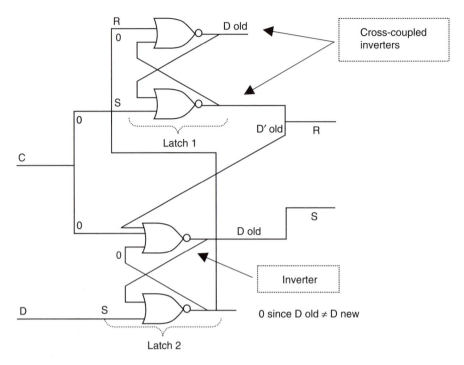

FIGURE 7.8.3
Schematic of Latch 1 and Latch 2 of Figure 7.8.1 with Clock, C = 0 and with D Changing

value D. Since the lower NOR gate of latch 2 receives both the old and new value of D, its output is forced to 0. This in turn forces one of the inputs of the top NOR gate of latch 1 to 0. Since $c = 0$, two of the inputs to the lower gate of latch 1(gate 2) assume a value of 0 ($c = 0$ and preset = 0). As a result, the top latch behaves as a cross-coupled inverter that stores the old values of D and its complement, D'. Similarly, the top NOR gate of latch 2 acts as an inverter that outputs D. Figure 7.8.3 shows a schematic of the discussion.

The effect of changing the D value while the clock assumes a value of 0 is summarized in Figure 7.8.4. The NOR gates were replaced with inverters based on the input conditions. As can be seen from the figure, the old values of D remain on the inputs of latch 3 and, as a result, changes in D while the clock assumes a value of 0 do not affect the outputs of the edge-triggered flip-flop. Row 5 in Table 7.8.1 reflects this discussion.

7.8.5 Clock Makes Transition from 0 to 1

As the clock makes a transition from 0 to 1, the lower NOR gate of latch 1 and the upper NOR gate of latch 2 (gates 2 and 3) are forced to 0 and, as a result, the contents of the flip-flop remain unchanged. This is reflected in the sixth row of Table 7.8.1.

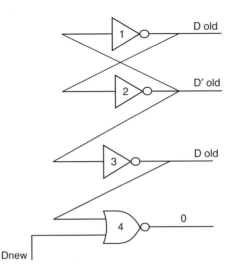

FIGURE 7.8.4
Figure 7.8.3 Redrawn with the NOR Gates Replaced by Invertors

From this discussion, over an entire clock cycle, the flip-flop changes states during the falling edge of the clock only, i.e., the inputs to the flip-flop are sampled at the falling (negative) edge of the clock to determine their effect on the outputs.

7.9 Block Diagrams and Timing Constraints

In this section, we present the block diagrams (or logic symbols) of the latches and flip-flops discussed earlier. In addition, we discuss timing constraints on the inputs imposed by actual designs. First, we summarize the results obtained.

In the discussion of latches and flip-flops, we considered when the outputs sample the inputs as an important factor. In asynchronous latches, the outputs continually sample the inputs and can change whenever the inputs change. Gated latches are subject to change during specific time intervals (for example, the high level of a clock). During this interval, the latch outputs continually sample the inputs and change accordingly.

Both types of latches cause oscillation. To remove oscillation, we used master–slave flip-flops in which the master samples the inputs during the high (or low level) of the clock. The output, however, is seen at the falling edge (or rising edge) of the clock. The design of a master–slave flip-flop removed the problem of oscillation but the design included a ones-catching property. To remove the ones-catching property, we use edge-triggered flip-flops in which the outputs sample inputs during the falling (or rising) edge of the clock only.

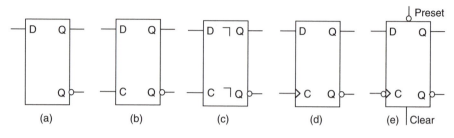

FIGURE 7.9.1
Logic Symbols of Latches with Different Input/Output Notation

We use different logic symbols to distinguish between the different types of latches and flip-flops, as shown in Figure 7.9.1. In Figure 7.9.1(a), we see the logic symbol of a D latch. We introduce a small bubble to represent the complement of Q. The bubble interpretation depends on its use with the associated signal as follows in the discussion. Figure 7.9.1(b) shows the logic symbol of a gated D latch. The enable input to the latch is shown as C. Figure 7.9.1(c) shows the logic symbol of a master–slave flip-flop. Note the use of the pulse symbol by the outputs; the symbol indicates the slave outputs are present on the falling edge of the clock. To represent a master–slave latch with outputs changing on the rising edge of the clock, we replace the above symbol with a ⌐.

Figure 7.9.1(d) and (e) represent the logic symbols for edge-triggered D flip-flop. In both cases, we use the triangular shape by the clock input to indicate the flip-flop is an edge-triggered flip-flop. The absence of a bubble indicates the flip-flop is sampled at the rising (positive) edge of the clock. A bubble in front of the clock indicates that the flip-flop is sampled on the falling (negative) edge of the clock.

In Figure 7.9.1(e), the additional inputs with labels "preset" and "clear" represent asynchronous preset and clear inputs. For the preset input, the presence of a bubble indicates that in order to preset the latch output to a value of 1, this input should be assigned a value of 0. For the clear input, in order to asynchronously clear the input to 0, the input is assigned a value of 1. Finally, in order for the flip-flop in Figure 7.9.1(e) to function in normal mode (as intended), the preset and clear inputs should have no effect (preset is assigned a value of 1 and clear is assigned a value of 0).

The above diagram can be used to construct the logic symbols of the remaining latches and flip-flops. For each latch or flip-flop, we replace the D input with the proper latch or flip-flop inputs.

7.9.1 Timing Constraints

From an actual design point of view, the responses of latches to input signals must conform to the following constraints:

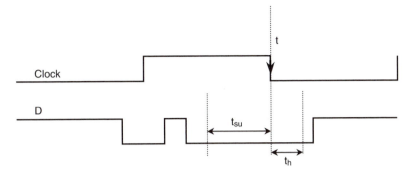

FIGURE 7.9.2
Sample Timing Diagram with the Timing Constraints

1. Setup time, t_{su}, is the minimum time window the input signal should remain unchanged before it is sampled.
2. Hold time, t_h, is the minimum time window where the input should not change after it is sampled.

The two times ensure that the input does affect the outputs as intended. The times are a result of the propagation delays and feedback loops found in the design of the latches and the flip-flops.

We use Figure 7.9.2 to show a sample timing diagram with the timing constraints included. In the figure, we assume the changes in the memory elements (flip-flops) occur at the falling edge of the clock. As a result, the times given are relative to the falling edge event.

From the figure, assuming the falling edge occurs at time t, the D input remains unchanged in the time window $t - t_{su}$ to $t + t_h$. Since the input satisfies the setup and hold times indicated, the edge-triggered flip-flop responds to the input correctly by storing 0 as the next output of the flip-flop. In general, this output is produced after some time delay, as was discussed earlier.

With this discussion of the primitive memory elements of a sequential circuit, we will next discuss the analysis aspects of sequential circuits; by "analysis," we mean determining the input output relation of the circuit.

7.10 Analysis of Sequential Circuits

Consider the circuit shown in Figure 7.10.1. What does this circuit do? This question is similar to questions asked with regard to the analysis part of combinational circuits, where the schematic of the circuit is given and the functionality of the circuit is to be determined. In combinational circuits, the

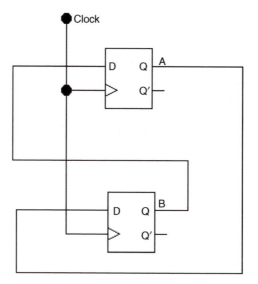

FIGURE 7.10.1
An Example of a Sequential Circuit

primitive building blocks used were logic gates. In sequential circuits, the primitive blocks used in the circuit include the logic gates and the flip-flops (or latches) we discussed earlier.

For combinational circuits, the analysis part may involve the creation of a truth table by applying inputs to the circuit and propagating the inputs through the gates to determine the outputs. The analysis part of sequential circuits may use a similar table, the characteristic or state table. An additional analogy to the analysis of combinational circuits, sequential circuits analysis may involve the computation of the external output equations as well as the next output equations of its memory elements.

In the following discussion, we present some of the common forms of analyzing sequential circuits:

- Characteristic or state table
- Characteristic equations
- State diagrams
- Timing diagram

Before we discuss the different representations, we first discuss the functionality of the above circuit.

The circuit is composed of two D edge-triggered flip-flops. The input to each flip-flop is the output of the other flip-flop in the circuit. We will assume the flip-flops are master–slave flip-flops, with the master latch turned on during the low level of the clock and the slave turned on during the high level of the clock.

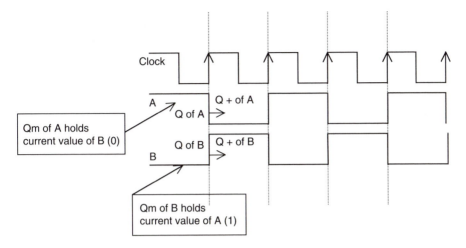

FIGURE 7.10.2
Timing Diagram of Circuit Given in Figure 7.10.1

For the circuit, the same clock signal is used as clock input to the two flip-flops. As a result, when one of the master latches is turned on, the other master latch is turned on as well, and both slave latches are turned off. Hence, during the low level of the clock the master latches store the current latch outputs. When the clock makes a transition from 0 to 1, both slave latches are turned on and both master latches are turned off. In this transition, the stored values in the master latches are moved to the outputs.

The timing diagram in Figure 7.10.2 is used as an illustration. Note on the first clock transition the current state of each flip-flop is seen on the left of the positive transition. The next state is seen on the right of the clock transition. From the timing diagram, we note that the above circuit continually swaps the inputs of the two latches on each positive clock transition. It is important to note that the master latch processes the current outputs of slave latch, Q, and not the next latch output, $Q+$.

We next formalize the analysis procedure for arbitrary circuits. First, we present a block diagram model of sequential circuits.

7.10.1   Sequential Circuits Block Diagram Model

We model sequential circuits as shown in the block diagram shown in Figure 7.10.3. Other alternative models exist by rearranging the sequential and combinational blocks. In the model, the combinational circuit block is used to realize the external outputs to the circuit and the next state equations (these are labeled excitation equations in the diagram). The inputs to the combinational circuit are the external inputs and the current memory element values as seen. The memory element block is composed of flip-flops. The circuit is called a synchronous sequential circuit since the memory elements sample their inputs by a clock signal.

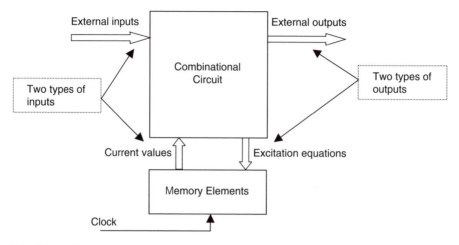

FIGURE 7.10.3
Model of a Sequential Circuit in Block Diagram

In this model, the effect of previous inputs to the circuit is captured in the memory elements' values. Based on these values and the current external inputs, the circuit will produce a specific output and cause the circuit to assume a new memory configuration. We will look at the details of the model in the remainder of this chapter and in the next chapter.

7.10.2   Characteristic Equations

The characteristic equations of the circuit are used to describe its behavior in algebraic form. By referencing the circuit in Figure 7.10.3, the equations should include external output equations as well as equations that cause transitions in the memory blocks (the excitation equations). The equations are based on two types of variables entering the combinational block: the external input variables and the current outputs (stored values) of the memory elements (flip-flops) in the circuit. With each memory element of the circuit, we associate a characteristic equation. Similarly, we associate a Boolean equation with each external output.

In forming the characteristic equations of a sequential circuit, the following steps are carried:

1. All outputs of the memory elements in the circuit are assigned variable names. This is done to distinguish between the different memory elements found in the circuit, since these elements are usually given at the outputs of flip-flops and, as a result, they have the same label (Q or Q').

2. According to the variable names assigned to the outputs of the flip-flops, the corresponding input labels are assigned the same name of the input but with a subscript used to identify the output it will affect.

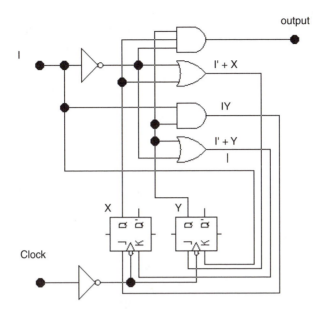

FIGURE 7.10.4
An Example Sequential Circuit Used in Analysis

For example, if the flip-flop used in the design is a JK flip-flop and the output is assigned the label X, then the J input of the flip-flop will be assigned the label J_x and its K input is assigned the label K_x.

3. The inputs to each flip-flop are, in general, functions that involve both external inputs and current outputs of memory elements in the circuit. For each flip-flop input, the Boolean function associated with the input is derived. The equations derived are called excitation equations.

4. The characteristic equation of a flip-flop can then be derived from the corresponding characteristic equation by (1) replacing the $Q+$ and Q outputs with the name assigned to the flip-flop, and (2) replacing each input in the flip-flop equation with the corresponding excitation equation.

We illustrate the above procedure on the example circuit given in Figure 7.10.4. In the example circuit in the figure, the sequential circuit has two JK flip-flops as the memory elements. According to the above procedure, we do the following:

1. Assign variable names to the outputs of the flip-flops. In the figure, the flip-flop outputs are named X and Y.

2. The input labels to the flip-flops would then be J_x, K_x, J_y, and K_y.

3. The excitation equations for each of the flip-flop inputs are then derived. The excitation equations are Boolean equations into the inputs of the flip-flops. From the figure, the equations are

$$J_x = IY$$

$$K_x = I' + Y$$

$$J_y = I' + X$$

$$K_y = I$$

4. The characteristic and output equations are then derived from the characteristic equations for the flip-flops and the above excitation equations. Both flip-flops used in the design of the above circuit are JK type flip-flops with the general characteristic equation

$$Q^+ = JQ' + K'Q$$

Using X, X^+, J_x, and K_x to substitute, respectively, for Q, $Q+$, J, and K in the above equation, we obtain

$$X^+ = J_x X' + K'_x X$$

Substituting the excitation equations for J_x and K_x in the above equation, we get

$$X^+ = (IY)X' + (I' + Y)'X$$

Similarly, for the characteristic equation for Y^+, we get

$$Y^+ = (I' + X)Y' + I'Y$$

The output equation is

$$\text{Output} = I'XY$$

The characteristic equations for the circuit and the output equations are grouped below.

$$X^+ = X'YI + XIY'$$

$$Y^+ = (I' + X)Y' + I'Y$$

$$\text{Out} = XYI'$$

It is important to note that the output produced is a function of the current memory elements and external input values.

7.10.3 Characteristic or State Table Construction

The above equations are similar to the Boolean equations we discussed in combinational circuits with one difference. The equations are based on the current memory elements as well as external outputs. The characteristic (state) table for a sequential circuit is a tabular representation similar to truth tables. The table can be constructed from its characteristic equations. This can be done by

1. Assigning values to its external inputs and the memory elements
2. Evaluating the outputs and the next value of the memory elements

The table constructed will have in its input section a column corresponding to each of the external inputs and a column corresponding to each of the current memory elements. The output part of the table will include a column for each of the external outputs and an additional column for each of the next memory element values. To complete the table, we compute the output and characteristics equations corresponding to each entry in the table. We illustrate the state table construction on the example circuit given in Figure 7.10.4.

The characteristic table for the above circuit has three columns in its input section. One column corresponds to the external input I; the other two columns correspond to the current X and current Y values, respectively. The output section has a column corresponding to each of the memory elements X^+ and Y^+ and an additional column for the output. To complete the table for the output section, each of the equations for X^+, Y^+, and output is computed for the given input assignment.

We illustrate the construction of the table in the figure by referring to the row with input part $XYI = 011$. For this input, we have

$$X^+ = X'YI + XY'I = 1 + 0 = 1$$

$$Y^+ = (I' + X)Y' + I'Y = 0 + 0 = 0$$

$$\text{Output} = I'XY = 0$$

The above values are found in the corresponding output part. In the computation, it is important to note that the X^+ and Y^+ are computed concurrently on the old X and Y values. With respect to timing, we will look at when the transitions in the above table take place when we discuss timing diagrams.

7.10.4 State Diagrams

The analysis part of sequential circuits may involve the construction of state diagrams as well. State diagrams are also called transition diagrams. The state diagram associated with a sequential circuit is a directed graph with

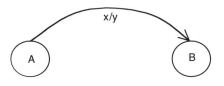

FIGURE 7.10.5
Figure Used to Illustrate Construction of State-Diagrams

labeled edges. A directed graph is composed of nodes (vertices) and directed edges. For the case of a sequential circuit, the diagram constructed has the following properties:

1. The number of vertices in the diagram is equal to the number of states. By "state" we mean the collective set of values associated with its memory elements at a specific instant of time. The collective binary assignment is the state of the sequential circuit. For the example above, the memory elements of the circuit are X and Y. As a result, the number of memory values the circuit could have is equal to four (one for each possible combination of the XY values, i.e., $XY = 00, 01, 10,$ or 11). The machine could then be in one of the four states: 00, 01, 10, or 11 state. Each vertex will be labeled by the state it represents.

2. The edges are labeled directed edges. A label to an edge has the form "x/y," where x represents a specific input assignment to all external inputs and y represents a specific output value. For the sequential circuit example, each edge will have a label with one bit representing its external input, I, and one bit representing its external output.

We use Figure 7.10.5 to illustrate state diagram construction. The interpretation of the partial state diagram is

> If the current state of the machine is A and its current input is x, then its output is y and its next state is B.

In the sequential circuit example given above, one can construct the state diagram from its characteristic table by converting each row in the table to a state transition as follows:

1. The current flip-flop outputs represent the label A in Figure 7.10.5.
2. The input, I, represents the label x.
3. The output represents the label y.
4. The next flip-flop output corresponds to the label B.

TABLE 7.10.1

Characteristic Table of Figure 7.10.4

X	Y	I	X+	Y+	Output
0	0	0	0	1	0
0	0	1	0	0	0
0	1	0	0	1	0
0[a]	1	1	1	0	0
1	0	0	0	1	0
1	0	1	1	1	0
1	1	0	0	1	1
1	1	1	0	0	0

[a] On current memory XY = 01 and input I,
the output is 0 and the next state is 10.

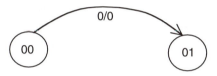

FIGURE 7.10.6
Partial State Diagram of Figure 7.10.4

As an example, the first row of Table 7.10.1 produces the partial state diagram as shown in Figure 7.10.6. The diagram in the figure is read as follows:

> If the current state of the circuit is 00 and the current input is 0, then the output is 0 and the next state of the circuit is 01.

The complete state diagram can be computed from the characteristic table as shown in Figure 7.10.7. We make the following remarks about the figure:

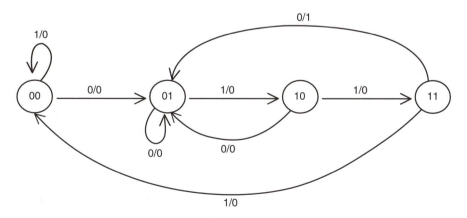

FIGURE 7.10.7
State Diagram of Sequential Circuit in Figure 7.10.4

- The nodes of the sequential circuits represent the memory of the circuit.

- The number of nodes associated with the circuit is determined from the number of flip-flops. With each binary assignment to the flip-flop output values, we associate a node in the state diagram. This is the case since each binary combination represents a different state of the circuit. For a circuit with n flip-flops, the number of nodes, in the corresponding state diagram, is 2^n.

- The number of edges leaving each node depends on the number of external inputs to the circuit. For a given node and a list of inputs, each possible input assignment is used to label one of the edges leaving the given node. For example, for a circuit with two inputs, the number of edges leaving each node is four (the input labels of the edges are 00, 01, 10, and 11). In general, for a circuit with m external inputs, the number of edges leaving a given node is 2^m.

7.10.5   Timing Diagrams

We could capture the description of sequential circuits in timing diagrams similar to the diagrams used to discuss flip-flops and latches. Timing diagrams have the advantage of describing changes in the circuit as a function of the clocking sequence applied. We illustrate the construction of the timing diagrams using Figure 7.10.4. The flip-flops in the circuit are JK flip-flops with the inputs sampled at the positive edge of the clock. This is due to the inverter circuit preceding the clock input. The timing diagram is given in Figure 7.10.8.

We note two properties of the timing diagram. The first property has to do with state transitions. By observing the timing diagram, state transitions occur at the rising edge of the clock only. As a result, over the remaining period of the clock (until the next transition), the state values remain unchanged. The second property has to do with the observed output. The observed output is a function of both the current state and the current input. As a result, changes in the output could occur any time there are changes in the current state or the current input.

When the external outputs are a function of current states as well as external inputs, the machine (sequential circuit) designed is called a Mealy machine. Similarly, the state diagram is called a Mealy state diagram. When the external outputs of the circuit are a function of the current states only, the circuit is called a Moore machine.

As another analysis example, consider the circuit shown in Figure 7.10.9. The circuit is composed of two types of flip-flops. The circuit is a synchronous sequential circuit. The model layout is different than the block diagram model given earlier. Here, the memory part of the sequential circuit is modeled on the right-hand side of the circuit. The combinational part is shown on the left-hand side of the circuit. The external input to the circuit is X. The

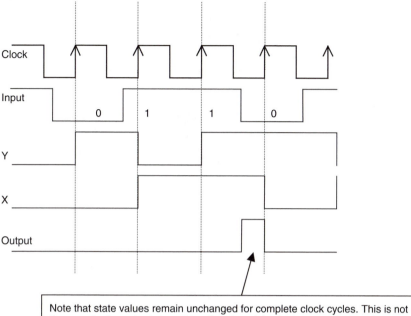

Note that state values remain unchanged for complete clock cycles. This is not the case for the output since it is a function of the inputs as well. Note the output changes to 1 for a short duration

FIGURE 7.10.8
Timing Diagram of the Sequential Circuit in Figure 7.10.4

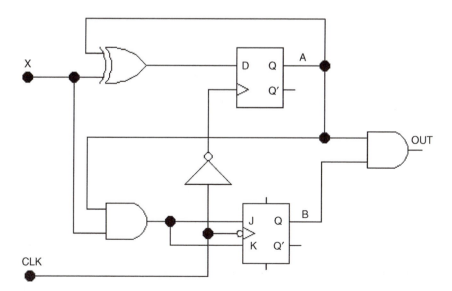

FIGURE 7.10.9
Sequential Circuit Used as an Example in Analysis

external output is OUT. Note that the D flip-flop is sampled on the positive edge of the clock and the JK flip-flop is sampled on the negative edge of the clock. To cause both flip-flops to sample inputs on the same edge of the clock, we added the inverter gate as shown in the figure.

As can be seen from the circuit diagram, the output is a function of the current state only. As a result, the circuit represents a Moore machine. Hence, unlike Mealy machines, the output of the circuit does not change as long as the memory element values do not change. Since the memory element values change only on the negative edge of the clock, the external outputs remain constant for a complete clock cycle that extends from one falling edge of the clock to the next falling edge.

We derive the characteristic and output equations of the circuit. For the memory element with label A, we use a D flip-flop. As a result we have

$$D_A = X \oplus A$$

Since for a D flip-flop we have $Q^+ = D$ and since Q^+ is A^+ and D is D_A, we have

$$A^+ = X \oplus A$$

For the JK flip-flop, using a similar procedure as was done earlier, we have

$$J_B = XA$$

and

$$K_B = XA$$

Substituting the above excitation equations in the characteristic equation for a JK flip-flop, we have

$$B^+ = J_B B' + K'_B B$$
$$= XAB' + (X' + A')B$$
$$= XAB' + X'B + A'B$$
$$= \Sigma\,(1, 3, 5, 6)$$

The output equation is

$$OUT = AB$$

The characteristic table for the above circuit has three columns in its input section. One column corresponds to the external input X; the other two columns correspond to the current A and B values. The output section has

TABLE 7.10.2

Characteristic Table of
Circuit in Figure 7.10.9

X	A	B	A+	B+	out
0	0	0	0	0	0
0	0	1	0	1	0
0	1	0	1	0	0
0	1	1	1	1	1
1	0	0	1	0	0
1	0	1	1	1	0
1	1	0	0	1	1
1	1	1	0	0	1

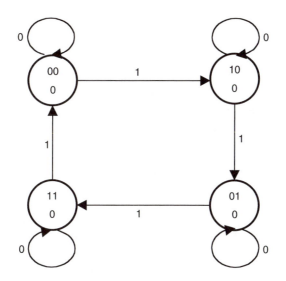

FIGURE 7.10.10
State Diagram of Circuit in Figure 7.10.9

a column corresponding to each of the memory elements A^+, B^+, and an additional column for the output. To complete the table for the output section, each of the equations for A^+, B^+, and OUT is computed for the given input assignments. Table 7.10.2 is the derived characteristic table of the circuit.

The edge of a state diagrams for the Mealy machine are labeled associated with the input and output data. For Moore machines, since the output of the machine is independent of the external inputs and depends only on the current state of the machine, the output is associated with a state instead of an edge of the diagram. Figure 7.10.l0 illustrates this. Note that each state in the state diagram has a state label as well as an output associated with the node. We will discuss this in the next chapter. Before we move to the next chapter, however, we will discuss alternative representations of state tables.

TABLE 7.10.3

State Table Format

Current State	Input	Next State (NS)	Output
25 cents	10 cents	35 cents	0
40 cents	10 cents	0 cents	1

7.10.6 Alternative Representations of State Tables

Consider Table 7.10.2, representing the state table of the circuit given in Figure 7.10.9. As discussed earlier, the input part of the table is composed of two parts, the external input part and the internal values of the flip-flop outputs (collectively representing the state of the circuit). The output part of the table is composed of two parts as well. The parts represent the external output and the next flip-flop output values (collectively representing the next state of the circuit).

When designing sequential circuits, the first step in the design is to generate state tables. As a result, there is no circuit used to derive the table. Instead, the first step in the design is to convert a word problem into a formal description, such as the construction of a state table, for example. This step initially may not involve the use of binary data. Instead, the states are given as generic labels that eventually have to be translated into binary labels as one of the steps in the overall design process (this will be discussed in the next chapter).

To illustrate the format of such state tables, we use the vending machine example by referring to the partial state table, as shown in Table 7.10.3. We assume a can of soda costs 50 cents. The states seen represent the total amount of coins deposited for a given transaction to complete (details of the construction will be given in several examples in Chapter 8). Two rows in the table are read as follows. Row 1 represents the current coin deposited (10 cents) and the previous total amount of coins deposited (current state, 25 cents). On this input and the current values, the next state (new memory) is 35 cents. In addition, the table contains an output of 0, indicating a can of soda is not released. The next row is read similarly for the input part. For the next state part and output part, the next state and output are 0 cents and 1, respectively. The 1 in the output indicates a can is released. The 0 cents represents the next state, a new transaction can be started with no coins deposited yet. The 0 cents state is called the initial state. All state tables have such an initial state representing the startup configuration of the circuit.

The state table representation obtained in circuit analysis and discussed for the vending machine example is not unique. Two alternative representations are shown in Table 7.10.4(a) and (b). In both representations, the present state is used as labels of the rows. In Table 7.10.4(a), the input, x, is used to label the columns of the table. The next state, NS, and output are the entries in the table and are given in the form NS/Output. For example,

TABLE 7.10.4

Alternative Representations of State Tables

(a)			(b)				
	NS/Output			Next State		Output	
Present State	$x = 0$	$x = 1$	Present State	$x = 0$	$x = 1$	$X = 0$	$x = 1$
A	B/0	C/0	A	B	C	0	0
B	C/0	D/1	B	C	D	0	1
C	B/0	E/1	C	B	E	0	1
D	D/1	F/1	D	D	F	1	1
E	E/1	F/1	E	E	F	1	1
F	F/0	A/1	F	F	A	0	1

for the present state B and for the input $x = 1$, the NS/output is read from the table as D/1. The alternative representation separates the next state and output into two sub-tables, as shown in Table 7.10.4(b).

Chapter 7 Exercises

7.1 In Figure 7.1.3, we showed the design of an SR latch using NOR gates. Replace the NOR gates by NAND gates and construct the characteristic table of the latch. Replace the S and R labels by X and Y, respectively.

7.2 Figure 7.1.3 of the design of an SR latch can be modified to include asynchronous preset and clear inputs. The inputs are used as inputs to the NOR gates. Modify the circuit design to include a preset and clear inputs.

7.3 Show the design of a gated SR latch using NAND gates only.

7.4 Construct the characteristic equations of the complement output (Q') of a JK latch.

7.5 Show the design of a JK flip-flop using T flip-flops.

7.6 Show the design of a T flip-flop using D flip-flops.

7.7 Given that a clock cycle width is 10 ns and that the clock assumes a value of 1 for 2 ns of the cycle time. Determine the frequency of the clock. Determine the duty cycle.

7.8 Complete the timing diagram of the SR latch shown in Figure E.7.1. Assume the top NOR gate delay is 1 ns and the lower NOR gate delay is 2 ns. Assume, initially, $Q = 0$ and $Q' = 1$.

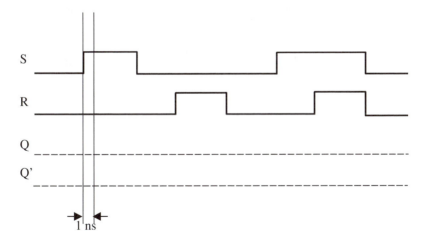

FIGURE E7.1

7.9 Show the design of a master-slave T flip-flop with changes occurring at the rising edge of the clock. Use block diagrams for the master and slave part of the flip-flop.

7.10 Show the design of a master-slave D flip-flop with changes occurring at the falling edge of the clock.

7.11 Given a sequential circuit with two JK flip-flops X and Y, an external input I, output out, and with

$$J_x = I, K_x = I,$$
$$J_y = IX, K_y = IX,$$
$$Out = IXY$$

Construct the characteristic equations of X and Y.

7.12 Draw the circuit schematics corresponding to the equations given in the previous question.

7.13 Construct the state diagram of the circuit with equations given in question 7.11.

7.14 Given the circuit shown in the Figure E7.2

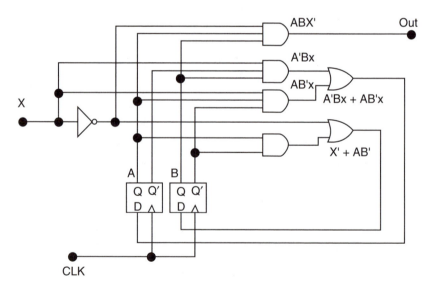

FIGURE E7.2

(a) Find the excitation equations of the inputs to the flip-flops.

(b) Find the characteristic equations of the flip-flops.

(c) Construct the state diagram of the circuit.

7.15 Construct the three alternative characteristic tables of the circuit given in the previous question.

7.16 For the circuit given in Figure E7.2, determine the sequence of states and outputs on the input 0110011101. Assume the initial state is AB = 00.

7.17 Given the circuit shown in the Figure E7.3. The circuit input is x as shown. The top T flip-flop input is set to 1.

(a) Find the characteristic and output equations of the circuit.

(b) Construct the state diagram of the circuit (note that the circuit represents a Moore circuit).

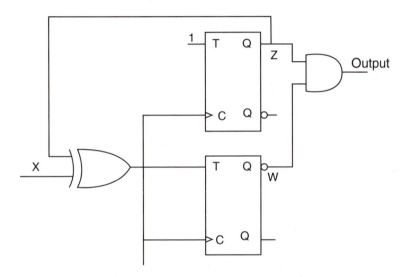

FIGURE E7.3

7.18 Complete the following timing diagram (Figure E7.4) of the circuit given in the previous question. Assume the changes occur on the rising edge of the clock (no delay). Assume the initial WZ value is 00.

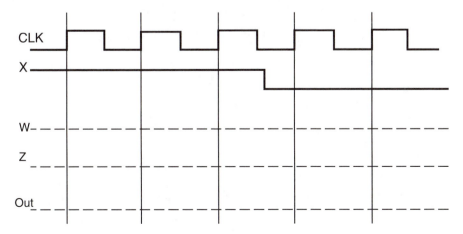

FIGURE E7.4

8

─────────────────────────

Design of Sequential Circuits and State Minimization

─────────────────────────

CONTENTS

In this chapter, we consider design procedures of sequential circuits. We discuss three methods of design in order of complexity with simplest considered first. We then discuss two different sequential circuit machines, the Mealy machine and the Moore machine, and consider conversions between the two machines. Finally, we discuss state minimization as a method to reduce the total design cost by reducing the number of circuit components needed in the design. We start with the simplest of the three methods of design.

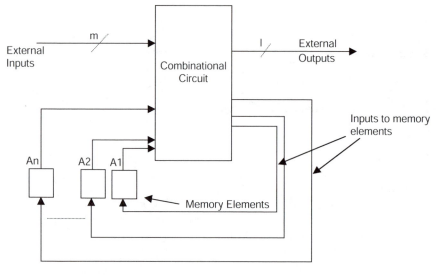

FIGURE 8.1.1
Block Diagram Schematic of a Sequential Circuit

8.1 Block Diagrams and Design from Excitation Equations

Before we discuss the three design procedures, we revisit the block diagram schematic of a sequential circuit, as shown Figure 8.1.1. The figure is a modified version of the block diagram given in Figure 7.10.3, which is used in the analysis section of the chapter. The block diagram shows m external inputs, l external outputs, and n memory elements with labels $A1$, $A2$, ..., An. In analysis, the details of the gate design within the combinational block as well as the type of memory elements used are given.

In sequential circuit design, our task is to

1. Determine the number of external inputs and external outputs
2. Determine the number of memory elements needed in the design and the type of these memory elements
3. Form the design of the combinational circuit part

To accomplish the itemized tasks, we move from an informal description of the problem (word problem description) to a formal representation using one or more of the representations discussed in analysis. The representation could be in the form of a state diagram, a state table, and/or state equations and output. From the formal description, a set of well-formed procedures are used to generate the design. In fact, using one of the formal descriptions of the functional behavior of the circuit, we could employ automated CAD tools that generate the design. These tools can be used to verify the correctness of design as well.

Since sequential circuit design is the reverse of analysis, our discussion of design starts with different initial conditions in the design process as related to analysis. Our goal is to relax these conditions until we tackle the general design procedure. The general procedure progresses by starting with the word description of the problem and ending in the design. We start with the simplest; we assume the excitation equations (input equations to flip-flops) and external output equations are given.

8.1.1 Design of Sequential Circuits Given the External Outputs and Excitation Equations

Having the excitation equations and the external output equations as the initial formal description of a sequential circuit reduces the problem of design to that of a combinational circuit. Here, the function of the combinational circuit block is described by the set of the equations. As a result, we employ standard combinational design procedures. These procedures may include minimizations of the given equations, for example.

Example 8.1.1
In the example, we design the sequential circuit with the following excitation and output equations:

$$J_A(A,B,x) = xB$$

$$K_A(A,B,x) = x' + B$$

$$J_B(A,B,x) = x' + A$$

$$K_B(A,B,x) = x$$

$$Out(A,B,x) = ABx'$$

From these equations, we conclude that the sequential circuit has two JK flip-flops as its memory elements. The circuit has a single external input, x, and a single external output, *Out*. The combinational circuit part is designed to realize the above equations. It has five outputs, *Out*, J_A, K_A, J_B, and K_B. The inputs to the circuit are the memory element outputs and the external input.

Before the design is completed, we minimize the above equations. By inspection, however, we find that each of the above equations is already given in its minimal form. The design of the circuit with the above equations is given in Figure 8.1.2.

We can conclude from the above that the design procedure from a set of excitation and output equations can be accomplished in a straightforward fashion. In fact, in any design, the goal of the design is to produce the needed

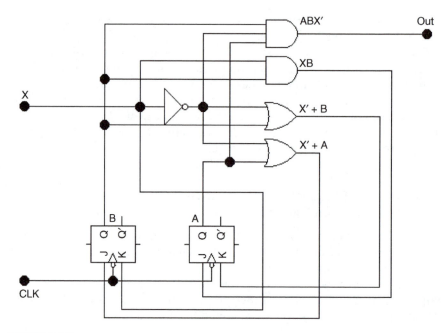

FIGURE 8.1.2
Circuit Design from Excitation Equations $J_A = xB$, $K_A = x' + B$, $J_B = x' + A$, $K_B = x$, $Out = ABx'$

excitation and output equations as the last step before the design. We will explain how these equations are obtained as we progress in our discussion of design.

In keeping with relating design to analysis, the next step in the analysis procedure is to form the characteristic equations of the memory elements and external outputs. As a result, to expand our task in terms of design, we assume the characteristic and output equations are given and the task is to design the sequential circuit from these equations.

8.2   Design Given the Characteristic Equations

In the analysis part of the previous chapter, we derived a set of characteristic and output equations from the given circuit. In obtaining the equations, we made use of the excitation equations that can be derived directly from the circuit. Here, however, our task is to design the circuit. How? From the above example, given the excitation equations, the design is reduced to a combinational circuit design that can be realized directly from the equations. As a result, our task in this method of design can be reduced to the task of obtaining the needed excitation equations.

We will see that the excitation equations can be derived directly from the characteristic equations, assuming we use D or JK flip-flop memory elements in the design. The examples below provide illustrations.

8.2.1 Design Using D Flip-Flops

Example 8.2.1

Assume one is to implement the sequential circuit described by the following characteristic and output equations using D flip-flops.

$$A^+(A,B,x) = \sum(3,5)$$

$$B^+(A,B,x) = \sum(0,2,4,5,6)$$

$$out(A,B,x) = \sum(6)$$

where x is an external input.

Procedure

1. We determine the number of memory elements. The circuit requires two memory elements (D flip-flops), one for each of the "A" and "B" characteristic equations. To distinguish between the two, we use A for the output of one of the flip-flops and B for the output of the other, as given in the equations.

2. We determine the number of inputs and outputs. The combinational circuit inputs are the memory element inputs (A, B, and their complements) and the external input x. The circuit has three outputs (one for the external output, one for each of the inputs to the D flip-flops, and "out"). The design of the output is a simple AND gate of the inputs listed in the equation.

3. We determine the excitation equations (the flip-flop inputs). The excitation equations are chosen so that the flip-flops realize the next state outputs A^+ and B^+. Since for the case of the D flip-flop we know that $Q^+ = D$, to realize A^+ we use it as an input into D_A. Similarly, we use B^+ as an input to D_B. As a result, the excitation equations are

$$D_A = A^+(A,B,x) = \sum(3,5)$$

$$D_B = B^+(A,B,x) = \sum(0,2,4,5,6)$$

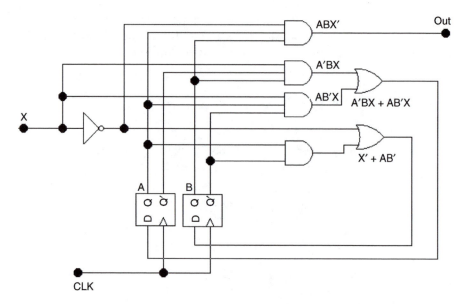

FIGURE 8.2.1
Design of Sequential Circuit from Characteristic Equations $A^+ (A,B,x) = \sum(3,5)$, $B^+ = \sum(0,2,4,5,6)$, $out = \sum(6)$

In obtaining the excitation equations, we have transformed this design problem to the problem of design from excitation equations as given above. Before the design, we could minimize the above equations if needed.

The excitation equations given above can be simplified to yield

$$D_A = A^+(A,B,x) = \sum(3,5) = A'Bx + AB'x$$

$$D_B = B^+(A,B,x) = \sum(0,2,4,5,6) = x' + AB'$$

4. We design the circuit. The circuit design is shown in Figure 8.2.1.

Before we discuss design using JK flip-flops, we relate the above design to the characteristic equations in terms of time. In the above circuit, the combinational circuit computes the flip-flops input equations A^+ and B^+ as a function of the current memory elements outputs (A and B) and the external output x. The changes in the next state value occur only at the rising edge of the clock. On the rising edge of the clock, these inputs are sampled and, in effect, are moved to the outputs of the D flip-flops. Finally, note that the circuit output is not synchronized with the clock; it could change any time the input x changes in value. We next discuss design using JK flip-flops.

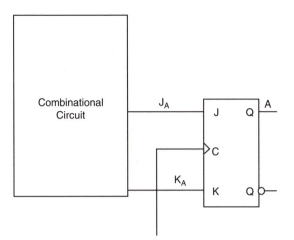

FIGURE 8.2.2

8.2.2 Design Using JK Flip-Flops

In design using JK flip-flops, we follow a similar procedure used for design using D flip-flops. The number of memory elements needed is equal to the number of characteristic equations. The combinational circuit inputs are the memory elements outputs (including their complements) and the external inputs as given by the equations. In terms of the outputs, the combinational circuit associates an external output with each external output equation and two excitation equations with each memory element. The excitation equations are for the J and K parts of each flip-flop. The design task is complete once the excitation equations are computed and the circuit is generated from these equations. We illustrate how one obtains the excitation equations from the state characteristic equations next.

Consider the circuit shown in Figure 8.2.2. In the circuit, J_A and K_A represent the excitation equations that the combinational circuit realizes for the JK flip-flop with label A. In order to find these equations, we make use of the characteristic equation for a JK flip-flop. In particular, we know that for a JK flip-flop with label A we have

$$A^+ = J_A A' + K_A' A$$

As can be seen from the equation, the J_A and K_A terms can be found from the characteristic equations by rewriting the equation in the form

$$A^+ = f_1 A' + f_2' A, \quad \text{to obtain}$$

$$J_A = f_1, \quad \text{and}$$

$$K_A = f_2$$

How does one find the functions f_1 and f_2 from a given set of characteristic equations? A given characteristic equation can be converted to a characteristic equation similar to the characteristic equation of a JK flip-flop by collecting all terms that include the Q' variable and factoring Q' out of these terms. The resulting term constitutes the Boolean function, f_1, associated with the J input. Similarly, to obtain the complement of the function, f_2, associated with the K input, we collect all the terms in the equation that include the variable Q. The resulting term formed after factoring the Q is the function f_2' associated with the input K.

Note that it is possible that some of the terms found in the characteristic equation may not contain the literal Q. These terms can be expanded to include the literal Q by using the rule

$$x = x(Q + Q') = xQ + xQ'$$

We illustrate the design process using the following example.

Example 8.2.2
Given the characteristic and output equations described below.

$$A^+(A,B,x) = A'Bx + AB'x$$

$$B^+(A,B,x) = x' + AB'$$

$$out(A,B,x) = ABx'$$

We would like to design the circuit realizing the above equations using JK flip-flops. The sequential circuit has a single input, x; a single output, *out*; and two memory elements (JK flip-flops) with outputs labeled A and B. To design the circuit, we need to implement the input (excitation) functions to each of the flip-flops (J_A, K_A, J_B, and K_B). To find the excitation equations for the A flip-flop, we rewrite the A^+ equation as

$$A^+(A,B,x) = A'Bx + AB'x$$

$$= (Bx)A' + (B'x)A$$

$$= (J_A)A' + (K_A')A$$

That is, the Boolean functions associated with the inputs are

$$J_A = Bx \quad \text{and} \quad K_A = (B'x)'$$

When applying a similar procedure to the B flip-flop, we obtain

$$B^+(A,B,x) = x' + AB'$$
$$= x'(B + B') + AB'$$
$$= (x' + A)B' + x'B$$
$$= J_B B' + K'_B B$$

That is, the Boolean functions associated with the inputs are

$$J_B = x' + A \quad \text{and} \quad K_B = x$$

The excitation equations obtained are the same equations used in the design example from excitation equations. As a result, the sequential circuit design produces the same circuit given earlier (Figure 8.1.2).

The design of sequential circuits does not start by forming the excitation equations or characteristic equations. Instead, it usually starts with an informal description of the problem. From this description we progress into formal descriptions using one of the behavioral description methods such as a state table or a state diagram. From the formal descriptions we proceed to designing the circuit by establishing the needed excitation equations. The discussion that follows tackles the design problem presented in state table or state diagram form. The design is general in nature as it applies to any of four memory elements. The previous design procedure was restricted to using D or JK flip-flops.

8.3 General Design Procedure of Sequential Circuits

Following is the general design procedure of the sequential circuits in the context of an example. We would like to design a sequential circuit with one input, x, and one output, y. On the input $x = 0$, the circuit makes transition between the state A, B, C, D, and back to A in the order listed. When the input is $x = 1$, the circuit makes transitions in the opposite order. The output of the circuit is 1 when the current state is D, i.e., the circuit output is independent of the current input.

8.3.1 Step 1

The first step in the design of sequential circuit is to derive the state table or state diagram from the word problem. For the above word problem, we obtain the state table shown in Table 8.3.1.

TABLE 8.3.1

An Example State Table

Present State	Next State x = 0	Next State x = 1	Output x = 0	Output x = 1
A	B	D	0	0
B	C	A	0	0
C	D	B	0	0
D	A	C	1	1

8.3.2   Step 2

The second step in the design procedure is to apply state minimization. State minimization is applied to the state table above. In state minimization, the objective is to reduce the number of states but maintain the same input and output relation. We will discuss state minimization in Section 8.7.

8.3.3   Step 3

The third step is to apply state assignment. What is state assignment? Table 8.3.1 is a description of the problem without reference to sequential circuits. Our task is to design a circuit that simulates the behavior as described in the table. Since the design processes binary data only, we need an encoding scheme that assigns a binary code word to each state in the state table. Since the states in the table represent the memory of the table, the binary codes in the design are associated with the memory elements of the circuit.

We determine the number of bits in a code word by relating the discussion to analysis. In analysis, the state of the machine is the current binary assignment on the outputs of its memory elements. For a circuit with two memory elements, the states are 00, 01, 10, and 11. Similarly, for a circuit with three and four memory elements, the number of states the machine could be in is eight and sixteen, respectively; and in general, for a machine with n memory elements, the machine could be in any of 2^n possible states.

In our case, we need two memory elements; call their outputs W and Z. The outputs of the memory elements are codes that represent the states in the state table. Since we have four states, the first state, A, could be assigned any of the four possible code words (there are four possible codes). For state B, we could assign any of the three remaining binary codes. Similar logic applies to the remaining states C and D, yielding a total of 4! = 24 possible assignments. Arbitrarily, we choose the assignment XY = 00, 01, 10, and 11 as code words for the states A, B, C, and D, respectively. With these assignments we reconstruct the state table as shown in Table 8.3.2; in (a) we have the original state table, and in (b) we have the modified state table based on the outputs of flip-flops in the sequential circuit to be designed.

TABLE 8.3.2

State Assignment, (a) Original Table, (b) Table with State Assignment

	(a)					(b)			
	Next State		Output			Next State		Output	
P.S.	x = 0	x = 1	x = 0	x = 1	P.S. WZ	x = 0	x = 1	x = 0	x = 1
A	B	D	0	0	00	01	11	0	0
B	C	A	0	0	01	10	00	0	0
C	D	B	0	0	10	11	01	0	0
D	A	C	1	1	11	00	10	1	1

We relate this table to the sequential circuit design. In the design, if the contents of the current memory elements are $WZ = 00$, and if the current input is $x = 0$, then from the table the next memory elements values are $WZ = 01$ and the output is 0. When we decode the states, 00 represents the current state A and 01 represents the next state B, as shown in Table 8.3.2(a).

Before we continue our discussion of the general design procedure, we note that Table 8.3.1 and Table 8.3.2 can be used to generate the characteristic equations of the memory elements as well as the output equations. To illustrate, Table 8.3.2(b) can be rewritten as shown in Table 8.3.3, from which the next state equations for Z and W as well as the output equation Y can be derived. The table contains truth values of Boolean functions (W^+, Z^+, and Y). As a result, the algebraic equations of these functions can be formed and minimized. From the minimized functions we could design the circuit using D or JK flip-flops as discussed earlier.

TABLE 8.3.3

Reconstructed Part (b)
of Table 8.3.2

XWZ	W$^+$	Z$^+$	Y
000	0	1	0
001	1	0	0
010	1	1	0
011	0	0	1
100	1	1	0
101	0	0	0
110	0	1	0
111	1	0	1

Since our objective is to design these functions using any of the memory elements, we continue the process of design and discuss how one can obtain the excitation equations for any of the four memory elements.

8.3.3.1 Flip-Flop Excitation Tables

The general procedure used to implement sequential circuits using any of the four types of flip-flops makes use of the excitation table of the circuit. The excitation table of the circuit is derived from the excitation tables of the individual flip-flops.

The excitation table for the flip-flops is composed of two parts. In the first part, we list the current flip-flop output and the desired next output. In the second part, we list the input requirements that will cause the flip-flop to change its value when its inputs are sampled. Hence, the first part contains the possible current Q and the desired Q^+ values. The second part contains

TABLE 8.3.4

Excitation Tables of the Four Flip-Flops

Q	Q⁺	S	R	J	K	D	T
0	0	0	x	0	x	0	0
0	1	1	0	1	x	1	1
1	0	0	1	x	1	0	1
1	1	x	0	x	0	1	0

the needed input values at the flip-flop inputs (SR, JK, D, or T) that cause the desired transition from Q to Q^+ as shown in Table 8.3.4.

The first and second columns of the table correspond to the current Q output and the desired next output Q^+ of a given flip-flop. The remaining columns of the table include the values on the proper flip-flops inputs that will cause the change. We illustrate the table construction for all flip-flops by referring to the row with $Q = 1$ and $Q^+ = 0$. For this row:

1. Using SR flip-flops, we could cause this transition from 1 to 0 by having $R = 1$ and $S = 0$ (this is shown in the third row, columns 3 and 4).

2. Using JK flip-flops, we could cause this transition from 1 to 0 by having the J input set to 0 and the K input set to 1. We could also cause Q^+ to become 0 by complementing the previous $Q = 1$ value, i.e., by setting both J and K to 1. In both cases, K must assume a value of 1. The J input, however, could be either 0 or 1. In the table, this is indicated by assigning an x to J and a 1 to K. An x indicates J can assume any of the two values.

3. Using D flip-flops, we could cause this transition from 1 to 0 by having the D input set to 0 since $Q^+ = D$.

4. Finally, using T flip-flops, we could cause this transition from 1 to 0 by setting the T input to 1.

We will use the above flip-flops excitation tables in the design of sequential circuits as seen next.

8.3.4 Step 4

Step four in the design process of sequential circuits is to form the excitation table of the circuit. What is the excitation table of the circuit? The excitation table of a circuit consists of two major parts. The first part is the characteristic (state) table of the circuit. The second part lists the conditions on the flip-flop inputs that cause the transitions as described in the first part (the

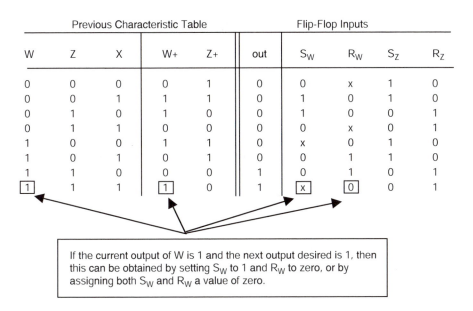

Previous Characteristic Table						Flip-Flop Inputs			
W	Z	X	W+	Z+	out	S_W	R_W	S_Z	R_Z
0	0	0	0	1	0	0	x	1	0
0	0	1	1	1	0	1	0	1	0
0	1	0	1	0	0	1	0	0	1
0	1	1	0	0	0	0	x	0	1
1	0	0	1	1	0	x	0	1	0
1	0	1	0	1	0	0	1	1	0
1	1	0	0	0	1	0	1	0	1
1	1	1	1	0	1	x	0	0	1

If the current output of W is 1 and the next output desired is 1, then this can be obtained by setting S_W to 1 and R_W to zero, or by assigning both S_W and R_W a value of zero.

FIGURE 8.3.1
Excitation Table Used in Sequential Circuit Design of Table 8.3.3

characteristic table). The format of the excitation table for the circuit at hand is given in Figure 8.3.1. The figure includes the associated function description of each of the flip-flops inputs (S_W, R_W, S_Z, and R_Z). It also includes the output description of the circuit.

The figure contains all the information needed in the design of the combinational circuit as given in Figure 8.3.2. This information includes the external output functions. It also includes the description of the input functions to the individual flip-flop inputs. The input functions are used to cause the transitions between states as described in the characteristic table. Note that the W^+ and Z^+ columns were used only to derive the input equations. With these columns removed, the table is reduced to a form similar to a truth table format: its inputs are W, Z, and X, its outputs are out, S_W, R_W, S_Z, and R_Z. The circuit design associated with the table will then follow standard procedures of designing Boolean functions from their truth table descriptions.

8.3.5 Step 5

The fifth step is to form the minimized excitation and output functions. When the K-map method of minimization is used, we obtain the tables in Figure 8.3.3. The design of the sequential circuit implementation is shown in Figure 8.3.4.

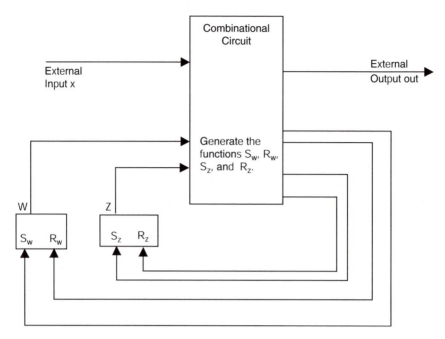

FIGURE 8.3.2
Block Diagram Circuit of Table in Figure 8.3.1

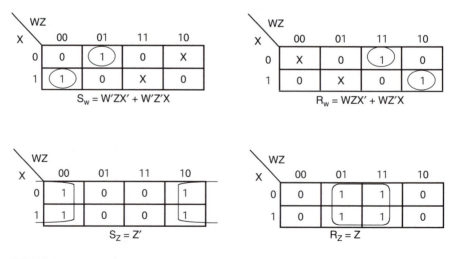

FIGURE 8.3.3
K-Maps of Table in Figure 8.3.1

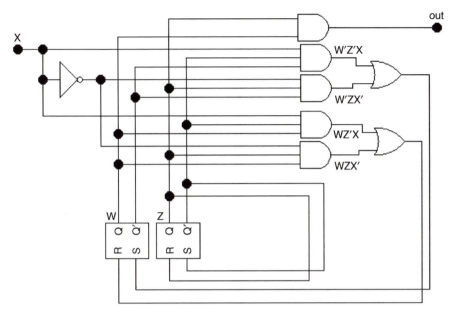

FIGURE 8.3.4
Circuit Design of Table in Figure 8.3.1

8.4 Machine Equivalence and State Assignments

In the general design procedure discussed in the previous section, we arbitrarily used SR flip-flops in the design. In addition, we arbitrarily used a specific state assignment in terms of states and the corresponding memory elements in the design. Changing the memory elements types or changing the state assignment produces different designs that realize the same functional behavior. In terms of the input and output behavior, the designs are equivalent, meaning that on the same inputs all designs produce the same outputs. The internal design of the circuit and the transitions within the internal memory elements are different, however.

This is similar to combinational circuits. In combinational circuits, the internal design of the same function may be different but the logical input and output behavior remains the same. This section considers additional design examples. First, we design the same problem as stated in the previous section using different flip-flops and different state assignments.

Example 8.4.1

We would like to apply the general design procedure on the same problem discussed in the previous section using JK flip-flops (instead of SR).

TABLE 8.4.1

Excitation Table of Circuit in Previous Section Using
JK Flip-Flops

Previous Characteristic Table						Flip-Flop Inputs			
W	Z	X	W⁺	Z⁺	Out	J_W	K_W	J_Z	K_Z
0	0	0	0	1	0	0	x	1	x
0	0	1	1	1	0	1	x	1	x
0	1	0	1	0	0	1	x	x	1
0	1	1	0	0	0	0	x	x	1
1	0	0	1	1	0	x	0	1	x
1	0	1	0	1	0	x	1	1	x
1	1	0	0	0	1	x	1	x	1
1	1	1	1	0	1	x	0	x	1

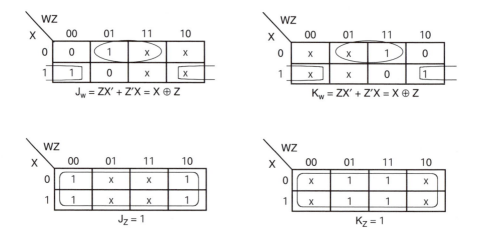

FIGURE 8.4.1
K-Maps of Table 8.4.1

Solution: Steps 1 and 2 are to form the state table and apply state minimizations. Both of these steps are done independent of design and, as a
result, are the same. The third step is to apply a state assignment (in the
process, we determine the number of memory elements needed). For this
step, we use the same state assignment. Step 4 is to form the excitation tables.
Since we are using JK flip-flops in the design with the same labels for the
outputs, we obtain the excitation table shown in Table 8.4.1.

Step 5 is to form the minimized flip-flop input functions and the minimized
output functions. The output function is out = WZ. The minimized flip-flop
input functions can be found using the K-map method, as shown in Figure
8.4.1. The final step is the design of the output equations and the above
excitation equations, as shown in Figure 8.4.2. Note that the circuit design
is similar in construction (in terms of having a combinational part and a

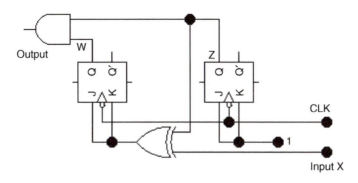

FIGURE 8.4.2
Circuit Design of Table 8.4.1

TABLE 8.4.2

Excitation Table Using T Flip-Flops

Previous Characteristic Table					Flip-Flop Inputs		
W	Z	X	W$^+$	Z$^+$	Out	T$_W$	T$_Z$
0	0	0	0	1	0	0	1
0	0	1	1	1	0	1	1
0	1	0	1	0	0	1	1
0	1	1	0	0	0	0	1
1	0	0	1	1	0	0	1
1	0	1	0	1	0	1	1
1	1	0	0	0	1	1	1
1	1	1	1	0	1	0	1

sequential part). The circuit can be reconstructed to the sequential circuit format given in block diagram format, as shown in Figure 8.1.1.

Example 8.4.2
In this example, we design the same word problem using T flip-flops. The inputs, outputs, state assignments, and number of memory elements is assumed to be similar to the previous two examples. As for the memory elements, we use T flip-flops. The excitation table with T flip-flops is given in Table 8.4.2. The minimized functions and the circuit design are shown in Figure 8.4.3.
Before we conclude this section, we present a final example of design of the same word problem using JK flip-flops but with different state assignments.

Example 8.4.3
This example deals with an alternative design of the same word problem using the following state assignments. The states *A*, *B*, *C*, and *D* are assigned the binary codes 00, 10, 11, and 01, respectively. The state assignment produces the new excitation table shown in Table 8.4.3. The minimized equations are

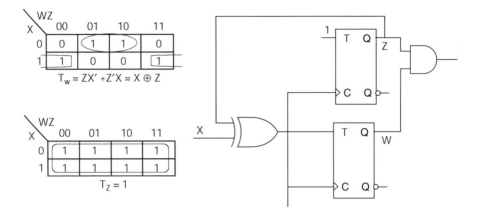

FIGURE 8.4.3
K-Map and Circuit Design of Table 8.4.2

TABLE 8.4.3

Excitation Table with Different State Assignment

Previous Characteristic Table						Flip-Flop Inputs			
W	Z	X	W⁺	Z⁺	Out	J_W	K_W	J_Z	K_Z
0	0	0	1	0	0	1	x	0	x
0	0	1	0	1	0	0	x	1	x
0	1	0	0	0	1	0	x	x	1
0	1	1	1	1	1	1	x	x	0
1	0	0	1	1	0	x	0	1	x
1	0	1	0	0	0	x	1	0	x
1	1	0	0	1	0	x	1	x	0
1	1	1	1	0	0	x	0	x	1

$$J_W = (X \oplus Z)'$$

$$K_W = X \oplus Z$$

$$J_Z = X \oplus W$$

$$K_Z = (X \oplus W)'$$

The design of the circuit is given in Figure 8.4.4. The design includes the switch inputs for the external inputs and the clock. In addition, it includes indicators for the outputs. As homework, using the Electronics Workbench verify the circuit above is a realization of the word problem given earlier. In your verification, construct the state diagram of the word problem first; then, using the state assignments, show that the same state diagram is obtained from the circuit except for the labels of the nodes in the state diagram.

The examples above are intended to illustrate the following. First, different initial state assignments yield different designs that realize the same word

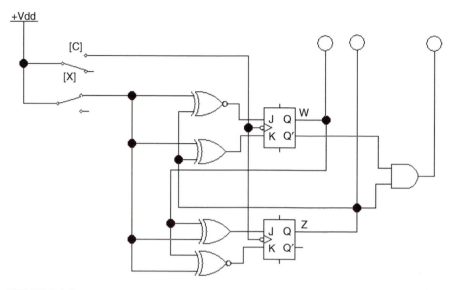

FIGURE 8.4.4
Circuit design of Table 8.4.3

problem. As a result, the initial state assignment affects the overall cost of design in terms of the number of gates used. Second, for the same state the use of different memory elements affects the design as well. For example, when T flip-flops were used in the design the combinational circuit part contained a single XOR gate and a single AND gate for the output. When SR flip-flops are used in the design, the combinational circuit included eight gates. We will next look at additional examples of sequential problems and discuss conversion between the two different representations of state machines: the Moore machine and the Mealy machine.

8.5 Mealy State Diagrams

Earlier we introduced state tables and state diagrams. State diagrams are directed graphs with labeled edges. When the output is part of the labeling of the edges of the diagram, the state diagram represents a Mealy model. In the Mealy model, the output is a function of both the current state as well as the current input. An alternative representation associates the output with the current state instead, i.e., the output does not depend on the current external input. This model is called a Moore model. In this section, we present several examples. A Mealy model construction of each example is given. In the next section, we consider the equivalent Moore model.

Example 8.5.1

Construct the state diagram for a simplified circuit of a soda vending machine with a single input and a single output. The input is one of two coins deposited (dimes or quarters). The output is a binary signal with 0 indicating no can of soda is released and 1 indicating a can is released. We assume the cost of a can of soda is 35 cents. In addition, we assume a different circuit handles the change returned.

Solution: In constructing the state diagram, we note that the memory of the circuit is the amount of coin deposited for a new transaction. An initial state is needed to indicate no coins have been deposited. We call this state "0," representing an amount of 0 cents deposited. From this state, we process two edges: one edge for an input of 10 cents and another edge for an input of 25 cents. On an input of 10 cents, we create a new state that represents a total of 10 cents is deposited. The output associated with the edge is 0 since the total amount deposited is less than 35 cents. Similarly, we generate a new state and label it 25 to represent the memory that 25 cents have been deposited.

We proceed from the two new states and process inputs from each state. From the 25 cents state, an input of 10 or 25 produces an output of 1 since the total amount deposited is at least 35 cents. The edges from this state are directed to the start state, indicating the transaction is complete and a new transaction can start. Following a similar analysis procedure on other states, we obtain the Mealy state diagram shown in Figure 8.5.1. Note that, with the exception of node 30, the number of edges leaving each node is equal to the number of possible input combinations. For simplicity, from node 30 we combined two edges into a single edge labeled 25/1, 10/1. This is equivalent to two edges labeled 25/1 and 10/1, respectively.

To gain familiarity with state diagrams, we trace the states of the diagram on the input, 10, 10, and 25 cents. Initially, the diagram is in state 0. On the

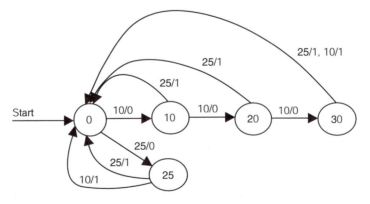

FIGURE 8.5.1

State Diagram for the Soda Vending Machine. The node with label 0 is the start node. The node labels represent the memory (coins deposited). The edge labeled 25/1, 10/1 represents two edges with indicated labels.

first input of 10 cents, the diagram makes a transition to state 10 and outputs a 0. On the second input of 10 cents and starting in the current state 10, the diagram makes transition to the next state 20 and outputs a 0 as well. Finally, from state 20 and on input 25 cents, the diagram outputs a 1 (a can is released) and a transition is made to the initial state to begin a new transaction.

The next two examples are sequence detector examples. The examples monitor the input for a specific binary sequence. The output is 0 when the sequence is not detected and 1 when the sequence is detected. For both examples, the circuit has a single input and a single output.

Example 8.5.2
Construct the state diagram of a sequential circuit with a single binary input and a single binary output. The circuit keeps track of the previous inputs as well as the current input. The output of the circuit is 0 until three consecutive 0s are entered at the input. The output is 1 afterward.

Solution: The circuit is sequential since it keeps track of the previous input. For the state diagram, the circuit requires at least four nodes:

1. An initial start node (no input is entered yet)
2. A node that represents a 0 is entered last
3. A node to represent two consecutive 0s are entered
4. A node to represent three consecutive 0s entered. The output is 1 on any input afterward.

The state diagram is shown in Figure 8.5.2. Note the need for the fourth node and that the state diagram loops in state *A* as long as the input entered is 1. As soon as a 0 is entered while in *A*, a transition is made to state *B* indicating a first 0 is entered. Now from *B* we process two inputs. On an input of 0, we move to another state, *C*, indicating two consecutive 0s entered. (Note that from *A* we get to *C* exactly when two consecutive 0s are entered.) On an input of 1, we move back to state *A*, indicating a restart of the process. Finally, once in state *D* (three consecutive 0s have been detected), the output produced is 1, independent of the current input. This is shown

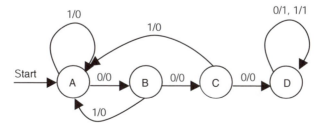

FIGURE 8.5.2
On the Input 01010001, the Circuit Output is 00000011. Assume inputs (outputs) are applied (observed) from left to right.

TABLE 8.5.1

Input 0000, Output 0011

Input	1	0	1	0	0	0	0	0	1	0
Output	0	0	0	0	0	1	1	1	0	0

by the edge that starts at D and loops back to D. Note that this edge cannot end in any of the previous states (A, B, or C).

Example 8.5.3

Construct the state diagram of a modified circuit as described in Example 8.5.2. For this circuit, the output is 1 whenever three consecutive 0s are entered. The output is 0 otherwise. To illustrate, Table 8.5.1 shows a sample of an input/output sequence. Note the overlap in the sequence, i.e., on an input of four consecutive 0s, the output is 1 on the third and fourth 0.

Solution: Similar to the previous problem, we use states as memory of how much of the string of 0s is recognized. Here, we need a state to indicate no string of the sequence is recognized; call it state A, the start state. Similarly, we need states as memory for the first 0 in the sequence is recognized and the second 0 in the sequence is recognized. Call these states B and C, respectively.

While in A, on input of 1 we loop back to A, on input of 0 we move to state B, indicating the last symbol entered is a 0. Similarly, from B on an input of 0 we move to C and an input of 1 we move back to A to start over. Since state C indicates the last two consecutive symbols are 0, on an input of 0 from this state the output should be 1 since the last three symbols entered would be the desired sequence (000). In addition, on this input the edge in the state diagram loops back to C due to the allowable overlap in the sequence. From C and on an input of 1, the next state is A, indicating that we need to start over. Therefore, no other states are needed. The complete state diagram is shown in Figure 8.5.3. The state diagram is not a unique solution. Similar analysis can be applied to the state diagram shown in Figure 8.5.4 to show that it is a solution to the above problem as well.

In the next section, we show that both state diagrams are solutions to the same problem (the state diagrams are equivalent). The next example we

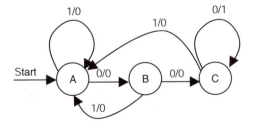

FIGURE 8.5.3
State Diagram of Example 8.5.3

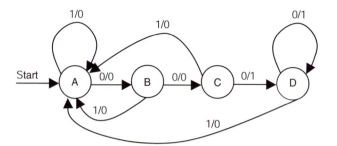

FIGURE 8.5.4
An Alternative State Diagram of Example 8.5.3

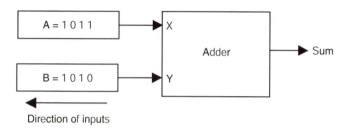

Direction of inputs

FIGURE 8.5.5
Block diagram of a 4-bit serial adder

consider deals with binary data for both inputs and outputs, as is the case for the previous two examples. For the example it is convenient to use binary data to label the states as well.

Example 8.5.4
A serial adder is a circuit that has two binary inputs and one binary output. The circuit adds two n-bit binary numbers, A and B. The numbers are entered in sequence, one bit at a time starting with the least-significant bits. For each pair of bits, the adder outputs the sum of three bits, the two bits to be added, and the carry from the previous addition. The diagram shown in Figure 8.5.5 is an example of two 4-bit numbers, A and B.

The diagram shows the direction of the inputs as applied. The inputs are applied from least significant to most significant. On the application of each input, the proper sum is produced. To produce the correct sum, the adder keeps track of the previous carry generated. As a result, the adder is a sequential circuit. The state diagram of the circuit contains two memory nodes representing a previous carry of 0 or 1, and labeled as 0 and 1, respectively. The number of edges leaving each node is four, corresponding to the four possible input combinations 00, 01, 10, and 11. The state diagram for the above circuit is shown in Figure 8.5.6.

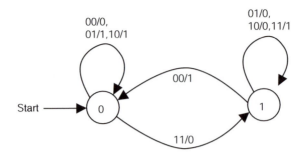

FIGURE 8.5.6
The State Diagram of Example 8.5.4. Note that the three edges are represented by a single edge with multiple input/output labels.

8.6 Moore Machines

The output of a Moore machine is a function of the current state only. As a result, the nodes in a state diagram corresponding to a Moore machine contain a label of the node, as well as the output associated with the node. In general, Moore machine state diagrams have a larger number of nodes as compared to the Mealy machine state diagrams. We illustrate the construction of Moore state diagrams based on the examples presented earlier.

Example 8.6.1
Construct the Moore machine state diagram for the soda machine example (example 8.5.1).

    Solution: In constructing the Moore machine state diagram, we refer to the Mealy model shown in Figure 8.5.1. A Moore state diagram can be constructed from this model by adding one extra state we call "done." This state represents an amount of coins deposited that is at least 35 cents. Note that this state cannot be any of the other states since the output in all other states should be 0. Figure 8.6.1 shows the Moore machine solution. Note that each state contains a label as well as an output.

    The state diagrams can be modified so as to output the change associated with a transaction as well. For the case of the Mealy machine, the number of states in the modified diagram remains the same. For the Moore machine example, however, the number of states will increase. The details of the construction will serve as an exercise.

Example 8.6.2
Construct the Moore machine state diagram of example 8.5.4.

    Solution: In the Mealy machine solution, the state diagram contained two states representing a carry of either a 0 or a 1. Since from each state it is possible to output a sum of 0 or 1, the Moore state diagram will contain two

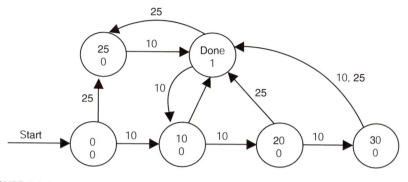

FIGURE 8.6.1
Moore Machine State Diagram of Soda Machine

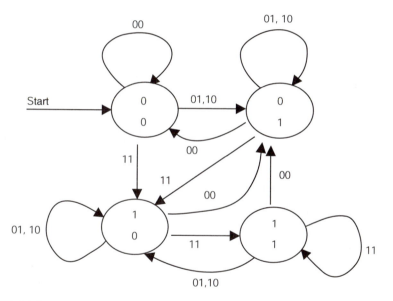

FIGURE 8.6.2
Moore Machine State Diagram of Example 8.5.4. The carry/output is listed in the upper/lower part of each node.

states associated with each state in the Mealy machine. The Moore model state diagram is shown in Figure 8.6.2.

We illustrate by processing inputs from the start state. The label of the state is 0 and the output is 0. On an input of 00, the sum is equal to 0 (the sum of the three bits 0, 0, and the carry of 0 is equal to 0). The carry is 0 as well. As a result, the edge loops back to this state. On an input of 01 or 10, however, we move to a new state since the sum is 1, even though the carry is still 0. Similar analysis can be applied on the remaining nodes. We next present a procedure that converts a Mealy state diagram to an equivalent Moore state diagram.

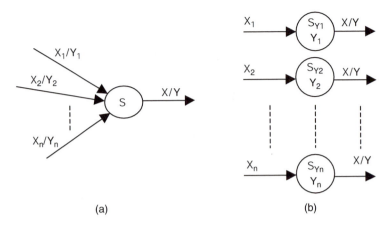

FIGURE 8.6.3
(a) Mealy State Transitions and (b) Equivalent Moore Transitions. Entering edges into S in (a) are routed to the proper representative state in (b). Edges starting at S are converted to edges starting at each of the representative states.

8.6.1 Conversion from Mealy to Moore Machines

The conversion from a Mealy state diagram to a Moore state diagram can be accomplished by replacing each state in the Mealy model with multiple representative states in the corresponding Moore model. In the Mealy model, for each state, s, with multiple edges entering the state and with n of these edges labeled with different outputs, we create n states in the corresponding Moore model. A transition into the original state, s, in the Mealy model is mapped to a transition into one of the representative states, as shown in Figure 8.6.3. In particular, the representative state with the same output is shown in the node.

Figure 8.6.3(a) shows the transitions into a state S in the Mealy model. Each of the edges produces a different output, Y_i. With each such output we create a representative state, with label S_{Yi} and output Y_i. This edge is then directed into the generated state, as shown in Figure 8.6.3(b). Finally, edges starting at state S in the Mealy model are converted to edges that leave each of the representative states in the Moore model. This is shown in the figure for the edge with label X/Y. We illustrate the construction procedure on the two examples discussed earlier.

Example 8.6.3
Convert the Mealy machine state diagram example for the soda machine to an equivalent Moore machine state diagram using the procedure outlined above.

Using the procedure above, we first determine the number of states of the Moore machine. For each set of edges with different outputs, Y_i, and each destination state, S, we create a set of representative states as discussed above. From the Mealy state diagram of the soda machine example, new

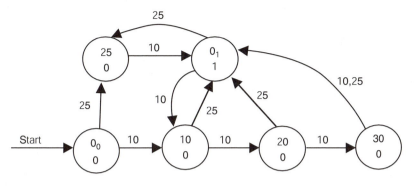

FIGURE 8.6.4
Moore Machine State Diagram of Soda Machine. Except for state names, the diagram is similar to the solution diagram of Example 8.5.1.

states are generated for state 0 only, since no other states receive edges with different outputs. Edges leaving each of the representative states are the same edges leaving the original state 0. Figure 8.6.4 shows the Moore machine state diagram. Note the similarity to the state diagram given in Figure 8.6.1.

Example 8.6.4
Use the conversion process of Mealy to Moore state diagram to construct the Moore state diagram for the serial adder circuit.

Solution: Since each state (0 or 1) receives edges with two different outputs, with each such state we associate two representative states. From each state we process four possible edges and choose the proper destination state using the conversion rules mentioned above. To obtain the diagram, replace the state names 0, 0, 1, and 1 in Figure 8.6.2, visited in clockwise fashion, with the names 00, 01, 11, and 10, respectively.

As we discussed earlier, the second step in the design of sequential circuits is to apply state minimization. State minimization is the process reducing the number of states in a state table or state diagram without affecting the input and output functionality of the circuit. We discuss state minimization next.

8.7 Machine and State Equivalence

We say that two state diagrams (machines) are equivalent if, on applying the same input to the two machines, the machines always produce the same output, i.e., one cannot distinguish between the two machines in terms of input and output. In the previous section, we presented different diagrams for the same problem (the Mealy and Moore machines). These state diagrams are then equivalent. In the section previous to that, we discussed different

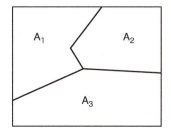

FIGURE 8.7.1
An Example of a Partition. The elements of the original set are contained within the rectangular area.

designs of the same problem based on using different state assignments and memory elements. The machines designed are equivalent since their input/output relationships are the same.

Equivalency can be applied to a pair of states instead of machines. Two sates, S_i and S_j, are said to be 1-equivalent if starting from either state and for any input, the output produced is the same. In the state table, two states are 1-equivalent if they have identical output rows.

Definition: In general, we say that two sates, S_i and S_j, are k-equivalent if, starting from either state and for any input of length k, the output produced is the same.

Definition: We say that two states, S_i and S_j, are equivalent if, on any input of any length, the output produced by starting at state S_i is the same as the output produced by starting at state S_j. Alternatively, we say that two states are equivalent if they are k-equivalent for any choice of k. Machine and state equivalence forms an equivalence relation. Each equivalence relation over a set, A, partitions the set A into equivalence classes.

Definition: A partition of a set, A, is a set $P = \{A_1, A_2, ..., A_n\}$ such that (1) each element A_i of P is a subset of the set A, (2) the intersection of any pair of element of P is empty, and (3) the union of all the elements of P is the entire set A.

Figure 8.7.1 shows a schematic of a partition with three sets. The original set is the entire rectangular area. In the figure, each A_i is called an equivalence class. Any two elements in an equivalence class are related (under the equivalence relation). Similarly, any two elements from two different A_i's are not related. In our discussion, the relation is 1-equivalence, k-equivalence, or machine equivalence. In addition, the original set A is entire set of states. The partitions will be a set of equivalence classes (each class is a set of states that are related under the equivalence relation). We illustrate the definitions and equivalence classes through the following examples.

Example 8.7.1
Find the 1-equivalence partition, P_1, for the state table shown in the Table 8.7.1.

TABLE 8.7.1

An Example Table Used to Find 1 Equivalence

Present State	Next State		Output	
	x = 0	x = 1	x = 0	x = 1
A	B	C	0	0
B	D	E	0	0
C	F	G	0	0
D	A	E	0	0
E	D	F	0	0
F	D	E	0	0
G	A	G	0	1

In forming the partition we note that the union of the partitions is the entire set of states given in the state table. In addition, we note that two states belong to the same partition, if from these two states and on all possible single inputs, the outputs produced are identical. This is the same as saying the two rows produce the same outputs. From the state table, states A, B, C, D, E, and F have identical rows of output (0 for $x = 0$ and 0 for $x = 1$). As a result, the states form a 1-equivalence class. State G is in equivalence class by itself. The partition P_1 is then composed of two subsets $A_1 = \{A, B, C, D, E, F\}$ and $A_2 = \{G\}$.

Notation: To simplify, in the above example we write A_1 and A_2 as $A_1 = (ABCDEF)$ and $A_2 = (G)$. In addition, we write the partition obtained by the 1-equivalance as $P_1 = (ABCDEF)(G)$ with 1 corresponding to 1-equivalence.

Definition: A refinement of a given partition, P, is another partition where some of the original elements (subsets) of P are further partitioned into smaller subsets.

In Figure 8.7.2, the original solid lines are the partition lines of some partition P. In the refinement, to obtain some other partition P', the original partitions boundaries (solid lines) are not changed. Instead, additional boundaries are added. As can be seen from the figure, the refinement produces five subsets A_{11}, A_{12}, A_{13}, A_2, and A_3; the original element A_1 from P is further partitioned with $A_1 = A_{11} \cup A_{12} \cup A_{13}$.

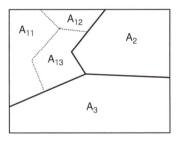

FIGURE 8.7.2

An Example of a Refinement. The original set of elements P_1 is partitioned into three disjoint subsets, as shown.

TABLE 8.7.2

Shows the Output Responses for All 2-Bit
Inputs, in Construction Refer to Table 8.7.1

	Output			
Present State	**x = 00**	**x = 01**	**x = 10**	**x = 11**
A	00	00	00	00
B	00	00	00	00
C	00	00	00	01
D	00	00	00	00
E	00	00	00	00
F	00	00	00	00
G	00	00	10	11

In the context of our discussions, the partitions formed from (k + 1)-equivalences classes are refinements of k-equivalence classes.

Example 8.7.2

Form the 2-equivalence partition of the previous example.

To form the 2-equivalence partition, we could construct the output produced by all inputs of length 2 by using states A through G as initial states. Table 8.7.2 shows the output responses for all 2-bit inputs. To generate the table, we refer to the original table (Table 8.7.1). On the input 00 and starting in state A, we move to state B and output 0 on the first 0 input. On the second 0 input, from state B we obtain the output 0. As a result from state A and input 00, the output produced is 00. This is shown in row 1 (current state A) and column 1 (input 00) of Table 8.7.2. Other entries are formed similarly.

From the table, the rows with labels A, B, D, E, and F have identical outputs. As a result, the corresponding states belong to the same equivalence class. Each of the remaining states is in a separate equivalence class. Hence, the partition, P_2, is $P_2 = \{A_1, A_2, A_3\}$ with $A_1 = (ABDEF)$, $A_2 = (C)$ and $A_3 = (G)$. Note that P_2 is a refinement of P_1. The new boundaries are added to the element $(ABCDEF)$ to produce two elements $(ABDEF)$ and (C). We will next discuss state minimization. Our discussion is based on the above definitions.

8.8   State Reduction and Minimal State Diagrams

Based on the previous discussion, we develop a procedure that reduces the number of states in a given state machine. For each state machine, the algorithm applied generates another equivalent machine with a minimum number of states. The reduction in number of states may yield a reduction in the number of memory elements needed in the design.

The algorithm we adopt is based on k-equivalence. It starts with partitions of the set of states formed from applying 1-equivalence. We obtain refinement of partitions by forming subsequent k-equivalence classes. The process of minimization stops when no further refinements are possible. This occurs when the partitions formed for some (k + 1)-equivalence are the same as those formed in the earlier k-equivalence partition. The procedure to form the successive refinements follows. It uses the following definitions.

Definition: For a given state, S_j, and a given input, i, define the i-successor (S_j) to be the state S_k, where S_k is reached from state S_j on input i.

For example, in the state table given in Table 8.7.1, 1-successor(C) is G. Similarly, 0-successor(A) is B. The above definition can be extended to a set of states.

Definition: For an input, i, and a set, A_j, the set of next states obtained by applying the input i to each state in the set A_j is called i-successor(A_j).

For example, assume given the partition, $P_1 = (ABCDEF)(G) = A_1 A_2$ as discussed in the previous section with regard to Table 8.7.1. Then, 0-successor(A_1) = (BDFADD).

We will make use of the above definitions in minimizing the number of states. To minimize the number of states in a given state machine, we:

Step 1: Form the partition of states, P_1 (example 8.7.1 is an illustration). On this set, we apply further refinements.

Step 2: Partition $P_{(k+1)}$ is obtained from partition P_k by processing each element of P_k. For each input, i, and each element, A_j, we form i-successor(A_j). The elements of A_i are partitioned according to i-successor(A_j). Two states in the set A_i are placed in two different sets if the i-successor states are in two different sets of P_K. To illustrate, assume $P_k = (A)(BCD)(F)$ with i-successor(BCD) = (AFF). From the discussion, the element (BCD) in P_k is partitioned to (B)(CD) in $P_{(k+1)}$ since states A and F belong two different sets in P_k.

Step 3: Step 2 is repeated until the new partition $P_{(k+1)}$ satisfies $P_{(k+1)} = P_k$, i.e., until the new partition is no longer a refinement partition. Note that step 2 is repeated a finite number of times since the number of states in a state machine is finite.

We illustrate the refinement procedure on the examples below.

Example 8.8.1
Construct all possible partitions P_k for the example state table given in Table 8.7.1.

From the example, we have $P_1 = (ABCDEF)(G)$. This is step 1 of the algorithm above.

For each set of states in the partition and for each input, we form the set of next states. Since our objective is to refine previous partitions, we consider sets with more than one state only.

For the set $(ABCDEF)$ and input 0, the 0-successor$(ABCDEF)$ set is $(BDFADD)$. Since the next states are elements of the same set in P_1, no partition on input 0 occurs. For the 1 input, the 1-successor$(ABCDEF)$ is $(CEGEFE)$. Of the states in the successor set state, G is not in the same set of states found in P_1 as the remaining successor sets. As a result, the set $(ABCDEF)$ is partitioned to $(ABDEF)(C)$ resulting in $P_2 = (ABDEF)(C)(G)$.

Since P_2 is not equal to P_1, step 2 of the algorithm is repeated. On the set $(ABDEF)$ and the input 0, the next states set obtained is $(BDADD)$. As a result, no separation (partition) of states occurs since the successor states belong to the same set in P_2. On the same set and an input of 1, the set of next sates obtained is $(CEEFE)$. The successor state results in $P_3 = (A)(BDEF)(C)(D)(G)$.

Since P_3 is not equal to P_2, we continue the above process on $(BDEF)$ with 0-successor$(BDEF) = (DADD)$ resulting in the refinement (BEF)(D), and 1-successor$(BDEF) = (EEFE)$. For P_4, we have $P_4 = (A)(BEF)(C)(G)$. On applying this step further, no additional refinements are made.

Since no separation of states occurs, the step of refinements stops with the states B, E, and F are equivalent states.

Example 8.8.2
Form all possible state equivalence partitions on the state table shown in Table 8.8.1.

From the table, we have $P_1 = (A)(BCF)(DE)$. Table 8.8.2 shows the successive application of step 2. Column 1 of the table contains the partitions with the corresponding elements to process. Column 2 contains the successor set for the given input. Column 3 contains the resulting partitions. In the table, since $P_2 = P_3$ the process of refinement stops.

Before we consider another example, we could make use of the definition to identify equivalent states from the state table in a preprocessing step. From the definition, two states are equivalent if they have identical rows, i.e., the next state rows as well as the output rows are the same. In Figure 8.8.1, A is equivalent to B since for any input sequence the output produced by starting at state A is the same as the output produced by starting at state B.

TABLE 8.8.1

State Table of Example 8.8.2

Present	Next State		Output	
State	x = 0	x = 1	x = 0	x = 1
A	B	C	0	0
B	C	D	0	1
C	B	E	0	1
D	D	F	1	1
E	E	F	1	1
F	F	A	0	1

TABLE 8.8.2

Partitions Obtained from Table 8.8.1

	Partition	i-successors		New Partitions
		i = 0	i = 1	
$P_1 =$	(A)(BCF)(DE)			
	(BCF)	(CBF)	(DEA)	(BC)(F)
	(DE)	(DE)	(FF)	(DE)
$P_2 =$	(A)(BC)(F)(DE)			
	(BC)	(CB)	(DE)	(BC)
	(DE)	(DE)	(FF)	(DE)

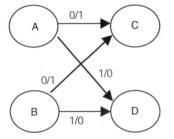

PS	x = 0	x = 1
A	C/1	D/0
B	C/1	D/0

FIGURE 8.8.1
From the Definition of State Equivalence. States A and B are equivalent

In a preprocessing step, we could identify equivalent states and from each set of equivalent states we could choose a representative element in a revised table. We illustrate the process in an example.

Example 8.8.3
Form the minimized reduced table of the state table given in Table 8.8.3.

From the table, in a preprocessing step we note that states *A* and *H* are equivalent since they have identical next state and output rows. In addition,

TABLE 8.8.3

Equivalent States, A and H Are
Equivalent, B and G Are Equivalent

Present State	Next State		Output	
	x = 0	x = 1	x = 0	x = 1
A	E	E	1	1
B	C	D	1	0
C	D	H	1	1
D	B	D	1	1
E	F	D	1	1
F	A	B	0	1
G	C	D	1	0
H	E	E	1	1

TABLE 8.8.4

Reduced Table, Obtained from Table 8.8.3

	Next State		Output	
Present State	x = 0	x = 1	x = 0	x = 1
A	E	E	1	1
B	C	D	1	0
C	D	A	1	1
D	B	D	1	1
E	F	D	1	1
F	A	B	0	1

state B and G are equivalent for the same reason. From this preprocessing step we form a reduced table with the G and H states removed. Note that state H is referenced from state C and on input $x = 1$. Since state H is removed from the reduced table, H is replaced by its equivalent state, A. The reduced table is given in Table 8.8.4.

From the above discussions for the partitions, we have $P_1 = (ACDE)(B)(F)$. For P_2 we process the 0 and 1 successors of $(ACDE)$ to get

$$(ACDE) \xrightarrow{0-successor} (EDBF) \xrightarrow{Partition} (AC)(D)(E)$$

and

$$(ACDE) \xrightarrow{1-successor} (EADD) \xrightarrow{Partition} (ACDE)$$

As a result, the new partition P_2 is $P_2 = (AC)(D)(E)(B)(F)$. Since P_1 is not equal to P_2, we continue the process of refinement. Note that there is at most one additional partition P_3 possible. If no refinements occur we stop the process ($P_2 = P_3$); if there is refinement on the other hand, then the refinement splits (AC) into (A) and (C) and, as a result, no additional refinements are possible. For the 0-successors of (AC), we have

$$(AC) \xrightarrow{0-successor} (ED) \xrightarrow{Partition} (A)(C)$$

Since each state is placed in its own partition, no further partitions are possible. Since P_3 is equal to $(A)(B)(C)(D)(E)(F)$. The reduced table above is the minimal state table.

8.8.1 The Reduced State Table

The above partition procedure is used to form the reduced state table as follows. The number of elements in the final partition is equal to the number of states in the reduced state table. Each element in the partition represents a state in the reduced state table. To form the transitions between states, we

TABLE 8.8.5

Final Reduced Table with Needed Transitions for Example 8.8.2, (a) the
Equivalent States from Table 8.8.2, (b) Table with Renamed States

(a)					(b)				
Present	Next State		Output		Present	Next State		Output	
State	x = 0	X = 1	X = 0	x =1	State	x = 0	X = 1	x = 0	x =1
(A)	(BC)	(BC)	0	0	A_1	A_2	A_2	0	0
(BC)	(BC)	(DE)	0	1	A_2	A_2	A_3	0	1
(DE)	(DE)	(F)	1	1	A_3	A_3	A_4	1	1
(F)	(F)	(A)	0	1	A_4	A_4	A_1	0	1

consult the original state table and the *i*-successors of the last partition
formed. Table 8.8.5 shows the reduced table with needed transitions for
example 8.8.2. The equivalent states shown in Table 8.8.2 are (A), (BC), (DE),
and (F).

To simplify from a notation point of view, the state labels can be renamed.
Table 8.8.5(b) of the table shows the equivalent state table. In the table, the
labels (A), (BC), (DE), and (F), are replaced, respectively, with the labels A_1,
A_2, A_3, and A_4.

Note that with the reduced state table the number of memory elements
needed in the design has decreased from three to two memory elements.

Chapter 8 Exercises

8.1 Given the characteristic equations, A^+ and B^+, and the output equation, out, such that

$A^+ (A, B, x) = A + xA'$

$B^+ (A, B, x) = B + (xA)'$

Out $= A + B$

Design the sequential circuit that realizes the above functions using D flip-flops.

8.2 Verify the circuit designed in question 1 is correct by generating the characteristic equations from the circuit design.

8.3 Given the characteristic equations, A^+ and B^+, and the output equation, out, such that

$A^+ (A, B, x) = ABx + A'B$

$B^+ (A, B, x) = Bx + AB'$

Out $= A B$

(a) Show the design of the circuit using JK flip-flops.

(b) Verify your design is correct by deriving the characteristic equations of the circuit and showing the equations are equal to above given equations.

8.4 Given the characteristic equations, A^+ and B^+, and the output equation, out, such that

$A^+ (A, B, x) = x + A'B$

$B^+ (A, B, x) = x + B$

Out $= (A B)'$

Design the circuit that realizes the above functions using JK flip-flops.

8.5 Given the state diagram constructed in example 8.5.2. Form a new state diagram with two memory elements X and Y and with the assignment $XY = 00, 01, 10,$ and 11 representing the states $A, B, C,$ and D, respectively.

8.6 Show the complete design procedure of example 8.5.2 based on the assignment given in question 8.5. Use D flip-flop for X and SR flip-flop for Y.

8.7 Repeat question 8.6 based on the assignment $XY = 00, 01, 10, 11$ representing $A, C, D,$ and B, respectively. Use JK flip-flops for both memory elements X and Y.

8.8 Show the complete design of the soda vending machine example given in Example 8.5.1. Use a normal binary encoding scheme to represent the states with 000 representing the state with the label 0, 001 representing the state with label 10, etc. Design your circuit using JK flip-flops.

8.9 Construct the Mealy state diagram of a sequential circuit with a single input. The circuit outputs a 1 whenever the binary input entered thus far is divisible by 5. Assume the number is entered from most significant to least significant. For example, on the input 110101 the output produced is 000001.

8.10 Construct the Moore machine state diagram of the circuit description given in question 8.9.

8.11 Construct the Mealy state diagram of a circuit that receives a single input. The circuit outputs a 0 until either of the sequences 000, 001, or 111 are detected. The output is 1 on all inputs afterward.

8.12 Show the design of the state diagram of the adder circuit given in example 8.5.4 using

(a) D flip-flops

(b) JK flip-flops

(c) T flip-flops

(d) SR flip-flops

8.13 Show the design of the circuit of the state diagram given in example 8.6.2 using

(a) D flip-flops

(b) JK flip-flops

(c) T flip-flops

(d) SR flip-flops

8.14 Show the design of a sequence detector detecting the sequence 10111 using D flip-flops.

8.15 Show the design of a sequence detector detecting the sequence 10111 using JK flip-flops.

8.16 Given the state table shown in Figure E8.1. Find the minimal state table.

Present State	Next State X = 0	x = 1	Output x = 0	x =1
A	B	C	0	0
B	D	E	0	0
C	F	G	0	0
D	A	E	0	0
E	D	F	0	0
F	D	E	0	0
G	A	G	0	1
H	B	C	0	0
I	D	E	0	0

FIGURE E8.1

8.17 Given the state table shown in Figure E8.2. Find the minimal state table.

Present State	Next State X = 0	x = 1	Output x = 0	x =1
A	B	C	0	0
B	G	D	0	1
C	D	A	0	0
D	C	B	1	0
E	C	F	1	0
F	A	D	0	1
G	B	C	0	0

FIGURE E8.2

8.18 Given the state table shown in Figure E8.3. Construct the corresponding state diagram. From the state diagram, construct the equivalent Moore state diagram.

Present State	Next State X = 0	x = 1	Output x = 0	x =1
A	B	A	0	0
B	B	C	0	0
C	D	A	0	0
D	B	C	1	0

FIGURE E8.3

9

Registers, Counters, and Memory Elements

CONTENTS

In this chapter, we discuss some of the common sequential circuits used in computer organization and design. The discussion is analogous to the discussion in Chapter 5, where we discussed iterative design procedures of common combinational circuits. In this chapter, we discuss common sequential circuits using an iterative procedure where needed. In particular, we discuss registers, counters, general-purpose registers/counters, register files, and random access memory (RAM). The circuits discussed are widely used as components in digital computer design. We start our discussion with registers.

9.1   Registers

A register is a sequence of storage memory elements that are treated as a single memory unit. Registers are used to hold temporary data for processing or for communication between two units in the computer. They are characterized according to (1) their size (the number of memory elements, flip-flops, they contain), (2) the method of reading the memory elements, and (3) the method of writing to the memory elements.

9.1.1   Parallel Registers

Information can be stored in a register in parallel. An n-bit parallel register is a register with n inputs. Each of the n inputs is used to store information in one of the n memory elements. Similarly, an n-bit parallel read register has n outputs; each output is used to read one of the 1-bit memory elements. The diagram in Figure 9.1.1 shows an example of a 4-bit parallel load and parallel read register. The design uses D flip-flops.

The inputs to the circuit, I_0 through I_3, can be stored into the memory elements during one clock cycle. This is the case since the same clock pulse samples all flip-flops simultaneously. The term "parallel load" is used since the contents of the memory elements are loaded in parallel during the same clock cycle. Similarly, the contents of the register can all be read at once at the output leads, Out_0 through Out_3, as shown in the diagram.

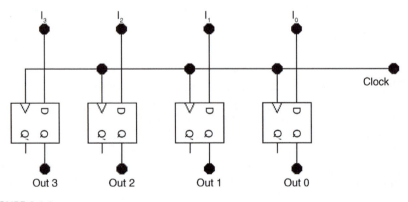

FIGURE 9.1.1
An Example of a 4-Bit Parallel Load and Parallel Read Register

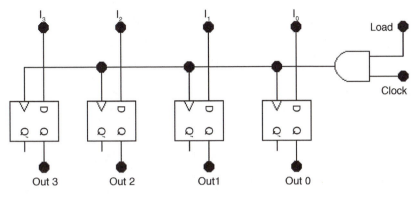

FIGURE 9.1.2
An Example of a 4-Bit Parallel Load and Parallel Read Register with a Load Control Input

The 4-bit register shown in Figure 9.1.1 is modified during each clock cycle. At the rising edge of the clock, the contents of the input lines are moved into the register, and hence possibly erasing the previous stored values. As we will see later in this chapter, it is possible to connect many registers to the same set of input lines. During a given clock cycle, the circuit may require that only one of theses registers be modified. As a result, one needs a mechanism by which only the desired register can store information while the contents of all other registers are left unchanged. To accomplish this, we add a control line. The line is used to control loading information into a register.

The circuit in Figure 9.1.2 shows this for a 4-bit register with the control line added. The register is similar to the circuit in Figure 9.1.1 but with an additional load input. In order for the inputs to be stored in the register, the load line must assume a value of one, and the clock must make a transition in logic value from low to high. When the load line value is 0, the contents of the registers are not affected by the values on the input line.

In Chapter 7, we discussed glitches as unwanted outputs that are caused by the different propagation delays of a given circuit. In synchronous sequential circuits, it is desired that the different memory units in the circuit are sampled at the same time. Here, a clock is used to send the needed signals in a synchronous fashion to all the circuit units. When gates are inserted in the path of a clock, the arrival time to the units will differ. The phenomenon is called "clock skew." To reduce clock skew, it is desirable to minimize the number of gates in the path of the clock signal. This will reduce the delay in arrival times of the clock signal to the different components of the circuit. Figure 9.1.3 shows a 4-bit register with the clock signal connected directly to the clock inputs of the flip-flops.

In the figure, if the load input is 0, then the inputs to each of the memory elements is the previous output value of the corresponding memory element. As a result, for this input the flip-flop contents do not change. If the load input assumes a value of 1, however, then the input to each flip-flop is the

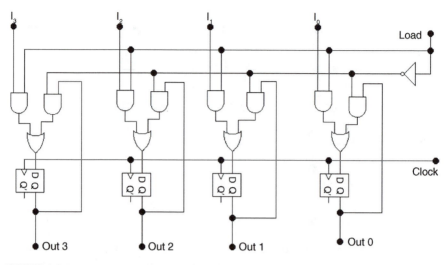

FIGURE 9.1.3
A 4-Bit Register with a Load Control Input and with the Clock Signal Connected Directly to the Clock Inputs of the Flip-Flops

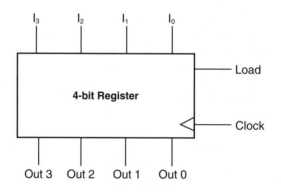

FIGURE 9.1.4
Block Diagram of a 4-Bit Register with a Load Input

corresponding external input, I_j. On the rising edge of the clock the inputs are stored in the corresponding memory elements. In block diagram, we could show the 4-bit register as given in Figure 9.1.4. Note that the register has four inputs and four outputs. This is not the case for shift registers, which are discussed next.

9.1.2   Shift Registers

Shift registers are used to store information in the register one bit at a time. Similarly, they can be designed to read information from register one bit at a time as well. Shift registers act on the stored information in a register by shifting its contents to the left or to the right. The topic of shifting an operand

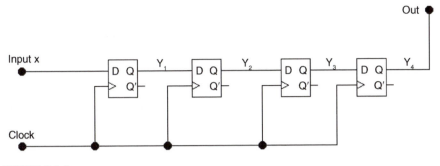

FIGURE 9.1.5
A 4-Bit Shift Register

TABLE 9.1.1

Input X = 1100 Is Shifted from LSB to MSB into 4-Bit Shift Register

Clock Cycle	Input X	Contents of the 4-bit register 			
		Y_1	Y_2	Y_3	Y_4
1	0	0	?	?	?
2	0	0	0	?	?
3	1	1	0	0	?
4	1	1	1	0	0

to the left was discussed in the arithmetic and logic unit (ALU) design section of Chapter 5.

In shift registers, the contents of one flip-flop are connected to the input of the adjacent flip-flop depending on method of shifting the stored information. In Figure 9.1.5, the diagram represents a 4-bit shift register. The information to be stored in the register is applied to the line with the input label. On the rising edge of the clock, the input is stored in the left-most memory element. At the same time, the values stored in the flip-flops are shifted to the flip-flop directly on their right. The register is a shift-right register. In order to store the needed data in the register, we apply the data in a serial fashion one bit at a time. By applying the input one bit a time, on the fourth clock cycle the register will contain the desired data.

Table 9.1.1 illustrates this for the input 1100. The symbol "?" is used to indicate that the contents of the register are not known. Initially, all outputs are assigned "?." On the rising edge of the first clock cycle, the left-most flip-flop input is sampled. As a result, its output stores the value at the input x. Note that all other flip-flop inputs are sampled as well; however, these flip-flop values remain "?." On the next clock cycle, the input x is stored in the left-most flip-flop (output Y_1). Similarly, the output of the left-most flip-flops is moved into Y_2. This is indicated in the table using arrows as shown.

As can be seen from the table, it takes four clock cycles to store information in the register. Similarly, in order to read information out, one must move

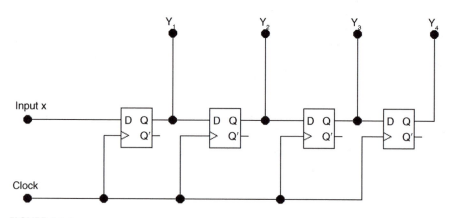

FIGURE 9.1.6
A 4-Bit Shift Register with Parallel Out

the contents of the memory elements to the output of the flip-flop with label "Y_4." In its current form, reading information out of the register will modify its contents. In general, when one reads information from a storage device, it is desired that the contents of the device do not change as a result of reading. The register design above can be modified to read information in parallel; Figure 9.1.6 illustrates this. The contents of the register are read at the outputs with labels Y_1 through Y_4. The contents of the register can be read during a single clock cycle.

To incorporate a load line, one can use the clock input as was done earlier for the case of the parallel register. Here, however, in order to store information in the register the load line should be held at one for four clock cycles. Figure 9.1.7 shows the modified register. The circuit design can be modified to remove clock skew. The design is used as an exercise.

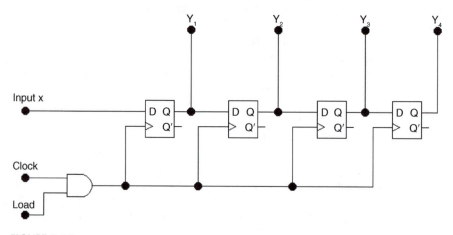

FIGURE 9.1.7
A 4-Bit Shift Register with Parallel Out and with a Control Load Input

9.2 Counters

Counters are sequential circuits similar to registers but follow a predetermined periodic sequence of outputs. When the periodic sequence of outputs is the binary counting sequence, the counter is called a binary counter. The counters we consider count the clock pulses generated externally. In the discussion that follows, we characterize counters as synchronous or asynchronous. In synchronous counters, all memory elements receive the same clock signal at their inputs. This is not the case for asynchronous circuits.

9.2.1 Mod-2^n Synchronous Counters

A modulo-m (mod-m) binary counter is a sequential circuit that counts in binary from 0 to $m - 1$. On application of the clock pulses, the binary sequence with decimal values equal to 0, 1, ..., $(m - 1)$ is repeated with 0 following the $(m - 1)$ count. When m is equal to 2^n, for some arbitrary n, the design of the counter can be achieved iteratively using n JK or T flip-flops. We illustrate the design using the standard design procedure first on the example that follows. From the example, we conclude an iterative generalized design procedure.

Example 9.2.1

We would like to design a mod-8 binary counter. The circuit has no inputs. Its outputs are the flip-flop outputs. On the application of clock cycles, the circuit repeatedly outputs the binary counts 000, 001, ..., 111, 000, ...

In the design, we would like to use T flip-flops. The number of flip-flops needed is three as shown in the generated binary count (1 flip-flop per bit of counting is needed). The excitation table for the design is shown in Table 9.2.1. The K-maps with the minimized functions are shown in Table 9.2.2. For the C flip-flop, the input T_C is equal to 1 since this bit of the counter changes on the application of each clock cycle. The design of the counter is

TABLE 9.2.1

Excitation Table of a Mod-8 Counter Using T Flip-Flops

A	B	C	A⁺	B⁺	C⁺	T_A	T_B	T_C
0	0	0	0	0	1	0	0	1
0	0	1	0	1	0	0	1	1
0	1	0	0	1	1	0	0	1
0	1	1	1	0	0	1	1	1
1	0	0	1	0	1	0	0	1
1	0	1	1	1	0	0	1	1
1	1	0	1	1	1	0	0	1
1	1	1	0	0	0	1	1	1

TABLE 9.22

K-maps Generated from the Excitation Table Given in Table 9.2.1

AB C	00	01	10	11
0	0	0	0	0
1	1	1	1	1

TB = C

AB C	00	01	10	11
0	0	0	0	0
1	0	1	1	0

$T_A = BC$

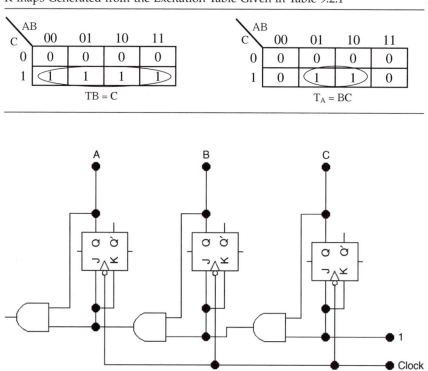

FIGURE 9.2.1
Mod-8 Counter Design of Excitation Table Given in Table 9.2.1

shown in Figure 9.2.1. Note the design is shown using JK flip-flops which are converted to T flip-flops. The design in the example is that of a synchronous counter. The counter design is synchronous since all flip-flops are sampled at the same time by the same falling edge of the clock. We contrast this with other designs shortly.

The above design can be generalized to design mod-2^n binary counters for an arbitrary large n. To illustrate we refer to the design above and a property of binary counting discussed in earlier chapters. In binary counters, in order for the bit at location i to change (toggle from 0 to 1 or from 1 to 0) all previous bits must be equal to 1. This is similar to the case of a decimal counter; in order for the decimal 6 to change to 7 in the number 672, for example, all previous digits must be equal to 9. Similarly for the binary number 1010, in order for the third bit (0) to change, all previous bits must assume a value of 1.

This property holds true in the design above. When using JK or T flip-flops, to change the output of the flip-flop the inputs are assigned a value of 1. For the case of the A flip-flop, for example, the flip-flop output changes

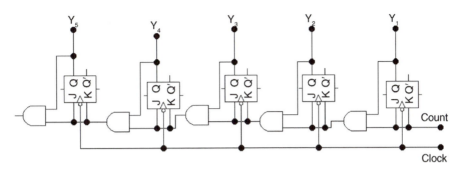

FIGURE 9.2.2
Design of a Mod-32 Binary Counter Using JK Flip-Flops

if all the previous bits assume a value of 1, i.e., the input to the flip-flop should be the product term BC. When both B and C assume a value of 1 and when the flip-flop inputs are sampled at the falling edge of the clock, the flip-flop output is changed (complemented).

Using this observation, we can extend the design procedure to a mod-2^n counter with outputs $Y_n Y_{(n-1)} \ldots Y_1$. For each flip-flop with output Y_i, we form the product $Y_{(i-1)} \ldots Y_1$. This product is used as an input to the flip-flop with output Y_i. The circuit diagram in Figure 9.2.2 shows an example of a mod-32 counter. We make three observations about the diagram. First, the circuit contains an additional input called count, as seen in the figure. When this input is assigned a value of 0, the inputs to all flip-flops assume a value of 0. As a result, the circuit outputs do not change. On the input count = 1, the circuit counts the clock pulses as intended. The count input is used as an enable to the circuit; when count = 1, the circuit counts the clock pulses as intended. On the other hand, the circuit stops counting when count = 0.

The second observation has to do with the AND gates. The gates are cascaded with the outputs of one gate used as inputs to the other. The cascading results in delays in obtaining a valid output at these gates. For example, consider the inputs to the flip-flop with output Y_5, the changes in Y_1 are rippled through four AND gates.

The final observation is with regard to the left-most AND gate. This gate is included to generate larger counters. For example, two mod-16 counters can be cascaded to generate a mod-2^8 binary counter. The two mod-16 counters receive the same clock signal at their clock inputs. The output of the AND gate associated with Y_4 is used as a count input into one of the cascaded counters as shown in Figure 9.2.3.

9.2.2 Mod-M Counters for General M

The above design procedures can be applied to mod-m counters when m is equal to 2^n for some integer n. For other cases where m is not a power of 2, we could apply the design procedure discussed in the previous chapter and

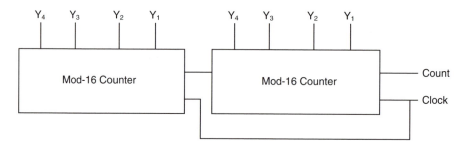

FIGURE 9.2.3
Design of Counters from Smaller Counters

applied in example 9.2.1. Alternatively, we could make use of the memory elements asynchronous clear. To accomplish the design, we use mod-2^n counters with

$$n = \lceil \log_2 m \rceil$$

We present examples of the two design procedures next.

Example 9.2.2
In the first example, we would like to design a mod-5 counter. The counter has no inputs. Its output is the repeated binary sequence 000, 001, 010, 011, 100. Following the 100 output, the circuit repeats the sequence by starting at 000.

The excitation tables for the circuit, using T flip-flops, are shown in Table 9.2.3. The K-maps and minimized outputs are shown in Figure 9.2.4. The design is given in Figure 9.2.5.

An alternative method of designing the above circuit is to make use of the asynchronous reset inputs of a mod-8 counter. In the design, when the count value is 100 the circuit is reset asynchronously to 0. This is done by using the output A as an input to the asynchronous clear of the flip-flops. We illustrate the design procedure in the following example.

TABLE 9.2.3

Excitation Table of a Mod-5 Counter Using T Flip-Flops

A	B	C	A⁺	B⁺	C⁺	T_A	T_B	T_C
0	0	0	0	0	1	0	0	1
0	0	1	0	1	0	0	1	1
0	1	0	0	1	1	0	0	1
0	1	1	1	0	0	1	1	1
1	0	0	0	0	0	1	0	0
1	0	1	x	x	x	x	x	x
1	1	0	x	x	x	x	x	x
1	1	1	x	x	x	x	x	x

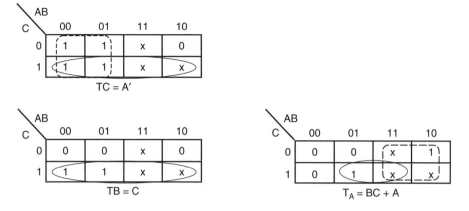

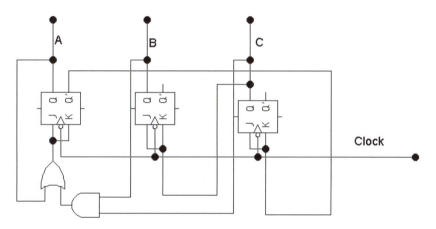

FIGURE 9.2.4
K-Map of Excitation Table, Table 9.2.3

FIGURE 9.2.5
Circuit Design of Excitation Table, Table 9.2.3

Example 9.2.3

We would like to design a mod-10 counter using a mod-16 counter with asynchronous preset and clear. The design is accomplished by causing the circuit to reset to the count 0000 following the maximum count value, 1001. This is shown in Figure 9.2.6.

In the figure, the counter functions in normal mode (counts as needed) if count is less than 1001. When the count output reaches 1001 (on the falling edge of the clock), the output of the AND gate with inputs Y_1 and Y_4 is set to 1. This output is used as an asynchronous clear input to each of the flip-flops. As a result, shortly after the output assumes a value of 1001, the circuit is reset to 0000 independent of the clock. Hence, the output at Y_1 is seen as a pulse with very short duration. This may result in undesirable design since the short duration of the pulse may not be observed by other units in the design.

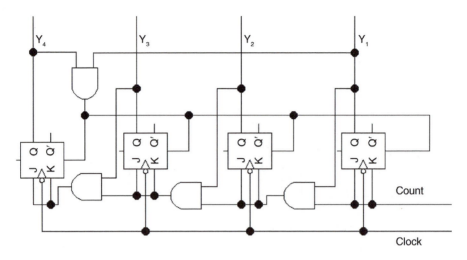

FIGURE 9.2.6
Design of a Mod-10 Counter from a Mod-16 Counter. Note the use of the asynchronous clear.

Current count value	Next count-down value
1110	1101
1101	1100
1111	1110
1100	1011

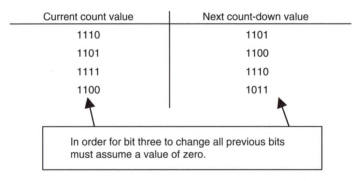

In order for bit three to change all previous bits
must assume a value of zero.

FIGURE 9.2.7
Counting Down in Binary

9.2.3   Binary Counters with Decreasing Counts

The above design procedures can be used to design circuits that can count
downward as well. The previous counters are called mod-m up-counters.
The counters considered here are called mod-m down-counters. In the
design, we consider the design of mod-2^n down-counter. As discussed earlier,
one can make use of counting properties to realize the design. For the case
of counting up, the inputs to a specific flip-flop (JK or T) received the product
of all previous bits in the count. In counting down, in order for a specific bit
to change (toggle), all the previous bits in the count must assume a value of
0, as shown in Figure 9.2.7. Hence, to cause the bit to change, we form the
product of the previous complemented bits. This product is used as an input
to the corresponding flip-flop.

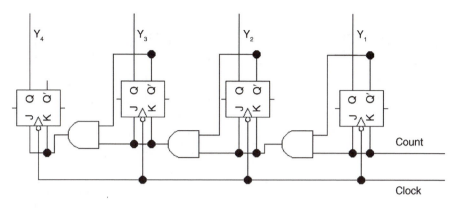

FIGURE 9.2.8
Mod-16 Count Down Binary Counter

Figure 9.2.8 shows the design of a mod-16 down-counter using JK flip-flops. Note the complemented outputs of the memory elements in the figure. These outputs are used as inputs into the AND gates, as is the case for counting up in binary counters.

9.3 Asynchronous, Ring, and Johnson Counters

9.3.1 Asynchronous Counters

Counters can be realized asynchronously as shown in the circuit example given in Figure 9.3.1. The design is asynchronous since the flip-flops are not sampled by the same clock signal. As can be seen from the figure, the clock input to the first flip-flop (with output Y_1) is the external clock input. This

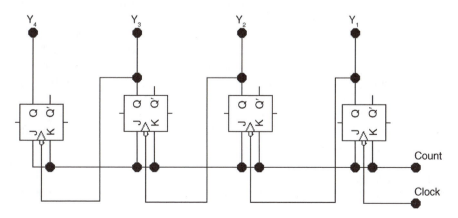

FIGURE 9.3.1
Ripple Counter

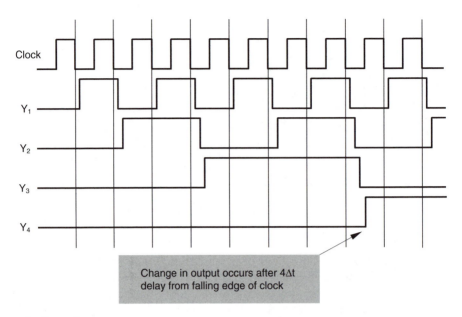

FIGURE 9.3.2
Ripple Counter Timing Diagram

is not the case for the remaining flip-flops. The clock input to the flip-flop with output Y_2 is Y_1. Similarly, the clock input to the flip-flops with output Y_3 and Y_4 are, respectively, Y_2 and Y_3. If count = 1, then the inputs to all flip-flops causes each flip-flop to toggle when sampled.

The circuit design is called a ripple counter. Ripple counters are among the simplest counters to design. In the design of ripple counters, the correct count is not obtained shortly after a clock transition. The delay in the memory elements are rippled through the counter with the least-significant bit producing the correct output first and the most-significant memory element producing the correct output last. We illustrate this using the timing diagram given in Figure 9.3.2. In the timing diagram, note the ripple delay effect from the falling edge of the clock (similar to the delay found in ripple adders). Assume the output associated with each flip-flop is delayed by Δt time units from the time the flip-flop inputs are sampled. With this assumption, the delay associated with Y_4 is $4\Delta t$ time units, as shown in the figure.

Earlier, we defined a counter as a circuit that periodically produces a sequence of outputs. The binary counter discussed earlier produced a sequence of binary counts. This sequence need not be a counting binary sequence but any arbitrary sequence that repeats periodically; ring counters and Johnson counters are examples. We will discuss the use of such counters when we look at the design of the control unit of a computer.

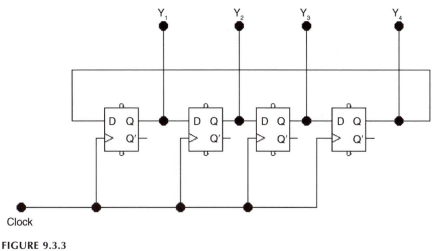

FIGURE 9.3.3
Ring Counter

9.3.2 Ring Counters

Ring counters are generated from shift registers. The counter is constructed by (1) connecting the last output of the shift register to the input of the first flip-flop, and (2) initializing exactly one bit in the register to 1 (the first bit). With these conditions, on the applications of clock pulses, the 1 bit is shifted to adjacent flip-flops in a circular fashion. Figure 9.3.3 is an example of a 4-bit ring counter. The initial memory element outputs are $Y_1 Y_2 Y_3 Y_4 = 1000$. On each rising edge of the clock, the output follows the sequence 1000, 0100, 0010, 0001. This sequence is repeated with 1000 following 0001.

Note that the outputs of the circuit satisfy the following two conditions. First, over one clock cycle, exactly one output assumes a value of 1. Second, the output is ordered where during the first clock pulse Y_1 assumes a value of 1. During the second clock pulse, Y_2 assumes a value of 1. Similar logic applies to the remaining outputs. We will see the importance of such circuits when we discuss computer cycles in Chapter 11. The timing diagram shown in Figure 9.3.4 reflects the order discussed.

An alternative method to generate the above sequence can be accomplished by using a 2-bit binary counter and a 2-to-4 decoder. Figure 9.3.5 illustrates this for a larger case. In the figure, the counter output is 000 initially. As a result, the output of the 3-to-8 decoder is 10000000. On the application of the clock pulses, the counter output follows the sequence 000, 001, 010, 111, 000. As a result, the decoder output follows the sequence 10000000, 01000000, 00100000, 000100000, 000000000.

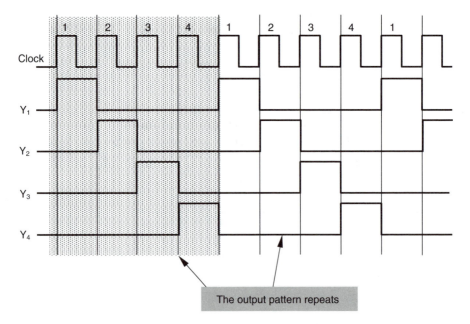

FIGURE 9.3.4
Timing Diagram Obtained from Ring counter in Figure 9.3.3

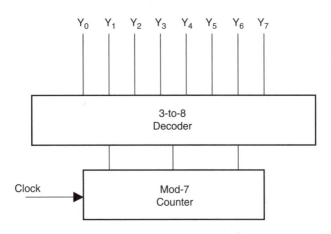

FIGURE 9.3.5
An Example Circuit that Generates 8 Timing Signals Instead of 4 Timing Signals as Given in Figure 9.3.4

9.3.3 Johnson Counters

Consider the circuit shown in Figure 9.3.6. The circuit is similar to a ring counter with the feedback connection changed. The complemented output of the last flip-flop is now connected to the input of the first flip-flop. Assuming the initial outputs of all flip-flops are 0, on the application of clock cycles

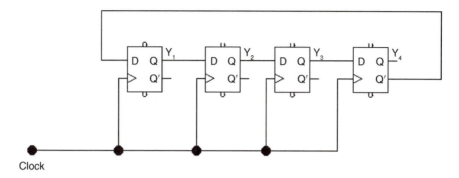

FIGURE 9.3.6
Johnson Counter

we obtain the repeated sequence 0000, 1000, 1100, 1110, 1111, 0111, 0011, 0001, 0000, etc.

We illustrate as follows. During the first clock pulse, the complement of the last flip-flop (right-most flip-flop) is shifted into the first flip-flop (left-most). Zeros are shifted in the remaining flip-flops. As a result, following the 0000 output, the next output obtained is 1000. On the next clock pulse, the last flip-flop output is still 0. As a result, 1 is shifted into the first flip-flop. The result of the shift is to obtain the next output in the sequence, 1100. This process continues until the output becomes 1111. Following this output, since the complement of the right-most flip-flop is 0, on the next clock pulse we obtain the new output 0111. The same logic is applied to obtain the remaining outputs in the sequence.

As can be seen from the sequence given above, with k-bit Johnson counter we generate $2k$ different sequences. In this sequence, one can inspect the binary code for each state and derive a unique expression. The expression should evaluate to 1 only when a particular sequence is currently at the output. The expression generated should evaluate to 0 otherwise. This is done so as to distinguish between the patterns in the sequence. Generating the minterms corresponding to each element of the sequence is sufficient. By inspection of outputs, however, one can generate a simpler set of product terms. Finding the set of product terms will be done as an exercise.

9.4 General-Purpose Register-Counter Circuits

In this section, we expand on the pool of sequential circuits by considering circuits that serve as both a register and a counter. We start by considering the diagram in Figure 9.4.1. In the circuit, if the T input assumes a value of 0, then the output of the XOR gate is Q. As a result, when the flip-flop inputs are sampled, we have $Q^+ = Q$, i.e., the flip-flop outputs remain unchanged.

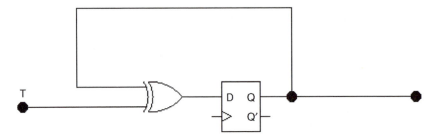

FIGURE 9.4.1
Design of T Flip-Flop from a D Flip-Flop

If the input T is 1, however, the output of the XOR gate is Q'. As a result, the next output Q^+ will be the complement of Q. From the discussion, the circuit functions as a T flip-flop.

The rationale for generating a T flip-flop from a D flip-flop is due to the fact that in register design it is best to use D flip-flops as the component memory elements. For binary counters, however, it is best use T flip-flops. With the T flip-flop design, the binary counter circuits discussed in the previous section can be designed iteratively using D flip-flops as well. To accomplish this, we replace each of the JK flip-flops (T flip-flops) by the circuit shown in Figure 9.4.1.

Our goal is to design circuits that could function as counters as well as being able to function as registers. Multiplexers can be used to design a circuit that serves as both a register and a counter. To illustrate we construct three circuits. The first circuit is used as a counter or a parallel register, as shown in the next example.

Example 9.4.1
In this example, we would like to design a circuit that functions as a 4-bit binary counter or a 4-bit register. We assume the circuit has a single control input, C. If C is equal to 1, then the circuit functions as a register. If C is equal to 0, however, the circuit functions as a binary counter.

Solution: To design the circuit, we make use of 2-to-1 multiplexers. The control input to the multiplexers is the C input. The circuit in Figure 9.4.2 shows the design using the T flip-flop construction from D flip-flops. The circuit function is based on the two possible values of the control input C. First for C = 0, the outputs of the multiplexers, from right to left, are I_0, I_1, I_2, and I_3. When the flip-flop inputs are sampled, these inputs are stored into the circuit. Hence, the circuit functions as a register.

Second for C = 1, the output of the right-most multiplexer is the complement of Y_0. Hence, on successive clock pulses this flip-flop output is continually complemented. This property is similar to counting. For the second multiplexer from the right, its output is either Y_1 or its complement. If the previous Y_0 value is 0, then the output of the multiplexer is Y_1. Hence $Q_1^+ = Q_1$. If Y_0 is 1, however, the output of the multiplexer is the complement of

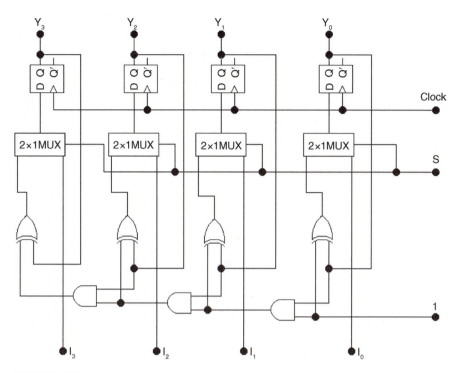

FIGURE 9.4.2
A Circuit That Functions as a Counter or a Register. On S = 0 the circuit is a register. On S = 1 the circuit is a counter.

Y_1. This property is again similar to the counting property in binary counters. By inspecting the circuit, we note that in order for Y_2 to change (from 0 to 1 or vice versa) both Y_0 and Y_1 must assume a value of 1. Similarly, in order for Y_3 to change, all least-significant bits Y_0, Y_1, and Y_2 must assume a value of 1; thus from the discussion, the circuit function as a mod-16 binary counter.

The previous circuit is always in one of two possible states: a count state or a register state. In general, we would like to have control inputs that cause the contents of the circuit to remain unchanged. To do this, we follow a procedure similar to that discussed above with a larger multiplexer and additional control inputs. We illustrate this with a second example.

Example 9.4.2
In this example, we would like to design a circuit that serves as a 4-bit register or a mod-16 binary counter as discussed earlier. Here, however, additional control inputs are used to allow for keeping the contents of the register circuit unchanged. We would like the circuit to function according to the description given in Table 9.4.1.

The circuit can be designed by expanding the design procedure given in the above example. In the design, we use 4-to-1 multiplexers. The circuit design is given in Figure 9.4.3. From the figure, if $S_1 S_0 = 00$, then the multiplexer

TABLE 9.4.1

Function Description of Register
in Figure 9.4.3

S_1	S_0	Circuit Function
0	0	Leave contents unchanged
0	1	Store inputs I_0 to I_3
1	0	Count up

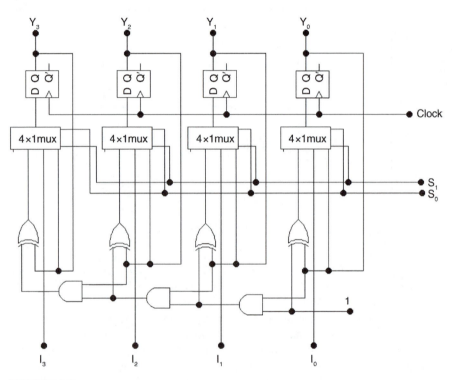

FIGURE 9.4.3
General-Purpose Register, Control Is S1S0

outputs are the previous Y_i outputs of the flip-flops. As a result, the circuit contents remain unchanged. For $S_1S_0 = 01$, the circuit function as a register since the flip-flops inputs are I_0 through I_3. Finally, if the control inputs are $S_1S_0 = 10$, then the circuit functions as a mod-16 counter.

In the circuit design, the function of the circuit is not specified when both of the control inputs assume a value of 1. We could increase the functionality of the circuit by making use of this unused case. To illustrate, we consider a third example.

TABLE 9.4.2

Function Description of Register
in Figure 9.4.4

S_1	S_0	Circuit Function
0	0	Leave contents unchanged
0	1	Store inputs I_0 to I_3
1	0	Count up
1	0	Count down

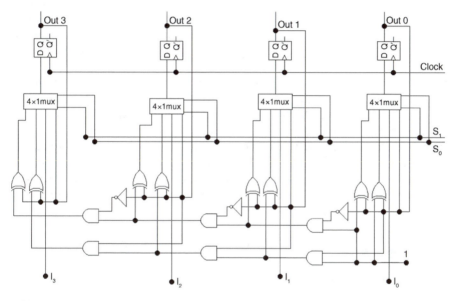

FIGURE 9.4.4
General-Purpose Register. Control is S1S0

Example 9.4.3

In this example, we would like to expand on the functionality of the previous
example by designing a circuit that functions as a down-counter as well. The
new function of the circuit is given in Table 9.4.2.

Using a procedure similar to what was done in the previous two examples
we obtain the circuit shown in Figure 9.4.4. In the circuit, the unused previous
multiplexer input is now used to cause the circuit to count down. In counting
down, as discussed earlier, a particular bit is left unchanged until all previous
bits assume a value of 0. These conditions are satisfied by the circuit design
given in Figure 9.4.4.

Before we conclude this section, we return to designing mod-m binary
counters where m is not a power of 2. (The three examples presented in this

section realize counters that are mod-2^n.) In the previous section, for designing counters that count from binary 0 to binary m where m is not a power of 2, we considered two methods of design. In the first method, we followed the general design procedure where we formed the excitation tables from the circuit description. From these tables we then could form the minimized flip-flop equations and complete the design. The method is tedious for counter circuits with many flip-flops. In the second method of the design procedure, we used a mod-2^n counter with asynchronous reset where

$$n = \lceil \log_2 m \rceil$$

The asynchronous reset caused the circuit output to assume the maximum value $(m - 1)$ for a very short duration of time. The short duration may result in design errors.

An alternative design procedure is to synchronously cause the counter to count mod-m by using the circuit given in example 9.4.1. To accomplish the design, we assign zeros to the parallel inputs of the register. When the count reaches the correct value of $m - 1$, we send a signal on the multiplexer select inputs to change the circuit function to store the contents of the inputs. As a result, on the next clock pulse, the memory elements are all set to 0. This pattern repeats, causing the circuit to function as a mod-m counter. The design of a mod-10 counter using this procedure is shown in Figure 9.4.5.

9.5   Memory Block Diagram

In this section, we discuss the block diagram organization of random access memory (RAM). RAM is a memory unit in the computer that is used to hold programs and data while the program is running. RAM is an example of a set of storage devices that hold information. Other devices include registers, hard disks, and diskettes. An example organization of RAM in a block diagram is shown in Figure 9.5.1.

In the figure, memory is composed of words. A word is a set of memory locations that can be moved out of or into memory as a single entity. As can be seen from the example block diagram, the memory contains 1024 words (word 0 to word 1023). A word is characterized by its content and its address. In the diagram, word 1 is the address of word 1; its content (or value) is (10101111). The contents of the word could represent either data or instructions, as will be discussed later. The size of the memory unit is the total number of bits. In the example, the memory unit size is 1024 × 8 (number of words × the size of each word).

The contents of a memory word can be accessed through the use of buses. A bus is a set of lines used to communicate between different units (e.g., the

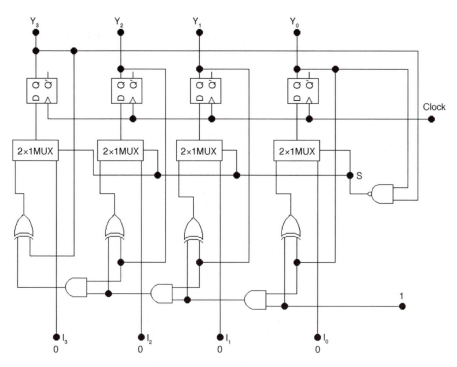

FIGURE 9.4.5
Synchronous Mod-10 Counter. On output 1001 the circuit functions as a register.

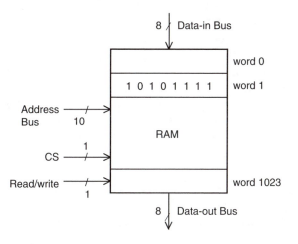

FIGURE 9.5.1
The Contents of Memory Location Is $(AF)_H$

CPU and memory). In Chapter 5, we considered the output of the ALU as a bus. In the figure, the memory block diagram shows three buses: the address bus, the data-in bus, and the data-out bus. The size of a bus is the number of lines used. In the figure, the data buses are 8 bits each. The address bus is 10 bits. The address and bus sizes are a function of the memory organization. In general, for a RAM with n words and m-bit word size, the number of address lines is given as

$$\lceil \log_2 n \rceil$$

The number of data-in and data-out lines is given as m, the size of each word. In the example figure, the size of the bus is 10 bits ($\lceil \log_2 1024 \rceil = 10$), with the address of word 0 given as $(0000000000)_2 = (0)_{10}$ and the address of the last word given as $(1111111111)_2 = (1023)_{10}$.

Reading from memory is the process of retrieving the contents of a word by placing its content on the data-out bus. This is done by placing the address on the address bus and informing memory of a read request (using read and write input signals). In the figure, there is one input line labeled read/write; a 1 on the line indicates a read request and a 0 indicates a write request. We will discuss the chip select later. Writing to memory is the process of modifying the contents of a memory word. Similar to reading, in order to write to memory we specify the address of the word on the address lines and place word contents on the data-in bus. We also indicate a write request on the read/write line.

In the block diagram of RAM given in Figure 9.5.1, the CS line is used to select a specific chip for reading or writing. This is done since general designs may have multiple RAM chips. These RAM chips may share a common set of data-in and data-out lines. The CS line is used to choose one of these chips for communication.

Before we conclude this section, however, we mention that the term "RAM" is used to indicate that words in memory can be accessed in any random fashion in approximately equal time. Contrast this with accessing information on a tape; accessing information at the beginning of the tape takes less time than accessing information toward the end of the tape (assuming the tape is rewound to the beginning). Another name used for RAM is read/write memory (RWM) to distinguish it from read-only memory (ROM).

9.6   Building Larger RAM from Smaller RAM

Physical limitations on the design of RAM impose a limit on the number of words that can be placed within a single memory chip. In this section, we present methods of constructing larger memories from individual smaller RAM chips. First, we look at Figure 9.6.1, a block diagram that represents the communication between the CPU and external memory. In the figure,

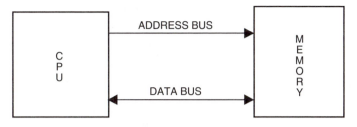

FIGURE 9.6.1
Block Diagram Schematic of Data and Address Buses between the CPU and Memory

the RAM representation is hypothetical; instead of a single RAM memory chip, the memory is formed from several RAM chips. To illustrate this, consider a CPU with 32-bit address bus (today, CPU address buses are 32 or 64 bits). As a result, the RAM needed may exceed 2^{32} words, approximately 4 G words. Today, RAM-chip word capacities are much smaller than 4 G. Hence, RAM is built from an array of smaller RAM chips. We use the following example to illustrate generating larger RAM circuits from smaller ones. The example uses a small address bus for illustration purposes only.

Example 9.6.1
Consider a CPU with an 8-bit address bus. With an 8-bit address bus, one can address 256 words of memory. Assume the available RAM chips contain 64 words, i.e., the address bus for each chip is 6 bits. The diagram in Figure 9.6.2 illustrates how one could create a larger memory with 256 words using four RAM chips.

To illustrate, assume the CPU issues the address $(0000\ 0000)_2$. Using the diagram in Figure 9.6.2, the location of the word with this address is found to be in location 0 of each of the RAM chips. From these, however, only one RAM chip (RAM0) is selected using the CS enable line. Similarly, the address $(1011\ 1111)_2$ is translated to the address of the last word in the third RAM chip (RAM2). As can be seen from the diagram, the first 6 bits in the address line of the CPU are used to identify the words within each RAM. This is due to the fact that words with the same six least-significant bits on the address bus are mapped to the same relative location with respect to each RAM. Similarly, by inspecting the figure, one notes that the two most-significant digits of the CPU address bus are the same for all words corresponding to a given RAM, 00, 01, 10, and 11, respectively.

In general, for a CPU with an address bus of n bits and RAM chips with 2^m words, in order to generate memory with 2^n words, one needs $2^{(n-m)}$ RAM chips and an $(n-m) \times 2^{(n-m)}$ decoder. The diagram in Figure 9.6.3 illustrates this for the case of a CPU with a 16-bit address bus and a RAM with 2^{10} words. From the above, one needs $2^{(16-10)} = 64$ RAM chips. In addition, one needs a 6×64 decoder.

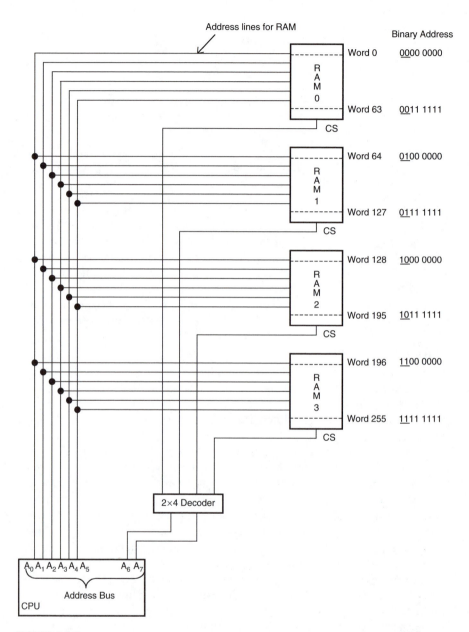

FIGURE 9.6.2
Building RAM with 256 Words from RAMs with 64 Words

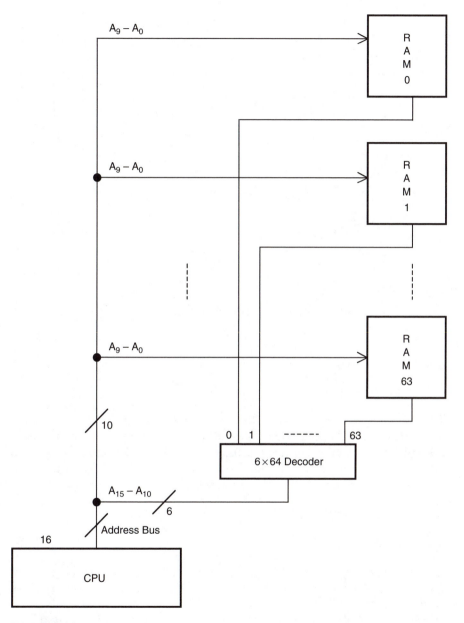

FIGURE 9.6.3
Building 64 K RAM from 1 K RAM Chips

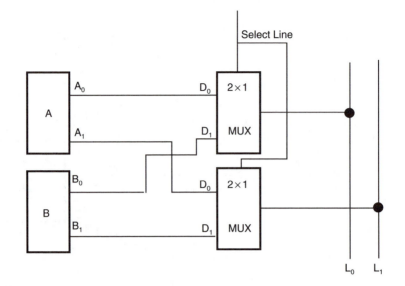

FIGURE 9.7.1
Connect Multiple Units to Common Data Lines L1 and L0

9.7   The Data Bus Connections

The previous discussion dealt with connections associated with the address bus component. The following discussion deals with the connections associated with the data bus. In the discussion, we use the concept of a common data bus that is used to communicate between the CPU and memory. In order for a unit to communicate with another unit, its contents must first be placed on the data bus.

9.7.1   Connections Using Multiplexers

One way to connect multiple units to the same set of lines is to use multiplexers as discussed in Chapter 5. Figure 9.7.1 illustrates this for the case of connecting two units to a single bus (set of lines). The units are labeled A and B, respectively, with each having two output lines. The bus is two lines labeled L_0 and L_1, as shown in the figure.

For this connection, one uses two 2-to-1 multiplexers, one for each line of the bus; a single select line is used to select A or B to be placed on the bus. As can be seen from the diagram, if a value of 0 is placed on the multiplexer select lines, then L_0 is connected to A_0 and L_1 is connected to A_1, i.e., unit A is placed on the bus. Similarly, if the select line of the multiplexer is set to 1, then unit B is placed on the bus line.

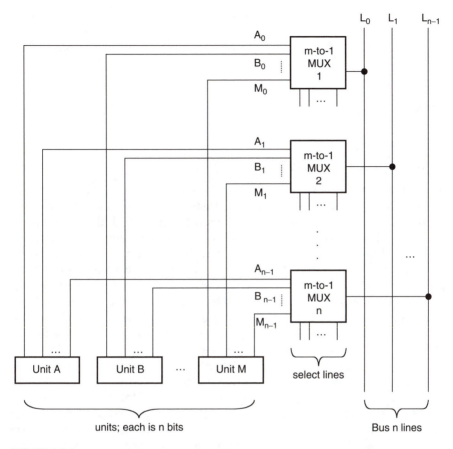

FIGURE 9.7.2
Connecting m Units to a Common Bus. Each unit is n bits.

In general, the number of multiplexers used in connecting multiple units to a common bus is a function of the size of the bus; with n lines, the number of multiplexers needed is equal to n. The number of data lines of each multiplexer is equal to the number of units. Figure 9.7.2 illustrates this. In the figure, we assume m units are connected to the bus. As a result, the multiplexers used are m-to-1 multiplexers. In addition, we assume that each unit is n bits (the bus size is n bits), and hence n multiplexers are needed.

We illustrate the function of the circuit by placing zeros on the select lines of the multiplexers. Zeros on the inputs of the multiplexers cause each multiplexer to place the contents of its first data line on the corresponding output. As a result, the data bus line with label L_0 receives the value A_0. Similarly, the remaining multiplexers outputs receive the values $L_1 = A_1, \ldots,$ and $L_{n-1} = A_{n-1}$, i.e., the contents of unit A are placed on the bus lines. Similar analysis can be used to verify that other units can be placed on the bus lines. This is done by placing the proper inputs on the select lines of each multiplexer.

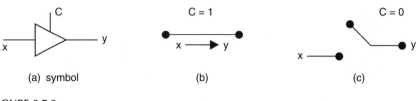

(a) symbol   (b)   (c)

FIGURE 9.7.3
Tristate Connections

9.7.2 Connections Using Tristate Gates

The use of multiplexers requires the use of many gates and, as a result, may be expensive. An alternative design uses tristate gates. A tristate gate is a circuit with one control input, c, one input, x, and one output, y. If the control input is equal to 1, then the output value follows the input value, i.e., $y = x$. If the control input is 0, however, the output is floating and is not connected to anything. Figure 9.7.3(a) shows the symbol for the tristate gate; Figure 9.7.3(b) and (c) show the equivalent connections as a result of $c = 1$ and $c = 0$, respectively. When the c control input is equal to 1, the value at the output, y, follows that of the value at the input, x. If $x = 0$, then y assumes a value of 0; similarly, if the input x assumes a value of 1, then the output y assumes a value of 1. In the figure, the arrow indicates that y receives the value of x but not vice versa.

In electrical engineering terms, Figure 9.7.3(c) corresponds to a connection with high impedance (resistance). High impedance means in physical terms that there is no connection between the input and output; that is, the value at the input does not affect the value at the output. Tristate gates offer alternative methods of connecting multiple units to the same bus. Figure 9.7.4 illustrates this for the case of connecting two units. Each unit is of size 2 bits. The decoder input is used to select between one of two units. In the figure, if the decoder input is 0, then unit A places its contents on the bus lines. This is the case since the B unit is not connected to the bus lines, as shown in Figure 9.7.5.

Figure 9.7.4 can be generalized to connect m units to a common bus with each unit of size n bits. For m units, one needs to use a decoder of size $k \times 2^k$ where

$$k = \lceil \log_2 m \rceil$$

Figure 9.7.6 illustrates this for the general case involving m units.

9.8 Internal Design of Memory

In this section, we present a gate design of RAM memory called static RAM (SRAM). Alternative designs of RAM are called dynamic RAM (DRAM).

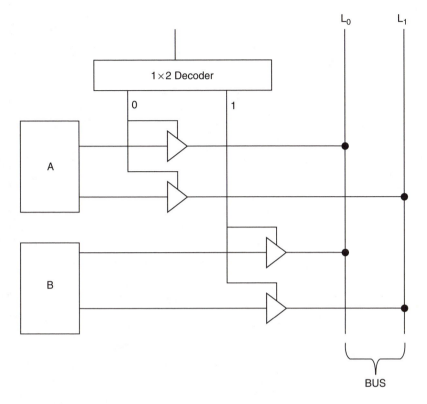

FIGURE 9.7.4
Connecting Multiple Units to Common Lines Using Tristate Gates with Decoders

DRAM designs are based on the concept of storing binary values as electric charge using capacitors, for example. DRAM design is not considered in the text.

9.8.1 Gate Design of a Single Memory Cell

At the gate level, static RAM can be modeled as composed of memory cells where each memory cell is designed by using latches or flip-flops. For each memory cell, one needs to be able to select the cell and indicate the request is for reading or for writing. The circuit diagram shown in Figure 9.8.1 illustrates this. The circuit in the diagram functions as shown in Table 9.8.1. Note that the access to the memory cell output is at the output of the tristate gate; if the select input is assigned the value of 0, then no changes to the memory cell can occur and the output to the cell is floating. To read or write, the select input must be set to 1. To read, a 1 on the R/W causes the output of the memory cell to be seen at the tristate output labeled out; to write, a 0 on the R/W input causes the S and R inputs to receive *in* and its complement, *in'*, respectively. As a result, this input is stored in the memory cell.

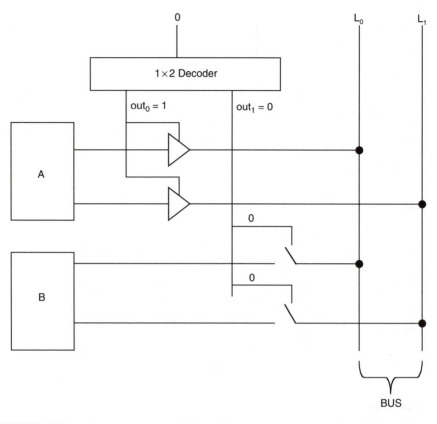

FIGURE 9.7.5
Effect of Assigning 0 to the Decoder Input

9.8.2 RAM Design with Two Data Buses

To design a RAM with 2^n words and with m bits per word, one needs $2^n \times$ m memory cells. Selecting words within memory is accomplished using an $n \times 2^n$ decoder. The decoder outputs are used to select one of the 2^n words for reading or writing. All the memory cells associated with a given word are selected simultaneously by the same decoder output. Figure 9.8.2 shows an example of a RAM with four words; each word is 3 bits in size. In the diagram, a memory cell (MC) corresponds to 1 bit of memory. The internal design of each is shown in Figure 9.8.1. The combination of the three memory cells on the same row constitutes the contents of a word in memory. The decoder is used to select which word to read from or to write to. This is done by specifying the address of the word on the address bus (the inputs to the decoder). The chip select of memory is the enable part of the decoder. If this value is set to 0, then all outputs of the decoder are set to 0; hence, no memory cell is selected.

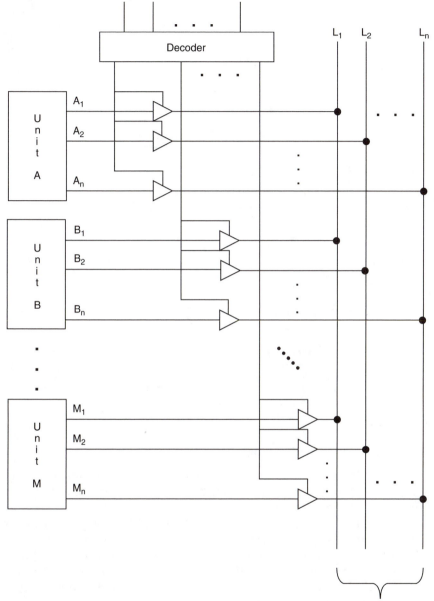

FIGURE 9.7.6
Connecting m Units to a Bus Using Tristate Gates

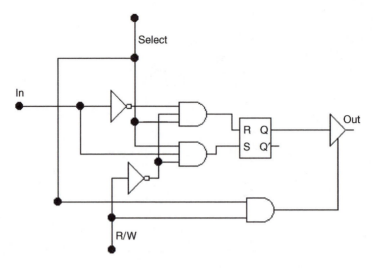

FIGURE 9.8.1
Design of a Memory Cell

TABLE 9.8.1

S	R/W	Q⁺	Out
0	x	Q	Floating
1	0	In	Floating (write to memory cell)
1	1	Q	Q (read from memory cell)

9.8.3   RAM Design with a Single Data Bus

The diagram in Figure 9.8.2 is an example of RAM with two data buses, one
for input and one for output. To reduce the number of communicating lines
between the CPU and memory, one can use a single data bus for both input
and output. This can be done using tristate gates. The diagram in Figure
9.8.3 shows this for an example device. As can be seen from the diagram,
the direction of information flow will be into the device if the R/W line is
set to 0. The direction of information, however, will be out of the device if
the R/W value is set to 1. When applied to the RAM circuit given in Figure
9.8.2, we obtain the RAM circuit shown in Figure 9.8.4. Note the pair of
tristate gates found in Figure 9.8.3 carries into the design in Figure 9.8.4.
These tristate gates are found as part of the memory cells.

The examples of RAM given above are for instructional purposes. Actual
physical RAM could exceed 256 M bits in size. (This is especially true when
the RAM is designed based on DRAM technology.) For the 256 M memory,
for example, one needs a very large decoder; the decoder should generate
all 228 possible minterms. The previous view of memory was based on a

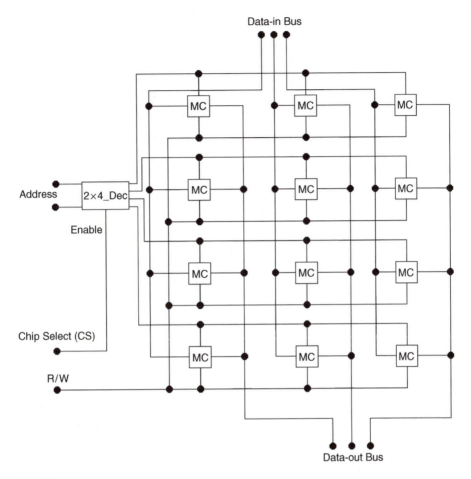

FIGURE 9.8.2

Design of a Small RAM from Memory Cells in Figure 9.8.1 with Data-In and Data-Out Separate Buses

one-dimensional address space view. In two-dimensional address decoding, one can significantly reduce the size of the decoder used for addressing. Figure 9.8.5 illustrates this view on words 1-bit in size. As can be seen in the figure, memory is organized into a two-dimensional array. To select a word, the CPU address is split into two decoders, a column and a row decoder. The intersection determined by the row and column addresses determines the 1-bit word for reading or writing. The two-dimensional view can be extended to include words of arbitrary size, as shown in Figure 9.8.6. In the figure, two decoders are used to select the proper column and proper row in the memory organization as discussed above.

The saving involved in using two-dimensional address decoding is given in Table 9.8.2. The table assumes an equal number of rows and columns. The size of the address on the address bus is given as n. This address is then

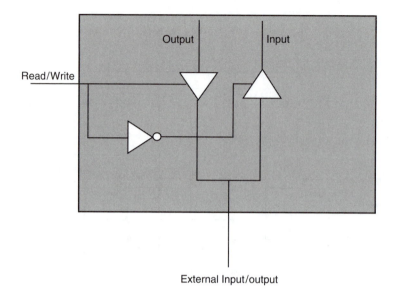

External Input/output

FIGURE 9.8.3
The Figure Shows How the Same External Lines Can Be Used as Input or Output Lines Using Tri-State Gates

split among the row and column decoders. In general, the number of minterms generated for a two-dimensional decoding is given as $2.2^{n/2} = 2^{(n/2)+1}$, where n is the size of the address bus. The savings in the number of minterms (as compared to one-dimensional decoding) is $2^n - 2^{(n/2)+1}$. This results in major savings in the cost of generating minterms. For example, for an address bus of size 20 bits, the saving in the minterm generation is approximately 98%.

9.9   Register Files

Register files are a form of memory that can be used within the CPU. An example block diagram of a CPU is shown in Figure 9.9.1. The detail of the design is given in the next chapter. In the diagram, the block labeled "Register File" contains a set of registers that communicate with the outside through two output buses and one input bus. The information placed on the bus can be processed using the ALU, as discussed in Chapter 5. The processed information can then be stored back in the register file using the input bus.

Selecting which register to place on the buses is done through the use of two decoders. Similarly, a decoder can be used to select the destination register to store the information found on the input bus. Figure 9.9.2 shows

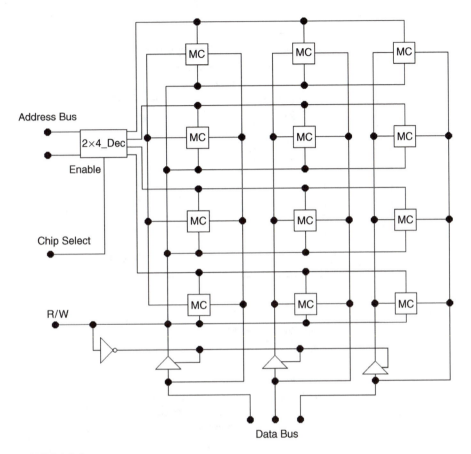

FIGURE 9.8.4
Design of a Small RAM from Memory Cells in Figure 9.8.1 with a Common Data-In and Data-Out Bus

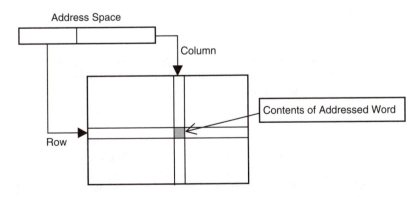

FIGURE 9.8.5
Two-Dimensional Address Decoding View of Memory. Word size is 1 bit.

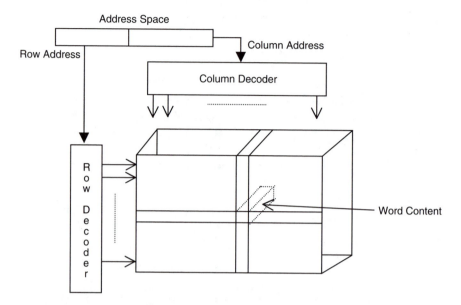

FIGURE 9.8.6
Two-Dimensional Address Decoding View of Memory

TABLE 9.8.2

Saving When Two Dimensional Decoding
Is Used, Saving Is Measured as a Reduction
in the Number of Minterms

	Number of Minterms	
Bus Size	One Decoder	Two Decoders
2	4	4
4	16	8
10	1024	64
20	1 M	2048

a partial design of a register file with two registers, each register of size 2 bits. The figure includes the bus system and a set of tristate gates to enable information to be connected to the bus.

As can be seen from the diagram, in order to place the contents of the top register on the bus with label A, one needs to enable the decoder associated with the bus. In addition, the address of the register (0) is placed on the decoder associated with the A bus. The tristate gates ensure that there are no conflicts in requests; for example, a request to connect the A bus to both registers simultaneously. Note that the design allows for placing the contents of the same register on both buses simultaneously, however.

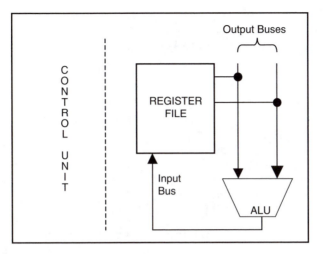

FIGURE 9.9.1
Block Diagram of CPU

The design of the register file can be generalized to include many registers of arbitary sizes. Figure 9.9.3 shows the general design of a register file with *n* registers and with each register of size *m* bits. Missing from the design are the tristate gates and the decoders needed to route information accordingly.

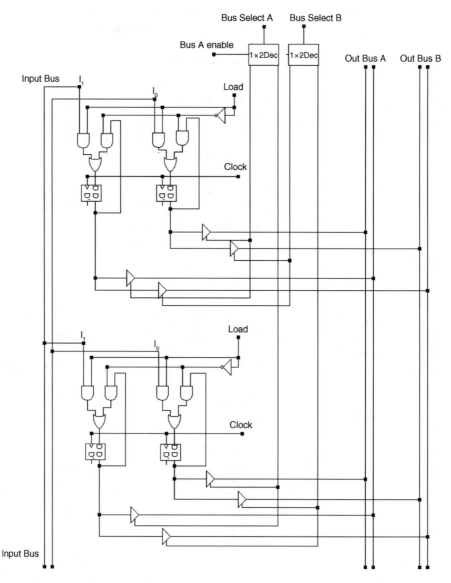

FIGURE 9.9.2
Register File Realization, Schematic Shows Two 2-Bit Registers Connected to Two Buses A and B

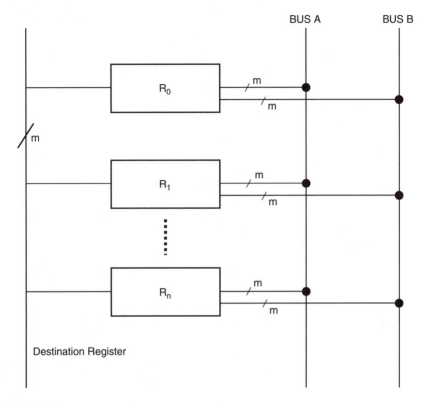

FIGURE 9.9.3
Block Diagram Representation of Register File Connections

Chapter 9 Exercises

9.1 Show the design of 4-bit parallel load register with a load line using SR flip-flops.

9.2 Show the design of a 4-bit parallel load register with a load line using T flip-flops.

9.3 Design a 4 bit shift-right register with a load line using D flip-flops.

9.4 Design a 4-bit rotate right register with a rotate control input, R. If R assumes a value of 0, then the contents of the register remain unchanged. If R assumes a value of 1, then the contents of the register are shifted to the right with the contents of the least-significant bit shifted into the contents of the most significant bit. Use D flip-flops in your design.

9.5 Repeat problem 9.4. Use JK flip-flops in the design.

9.6 Show the design of asynchronous mod-9 counter using mod-16 binary counters.

9.7 Show the design of a mod-5 asynchronous counter using a mod-8 binary counter.

9.8 Show the design of a mod-6 synchronous counter using a mod-8 counter.

9.9 Show the design of a counter with the sequence 1, 3, 5, 7. The sequence repeats with the count 1 following count 7. Use JK flip-flops in the design.

9.10 Show the design of a counter with an external input x. If x assumes a value of 1, then the counter is a mod-16 count-up counter. If x = 0, then the counter is a mod-16 count-down binary counter. Use JK flip-flops.

9.11 Design a 4-bit register with the following function. Use D flip-flops and multiplexers in your design.

Control Inputs ($C_1 C_0$)	Function
00	Synchronous clear the contents of the register
01	Load register in parallel
10	Serial shift-right contents
11	Serial shift-left contents

9.12 Repeat problem 9.11 with the design using JK-flip-flops instead.

9.13 Form the timing diagram for the circuit (Figure E9.1). The timing diagram should include the clock signal as well as the output of the

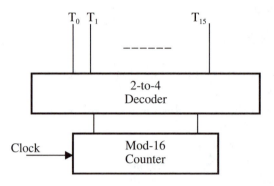

T_0 T_1 T_{15}

2-to-4
Decoder

Clock

Mod-16
Counter

FIGURE E9.1

decoder signals (T_0 through T_{15}). Include 20 clock cycles in the timing diagram.

9.14 How many flip-flops are needed if one is to design a circuit with a similar timing diagram as given in problem 9.13 using Ring counters?

9.15 How many flip-flops are needed to design a circuit with similar output to problem 9.13 using Johnson counters?

9.16 Show the design of a single memory cell using a D flip-flop. Except for the use of a different flip-flop in the design, the functionality of the cell should be similar to the memory cell discussed in the chapter.

9.17 Given a RAM unit with 1024 words and 16-bit word, what is the minimum number of inputs and outputs to the RAM unit? Construct the block diagram of the RAM and label its inputs and outputs.

9.18 Assume we are to build 1024 16-bit word RAM. Assume as well, the available RAM chips are 1024 8-bit words. Show the design of such a RAM from the available memory chips. Include the bus and data connections.

9.19 Construct a 1024 1-bit word RAM from 256 1-bit word RAM. Show the address bus connections.

9.20 Repeat question 9.19 but show the address bus as well as the data-bus connections. Assume two data buses are used in the design, a data-in and a data-out bus.

9.21 Show the address bus and data bus connections in the design of a 64-word, 4-bit RAM from 16 1-bit word RAM. Assume a bidirectional data bus RAM.

9.22 Assume one is to design a register file that contains 16 32-bit registers with the outputs connected to a single data-out bus and the inputs connected to a single data-in bus. Assume as well that multiplexers are used to select which register to place on the bus output and a decoder is used to select which register to load with the data-in bus contents. Determine the number and size of the multiplexers/decoders used in the design and the total number of gates in each.

9.23 Show the design of the register file described in problem 9.22. Use 2-bit registers, instead of 16-bit registers, for illustration.

9.24 Repeat problem 9.22, use tristate gates instead of multiplexers in your design.

9.25 Show the register file design of problem 9.24. Use 2-bit registers for illustration.

9.26 Show the design of a register file with four registers, each register is 4-bits. Assume the register file outputs are connected to two data buses A and B. Assume as well the input to the register file is a C bus. Use decoders and tristate gates to complete the bus connections. Assume the register labels are R_0, R_1, R_2 and R_3. Give the decoder values so as to simultaneously (1) place register R_1 on the A bus, (2) place register R_2 on the B bus, and (3) to store the C bus in register R_0.

10

Instruction Set Architecture

CONTENTS

10.1 Instruction Set of a Computer

Instruction sets of a computer are associated with the organization of the central processing unit (CPU) of the computer. We discuss the instruction sets of a computer by relating them to high-level languages. Consider a C++ statement for adding two variables, $x = x + y$. As you know from programming, the statement can be executed using the same processor or using different processors, assuming an appropriate compiler exists. The compiler is an example of a translator that translates high-level languages (such as C++) to a machine-dependent language. The language the compiler generates is a subset of instructions found in a computer's instruction set.

Each computer has a unique instruction set associated with it. The instruction set is composed of individual primitive instructions that instruct the hardware of the computer to specify a primitive task such as moving the contents of a memory location to a register within the CPU, or adding the contents of two CPU registers. The instructions generated depend on the organization

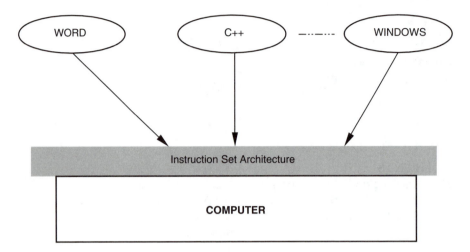

FIGURE 10.1.1
An Abstract View of the Interface between the CPU and the User. All programs must first be converted to the instruction set of the computer.

or architecture of the computer and, as a result, can be called instruction set architecture.

The instruction set of a computer is the language the computer can interpret. All programs must first be translated to the computer's instruction set before they can be run by the underlying machine (computer). Figure 10.1.1 shows sample programs such as Word, Windows, and C++ programs. In addition, we show the block diagram of the hardware part of the CPU presented conceptually as a block diagram. In order for those programs to run on the computer, they must first pass through the buffer block (the instruction set).

In the next sections, we present two different types of architectures and a hypothetical sample of instruction set associated with each. We then describe how one can translate high-level language constructs to the associated instruction set. In the following chapter, we look at the complete design of a simple CPU.

10.2 Accumulator-Based Instruction Set Architecture

Instructions are written so as to be intimately associated with the organization of the CPU. It addresses the question of which part of the CPU and/or memory a user can access in software. In this section, we discuss the accumulator-based instruction set and the corresponding CPU organization.

10.2.1 Accumulator-Based Architecture

First we emphasize that, in the context of memory of a computer system, memory is used to hold both data and instructions. Memory is a passive unit that is used exclusively for information storage. As a result, any processing of information is done outside of memory. For example, consider the for-loop construct in a high-level language. For this construct, memory can be used to store the value of a counter variable, i, used in the "for" loop. In order to increment the counter variable, the variable must first be read from memory into the CPU. The CPU contains temporary storage elements called registers, as discussed in the previous chapter. Once in the CPU the variable can be incremented using the arithmetic logic unit (ALU) of a processor, as discussed in Chapter 5. Finally, the incremented variable is stored back in memory.

In the accumulator-based architecture, in general, the user has control over one storage register in the CPU (this will become clearer as we progress in the subject discussion in this chapter). In order to process data, the data must be present in this special register called the accumulator (AC). The type of instructions the instruction set designer chooses is based on the functionality desired as well as the underlying architecture. A possible block diagram of an accumulator-based CPU is shown in Figure 10.2.1. The architecture includes additional registers that will be discussed later.

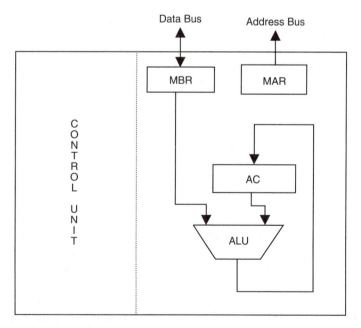

FIGURE 10.2.1
A Block Diagram of an AC-Based CPU

The figure is somewhat similar to the CPU organization presented in the previous chapter in the register file section. The three registers shown can be placed in the block diagram representing the register file part of the CPU. As can be seen from the diagram, the accumulator register serves as both a source and destination for one of the ALU inputs (operands). The other input to the ALU is the memory buffer register (MBR). As the name implies, the MBR is used to hold information as a buffer between the CPU and memory. In this organization of the CPU, all traffic, instructions, and data between the CPU and memory is temporarily stored in MBR, which is connected to the data bus of the CPU. The data bus was discussed in the previous chapter; it connects the CPU to the outside memory. The data bus is shown as a bidirectional data bus, i.e., it is used to move data out of and into the CPU.

In Figure 10.2.1, the register MAR (memory address register) contains the address of an instruction or data found outside the CPU, in memory for example. In the discussion of RAM in the previous chapter, we represented the data and address bus connections to memory. These buses were connected to the CPU. As can be seen from the diagram, the address bus contents are found in the register MAR. The data to be read or written is placed in MBR. We will discuss the details of these connections in the next chapter.

10.2.2   Accumulator-Based Instructions

With the accumulator-based (AC) CPU organization given earlier, the task of an instruction set designer is to form a set of primitive instructions. These instructions are used for communication between the outside and the hardware of the computer. All programs written in high-level languages must first be translated into the instruction set of the underlying computer before they can be executed. The same high-level language program may be translated into different instruction sets, depending on the computer used. We discuss some common accumulator based instructions next.

10.2.2.1   Load and Store Instructions

We have mentioned earlier that all instructions (programs) and data are stored in memory. We have also mentioned that processing data is done outside of memory, as memory is a passive unit. As a result, in order to increment a variable stored in memory, one needs to bring the variable from memory. The instruction set architecture then needs to include instructions that transfer data from memory to the CPU, load instructions, and store instructions. We use symbolic names for these instructions and relate them to high-level languages later.

A load instruction directs memory to place a content of a word on the data bus. This word is then stored in the CPU. As we have mentioned earlier, the word is stored in MBR. In the accumulator-based instruction, the accumulator is used implicitly as the final destination to load the word. To read a specific word in memory, one needs to specify its location. The method used in specifying the locations is called addressing mode. For now, we consider a special type of addressing mode called direct addressing. In direct addressing, one specifies the address of the word in memory where information is to be retrieved or stored. The specification is used as part of the instruction.

From the discussion, a load or store instruction will be composed of two parts, one indicating the type of operation used and the other indicating the address of the operand. For example, if we use the abbreviations LOD for load accumulator and STO for store accumulator, then LOD 100 has two parts, the operation part (LOD) and the address part (100). When this instruction is executed, the contents of memory at address 100 (assume decimal base is used) are loaded into the accumulator. Similarly, STO 100 will store the value of the accumulator into the memory word at memory location 100. Other symbolic names for LOD and STO are used such as LDA and lw for load and STA and sw for store. The abbreviations LDA, lw, STA, and sw stand for load accumulator, load word, store accumulator, and store word, respectively.

10.2.2.2   Arithmetic and Logic Instructions

The power of a computer is attributed to both the ability to store information and to process information with high speed. Performing arithmetic operations is part of the overall procedures of processing information. The instruction set of the computer is closely associated with the hardware design of the CPU. For example, if the ALU part of the CPU includes hardware for addition and subtraction, then the instruction set should include primitive add and subtract instructions.

In the accumulator-based computer organization as shown in Figure 10.2.1, for operations that require two operands such as add and subtract operations, one of the operands is assumed to be in the accumulator. Since the only accessible CPU register to a user is AC, the other operand (assuming direct addressing) is found in memory. In addition, in programming one usually performs arithmetic operations with the intention of storing the result in a variable using assignment statements as in the example $x = 2 + 3$. Here, the statement specifies the operation, the operands, and the location to store the result. Similarly at the instruction set architecture, one needs to specify the operation, the operands, and the location to store the result.

In the accumulator-based instruction set, both the source of one of the operands as well as the location to store the result is implicitly determined as the accumulator. From the discussion, for example, if we use ADD and SUB as abbreviations for add and subtract operations respectively, then ADD 100 would mean to add the contents of the accumulator to the contents of the word found at memory location 100. The result obtained is stored in the accumulator (replaces the previous value of the accumulator). Similarly, SUB 100 would mean subtract from contents of the accumulator the contents of the word found at memory location 100. The result obtained is stored in the accumulator (replaces the previous value of the accumulator).

TABLE 10.2.1

Example Register Transfer Instructions

Instruction Set	Register Transfer
LOD x	AC ← M[x]
STO x	M[x] ← AC
ADD x	AC ← AC + M[100]
SUB x	AC ← AC − M[100]
AND x	AC ← AC ∧M[x]
OR x	AC ← AC ∨ M[x]

In addition to add and subtract instructions, by referring to the ALU design in Chapter 5, we could include additional logic instructions. For example, such logic instructions maybe abbreviated as AND x and OR x.

In both cases, x is the address of one operand found in memory. The other operand is found in the accumulator. Both operations perform the bit-wise logic AND and logic OR, as discussed in Chapter 5.

10.2.2.3   Register Transfer Languages

The above operations can be described in register transfer notation as given in Table 10.2.1. More details will be given about register transfer languages in the next chapter. For now, we discuss the notation by referring to the table. In the table, the "←" is a symbol used to indicate transfer of information with the source on the right-hand side and the destination on the left-hand side. The transfer places a copy of the source in the destination without changing the contents of the source. An alternative is to place the source on the left-hand side of the transfer and use the symbol "→" instead. Both notations are used.

The source and destinations can be registers or memory contents as seen in the table. For memory, we use the symbol M to indicate a memory reference. In addition, as discussed in the previous chapter, memory is an array of words. To access a specific word for reading or writing, the register transfer language includes an address notation. In the table, we use brackets to enclose the memory address x. Hence M[100] refers to memory location 100. Finally, as can be seen from the table, the last four notations represent arithmetic and logic operations. For the add operation, for example, the symbol used is the "+" symbol to indicate arithmetic addition. The register transfer instruction is interpreted as follows. First, the contents of AC are added to the contents of memory location x using the ALU part of the CPU. Second, the result is stored in AC (the destination register) as indicated by the register transfer instruction. The remaining register transfer instructions are interpreted similarly with "−," "∧," and "∨" representing arithmetic subtraction, bit-wise logical AND, and bit-wise logical OR, respectively. Alternatively, the words AND, COMPLEMENT, and OR can be used to represent the bit-wise logic operations.

The set of instructions found in an instruction set architecture is composed of instructions that perform primitive tasks, e.g., ADD operation. As a result, complex arithmetic expressions that can be written as a single statement using high-level languages cannot be written as a single statement using the instruction set of a given computer. Part of the function of a compiler is to translate these complex arithmetic expressions to a set of instructions of the underlying instruction set of the computer. Example 10.2.1 illustrates this. In the example, we assume the variables x, y, z, and w are stored at memory locations with decimal values 100, 101, 102, and 103, respectively.

Example 10.2.1
Translate the high-level program expression $w = x - y + z$ into an accumulator-based (AC-based) instruction using the instructions described above and given in Table 10.2.1.
Solution: Using knowledge of precedence rules from high-level languages, we know that addition and subtraction are of equal precedence and, as a result, the expression is computed from left to right with subtraction done first and followed by addition. To translate the expressions into the instructions found in Table 10.2.1, we do the following steps:

1. Bring the needed operands from memory into the CPU (note that the translated instruction set is assumed to be in memory).
2. Apply the needed arithmetic operations on the operands.
3. Store the result in the memory location indicated by the high level-level expressions.

At this stage, we are not concerned with how this program is stored in memory. To form the first operations (subtraction), we need an instruction to bring the first operand (x at memory location 100) into the CPU (the accumulator). Once this is done, we could subtract y and add z. The set of instructions below is the solution desired.

$$
\begin{array}{ll}
\text{LOD} & 100 \\
\text{SUB} & 101 \\
\text{ADD} & 102 \\
\text{STO} & 103 \\
\end{array}
$$

To illustrate this process, we show the contents of memory and the accumulator as the sequence of instructions is executed, as shown in Figure 10.2.2. In the figure, we assume the operands for the variables x, y, z, and w are as shown in the first row of the table. Changes in contents as a result of the corresponding instruction are shown in bold.

The above discussion is intended to introduce AC-based instruction sets and formats. In the next chapter, we add to the above set of instructions and present the design of an AC-based CPU. In the next section, we discuss an

Instructions	AC	M[100]	M[101]	M[102]	M[103]
Initially	?	5	3	7	12
LOD 100	**5**	5	3	7	12
SUB 101	**2**	5	3	7	12
ADD 102	**9**	5	3	7	12
STO 103	9	5	3	7	**9**

Contents of memory and accumulator

FIGURE 10.2.2
The Changes Due to Each Instruction are in Bold

alternative instruction set architecture based on general purpose register-based architecture.

10.3 General Register-Based Architecture

Consider the example of swapping the contents of two memory locations, x and y. The C++ solution to swapping the contents is to assign one of the variables to a temporary variable; call it temp. The code is

$$temp = x$$
$$x = y$$
$$y = temp$$

The accumulator-based (AC-based) instruction set solution to the above code requires bringing the operands (variables) into the CPU and storing these variables in the proper memory locations. A possible code is

```
LOD   X
STO   temp
LOD   Y
STO   X
LOD   temp
STO   Y
```

In the above solution, we note that the temp memory location was stored in line 2 and then brought back into the CPU in line 5. This was needed because the user cannot access other registers in the CPU (outside of the accumulator register as defined by the instruction set). The process of moving information in and out of memory is expensive in terms of speed as memory access is slower than the CPU execution time. In a general register CPU

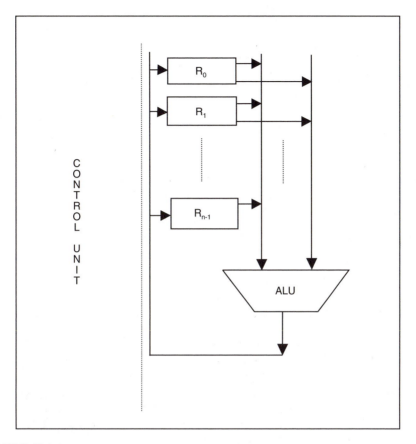

FIGURE 10.3.1

CPU Organization of a General Purpose Register Organization. The registers R_0 through R_{n-1} are used to replace the AC register.

organization, the CPU contains many registers that are directly accessible by the user through the provided instruction set. As a result, the user can store the temporary value of temp within one of the CPU registers, and hence reduce CPU-memory traffic. Figure 10.3.1 shows a hypothetical organization of a general register CPU organization. A similar figure was presented in the discussion of register files in the previous chapter.

In the diagram, it is shown that any of the n registers can be used as one of the operands to the ALU. For this organization, the instruction set may include load instructions that specify destination registers in the CPU (other than the accumulator). Similarly, store instructions may specify both the source register in the CPU and the memory location where the information is to be stored. Examples of such instructions are

$$\text{LOD} \quad R_1, 100$$
$$\text{STO} \quad R_3, 105$$

TABLE 10.3.1

Examples of General Purpose,
Register-Based Instructions

Instruction	Register Transfer
LOD R_1, 100	$R_1 \leftarrow M[100]$
STO R_3, 105	$M[105] \leftarrow R_3$

The register transfer interpretation of the instructions is given in Table 10.3.1. As can be seen from the register transfer, the LOD instruction reads the contents of memory into the register R_1. Similarly, the STO instruction stores the contents of R_3 into memory location 105. With this general register instruction set, the swap example can be rewritten as

```
LOD     R₁, X
LOD     R₂, Y
STO     R₁, Y
STO     R₂, X
```

Note that with this CPU organization one reduces the number of memory access from 6 to 4; or the memory traffic is reduced by one third of the amount used by the accumulator-based instruction set. Note that although the high-level language made use of a temp variable, the general register solution made no use of this variable.

Associated with the above architecture is an instruction set that makes use of the registers as discussed in the example swap given. Before we look at the type of instructions included in such an instruction set, we look at the machine-level representation of instructions.

10.4   Machine-Level Instructions

In describing the instruction set in the previous sections, we used symbolic names for the type of operations used. At the machine level, these operations must be translated to a binary sequence. Each symbolic instruction is called an assembly instruction. In general, assembly instructions form a one-to-one correspondence with the corresponding machine instruction. As a matter of fact, assembly instructions are derived from machine instructions. This is done for ease of understanding the function of a machine instruction; it is easier to understand the function in symbolic notation rather than a sequence of binary digits. In this section, we look at the instruction set of a computer at the machine level and relate it to its representation at the assembly or symbolic level.

Consider the instruction "ADD X" in the accumulator-based instruction set architecture. The instruction can be broken into two parts, an operation part and an operand part.

This logical distinction between the two parts of the instruction is presented in binary as a machine instruction with two fields: (1) a field that identifies the type of operation to be performed, called the opcode field (operation field); and (2) a field that identifies the operand location to be used, called the address field. For machine instruction formats, it is customary to represent the instructions as a rectangular block that contains sub-rectangles identifying the different fields. For the set of accumulator-based instructions described earlier, this is represented as

| Opcode Field | Address Field |

Both the opcode field and the address field are stored in memory as a sequence of binary digits (bits). We assume the instruction is stored in a memory word. As discussed in the previous chapter, the memory word size (number of bits) is determined by the data bus size. To determine the data bus size, we determine the number of bits found in a machine instruction. As can be seen from the instruction format, the word size is the sum of the sizes of the opcode field and the address field.

To determine the size of each field, one needs to determine the maximum allowable addressable memory as well as the maximum allowable machine instructions of the form presented above. Both field sizes are parameters determined by the instruction set designer. For the opcode field, for example, if the designer desires m such instructions (with opcode and direct address field), then the opcode field must include a binary code associated with each such operation. Each binary code corresponds to an opcode representing one of the m operations. Hence, the opcode field size is equal to

$$\lceil \log_2 m \rceil$$

As for the address field, in direct addressing the address field is used to reference words in memory. As a result, the size of this field is related to the addressable memory. In fact, the size of this field is equal to the size of the address bus.

Example 10.4.1
In this example, we would like to determine the instruction size for an accumulator-based CPU with the following. For the external memory, assume a maximum addressable memory of 64 k words. For the number of operations with memory address, we assume a maximum of 16 allowable operations. In this case, the opcode field is at least 4 bits in width. Each opcode binary assignment represents one of the 16 operations. As to the address field size, since the addressable external memory contains 64 k

words $= 2^{16}$ words, the address bus size is 16 bits. As a result, the address field size of the machine instruction is 16 bits as well. The instruction format in rectangular form is given as

Opcode Field	Address Field
4 bits	16 bits

Example 10.4.2

In this example, we would like to convert the ADD $(105)_{16}$ assembly instruction into the corresponding machine instruction based on the previous conditions found in example 10.4.1. We assume that the opcode field for the ADD operation is $(0)_{16}$ as determined by the instruction set designer. Note that the instruction memory address part is given in hexadecimal format for simplicity of conversion.

By replacing the opcode field and address field by the proper binary code, we obtain the machine instruction

0000	0000 0001 0000 0101
Opcode Field	Address Field

As can be deduced from the above discussion, it is much easier to understand the function of the instruction when it is represented in assembly form rather than in machine form. The instruction in memory is stored in machine form, however. To simplify the task of a designer/programmer, one can write the instructions in assembly code and pass the code to an assembler program. Part of the function of the assembler program is to translate the assembly code into machine code. The machine code generated can then be stored in memory for program execution.

Before we conclude this section, we discuss the machine instruction format of a general register-based CPU in the context of the accumulator-based CPU discussed previously. We consider the instruction LOD R_1, X, for example. The machine instruction associated with this instruction is composed of three fields. Two of these fields are analogous to the accumulator-based machine instruction, the opcode field and the address field. The third field represents an address of a register within the CPU. To be able to address n registers within the CPU, the size of the register field must not be less than

$$\lceil \log_2 n \rceil$$

Example 10.4.3

In this example, we would like to determine the field sizes of a general register CPU on an instruction of a form similar to LOD R_1, X. Assume a maximum of 16 different operations are required. Assume as well the addressable memory is 64 k words. Finally, assume the CPU contains 16 general purpose registers.

In determining the field sizes for the opcode and address part, we follow a similar procedure as given in the examples above. The instruction includes a register address field as well. The size of this field is

$$\lceil \log_2 16 \rceil = 4.$$

As a result, the instruction format with field sizes is

Opcode Field	Register Address	Address Field
4 bits	4 bits	16 bits

Example 10.4.4

In this example, we assume the opcode for an LOD instruction is $(7)_{16}$. We would like to convert LOD 5, 1023 to machine instruction (we assume the operands are presented in base 10 and the CPU contains 32 general purpose registers). Assuming the same number of external memory words, we obtain the following machine instruction:

0111	00101	0000 0011 1111 1111
4 bits	5 bits	16 bits

The general register CPU instructions have two address fields: one field refers to a register within the CPU, the other field refers to an address of an operand in memory. Later in the discussion of instruction sets, we classify instructions based on the number of address fields they contain.

The term addressing mode refers to the method of obtaining the actual operand of an instruction. For example, in the above example one of the operands is the value of a register, and the other is the content of a memory location. Classification of instructions is also done according to the addressing mode chosen.

10.5 The Computer Instruction Cycles

In this section, we consider the computer instruction cycle for the case of the accumulator–based CPU. We first distinguish between instructions and data in the CPU and use for this distinction the swap example presented earlier.

For this, we assume that the instruction size of the accumulator-based CPU is 20 bits with 16 bits reserved for the address field and 4 bits reserved for the opcode field. Both instructions and data are stored in memory.

Table 10.5.1 lists the set of instructions used and the corresponding machine instruction in tabular form. The format of the machine code is arbitrary and is chosen as an example. Assume that instructions are stored

TABLE 10.5.1

Machine Instruction Examples

Assembly Instruction	Machine Instruction
LOD x	0001 xxxxxxxxxxxxxxx
STO x	0010 xxxxxxxxxxxxxxx

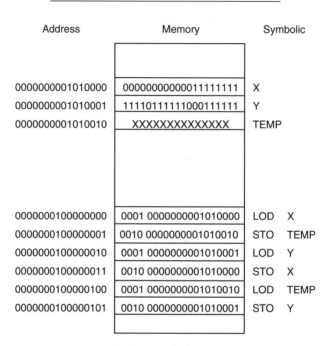

Address	Memory	Symbolic	
0000000001010000	00000000000011111111	X	
0000000001010001	11110111111000111111	Y	
0000000001010010	XXXXXXXXXXXXXX	TEMP	
0000000100000000	0001 0000000001010000	LOD	X
0000000100000001	0010 0000000001010010	STO	TEMP
0000000100000010	0001 0000000001010001	LOD	Y
0000000100000011	0010 0000000001010000	STO	X
0000000100000100	0001 0000000001010010	LOD	TEMP
0000000100000101	0010 0000000001010001	STO	Y

FIGURE 10.5.1
The Address, the Contents, and the Symbolic Codes are Read from Left to Right

in memory as words, i.e., the size of a memory word is 20 bits. In addition, assume that instructions are stored starting at location, $(0100)_{16}$; and the data for the variables are stored in consecutive locations starting at memory location $(50)_{16}$, as shown in Figure 10.5.1. (The allocation of memory for storing instructions and data is part of the overall task of converting a high-level language to machine level through compilation. This topic is outside the scope of the text.)

In Figure 10.5.1, we show three labels: (1) the address of memory labels, (2) the contents of the corresponding memory words, and (3) the symbolic (assembly) code. In order for the computer to perform the swap operation, it needs to execute the set of six instructions starting at location $(0100)_{16}$. The processing is done in the CPU. For each instruction, the CPU first brings the instruction from memory. The process of bringing the instruction from memory into the CPU is referred to as the fetch cycle. (We will discuss this and the following steps in the next chapter.) Next, the control unit in the CPU determines the type of instruction fetched from its opcode field. This process of finding the type of instruction fetched is called the decode cycle. Here, the control determines that the instruction is a load instruction. Finally, the computer executes the instruction fetched; this process is called the execute cycle.

In order to execute the first instruction, the CPU needs to reference memory again. This is the case since the operand is still in memory. This is done by placing the address of the operand on the data bus (the address is 0000000001010000). A read is then initiated and the operand is brought into the CPU, i.e., for the LOD instruction to be completed the CPU must reference memory twice. The first reference is to fetch the instruction; the second reference is to bring the operand into the CPU.

The state of the CPU is determined by the contents of its storage elements. Of these storage elements we consider the two registers MAR and MBR found in Figure 10.2.1. The memory address register, MAR, contains the address of the instruction or of the operand that needs to be fetched from memory. For a read, the memory buffer register (MBR) is used to retrieve the instruction or data. For a write (store), MBR contains the data to be stored in memory. To illustrate, we use Figure 10.5.2, which shows a schematic of the CPU and memory with contents of MAR used to fetch the first instruction in the swap procedure. The diagram includes the contents of the address bus and the data bus in hexadecimal notation. Note the contents of MAR are used to set the data bus values to point to the first instruction in the assembly code. The read operation brings the contents of this memory word (the LOD instruction) into the CPU and places it in MBR. Once the instruction is decoded, the computer places the address of the operand in MAR (address is 0000000001010000) and initiates a read signal. This is done to bring the operand into the CPU. Note that the circuit is missing many connections needed to complete the instruction cycle. These will be covered in detail in the next chapter. By following similar analysis on the remaining instructions, we determine the total number of memory accesses needed to execute the program is 12.

10.6 Common Addressing Modes

In the previous sections, we considered a special kind of addressing mode called direct addressing. Addressing modes have to do with the method of retrieving an operand. We illustrate the need for different addressing modes by referring to high-level languages. From high-level languages, we know that arithmetic expressions may contain a constant as well as a variable as part of the expression. Consider, for example, the expression $x = w + 2$. Using direct addressing, in order to write a set of instructions to compute the above expression one needs to treat the constant 2 as a variable. That is, a memory location must be preserved for the constant and the value 2 must be stored

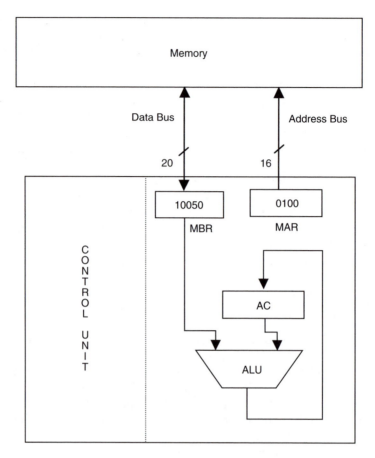

FIGURE 10.5.2
Contents of MAR and MBR during a Fetch Instruction. MAR = $(0100)_{16}$, MBR = $(10050)_{16}$.

in it. In doing so, an LOD instruction is first used to bring the number 2 into the CPU. This instruction will take two memory accesses to complete, the fetch of the instruction and the fetch of the operand.

Instruction set architecture designers realized that one can reduce the number of memory accesses by including the constant as part of the instruction. As a result, when the instruction is fetched, the operand is brought into the CPU as well. This can be done by treating the address part of the instruction not as an address but as an operand. For this to occur, the instruction needs to contain a mechanism that tells the CPU how to interpret the address field. To distinguish between the different interpretations of the address field of the instruction, the instruction contains a special field called addressing mode field. This form of addressing is called immediate addressing. For an instruction set architecture that allows for two different addressing modes, one can simply add 1 bit to distinguish between the two modes. A possible instruction format would then be

| Opcode Field | Addressing Mode Field | Address Field |

An add instruction is determined from the opcode field. The addressing mode field determines the location of the operand. To illustrate, we write the code for the expression $x = w + 2$. In the example, we distinguish between direct and immediate addressing modes by using the letter I for immediate. The code is

LOD		W	#	Load value of W into AC
ADD	I	2	#	Add the constant 2 to AC
STO		X	#	Store AC in memory location X

The solution contains comments similar to those found in high-level languages. In the example, we use the # as an indicator of the start of a comment. The comment terminates with the end of line marker. We now discuss other common addressing modes; in the discussion, we refer to accumulator-based and the general purpose register-based architectures. We start with an addressing mode called implied addressing. To discuss this addressing mode, we refer to special instructions. We consider the accumulator-based CPU and an instruction that implicitly increments the accumulator. An abbreviated form for the instruction can be INC. When the instruction is fetched and executed, the result is to increment the contents of the accumulator. The instruction INC has no operand field; the operand AC is implied.

The next address mode field we consider is related to general purpose register CPU organization. Consider the instruction LOD R_1, X. This type of an instruction has two address fields: (1) a field specifying the destination of the load (in this case register R_1), and (2) a field specifying the address of the source (in this case a memory location with address x). Instructions can be classified according to the number of addresses/operands in the address field. A two-address instruction may have the form

| Opcode Field | Address Mode Field1 | Address Mode Field2 | Address Field1 | Address Field2 |

where the interpretation of Field1 and Field2 depends on the addressing mode associated with each. In register addressing mode, one of the address fields specifies the address of a register; the contents of the specified register serve as one of the operands used in an instruction. The register is found in the CPU of the computer. This has the advantage of using a small address field, 5 bits in the case of a CPU with 32 registers.

As an example of two-address instructions with a register addressing mode, consider ADD R_1, X, with the register transfer interpretation $R_1 \leftarrow R_1 + M[X]$. From the register transfer, we conclude the instruction uses two addressing modes, a register mode and a direct address mode.

Other addressing modes include indirect addressing and register indirect addressing modes. In indirect addressing, the address of the operand is found in the word with address given in the instruction. To illustrate this,

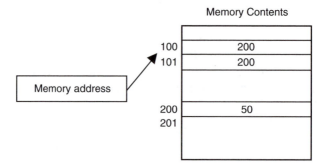

FIGURE 10.6.1
The Three Addressing Modes: Immediate, Direct, and Indirect

we use the load instruction in the accumulator-based CPU. Consider the memory organization as shown in Figure 10.6.1.

For simplicity, we assume both the contents of memory as well as the memory addresses are given in base 10. In addition we assume the addresses given in the LOD instructions are given in base 10. Using the three addressing modes, immediate, direct and indirect, respectively, we show the contents of the accumulator as shown in the comment section of the instruction sets below:

```
LOD 100   #   For immediate addressing, we have
          #   AC ← 100
LOD 100   #   For direct addressing, we have
          #   AC ← M[100], or AC ← 200
LOD 100   #   For indirect addressing, we have
          #   AC ← M[M[100]] = M[200]
          #   or AC ← 50
```

Similar to indirect addressing, in register indirect addressing the instruction contains an address of a register in the CPU. The CPU register identified in the instruction holds the actual address of the operand in memory. Figure 10.6.2 illustrates this. As can be seen from the above figure, the contents of the register specified in the instruction, in this case 3, are used as an address of the operand in memory, i.e.,

$$AC \leftarrow M[R_3]$$
$$AC \leftarrow M[150]$$
$$AC \leftarrow 20$$

The last two addressing modes we consider are the index and relative addressing modes. Index addressing mode can be used in the implementation of the array data structure. Arrays are normally stored in consecutive locations in memory. By adding an index value to an offset, representing the location of the first element of the array in memory, one can access the individual elements of the array accordingly. In index addressing, a special CPU register,

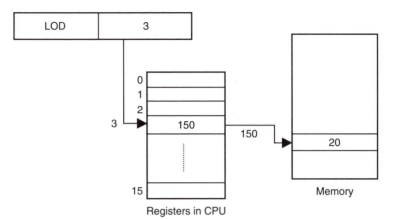

FIGURE 10.6.2
Register Indirect Addressing

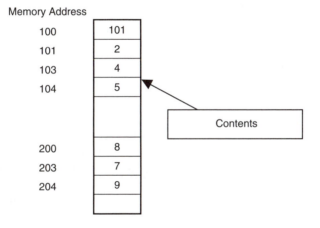

FIGURE 10.6.3
Memory Contents Used with the Different Addressing Modes

Ri, is identified as the index register. For a given instruction containing x in its address field, x + Ri constitutes the address of the operand in memory.

Relative addressing is similar to index addressing. Here, however, a special register called the program counter, PC, is used in determining the address of the operand. For example in relative addressing, LOD X will result in $AC \leftarrow M[X + PC]$. We illustrate the addressing modes in the following example.

Example 10.6.1
Given the memory contents as shown in Figure 10.6.3, assume the values of the program counter, PC, and register R1 are 96 and 200, respectively. Assume an AC-based instruction set. Determine the accumulator value after the instruction LOD x is performed with the addressing modes:

1. Immediate (address field, x, contains 100)
2. Direct (address field, x, contains 100)
3. Indirect (address field, x, contains 100)
4. Register indirect (address field, x, contains 1)
5. Register 1 index (address field, x, contains 3)
6. Relative (address field, x, contains 7)

The answers are given in register transfer form as

1. $AC \leftarrow 101$
2. $AC \leftarrow M[100] = 101$
3. $AC \leftarrow M[M[100]] = M[101] = 2$
4. $AC \leftarrow M[R1] = M[200] = 8$
5. $AC \leftarrow M[R1 + 3] = M[203] = 7$
6. $AC \leftarrow M[PC + 7] = M[103] = 4$

10.7 Macros

In the next chapter, we discuss the design of an instruction set that uses a small number of instructions. For example, the instruction set is chosen so as to perform addition only. In the context of our discussion, such an instruction is to be realized in hardware as there is an adder unit found in the CPU to perform the addition. As we have discussed in Chapter 5, subtraction can be performed using addition. When the hardware does not include units that perform a specific operation, the operation may be realized in software as a set of instructions. These instructions can then be grouped together and referred to as a macro. The macro is given a name. Whenever the name of the macro is present in symbolic code, the set of instructions associated with the macro are inserted in place of the macro reference. In this section, we give some examples and show how additional operations can be realized in software.

Example 10.7.1

In this example, we would like to write a subtraction macro. We assume the hardware does not contain a subtract instruction. We use the 2's complement procedure to perform subtraction. In addition, we do not test for overflow or underflow.

To form $A - B$, we need to form the 2's complement of B. We then add A to the 2's complement of B. The following set of instructions will accomplish this:

LOD B	#	Bring B into AC
CMP	#	This instruction complements the contents of AC
INC	#	The instruction adds 1 to the contents of AC
ADD A	#	AC ← B' + 1 + A (AC contains A − B)

As can be seen from the example, to perform subtraction in software we have to perform the above four instructions. Note that the two introduced instructions (CMP and INC) have implied addressing mode, the AC register. As a result, each of these instructions requires only one reference to memory (the fetch instruction). The total number of memory references needed is six.

In the next example, we assume the instruction set contains two logic operations only, the complement (as given in the above example) and the bit-wise AND.

Example 10.7.2

In this example, we would like to write a macro for the bit-wise logic expression A OR B. We assume the instruction set contains a COMPLEMENT and an AND instructions logic expressions only.

We could form A OR B based on the use of DeMorgan's rule, as discussed earlier. In particular, we note A OR B = (A' AND B')', which can be written in assembly as

LOD A	#	AC ← A
CMP	#	AC ← A'
STO TEMP1	#	Store A' in temp1
LOD B	#	AC ← B
CMP	#	AC ← B'
AND TEMP1	#	AC ← A' AND B'
CMP	#	AC ← (A' AND B')'

The two examples are intended to illustrate the difference between operations that are realized in hardware and those that are realized in software. The user would like the instruction set to include many arithmetic and logic operations as, in general, these will speed program execution. This increases the hardware requirements, however, and makes the design more expensive. In the next chapter, we present a small instruction set and discuss a CPU design for such a set.

Chapter 10 Exercises

10.1 Write an AC-based assembly instruction for the expression

$$X = (Y + Z * X) - W + D$$

Assume direct addressing mode.

10.2 Convert the address part of the above instruction solution into hexadecimal. Assume the variables D, W, X, Y, and Z are in memory locations 100, 101, 102, 103, and 104, respectively. (Each memory location is given in base 10.) Assume the total addressable memory is 4096 words.

10.3 Determine the total number of memory references resulting from your solution to problem 10.1.

10.4 Given the arithmetic expression $X = (2 + 3) - W * D$. Assume an AC-based instruction set with a direct and immediate addressing mode. Convert the expression into assembly. Your code should result in a minimum number of memory references.

10.5 Assume the instruction set of an AC-based instruction set contains 7 instructions that require reference to memory. Assume the AC-based instruction set uses three addressing modes and can address a total of 2048 memory words.

(a) In block representation (rectangular format), show the instruction fields and give the size of each.

(b) Many instructions can be completed without the need to reference memory; consider the CMP instruction in example 10.7.2. With the instruction format as given, determine the total possible number of such instructions that can be added.

10.6 An alternative to an AC-based instruction set architecture is to have both operands of a binary operation in memory. In addition, the result of the operation is stored in memory. An ADD X, Y, Z, for example, may mean $M[X] \leftarrow M[Y] + M[Z]$. Convert the expression

$$X = (Y + Z * X) - W + D$$

considered in question 1 to assembly instructions of the format in this question.

10.7 For the instruction set of question 10.6, assume 3 addressing modes are possible with each operand. In addition, assume the total number of addressable memory words is 4096. If the total number of memory reference instructions is 15, determine the instruction format in terms of the number fields and the size of each field.

10.8 Based on your answers to questions 10.6 and 10.7, determine

(a) The number of bits in the assembly solution to question 10.6

(b) The total number of memory reference instructions

10.9 An alternative to the instruction set architecture presented in question 10.6 is an instruction set architecture called reduced instruction set architecture. In this architecture, except for load and store instructions, all operands are found in registers in the CPU. This is done to reduce memory traffic. As a result ADD X, Y, Z, for example, may mean $R_X \leftarrow R_Y + R_Z$ with R_i representing register i in the CPU. Convert the expression $X = (Y + Z * X) - W + D$ into this instruction set. Use the instructions lw R_i, X and st R_i, X to mean $R_i \leftarrow M[X]$ and $M[x] \leftarrow R_i$, respectively.

10.10 Compute the total number of memory reference instructions in your solution of problem 10.9.

10.11 Assume a total of 32 general-purpose registers are used in question 10.9. Assume an opcode field of 4 bits, one addressing mode, and a total of 4 G addressable words. Determine the instruction formats in terms of number of fields and size of each field.

10.12 Assume an AC-based instruction set with one logic operation only, NAND X to mean AC ← (AC AND M[X])', i.e., the AND and CMP operations are replaced by the NAND operation.

(a) Write a set of instructions (macro) that perform the complement of a memory locations X and places the result in AC.

(b) Write a set of instructions that performs the AND logic operation (AND X means AC ← AC AND M[X]).

(c) Write a set of instructions that performs the OR logic operation (OR X means AC ← AC OR M[X]).

10.13 Assume one is to perform the following set of expressions:

$X = X + Y;$

$Y = X - Y;$

$W = X * Y;$

$U = X/Y;$

(a) Convert the above set of expressions to AC-based instructions.

(b) Convert the above instructions into the format presented in question 10.6.

(c) Convert the above set of expressions into reduced instructions set format.

10.14 Assume given the memory contents as shown in Figure E10.1. Assume the values of the program counter, PC, and register R_1 are 105 and 197, respectively. Assume an AC-based instruction set. Determine the accumulator value after the instruction LOD x is performed with the addressing modes:

(a) Immediate   (address field, x, contains 100)

(b) Direct   (address field, x, contains 101)

(c) Indirect   (address field, x, contains 101)

(d) Register indirect   (address field, x, contains 1)

(e) Register 1 index   (address field, x, 99)

(f) Relative   (address field, x, contains 3)

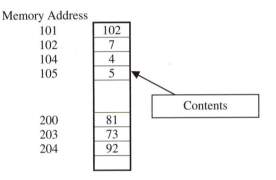

FIGURE E10.1

The remaining questions are with respect to an alternative instruction set architecture called stack-based instruction set architecture. In this architecture operands are stored as the top two elements of the stack. In this architecture, the operands of an arithmetic instruction are implicitly assumed to be the top of the stack. Examples are

ADD $M[SP - 1] \leftarrow M[SP] + M[SP - 1], SP \leftarrow SP - 1$

SUB $M[SP - 1] \leftarrow M[SP] - M[SP - 1], SP \leftarrow SP - 1$

MUL $M[SP - 1] \leftarrow M[SP] * M[SP - 1], SP \leftarrow SP - 1$

PUSH X $M[SP] \leftarrow M[X], SP \leftarrow SP + 1$

POP X $M[X] \leftarrow M[SP], SP \leftarrow SP - 1$

In this architecture, the stack is stored in memory with the top of the stack address stored in a special register called the stack pointer, SP. For an example of expression translation into this architecture, we consider the instruction

$$X = X + Y$$

The above expression can be translated to

    PUSH X
    PUSH Y
    ADD
    POP X

10.15 Construct the stack instructions of the expression

$$X = (X + Z) - W * D$$

10.16 Compute the total number of memory references used in solving question 10.15.

10.17 Assume a total of 4096 addressable memory words. Assume a total of two addressing modes and an opcode field of 3 bits. Based on the stack-based instructions presented above, determine the different instruction formats in terms of number of fields in an instruction and the size of each field.

11

Design of a Simple AC-Based CPU

CONTENTS

11.1 Microoperation and Register Transfer Languages

Our discussion has progressed from Boolean algebra to designs of combinational and sequential circuits. In the design, we moved from simple logic gates to designs of arithmetic logic units, registers, counters, and memory elements. In this chapter, we progress further by considering the units discussed in the previous chapter as the building blocks in the design of larger systems. In particular, we consider the design of a simple AC-based CPU.

The description of the design at this level can be accomplished by using a set of microoperations. What is a microoperation? A microoperation is a primitive hardware operation that can be accomplished during one clock cycle. With the registers and counters used as part of the building blocks of a system, a microoperation may mean clearing the contents of a register or incrementing the contents of a counter, for example. These elementary operations can be completed in one clock cycle. We will discuss this later.

In the previous chapter, we presented assembly code in symbolic format. For example, when the AC-based architecture was discussed, ADD x was presented as $AC \leftarrow AC + M[x]$. A register transfer language follows a similar notation. The intention of using the language is to provide a description of microoperations that is more precise than using word sentences, for example. The term "register transfer" is used because in general the language describes transfer of data between registers. In addition to transfer of data, the language includes operations to perform on the data before the transfer occurs. The + operation is an example. Finally, the language allows a conditional transfer of data. We illustrate as follows.

Let X, Y, and Z represent three registers and let C represent a Boolean expression. The following are examples of register transfer statements:

$$X \leftarrow Y, X \leftarrow Y + Z, \text{ if } (C = 1) \text{ then } Y \leftarrow Z$$

This is three statements separated by commas. We say each of the register transfer statements represents a microoperation that can be completed during one clock cycle. To accomplish this, it is assumed the needed hardware exists to accomplish the task. In the first example, the contents of register Y are copied (replace) to the contents of register X without modifying the contents of register Y. In the second statement, the sum of the contents of the two registers Y and Z is computed. This sum is used then to replace the contents of register X. The last example statement is a conditional statement. For this statement, the completion of the transfer of the contents of register Z into register Y is based on the Boolean condition C. The transfer occurs only if C is true.

In general, register transfer statements are executed under specific machine conditions as indicated in the last register transfer statement example above. As a result, the statement

$$\text{if } (C = 1), \text{ then } Y \leftarrow Z$$

is abbreviated as

$$C: Y \leftarrow Z$$

In this register transfer notation, the term to the left of the ":" represents a Boolean condition. The term to the right represents the action to be performed if the Boolean condition C is true. The Boolean condition C is a Boolean expression. As a result, it may include Boolean operators. In the previous chapters, we used + to represent the OR Boolean operator. In register transfer, we distinguish between the sum operator (+) and the Boolean OR operator by using the word OR or the symbol $\vee$ to represent the bit-wise OR. Similarly, we use the symbol $\wedge$ or the word AND to represent the bit-wise AND. With this notation, for example, the register transfer statement

$$C1.C2: Y \leftarrow Z + X$$

is interpreted as follows: if the Boolean expression $C1.C2$ (the "." represents logical AND) is true, then the contents of register Y are replaced by the binary sum of registers X and Z. Similarly, the register transfer

$$C1 + C2: Y \leftarrow Z \wedge X$$

is interpreted as follows: if the Boolean expression $C1 + C2$ (the "+" represents logical OR) is true, then the bit-wise AND of registers Z and X replace the contents of register Y. Finally, the two register transfer statements

$$C1: Y \leftarrow Z \vee X$$

and

$$C1: \leftarrow Z \text{ OR } X$$

are identical. Before we conclude this section, we discuss two more notations that we use in the design of the CPU.

First, it is possible that more than one register transfer is desired if a certain Boolean condition holds true. To do this, we include the needed register transfers under the same condition but separate the conditions by a ",". For example, the statement

$$C: Y \leftarrow X, Z \leftarrow 0, W \leftarrow W + 1$$

means when C holds true, the three listed register transfers can be computed simultaneously, i.e.,

1. The contents of X replace the contents of Y
2. The contents of register Z are cleared to 0
3. The contents of register W are incremented

By using the proper hardware design, we will see that it is possible to accomplish the above statements simultaneously.

Second, the register transfer statements do not need to refer to registers only. For example, the operands could be a single flip-flop, a subset of a register contents, a memory location, or a bus line. To designate a specific part of the register transfer, we use R[k–m] to mean bits k through m of register R. Similarly, to designate a memory location with address R we use M[R], where M represents memory and R represents the address of the word in memory. The organization of memory was discussed in the previous chapter as composed of words starting at word 0. For the register part, we assume the least-significant bit of a register is assigned location 0. Hence, if R is a 16-bit register, then R[0–7] refer to the 8 least-significant bits of register R.

11.2   Design of RTL Statements

In the previous section, we assumed that the register transfer statements are associated with a hardware that realizes the statements. The hardware that realizes the statements is not unique. We consider examples of statements and possible hardware to realize them.

We start with the simple statement $X \leftarrow Y$, from which we conclude that the output of register Y must be connected to the inputs of register X explicitly (through direct connections) or implicitly (through a bus system, for example). Figure 11.2.1 shows the two possible block diagram realizations. In Figure 11.2.1(a), the outputs of register Y are directly connected to the inputs of register X. The circuit is clocked. Hence, when the register inputs are sampled, the contents of register Y are copied into register X. In Figure 11.2.1(b), the registers are connected through the bus lines. As a result, control signals are added to place the contents of register Y on the bus and for the contents of the bus to be stored in register X. Since both are valid realizations, one of the steps of the design is to determine *a priori* the type of hardware organization employed in the design (is the design based on a bus system, for example).

To make the transfer conditional, as in C: $X \leftarrow Y$, we use registers with a load control as discussed in the previous chapter. For parallel-load register, we require the C signal to assume a value of 1 for a complete clock cycle. During this cycle, when the register inputs are sampled the transfer is completed. The design in block diagram is shown in Figure 11.2.2(a). In the figure,

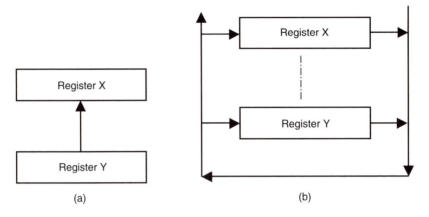

FIGURE 11.2.1
Two Possible Realizations of X ← Y: (a) Direct Connections; (b) Bus Connections

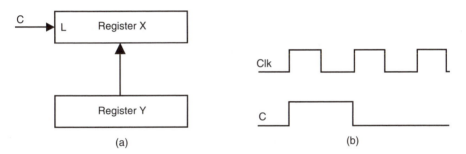

FIGURE 11.2.2
(a) Realization of C: X ← Y; (b) Timing Relation

C is used as an input into the load line, L, of the register. In Figure 11.2.2(b), we show the timing relation of C to the clock. As can be seen from the figure, the C control input is held at 1 for a complete clock cycle.

To realize the statement C: X ← Y using a bus organization, we need to place the contents of register Y on the bus. In addition we need to enable the load line of register X so as to store the bus contents. Hence, additional hardware signals are included in the design; in particular, the signals to place register Y on the bus. Note that these signals are implied from the statement and the underlining hardware organization. The bus system shown in Figure 11.2.1(b) is similar to the register file organization discussed in the previous chapter. Hence, the selection can be accomplished using a multiplexer realization of the bus connections or, alternatively, the selection can be accomplished from a combination of tristate and decoder realization of the bus connections.

We further illustrate the realization of RTL statements with several examples.

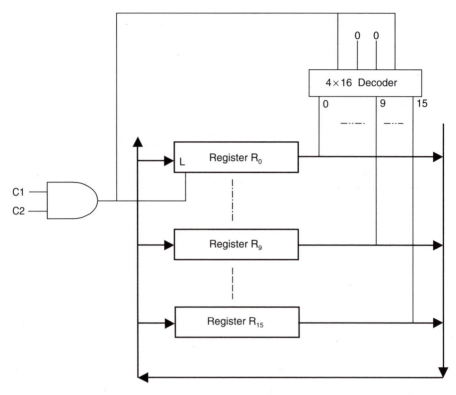

FIGURE 11.2.3
Bus Realization of C1.C2: $R_0 \leftarrow R_9$. C1.C2 = 1 for a Complete Clock Cycle

Example 11.2.1
In this example, we show the block diagram realization of C1.C2: $R_0 \leftarrow R_9$. We assume a bus organization with 16 registers and the conditions C1 and C2 are available. (Later we show that the control unit generates such signals.)

To realize the transfer, the contents of register R_9 are placed on the bus. In addition, the load line of register R_0 is activated. This is done under the condition C1.C2 holding true. To place the contents of the register R_9 on the bus, we place the binary value 1001 on the inputs of decoder associated with the bus (please refer to the tristate implementation of the register files in Chapter 9). Note that a 4-to-16 decoder is used to choose one of the 16 registers (registers R_0 to R_{15}). The design is shown in Figure 11.2.3. Note the use of the AND gate with output C1.C2 used as input to the load line of register R_0 and as input to two of the 4-to-16 decoder inputs. When the AND gate output assumes a value of 1, the contents of register R_9 are placed on the bus. In addition, when register R_0 samples the inputs (since C1.C2 = 1), the contents of the bus are stored in R_0.

In the next example, we expand on the design process by realizing multiple register transfer statements simultaneously.

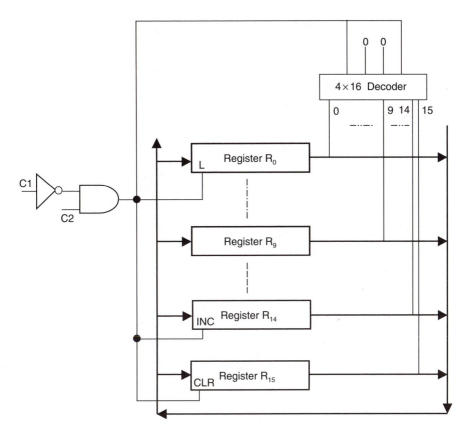

FIGURE 11.2.4
Bus Realization of C1'.C2: $R_0 \leftarrow R_9$, $R_{15} \leftarrow 0$, $R_{14} \leftarrow R_{14} + 1$

Example 11.2.2
In this example, we would like to realize the RTL statement C1'.C2: $R_0 \leftarrow R_9$, $R_{15} \leftarrow 0$, $R_{14} \leftarrow R_{14} + 1$. In the realization, we use a bus system as discussed in the previous example.

Figure 11.2.4 shows the design. Similar to the previous example the condition C1'.C2 is used to place the contents of register R_9 on the bus and to store the contents of the bus into register R_0. In addition, the signal is concurrently used to clear the contents of register R_{15} as well as increment the contents of register R_{14}.

As can be concluded, the registers used with the bus system are general purpose registers that are capable of performing three operations (loading the register, causing the register to function as a counter, and clearing the contents of the register). The design of such general purpose registers is very similar to the design of general purpose registers discussed in Chapter 9. Figure 11.2.5 shows the design. Note the use of the three control inputs INC, CLR, and Load. At most, one of the control inputs may assume a value of

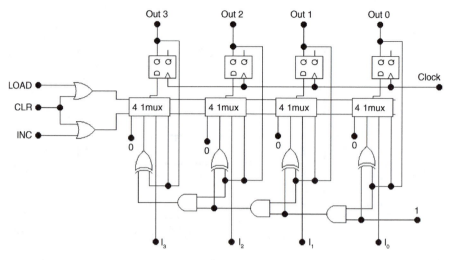

FIGURE 11.2.5
A General Purpose Register Used in the Design of the Simple CPU

TABLE 11.2.1

Description of Figure 11.2.5

CLR	INC	LOAD	S_1	S_0	RTL Function
0	0	0	0	0	$R \leftarrow R$
0	0	1	0	1	$R \leftarrow$ Input
0	1	0	1	0	$R \leftarrow R + 1$
1	0	0	1	1	$R \leftarrow 0$

1. The function of the circuit is described in Table 11.2.1. When the control inputs assume a value of 0, the contents of the register remain unchanged. The contents of the register are cleared to 0 when the input CLR = 1 zeros are placed at the outputs of the multiplexers. These values are stored in the flip-flops when the clock makes a transition from 0 to 1.

Register transfer statements may refer to a single flip-flop. We will see the use of such statements when we consider the design of a simple CPU. First, we present the instruction set architecture of the simple CPU.

11.3 Instruction Set of the Simple CPU

11.3.1 Instruction Set Completeness

The instruction set of a computer is chosen so as to be able to translate high-level languages to the instruction set of the computer. As a result, the instruction set should allow for the following.

11.3.1.1   Arithmetic Instructions

The CPU should contain arithmetic instructions. The CPU we consider will contain an add instruction. As discussed in Chapter 5 and Chapter 10, one can perform subtraction with addition. Since multiplication can be obtained by repeated addition, one can perform multiplication as well. As a result, in order for a computer to perform the arithmetic operations, an add instruction could serve as a representative instruction for the remaining arithmetic basic instructions.

11.3.1.2   Logic Instructions

Logic instructions are needed for conditional statements as in the case of if-then-else statements and loop statements. Earlier in the text we discussed logical completeness. With an instruction set that includes the operations of a logically complete set, one can generate all other logic operations. As a result, the instruction set chosen needs to include at least the operations found in a representative logically complete set.

11.3.1.3   Branch (Jump Instructions)

These instructions in conjunction with logic instructions are used to alter the sequential execution of program statements. Their effect is to cause the program conditionally or unconditionally to jump to specific locations in memory and, as a result, simulate the behavior of a loop or if-then-else construct.

11.3.1.4   CPU and Memory Instructions

In addition to the above instruction types, the instruction set should include instructions that move data between the CPU and memory. Input and output instructions can be thought of as part of the CPU communication with memory. That is, part of the CPU reference to memory can be interpreted as input/output instruction. The CPU treats the reference to memory and input/output as if there is no distinction between them. This scheme is called memory mapped.

11.3.2   The Instruction Set of the Simple CPU

With the previous subsection we present the instruction set shown in Table 11.3.1 as our working AC-based CPU instruction set.

Table 11.3.1(a) represents memory-reference instructions. In order for these instructions to complete, in addition to the fetch reference to memory, memory is referenced again to obtain an operand or store an operand. Table 11.3.1(b) contains register-reference instructions. With the exception of fetching the

TABLE 11.3.1

(a) Memory Reference Instructions, (b) Register
Reference Instructions

Instruction	Meaning	Assigned Opcode
(a) Memory Reference		
LW XXX	AC ← M[XXX]	0XXX
ST XXX	M[XXX] ← AC	1XXX
ADD XXX	AC ← AC+M[XXX]	2XXX
AND XXX	AC ← AC AND M[XXX]	3XXX
JMP XXX	PC ← XXX	4XXX
SKZ XXX	If M[X] = 0 then PC ← PC + 1	5XXX
SKP XXX	If M[X] > 0 then PC ← PC + 1	6XXX
(b) Register Reference		
CMP	AC ← AC′	8xxx
CLA	AC ← 0	9xxx
INC	AC ← AC + 1	Axxx
CLV	V ← 0	Bxxx
SKV	If V = 1 then PC = PC + 1	Cxxx

instruction, register-reference instructions do not need to access memory as the operand of these instructions is found in the CPU.

The size of the memory address is given as xxx with each x representing a hexadecimal number. As a result, the address field size is 12 bits. In addition, we use an opcode field of size 4 bits. Finally, we use one addressing mode only (direct addressing). As a result, no addressing mode field is needed. Since memory words are used to store instructions and data, and since the instruction size is 16 bits, we conclude that the memory word size is 16 bits. This word size is used to store data as well. Based on the above, the instruction format is

Opcode	Operand
4 bits	12 bits

In the instruction set given in Table 11.3.1, the V is an overflow bit used as an extension of the accumulator for arithmetic operations that require additional bits to store.

In addition to the absence of input/output instructions, the instruction set does not include interrupt instructions. One of the functions of the interrupt instructions is to be used by the operating system to switch between different programs in a multi-user or Windows environment. This topic is not covered in the text.

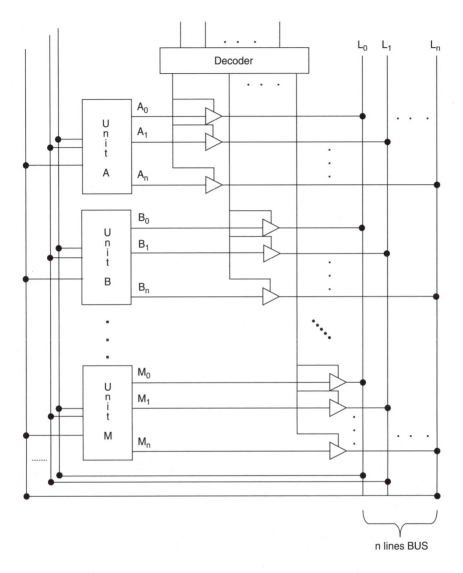

FIGURE 11.4.1
Registers (Units A through M). The figure contains one n-bit bus

11.4 CPU Organization Data Path

The data path organization is based on bus connections as shown in Figure 11.4.1, which is similar to Figure 9.7.6. The connections form the register file part of the data path. The data path contains an ALU unit as well. As can be seen from the figure, units A through M can place their contents on the bus. The decoder ensures one of these units at most can place its contents on the bus. The bus is connected to the inputs of all units. To move the contents of unit A to unit B, for example, the decoder inputs are set to decimal 0. This places the contents of unit A on the bus. In addition, unit B is activated to store the contents of the bus.

The data path of the CPU used in the design is similar to Figure 11.4.1 with units A through M replaced by needed registers and with an ALU added for computations. To determine the needed registers, we refer to the type of architecture used (AC-based, general purpose register-based, etc). The architecture chosen is an AC-based instruction set architecture. As a result, the CPU contains this single register to access by the user (this is in addition to a single bit, V, discussed later). In addition to this register, we need registers used for communication with the memory unit. In particular, we need a program counter (PC), a memory address register (MAR), and a memory buffer register (MBR). For the decoding aspect of the instruction, the CPU contains an additional register, the instruction register (IR). The register is used to hold the instruction on a temporary basis. These registers were discussed in the previous chapter. More details on their use are given in this chapter.

In terms of the sizes of the registers, MAR and PC are 12 bits since these registers hold the address of the instruction. AC and MBR are 16 bits each since they hold the contents of a word (data or instruction). Since the instruction register holds the contents of the instruction on a temporary basis, the size of the register is 16 bits as well. Finally, the memory unit is composed of 2^{12} 16-bit words. The details of the connections between the registers and the details of the contents of the control unit are the subject of chapter.

We progress by representing the data path in block diagram format as shown in Figure 11.4.2. Note the use of a single bus to communicate between the different registers, and that the AC register inputs are not directly connected to the bus. In order to access the inputs of AC, the data must first be moved into MBR. We make five additional observations:

1. The outputs of MAR are connected to the bus but are also routed separately as an address bus into memory.

2. The data bus connecting the CPU to memory is connected to the CPU bus and is bidirectional. The design of memory was covered in Chapter 9.

3. With the exception of AC, the inputs and outputs to/from the registers are placed on the same side to simplify the schematic. Similarly, the decoder and tristate gates are removed to simplify the schematic.

4. The registers used are capable of storing information in parallel, clearing to 0, and incremented. A schematic of these registers was given in Figure 11.2.5.

5. The inputs to the ALU are directly connected to the outputs of MBR and AC, i.e., the bus is not needed for these inputs.

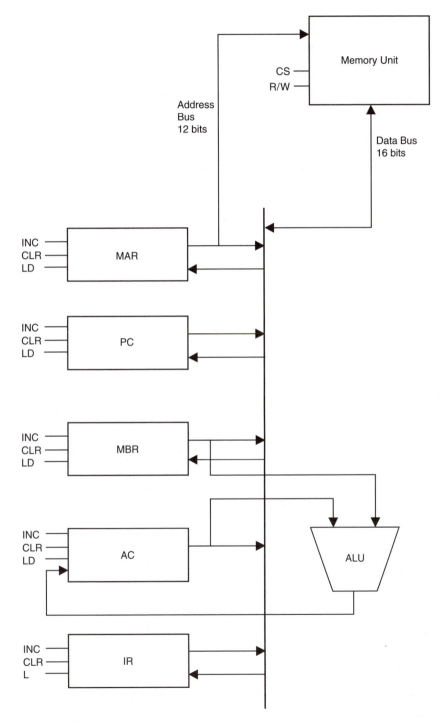

FIGURE 11.4.2
Data Path and Memory Connection of the AC-Based CPU

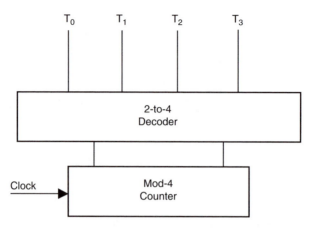

FIGURE 11.5.1
A Schematic of Generating Four Nonoverlapping Control Signals T_0, ..., T_3.

11.5 The Control Unit

In the previous section, we presented the data path and the memory connection of the simple CPU design. We continue the presentation of the simple CPU design by discussing the design of the control unit. In the previous chapter, we mentioned that both instruction and data are located in memory. The instructions of a given program are executed by moving them into the CPU and by storing the results back into memory, if needed. The control unit is that part of the CPU that initiates the needed control signals to accomplish this. The order of initiating the signals is important; for example, the decoding cycle must be preceded by the fetch cycle.

The clock synchronizes the movement of information between the units of the computer. Based on the clock signals one can impose an order on the control signals where a control signal may remain active for a complete clock cycle. We refer to the circuit given in Figure 9.3.5 and repeated in Figure 11.5.1 for the case of mod-4 counter. The timing diagram for the circuit is shown in Figure 11.5.2. The outputs are measured at T_0 through T_3. The counter counts the clock pulses that are continually generated by a clock generator. The counter is assumed to change states on the rising edge of the clock. In addition, the counter is assumed to have a clear input that causes its value to be reset to 0 synchronously. Please refer to Figure 9.4.5 for illustration. From the timing diagram (over the shaded area) we note that the T_j outputs are ordered with T_0 preceding T_1 and T_1 preceding T_2, etc. The diagram can be modified to output a larger sequence of ordered signals. For example, using a mod-16 counter and a 4-to-16 decoder, one can generate 16 such ordered signals.

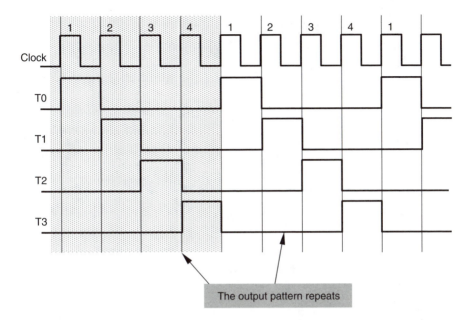

FIGURE 11.5.2

T_0 Assumes a Value of 1 for an entire clock cycle. This is followed by T_1, T_2, and T_3 assuming a value of 1 in the listed order. The sequence repeats.

As we will discuss later, the number of clock cycles needed to complete an instruction depends on the type of instruction. As a result, in addition to the counter and decoder circuit used to generate the ordered signals, the control unit contains circuit elements used to determine the type of the current instruction being executed. The schematic of the control unit we use is given in Figure 11.5.3; the decoder used for the timing signals is removed (the reason will be discussed later). We present next the details of the design of the combinational part of the control unit, and the details of how the control signals are connected to the data path and to memory. Note that since the sequence counter is a 3-bit sequence counter, one can generate eight timing signals T_0 through T_7.

11.6 The Three Cycles

In the design of the computer, each instruction passes through the fetch, decode, and execute cycles.

In fetch, the instruction is brought from memory. The program counter contains the address of the next instruction. From the data path organization, MAR addresses memory directly. As a result, the first step in the fetch cycle is to place the contents of the program counter on MAR. Once this is done,

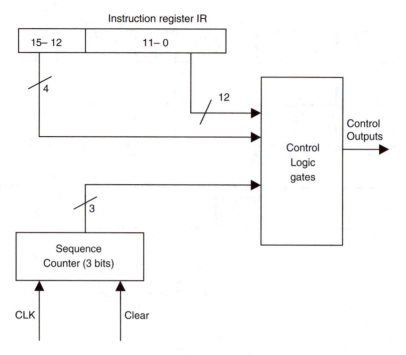

FIGURE 11.5.3
Control Unit of the Basic Computer

memory is read into IR where the instruction will be decoded next. In addition, PC is incremented as the computer assumes the next instruction to be executed is the next instruction in the sequence. (We will see how the PC contents change in branch instructions later.) The sequence counter value distinguishes between the three cycles. The fetch cycle, for example, is initiated by the condition $SC = 0$, $T_0 = 1$. The fetch cycle can be described more formally using the following microoperations.

$$T_0: MAR \leftarrow PC$$

$$T_1: IR \leftarrow M[AR], PC \leftarrow PC + 1$$

At the end of the T_1, the contents of the instruction are found in the instruction register (IR) and the PC contains the address of the next instruction. The next step is to decode the fetched instruction.

Decoding the instruction is to determine its type. This can be done in the control unit during the timing signal T_2, $SC = 2$. During this time interval as well, the address of the operand (in case the instruction is a memory-reference instruction) is placed in MAR. If the instruction is a memory-reference instruction, the operand can be brought into the CPU during the following timing signal. As a result, the next microoperation is

$$T_2: \text{MAR} \leftarrow \text{IR}[0\text{--}11]$$

The next cycle considered is the execute cycle. The execute cycle starts at time T_3.

11.7 Computer Cycles Execute Microoperations

Following decoding, the computer executes the instruction fetched from memory. This is done starting at time T3 and depends on the opcode value found in the opcode field of the instruction. We associate with each valid opcode the letter αi where αi is true when the opcode decimal value is i (αi is similar to the minterms discussed earlier).

Based on the opcode field, the control unit generates the needed control signals used to complete the corresponding instruction. Figure 11.7.1 shows the distinction between the two groups of instructions we will consider. If the most-significant bit of the opcode field assumes a value of 1, then the instruction is a register-reference instruction. If the bit assumes a value of 0, then the instruction is a memory-reference instruction. We next list the microoperations associated with each instruction.

11.7.1 The Memory-Reference Instructions

11.7.1.1 The LW Instruction

From Table 11.3.1, we note that the opcode field for this instruction is 000. The microoperations needed to complete this instruction are

$$\alpha_0 T_3: \text{MBR} \leftarrow \text{M[MAR]}$$

$$\alpha_0 T_4: \text{AC} \leftarrow \text{MBR, SC} \leftarrow 0$$

Before we move to the next instruction, we justify the above two microoperations from a data path completion point of view. The LW xxx instruction

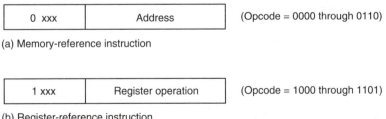

(a) Memory-reference instruction

(b) Register-reference instruction

FIGURE 11.7.1
The Two Groups of Instructions: (a) Memory-Reference, and (b) Register-Reference

places the contents of memory location xxx into the accumulator. During T_2 the address xxx was stored in MAR. As a result, during T_3 the contents of memory at this location can be read into the CPU (stored into MBR). Note that the contents cannot be directly stored into the AC as the AC inputs are not connected to data bus. During T_4, these contents can be moved into AC through the ALU. (Recall from Chapter 5, the ALU designed at the end of the chapter allowed moving the contents of one of the operands to its output.)

Since at the end of T_4 the contents of AC contain the memory operand, the instruction execution is complete and the CPU can start fetching the next instruction in memory. Since the fetch cycle starts at time T_0, the sequence counter is reset synchronously to 0. On the next clock cycle, the process of fetch, decode, and execute resumes.

11.7.1.2   The ST Instruction

The store instruction, ST xxx, moves the contents of the AC to memory location xxx. This can be completed in one clock cycle at time T_3 as given in the microoperation.

$$\alpha_1 T_3: \text{M[MAR]} \leftarrow \text{AC, SC} \leftarrow 0$$

We illustrate by referring to the data path as discussed earlier. In order for the transfer from AC to memory to occur, the control unit places the contents of AC on the CPU bus. This is done by placing the proper inputs on the decoder associated with the bus. The bus is connected to the data bus of the memory unit. The transfer occurs when the chip select input of memory is set to 1 and the read/write input is set to 0 (please refer to the design of memory in the previous chapter). In our discussion, we assume memory can be read or written in one clock cycle. Since the instruction is completed, the sequence counter is reset to 0 to start fetching the next instruction. This is done by placing a 1 on the CLR input of a 3-bit general purpose register (converted into a counter) as shown in Figure 11.2.5. A 3-bit counter is generated by reducing the number of memory elements by one flip-flop.

11.7.1.3   The ADD Instruction

The microoperations

$$\alpha_2 T_3: \text{MBR} \leftarrow \text{M[MAR]}$$

$$\alpha_2 T_4: \text{AC} \leftarrow \text{AC + MBR, V} \leftarrow \text{ALU.CO, SC} \leftarrow 0$$

are used to complete the add instruction. The ALU is assumed to contain the needed hardware to perform the arithmetic and logic operations. The ALU contains an additional output (ALU.CO) the carry-out needed for over-flow. This output is stored into the overflow flip-flop, V.

11.7.1.4 The AND Instruction

Similar to the ADD instruction, the following microoperations are used to execute the AND instruction:

$$\alpha_3 T_3\text{: MBR} \leftarrow \text{M[MAR]}$$

$$\alpha_3 T_4\text{: AC} \leftarrow \text{AC AND MBR, SC} \leftarrow 0$$

11.7.1.5 The JMP Instruction

The jump instruction, JMP xxx, causes the execution of the program to start at location xxx. The PC contains the address of the next instruction in memory. Since memory address xxx was stored in MAR during T_2, during T_3 we move this address to PC. When the next instruction is fetched, execution starts at memory location xxx. The above is captured in the single microoperation.

$$\alpha_4 T_3\text{: PC} \leftarrow \text{MAR, SC} \leftarrow 0$$

The remaining two instructions are somewhat similar.

11.7.1.6 The SKZ and the SKP Instructions

Depending on the operand value of a memory location, both instructions may cause the program to skip the next instruction in the sequence. Since PC contains the address of the next instruction, on the condition being true the next instruction is skipped by incrementing the contents of PC. The microoperations for SKZ are

$$\alpha_5 T_3\text{: MBR} \leftarrow \text{M[MAR]}$$

$$\alpha_5 T_4\text{: If MBR} = 0 \text{ then PC} \leftarrow \text{PC} + 1, \text{SC} \leftarrow 0$$

For the SKP instruction, we obtain

$$\alpha_6 T_3\text{: MBR} \leftarrow \text{M[MAR]}$$

$$\alpha_6 T_4\text{: If MBR} > 0 \text{ then PC} \leftarrow \text{PC} + 1, \text{SC} \leftarrow 0$$

11.7.2 Register-Reference Instructions

The remaining instructions to consider are the register-reference instructions. These instructions can be completed without having to get additional operands from memory. The instructions are distinguished from memory-reference instructions by the value in the opcode field. All register-reference instructions have a 1 in the MSB of the opcode field.

TABLE 11.7.1

Microoperations of Register-Reference Instructions

Instruction	Condition	Register Transfer
CMP	$\alpha_8 T_3$	AC ← AC′, SC ← 0
CLA	$\alpha_9 T_3$	AC ← 0, SC ← 0
INC	$\alpha_{10} T_3$	AC ← AC +1, SC ← 0
CLV	$\alpha_{11} T_3$	V ← 0, SC ← 0
SKV	$\alpha_{12} T_3$	If V = 1 then PC ← PC +1, SC ← 0

TABLE 11.7.2

Microoperations for the Simple CPU

Instruction	Time	Operation
	T_0	MAR ← PC
	T_1	IR ← M[MAR], PC← PC + 1
	T_2	MAR ← IR[0–11]
LW	$\alpha_0 T_3$	MBR ← M[MAR]
	$\alpha_0 T_4$	AC ← MBR, SC ← 0
ST	$\alpha_1 T_3$	M[MAR] ← AC, SC ← 0
ADD	$\alpha_2 T_3$	MBR ← M[MAR]
	$\alpha_2 T_4$	AC ← AC + MBR, V ← ALU.CO, SC ← 0
AND	$\alpha_3 T_3$	MBR ← M[MAR]
	$\alpha_3 T_4$	AC ← AC AND MBR, SC ← 0
JMP	$\alpha_4 T_3$	PC ← MAR, SC ← 0
SKZ	$\alpha_5 T_3$	MBR ← M[MAR]
	$\alpha_5 T_4$	**If MBR = 0 then PC ← PC + 1, SC ← 0**
SKP	$\alpha_6 T_3$	MBR ← M[MAR]
	$\alpha_6 T_4$	**If MBR > 0 then PC ← PC + 1, SC ← 0**
CMP	$\alpha_8 T_3$	AC ← AC′, SC ← 0
CLA	$\alpha_9 T_3$	AC ← 0, SC ← 0
INC	$\alpha_{10} T_3$	AC ← AC +1, SC ← 0
CLV	$\alpha_{11} T_3$	V ← 0, SC ← 0
SKV	$\alpha_{12} T_3$	**If V = 1 then PC ← PC + 1, SC ← 0**

The microoperations for the register-reference instructions are given in Table 11.7.1. A summary of the microoperations associated with the simple AC-based CPU is given in Table 11.7.2.

We are at a point where we consider the design of the AC-based CPU. The design involves generating the needed control signals and routing these signals to the proper units within the CPU as well as to the external memory. In the design, we consider the needed inputs to the combinational part of the control units. We will also consider the needed output signals.

11.8 Inputs and Outputs of the Combinational Part of Control Unit

11.8.1 Input Part

To determine the needed inputs to the combinational part of the control unit, we scan the table of microoperations. The list of conditions found on the left-hand side of each microoperation is used to determine part of the set of inputs. From Table 11.7.2 and our earlier discussion, the set of inputs should include the opcode field part of IR (IR[12–115]) and the sequence counter inputs.

To determine other inputs, we inspect the right-hand side of each microoperation as well. In particular, we identify those microoperations with a conditional transfer (using if-then) found as part of the register transfer. The table shows there are three such statements as shown with highlighted (bolded) rows. The three statements cause PC to be incremented based on the contents of the MBR register or the V bit. As a result, the control unit must inspect the values of MBR and V as well. In the first section of this chapter, we mentioned that a statement of the form

$$\text{if } (C = 1) \text{ then } Y \leftarrow Z$$

can be written as

$$C: Y \leftarrow Z$$

Hence, the "if" conditions associated with the right-hand side of each microoperation can be moved to the left-hand side. For example, the statement

$$\alpha_5 T_4: \text{If MBR} = 0 \text{ then PC} \leftarrow \text{PC} + 1, \text{SC} \leftarrow 0$$

can be written as the two statements

$$(\text{MBR} = 0) \; \alpha_5 T_4: \text{PC} \leftarrow \text{PC} + 1$$

$$\alpha_5 T_4: \text{SC} \leftarrow 0$$

By inspecting Table 11.7.2, we note that three additional inputs are required: an input V and two inputs representing MBR > 0 and MBR = 0. We will determine how these inputs are generated later.

11.8.2 Output Part

The output part of the control unit is the set of control lines used to initiate the different functions in the proper order. Among the set of output lines, for example, are the bus control lines used to move data between the different registers and/or memory. As another example, one needs control lines to select the proper data operation associated with the ALU.

We start with determining the needed lines of the ALU. Similar to the bus select part, to minimize the needed ALU lines we use a decoding scheme. We first determine the total number of arithmetic and logic operations needed. To do this we refer to Table 11.7.2 and to the data path organization of the CPU. From the table, we identify the microoperations that affect the AC register (microoperations of the form AC ← X). Note that the AC is the only register considered since the AC is the only register connected to the output of the ALU. As a result, other arithmetic operations that are performed on the remaining registers (e.g., MBR ← MBR + 1 and PC ← PC + 1) are done independent of the ALU. In fact, this is the reason the registers considered include an increment input. To increment PC using the ALU, we could have placed its contents on MBR using the bus. We then follow that by adding 1 to the contents of MBR through the ALU unit. The result of the ALU is then stored on AC and routed back to PC. As you may have concluded, this is a lengthy process.

From Table 11.7.2, the microoperations that affect the output of the ALU are

$$\alpha_0 T_4: \text{AC} \leftarrow \text{MBR}$$

$$\alpha_2 T_4: \text{AC} \leftarrow \text{AC} + \text{MBR}$$

$$\alpha_3 T_4: \text{AC} \leftarrow \text{AC AND MBR}$$

$$\alpha_8 T_3: \text{AC} \leftarrow \text{AC}'$$

$$\alpha_9 T_3: \text{AC} \leftarrow 0$$

$$\alpha_{10} T_3: \text{AC} \leftarrow \text{AC} + 1$$

Of the above microoperations, the last two (AC ← 0, and AC ← AC + 1) can be accomplished by using the clear and increment inputs of AC. The remaining four can be realized through the ALU. As a result, similar to Chapter 5, we use select lines to choose the function we would like the ALU to perform. We label the select lines as ALU.S_0 and ALU.S_1 with the corresponding function as given in Table 11.8.1. As can be seen from the table, depending on the select lines, one of the four microoperations can be placed at the output of the ALU.

TABLE 11.8.1

ALU Function According to Select Lines

ALU.S_1	ALU.S_0	Function
0	0	AC ← MBR
0	1	AC ← AC + MBR
1	0	AC ← AC AND MBR
1	1	AC ← AC'

For the bus part, the control unit outputs three functions, BUS.S_1, BUS.S_2, and BUS.S_3. These outputs are used as inputs into the decoder to determine which of the registers (memory included) is selected to place its contents on the bus. We assume the association is as given in Table 11.8.2.

In addition, the following outputs are needed: outputs associated with the increment, load, and clear inputs of the registers; outputs that affect the value of the V flip-flop; memory control outputs (chip select and read/write); and one output that resets the sequence counter so as to start the fetch cycle when needed.

We next construct the functions for each of the above outputs.

TABLE 11.8.2

Bus Connections

BUS $S_2 S_1 S_0$	Unit Connected
0 0 0	None
0 0 1	Memory
0 1 0	MAR
0 1 1	PC
1 0 0	MBR
1 0 1	AC
1 1 0	IR
1 1 1	None

11.9 The Control Unit Output Functions

In constructing the functions, we refer to the set of microoperations given in Table 11.7.2. With each microoperation we determine the conditions that must be satisfied to complete the microoperation.

We start at time T_0. During this time, the control unit generates signals that cause the contents of PC to be stored into MAR. To store PC into MAR, we place PC on the bus, assigning 011 to the select lines of the bus which selects PC. In addition, assigning 1 to the load input of MAR causes the contents of the BUS to be stored into MAR on the rising edge of the clock. Note that from our discussion of the timing signals earlier, T_0 assumes a value of 1 for an entire clock cycle. The changes in MAR occur during this clock cycle.

At time T_1, the following two microoperations are to be completed

$$IR \leftarrow M, \text{ and } PC \leftarrow PC + 1$$

The first part, the memory read, is completed by reading memory on the bus and activating the load line of IR. (Note we replaced M[MAR] by M for simplicity.) To place the contents of memory on the bus we (1) set the chip select line to 1, (2) set the read/write input to 1, and (3) place 001 on the select lines of the bus. In addition, we set the load line of IR to 1. In addition to reading memory in IR, the contents of the PC are incremented during T_3. This can be done concurrently with reading memory by assigning 1 to the increment input of the PC.

We give a more formal description of the above microoperations in rows 1 and 2 of Table 11.9.1. As can be seen from the table, we use MAR.L to refer

TABLE 11.9.1

Sample Microoperations with the Corresponding Control Outputs Needed
in the Design

Time	Operation	Control Signals Needed
T_0	MAR ← PC	BUS.SELECT = 3, MAR.L = 1
T_1	IR ← M, PC ← PC + 1	BUS.SELECT = 1, CS = 1, R/W = 1, IR.L = 1, PC.INC = 1
T_2	MAR ← IR[0–11]	BUS.SELECT = 6, MAR.L = 1
$\alpha_0 T_4$	AC ← MBR, SC ← 0	AC.L = 1, ALU.SELECT = 0, SC.CLR = 1
$\alpha_2 T_4$	AC ← AC + MBR, V ← ALU.CO, SC ← 0	AC.L = 1, ALU.SELECT = 1, V.L = 1, SC.CLR = 1
(MBR > 0) $\alpha_6 T_4$	PC ← PC +1	PC.INC = 1
$\alpha_6 T_4$	SC ← 0	SC.CLR = 1
$\alpha_{10} T_3$	AC ← AC +1, SC ← 0	AC.INC = 1, SC.CLR = 1
$\alpha_{11} T_3$	V ← 0, SC ← 0	V.C = 1, SC.CLR = 1

to the load line of the MAR register. We also refer to the select lines of the
bus as BUS.SELECT. A decimal assignment of 3 indicates the contents of PC
are placed on the bus. Note that only 12 bits of the IR registers are moved
in the MAR during T_2. This is done by connecting the 12 least-significant
bits of the bus to the inputs of MAR. The table contains additional sample
representative microoperations with the needed control signals. Later, we
will use these to build the complete input/output table of the combinational
part of the control unit.

In the table, when the condition $\alpha_0 T_4$ holds true, then MBR is moved into
AC. In this sample microoperation, we do not need to use the bus. Instead,
we use the ALU to move MBR into AC. From the description of the ALU
function, we assign ALU.SELECT the decimal value 0. In addition, we make
AC.L = 1. Finally, the sequence counter value is cleared (SC.CLR = 1). When
the timing signal T_4 is completed, the sequence counter output is set to 0
and, as a result, a new fetch cycle is started. The next microoperation associated with the condition $\alpha_2 T_4$ selects the add operation of the ALU. It also
causes the carry-out of the sum of to be stored in the overflow bit, V (the
V ← ALU.CO indicates this).

The microoperations discussed so far are pair-wise mutually exclusive.
That is, no two Boolean conditions associated with two microoperations can
be equal to 1 simultaneously. The next two microoperations in the table are
not mutually exclusive. In fact, these two operations are derived from the
microoperation

$$\alpha_6 T_4: \text{if (MBR > 0) then PC ← PC + 1, SC ← 0}$$

The statement is written as two statements as shown in the table with
(MBR > 0) evaluating to 1 if MBR > 0 and evaluating to 0 otherwise.

The following microoperation in the table is associated with the condition
$\alpha_{10} T_4$. For this statement we note that to increment AC, the ALU is not used.

Instead, AC.INC is set to 1. The last statement causes the V bit to be cleared to 0 ($V \leftarrow 0$).

With the above sample conditions, and by inspecting the set of micro-operations found in Table 11.7.2, one can derive the input/output table given in Table 11.9.2. In the table, column 1 corresponds to V. An entry in this column is assigned one of three possible values 0, 1, or x. A 0 indicates that V assumes a value of 1, a 1 indicates that V assumes a value of 0, and an x corresponds to a "don't-care" condition. The next two columns refer to MBR with one column indicates MBR = 0 and the other indicates MBR > 0. For the output part, we associate with each element the set of lines of interest. For example, with memory we associate two columns with labels CS and R/W. A comma separates the labels. As another example, we associate three columns with the AC registers. The label L,C,I indicates that the AC field is 3 bits with the first bit corresponding to load, the second to clear, and the third to increment.

As can be seen, the table contains an input part and an output part as well. The output part was derived based on the discussion presented earlier in this section. For each condition, we derive the input part and output part of the row containing the condition. To illustrate, for the condition T_0 to hold true the sequence counter output must be 000 (this corresponds to T_0). Note that this is the only requirement that the inputs must satisfy. As a result, all remaining inputs in the table are assigned x values, the don't-care condition. As to the output part, it is derived based on the discussion carried in constructing Table 11.9.1 above. The output entries in the table with no assignments mean these outputs are assigned a value of 0.

11.10 Design of the AC-Based CPU

The design of the CPU is based on the generation of the control signals found in the previous section, and connecting these lines to the appropriate locations in the data path. The data path does not include the V flip-flop. As a result, the design includes determining the needed connections for this flip-flop.

We first start with the design of Table 11.9.2. By removing the control column from the table, the table is reduced to a table similar to a truth table with 18 outputs and 10 inputs. The table is abbreviated as many of the entries in the input part are don't-care inputs. The number of rows in the table is 23. One can realize the table using AND-OR gates or a programmable logic device, e.g., a PLA or PAL. The PLA programming table is shown in Table 11.10.1. The PLA programming table is obtained directly from 11.9.2. From the table, one can generate (program) the needed connections of the PLA. The outputs of the PLA are connected to the proper locations within the control unit (the sequence counter) and to the data path signals (the bus, ALU, register controls, and memory, for example).

TABLE 11.9.2

Input and Output Relations of the Control Unit Combinational Part

Inputs						Outputs									
	MBR					MEM	MAR	AC	MBR	PC	IR	SC	V	BUS	ALU
V	$=0$	>0	Opcode $IR_{15}IR_{14}IR_{13}IR_{12}$	SC $X_2X_1X_0$	Control	CS, R/W	L	L,C,I	L	L,I	L	C	L,C	$S_2S_1S_0$	S_1S_0
x	x	x	xxxx	000	T_0		1							011	
x	x	x	xxxx	001	T_1	11				01	1			001	
x	x	x	xxxx	010	T_2		1							110	
x	x	x	0000	011	$\alpha_0 T_3$	11								001	
x	x	x	0000	100	$\alpha_0 T_4$	00		100	1			1			00
x	x	x	0001	011	$\alpha_1 T_3$	10						1			
x	x	x	0010	011	$\alpha_2 T_3$	11								101	
x	x	x	0010	100	$\alpha_2 T_4$			100	1			1	10	001	01
x	x	x	0011	011	$\alpha_3 T_3$	11						1		001	
x	x	x	0011	100	$\alpha_3 T_4$			100	1			1			10
x	x	x	0100	011	$\alpha_4 T_3$				1	10		1		010	
x	x	x	0101	011	$\alpha_5 T_3$	11								001	
x	1	x	0101	100	(MBR = 0) $\alpha_5 T_4$					01		1			
x	x	x	0101	100	$\alpha_5 T_4$							1			
x	x	x	0110	011	$\alpha_6 T_3$	11								001	
x	x	1	0110	100	(MBR > 0) $\alpha_6 T_4$					01		1			
x	x	x	0110	100	$\alpha_6 T_4$				1			1			
x	x	x	1000	011	$\alpha_8 T_3$			100				1			11
x	x	x	1001	011	$\alpha_9 T_3$			010				1			
x	x	x	1010	011	$\alpha_{10} T_3$			001				1			
x	x	x	1011	011	$\alpha_{11} T_3$							1	01		
1	x	x	1100	011	(V = 1) $\alpha_{12} T_3$					01		1			
x	x	x	1100	011	$\alpha_{12} T_3$							1			

TABLE 11.10.1

Programming Table of the Combinational Part of the Control Unit

Product	MBR $V=0=0$	MBR >0	Opcode $IR_{15}IR_{14}IR_{13}IR_{12}$	SC $X_2X_1X_0$	MEM CS, R/W	MAR L	AC L,C,I	MBR L	PC L,I	IR L	SC C	V L,C	BUS $S_2S_1S_0$	ALU S_1S_0
$X_2'X_1'X_0'$	–	–	– – – –	000	00	1	000	0	00	0	0	00	011	00
$X_2'X_1X_0$	–	–	– – –	001	11	0	000	0	01	1	0	00	001	00
$X_2'X_1X_0'$	–	–	– – –	010	00	1	000	0	00	0	0	00	110	00
$IR_{15}'IR_{14}'IR_{13}IR_{12}'X_2'X_1X_0$	–	–	0000011		11	0	000	1	00	0	0	00	001	00
$IR_{15}'IR_{14}'IR_{13}'IR_{12}'X_2X_1'X_0'$	–	–	0000100		00	0	100	0	00	0	1	00	000	00
$IR_{15}'IR_{14}'IR_{13}IR_{12}'X_2'X_1X_0$	–	–	0001011		10	0	000	1	00	0	1	00	101	00
$IR_{15}'IR_{14}'IR_{13}IR_{12}'X_2'X_1X_0$	–	–	0010011		11	0	000	0	00	0	1	00	001	00
$IR_{15}'IR_{14}'IR_{13}IR_{12}'X_2X_1'X_0'$	–	–	0010100		00	0	100	1	00	0	1	10	000	01
$IR_{15}'IR_{14}'IR_{13}IR_{12}'X_2X_1X_0$	–	–	0011011		11	0	000	0	00	0	0	00	001	00
$IR_{15}'IR_{14}'IR_{13}IR_{12}'X_2X_2'X_1X_0$	–	–	0011100		00	0	100	0	10	0	1	00	010	10
$IR_{15}'IR_{14}'IR_{13}IR_{12}'X_2X_2'X_1X_0'$	–	–	0100011		11	0	000	1	00	0	1	00	001	00
$IR_{15}'IR_{14}'IR_{13}'IR_{12}'X_2'X_2X_1'X_0$	–	–	0101100		00	0	000	0	10	0	1	00	000	00
$M_=IR_{15}'IR_{14}IR_{13}IR_{12}'IR_{12}X_2X_2X_1'X_0'$	–	1	0101100		11	0	000	1	00	0	0	00	000	00
$IR_{15}'IR_{14}'IR_{13}IR_{12}'X2X1'X0$	–	–	0101100		00	0	000	0	01	0	1	00	000	00
$IR_{15}'IR_{14}IR_{13}IR_{12}'X_2X_2X_1X_0$	–	–	0110011		11	0	000	1	00	0	0	00	001	00
$M_>IR_{15}'IR_{14}IR_{13}IR_{12}'X_2X_2X_1'X_0'$	–	1	0110100		00	0	000	0	01	0	1	00	000	00
$IR_{15}'IR_{14}IR_{13}'IR_{12}'X_2X_2X_1'X_0'$	–	–	0110100		00	0	000	0	00	0	1	00	000	00
$IR_{15}IR_{14}IR_{13}'IR_{12}'X_2X_2X_1X_0$	–	–	1000011		00	0	100	0	00	0	1	00	000	11
$IR_{15}IR_{14}IR_{13}'IR_{12}X_2X_2X_1X_0$	–	–	1001011		00	0	010	0	00	0	1	00	000	00
$IR_{15}IR_{14}IR_{13}'IR_{12}'X_2X_2X_1X_0$	–	–	1010011		00	0	001	0	00	0	1	01	000	00
$IR_{15}IR_{14}IR_{13}'IR_{12}X_2X_2X_1X_0$	–	–	1011011		00	0	000	0	00	0	1	00	000	00
$VIR_{15}IR_{14}IR_{13}'IR_{12}'X_2X_2X_1X_0$	1	–	1100011		00	0	000	0	01	0	0	00	000	00
$IR_{15}'IR_{14}IR_{13}'IR_{12}'X_2X_2X_1X_0$	–	–	1100011		00	0	000	0	00	0	1	00	000	00

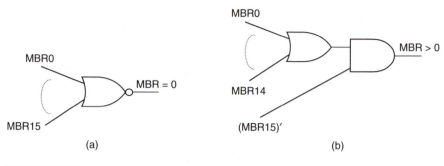

FIGURE 11.10.1
(a) Design of MBR = 0; (b) Design of MBR > 0

We illustrate the relation of the PLA design to the overall design by considering some examples. Consider the MAR.L output of the PLA. This output is the logical OR of two entries $(X_2' X_1' X_0' + X_2' X_1 X_0')$. When either of these conditions holds true, the output of the OR gate assumes a value of 1 and, as a result, the contents of MAR are cleared. Note that there is no other Boolean condition that causes MAR.L to be set to 1. This can be deduced from the table by observing the remaining input assignments to the MAR 1.

In order for the PLA circuit to work, all its inputs must be available. In our discussion, the IR opcode and SC part are given as part of the control unit. Missing are the inputs representing the status of V and the status of MBR. The status of V can be obtained by directly connecting the V output to the input of the PLA. The MBR part can be obtained with minor additional gates. For example, the input to test if MBR = 0 is obtained by simply feeding all the MBR bits into a single NOR gate. The output of the NOR gate is 1 if and only if MBR = 0. We use a similar procedure to generate the input MBR > 0, with this input assuming a value of 1 if and only if MBR > 0. To do this, we assume the number is presented in 2's complement. As a result, in order for MBR to be greater than 0, the most-significant bit, MBR_{15} must be 0 and at least one of the remaining bits must be equal to 1. To generate the inputs MBR = 0 and MBR > 0, we form the circuit shown in Figure 11.10.1(a) and (b), respectively. The output of each OR gate is used as an input to the PLA of the control unit.

The remaining circuit design not considered is that of the V flip-flop. As can be concluded from Table 11.9.2, depending on the condition in the table, the V flip-flop needs to be cleared or loaded from the ALU. The design of this flip-flop is left as an exercise.

Chapter 11 Exercises

Questions 11.1 through 11.5 deal with RTL design that is not bus based, i.e., assume connections can be made to the inputs of the registers or flip-flops directly.

11.1 Show the design of the following RTL statements with X referring to a single SR flip-flop, and P1 and P2 are mutually exclusive signals.

P1: $X \leftarrow 0$

P2: $X \leftarrow 1$

11.2 Show the design of the following RTL with X referring to a JK flip-flop. Assume P1, P2, and P3 are mutually exclusive signals.

P1: $X \leftarrow 0$

P2: $X \leftarrow 1$

P3: $X \leftarrow X'$

11.3 Show the design of the following RTL statements using an SR flip-flop. The P conditions are mutually exclusive Y and Z are outputs of flip-flops.

P1: $X \leftarrow 0$

P2: $X \leftarrow 1$

P3: $X \leftarrow Y$

P4: if (P5 = 1), then $X \leftarrow Z$

11.4 Repeat problem 3 on

P1: $X \leftarrow 0$

P2: $X \leftarrow 1$

P3: $X \leftarrow Y$

P4: if (P5 = 1), then $X \leftarrow Z$

P6: $X \leftarrow 0$

P7: $X \leftarrow 1$

11.5 In the design of the AC-based CPU, we left the design of the V flip-flop as an exercise. Show the needed connections to the V flip-flop. Assume V is a JK flip-flop.

11.6 Many of the Boolean conditions used in constructing the programming table in the chapter are mutually exclusive. Identify and list those that are not.

11.7 Use bus connections to show the design of the following RTL Statements. Assume A_i refers to register I. Assume the bus connections are accomplished through the use of tristate gates with only four registers connected to the bus.

> P1: $A_1 \leftarrow A_2$
>
> P2: $A_1 \leftarrow A_3$
>
> P3: $A_1 \leftarrow 0$
>
> P4: if (P5 = 1) then $A_1 \leftarrow A_1 + 1$

11.8 Identify the PLA outputs that affect the fetch cycle of the AC-based CPU.

11.9 For realizing the fetch cycle, show all needed connections from the control unit to the data-path and memory of the AC-based CPU.

11.10 Assume the contents of PC are $(100)_{16}$ and memory location 100 contains $(9100)_{16}$. To complete the instruction from fetch to execute, show the contents of PC, MAR, MBR, IR, SC, AC, IR, the bus decoder inputs. and the ALU select inputs for each of the timing signals (T_i). Use "?" for those entries that are not known.

11.11 By referring to question 11.10, assume the next instruction at location $(101)_{16}$ is $(2020)_{16}$ with memory location $(020)_{16}$ equal to $(AB11)_{16}$. To complete the instruction from fetch to execute, find the contents of PC, MAR, MBR, IR, SC, AC, IR, the bus decoder inputs, and the ALU select inputs for each of the timing signals (T_i). Use "?" for those entries that are not known. Assume the previous instruction was completed successfully.

11.12 Show the needed connections from the control unit to the data-path and memory to complete the LW instruction from fetch to execute.

11.13 Repeat question 12 for the SKZ instruction.

11.14 As discussed in the macro section of the previous chapter, one can write macros for common tasks. Write the needed set of instruction for the statement

$$\text{if } (A >= B) \text{ then } A = 0;$$

Assume A and B are memory locations. To exit the macro, use JMP EXIT.

11.15 Repeat problem 14 on

> if $(A >= B)$ then $A = 0$
>
> else
>
> $A = A + B;$

11.16 Write a macro for multiplying two positive numbers A and B.

Appendix A

References

1. J. Hayes, *Introduction to Digital Logic Design*, Addison-Wesley, 1993.
2. R. Tocci and N. Widmer, *Digital Systems Principles and Applications*, Prentice Hall, 1998.
3. M. Mano, *Digital Design*, 2nd edition, Prentice Hall, 1991.
4. A. Clements, *The Principles of Computer Hardware*, 3rd edition. Oxford, 2000.
5. G. Karam and J. Bryant, *Principles of Computer Systems*, Prentice Hall, 1992.
6. Richard S. Sandige, Cal Poly, San Luis Obispo, *Digital Design Essentials and XILINX SE 4.21 Package*, Prentice Hall, 2003.
7. M. Morris Mano, *Digital Design*, 3rd edition, Prentice Hall, 2002.
8. M. Morris Mano, *Logic and Computer Design Fundamentals and Xilinx 4.2 Package*, 2nd edition, Prentice Hall, 2002.
9. Daniel D. Gajski, *Principles of Digital Design*, Prentice Hall, 1997.
10. Victor P. Nelson, H. Troy Nagle, Bill D. Carroll, and David Irwin, *Digital Logic Circuit Analysis and Design*, Prentice Hall, 1995.
11. Ken Coffman, *Real World FPGA Design with Verilog*, Prentice Hall, 2000
12. Jayaram Bhasker, *VHDL Primer, A*, 3rd edition, Prentice Hall, 1999
13. John Vyemura, *A First Course in Digital System Design*, Brook/Cole Publishing, 2000.
14. John Wakerly, *Digital Design Principles and Practices*, Prentice Hall, 2001.
15. Steve Waterman, *Digital Logic Simulation with CPLD Programming*, Prentice Hall, 2003.
16. William Stallings, *Computer Organization and Architecture: Designing for Performance*, 6th edition, Prentice Hall, 2003.
17. Randal E. Bryant and David R. O'Hallaron, *Computer Systems: A Programmer's Perspective*, Prentice Hall, 2003.
18. G. Karam and J. Bryant, *Principles of Computer Systems*, Prentice Hall, 1992.
19. J. Carpinelli, *Computer Systems Organization and Architecture*, Addison-Wesley, 2001.
20. V. Hamacher, Z. Vranesic, and S. Zaky, *Computer Organization*, 4th edition, McGraw-Hill, 1996.
21. V. Heuring and H. Jordan, *Computer System Design and Architecture*, Addison-Wesley, 1997.
22. P. Abel, *IBM PC Assembly Language and Programming*, Prentice Hall, 1995.
23. J. Hayes, *Computer Architecture* and *Organization*, 3rd edition, McGraw-Hill, 1998.

24. M. Murdocca and V. Heuring, *Principles of Computer Architecture*, Prentice Hall, 2000.
25. J. Hennessy and D. Patterson, *Computer Architecture: A Quantitative Approach*, 2nd edition, Morgan Kaufmann, 1996.
26. J. Hennessy and D. Patterson, *Computer Organization and Design: The Hardware/ Software Interface*, 2nd edition, Morgan Kaufmann, 1998.
27. M. Mano, *Computer System Architecture*, 3rd edition, Prentice Hall, 1993.
28. W. Stallings, *Computer Organization and Architecture*, 5th edition, Prentice Hall, 2000.
29. Andrew S. Tanenbaum, *Structured Computer Organization*, 4th edition, Prentice Hall, 1999.
30. James Evans, *Itanium Architecture for Programmers: Understanding 64-Bit Processors and EPIC Principles*, Prentice Hall 2003.

Appendix B

Answers to Selected Problems

Chapter 1

1.1 (a) $(33)_{10}$, (b) $(22)_{10}$, (c) $(146095)_{10}$

1.3 $(676.16)_8$

1.5 $(3BE.38)_{16}$

1.7 $(6E.4)_{16}$

1.9 (a) $(111111100.01)_2$, (b) $(774.2)_8$, (c) $(1FC.4)_{16}$

1.11 $(100100110)_2$

1.13 $(3230)_5$

1.15 $(2260.555)_8$

1.17 $(01010000)_2$

1.19 $(007550)_8$

1.21 10's complement: 877, 9's complement: 876

1.23 8's complement: 6506777, 7's complement: 6506776

1.25 (a) 8931, (b) 35121, (c) − 2353 (d) −30414, (e) −30415

1.27

0	1011	101010

Chapter 2

2.1

			(a)	(b)	(c)
X	Y	Z	XY + Z	X'Y'+ZZ'	XYZ+(X+Y)'
0	0	0	0	1	1
0	0	1	1	1	1
0	1	0	0	0	0
0	1	1	1	0	0
1	0	0	0	0	0
1	0	1	1	0	0
1	1	0	1	0	0
1	1	1	1	0	1

2.3 (a) $(x + y)(z + w(x' + y'))$

(b) $x' + y' + 0.x$

(c) $(x + y + z)(xy)'$

2.5 The expression x where x is a Boolean variable

2.7 Complement individual variables in dual expression to get $G + (A' + B' + CD')(E' + DF' + (A'B')')$

2.9 No, by definition the two expressions can not be equal.

2.11 (a) $x' + y + z$

(b) $y' + z$

(c) $x'z' + x'w + xyz$

2.13

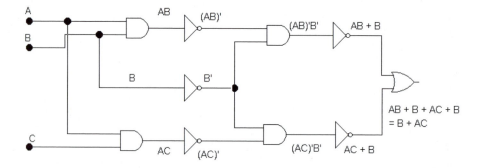

2.15 The verification can be done by connecting the outputs of the circuits to the logic converter of the Electronics Workbench and verifying the circuit and the corresponding simplified circuit produce the same truth table.

2.17 $V_A = 10 - (100I_1) = 2.083$

2.19

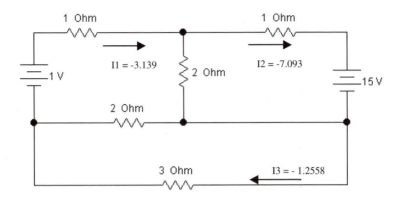

───────────

Chapter 3

3.1 Since the minterms are different then their representation differ in at least one location where a variable x_i is complemented in one minterm but not in the other. Hence the product can be written as

$$e_1\, x_i \cdot e_2\, x_i' = (e_1 \cdot e_2).(\, x_i \cdot x_i'\,) = 0$$

3.3 (a) $f(A,B,C) = A'B'C' + A'BC + AB'C + ABC' + ABC$
   (b) $f(A,B,C) = (A+B+C')\,(A+B'+C)(A'+B+C)$
   (c) $f'(A,B,C) = A'B'C + A'BC' + AB'C'$
   (d) $f'(A,B,C) = (A+B+C)(A+B'+C')(A'+B+C')(A'+B'+C)(A'+B'+C')$

3.5 (a) $f(A,B,C) = \Sigma(0,3,5,6,7)$
   (b) $f(A,B,C) = \Pi(1,2,4)$
   (c) $f'(A,B,C) = \Sigma(1,2,4)$
   (d) $f'(A,B,C) = \Pi(0,3,5,6,7)$

3.7 (a) None due to $(AB)'$ term
   (b) Sum of product
   (c) Sum of product and canonical sum
   (d) Sum of product and product of sum
   (e) Sum of product, product of sum and canonical product
   (f) None due to $A'\,(B'+C)$ term

3.9 $F(A,B,C) = A + B$

$\qquad\qquad = A(B+B')(C+C') + B(A+A')(C+C')$

$\qquad\qquad = A'BC' + A'BC + AB'C' + AB'C + ABC' + ABC$

3.11 (a) $f(A,B,C) = A'B'C' + A'BC + AB'C + ABC' + ABC$

$\qquad\qquad\qquad = A'B'C' + BC + AC + AB$

  (b) $f' (A,B,C) = A'B'C + A'BC' + AB'C'$ simplified

  (c) For the design, first write the function in:

    (i) sum of product

    (ii) product of sum (complement f')

    (iii) sum of product

    (iv) product of sum

  (d) For the design first:

    (i) Design f' in sum of product and then invert

    (ii) Design f' in product of sum and invert

3.12 Yes, when AND is followed with NOR the resulting circuit is similar to AND-OR-Invert.

3.13 Similar to 3.12. The resulting circuit is OR-AND-Invert, however.

Chapter 4

4.1 $f(A,B,C)= \Sigma(0,1,4,5)$

$\qquad\qquad = A'B'C' + A'B'C + AB'C' + AB'C$

The table below shows adjacency an x in the table means the minterms are adjacent.

	$A'B'C'$	$A'B'C$	$AB'C'$	$AB'C$
$A'B'C'$		x	x	
$A'B'C$	x			x
$AB'C'$	x			x
$AB'C$		x	x	

4.3 (a)

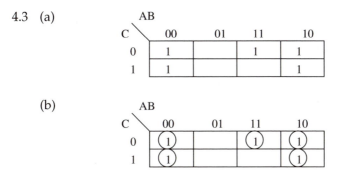

(b)

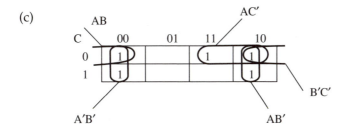

Algebraic are same as minterms.

(c)

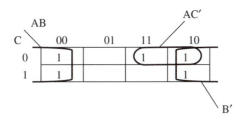

(d) No, subcube size must be 2k for some integer k.

(e)

AB

C	00	01	11	10
0	1		1	1
1	1			1

(f) Prime implicants are shown in the table below.

AC′

AB

C	00	01	11	10
0	1		1	1
1	1			1

B′

4.5

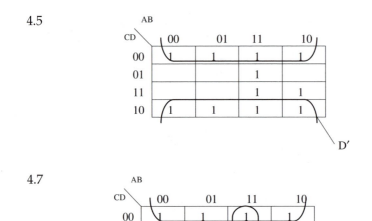

4.7

4.9 Each implicant is essential. Hence one minimum $D' + AB + AC$.

4.11 $c = B + C' + D$

4.13 $e = B'D' + CD'$

$f = A + B + C'D'$

$g = A + B'C + BC' + BD'$, or

$g = A + B'C + BC' + C'D'$

4.15 $f' = A'BC' + BC'D' + ACD'$. Hence

$f = f'' = (A+B'+C)(B'+C+D)(A'+C'+D)$

4.17 Prime implicants, PI's, P1 = (0, 4), P2 = (4, 5), P3 = (5, 13), P4 = (10, 11),

P5 = (11, 15), P6 = (13, 15).

4.19 $f = B'E' + C'DE' + CD' + CE$

Chapter 5

5.1 For C_2 delay is 7 ns, for C_3 delay is 14 ns.

5.3 $C_6 = G_5 + G_4P_5 + G_3P_5P_4 + G_2P_5P_4P_3 + G_1P_5P_4P_3P_2 + C_1P_5P_4P_3P_2P_1$

5.5

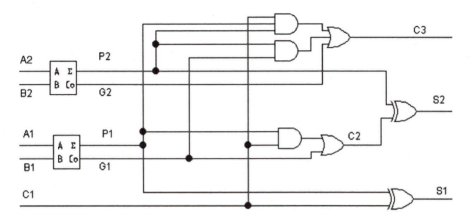

5.7

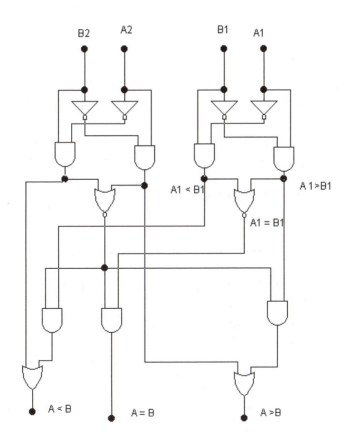

5.9   7 ns. 7 ns.

5.11

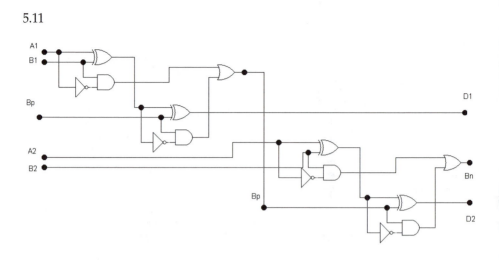

5.13   The result for Bp = 0 and Bp = 1 is, respectively, $D_2D_1B_n$ = 111 and $D_2D_1B_n$ = 101.

5.15   Form 0101101 + 0111001 = 1100110; MSB = 0, overflow occurred.

5.17   Append the sign bit to the 4 most significant bits (A = 00000011 and B = 11111011). The sign bit is copied into the added bits. The method is called sign extension.

5.19   (a)   10001010 + 01101100 = 11110110; cin into sign bit = cout, no overflow.

        (b)   10001010 + 10010100 = 00011110; cin into sign bit not equal cout, overflow.

        (c)   90010 + 99499 = 1 89509; overflow.

        (d)   91501 + 02345 = 93846; no overflow.

5.21   Number of adders is 1 less than the size of B = 7 adders. The size of each is equal to the size of A, 16. The number of AND gates is the equal to the product of the operand sizes, 16 × 8 = 128.

5.23   (a)   11110000 AND 10101100 = 10100000, 11110000 OR 10101100 = 11111100, A' = 00001111 and B' = 01010011.

        (b)   00000000 AND 10101111 = 00000000, 00000000 OR 10101111 = 10101111, A' = 11111111, B' = 01010000.

        (c) AF AND 91 = 10101111 AND 10010001 = 10000001; OR results in 10111111, A' = 01010000, B' = 01101110.

Chapter 6

6.1

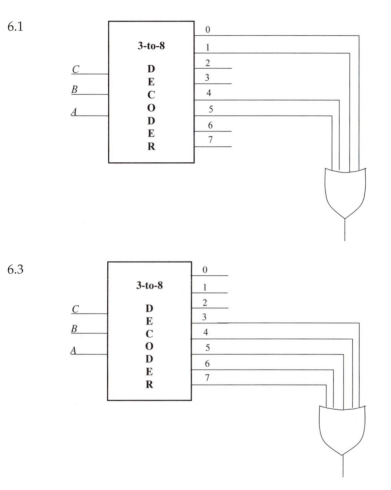

6.3

6.5

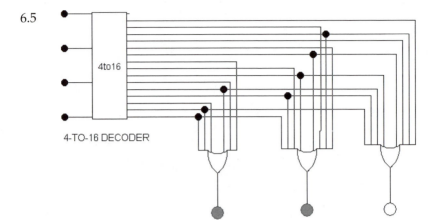

4-TO-16 DECODER

6.7

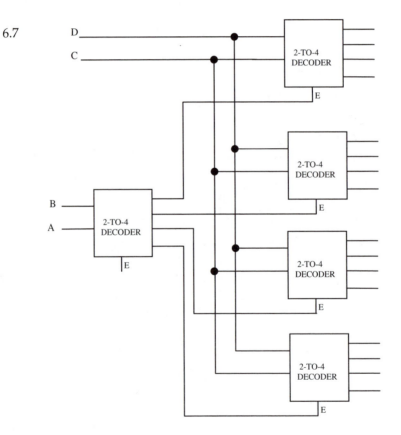

6.9

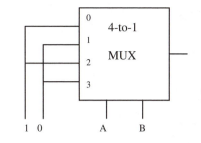

6.11 From Figure 5.4.1 we obtain

A	B	Bn	D
0	0	Bp	Bp
0	1	1	Bp'
1	0	0	Bp'
1	1	Bp	Bp

6.13

	Inputs				Outputs		
Product Terms	A_2	A_1	B_2	B_1	C_3	S_2	S_1
$A_2'A_1'B_2'B_1'$	0	0	0	0	1	1	1
$A_2'A_1'B_2'B_1$	0	0	0	1	1	1	0
$A_2'A_1'B_2B_1'$	0	0	1	0	1	0	1
$A_2'A_1'B_2B_1$	0	0	1	1	1	0	0
$A_2'A_1B_2'B_1'$	0	1	0	0	1	1	0
$A_2'A_1B_2'B_1$	0	1	0	1	1	0	1
$A_2'A_1B_2B_1'$	0	1	1	0	1	0	0
$A_2'A_1B_2B_1$	0	1	1	1	0	1	1
$A_2A_1'B_2'B_1'$	1	0	0	0	1	0	1
$A_2A_1'B_2'B_1$	1	0	0	1	1	0	0
$A_2A_1'B_2B_1'$	1	0	1	0	0	1	1
$A_2A_1'B_2B_1$	1	0	1	1	0	1	0
$A_2A_1B_2'B_1'$	1	1	0	0	1	0	0
$A_2A_1B_2'B_1$	1	1	0	1	0	1	1
$A_2A_1B_2B_1'$	1	1	1	0	0	1	0
$A_2A_1B_2B_1$	1	1	1	1	0	0	1

6.15 Equations can be minimized separately:

$$F_{A<B} = A_2'A_1'B_1 + A_2'B_2 + A_1'B_2B_1$$

$F_{A=B}$ can not be minimized

$$F_{A>B} = A_1B_2'B_1' + A2B_2' + B_1'A_2A_1$$

Hence the PAL needed should contain at least 3 OR gates and 10 AND gates. One of the inputs to the OR gates must receive four product terms. Each of the others must receive 3 inputs each.

6.17 From 6.5, the decoder of the ROM must be 4-to-16 decoder; the OR
      array must include at least 3 OR gates.

6.19 Minimized equations needed for parts (b), (d) and (e) are

$$F1 = ABC + ABD$$
$$F2 = A'BD + A'BC + AB' + AC'D'$$
$$F3 = B'C + BC'D' + CD$$
$$F4 = B'D + BD'$$

For part (c), the minimized equations needed are

$$F'1 = A' + B' + C'D$$
$$F'2 = A'B' + A'C'D' + ABC + ABD$$
$$F'3 = C'D + B'C' + BCD'$$
$$F'4 = B'D' + BD$$

Chapter 7

7.1 Circuit design is

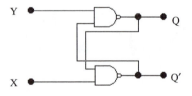

Characteristic table is

X	Y	Q	Q⁺	Q'⁺
0	0	0	1	1
0	0	1	1	1
0	1	0	1	0
0	1	1	1	0
1	0	0	0	1
1	0	1	0	1
1	1	0	0	1
1	1	1	1	0

7.3 From question 7.1, X and Y can be thought of as S and R if they are inverted first. Hence, design is

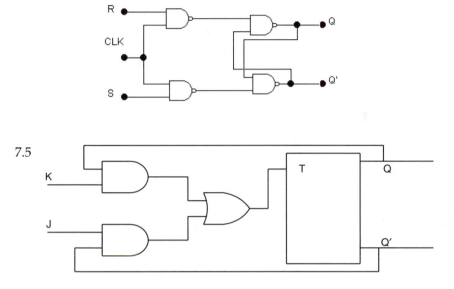

7.5

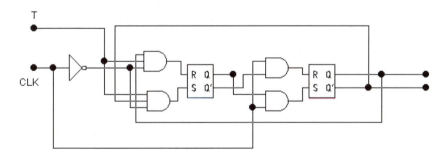

7.7 $f = 1/T = 1/10$ ns $= 100$ MHz. Duty cycle $= \%$ of T when clock is equal to $1 = 2/10 \times 100 = 20\%$.

7.9

7.11 $X^+ = J_x X' + K'_x X = IX' + I'X$

$Y^+ = J_y Y' + K'_y Y = (IX)Y' + (IX)\,'Y$

7.13

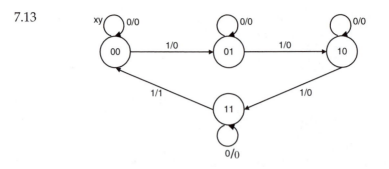

7.15   The Three Representations

A	B	X	A⁺	B⁺	OUT
0	0	0	0	1	0
0	0	1	0	0	0
0	1	0	0	1	0
0	1	1	1	0	0
1	0	0	0	1	0
1	0	1	1	1	0
1	1	0	0	1	1
1	1	1	0	0	0

(a)

	NS/output	
Present State	*x* = 0	*x* = 1
00	01/0	00/0
01	01/0	10/0
10	01/0	11/0
11	01/1	00/0

(b)

	Next State		Output	
Present State	*x* = 0	*x* = 1	*x* = 0	*x* = 1
00	01	00	0	0
01	01	10	0	0
10	01	11	0	0
11	01	00	1	0

(c)

7.17 $Z^+(W,Z,X) = 1 \oplus Z = \sum(0,1,4,5)$

$W^+(W,Z,X) = T_W \oplus W = W \oplus X \oplus Z = \sum(1,2,4,7)$

$Output(W,Z,X) = WZ = \sum(6,7)$

Chapter 8

8.1

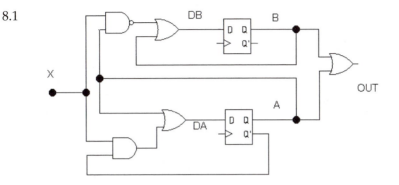

8.3 (a) In the design use $J_A = B$, $K_A = (BX)'$, $J_B = A$, and $K_B = X'$. (b) In the design we get the correct characteristic equations by deriving J_A, k_A, J_B, K_B and substituting these in the characteristic equations of a JK flip-flop.

8.5 From Figure 8.5.2 and the assignment XY = 00, 01, 10, and 11 representing A, B, C, and D we have

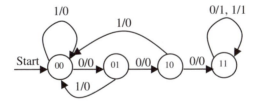

8.7 Excitation equations obtained are

$$J_X = I', K_X = Y, J_Y = X'I', \ K_Y = I + X', \text{and } OUT = XY'$$

8.9 The states are used to store the remainders of division by 5.

8.11 The states keep track of the last three inputs entered.

8.13 The excitation equations are

(a) $D_W = WZ + WY + YZ$

   $D_X = WY'Z' + W'Y'Z + WYZ + W'YZ'$

   $Out = x$

(b) $J_W = YZ$

   $K_W = Y'Z'$

   $J_X = WY'Z' + W'Y'Z + WYZ + W'YZ'$

   $K_X = W'Y'Z' + WY'Z + W'YZ + WYZ'$

(c) $T_W = WY'Z' + W'YZ$

   $T_X = W \oplus X \oplus Y \oplus Z$

(d) $S_W = YZ$

   $R_W = Y'Z'$

   $S_X = WY'Z' + W'Y'Z + WYZ + W'YZ'$

   $R_X = W'Y'Z' + WY'Z + W'YZ + WYZ'$

8.15 Need three memory elements A, B, and C with excitation equations

$$J_A = BCI, \quad K_A = 1$$

$$J_B = AI' + CI', \quad K_B = C'I' + CI$$

$$J_C = I, \quad K_C = B + I'$$

$$OUT = AI$$

8.17 Partition $P = (AG)(BF)(C)(DE)$

Chapter 9

9.1

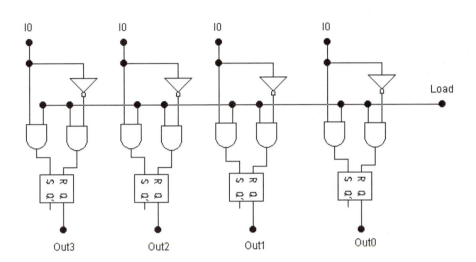

9.3

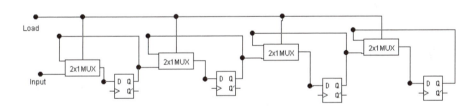

9.5 First convert the JK flip-flops into D. Follow that with design as in question 9.4.

9.7 The design is similar to Figure 9.4.5. Use a 3-bit counter/register instead. The inputs to the NAND gate are bits Y2 and Y0.

9.9 For the two most significant bits, the design is similar to a mod 4 counter. The least significant bit is always equal to 1.

9.11

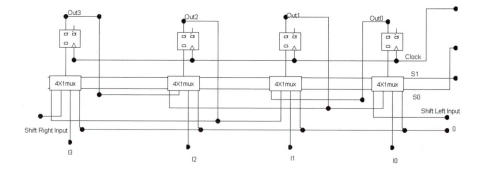

9.13   The timing diagram is similar to the diagram given in Figure 9.3.4. Here, however, the pattern repeats after 16 clock cycles instead of 4.

9.15   Eight flip-flops are needed.

9.17   Twenty-eight inputs/outputs are needed as shown.

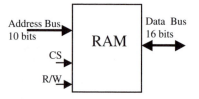

9.19

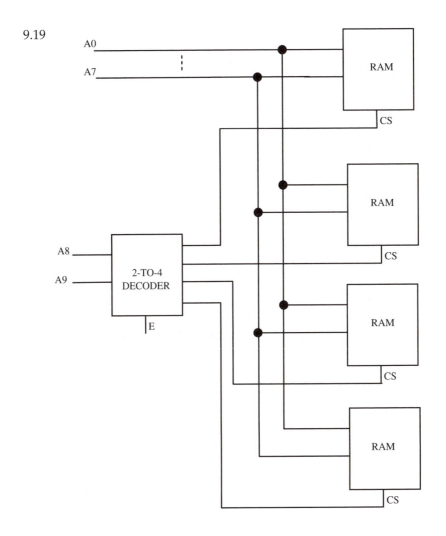

Chapter 10

10.1   LOD Z
      MUL X
      ADD Y
      SUB W
      ADD D
      STO X

10.3   12 memory references

10.5 (a)

3 bits	2 bits	11 bits
OPcode	Addressing Mode	Address Field

(b) 8192

10.7

4 bits	2 bits	2 bits	2 bits	12 bits	12 bits	12 bits
OPcode	3 Addressing Mode			3 Addressing Fields		

10.9 LW R_0, Z
      LW R_1, X
      MUL R_0, R_0, R_1
      LW R_1, Y
      ADD R_0, R_0, R_1
      LW R_1, W
      SUB R_0, R_0, R_1
      LW R_1, D
      ADD R_0, R_0, R_1
      ST R_0, X

10.11 Two types of instructions: arithmetic and load/store. Arithmetic 4 fields of sizes 4, 5, 5, and 5. Three fields for load/store with field widths of 4, 5, and 32 bits.

10.13 (a) LOD   X
          ADD   Y
          STO   X   #X = X + Y
          LOD   X
          SUB   Y
          STO   Y   #Y = X − Y
          LOD   X
          MUL   Y
          STO   W   #W = X * Y
          LOD   X
          DIV   Y
          STO   U   #U = X / Y
     (b) ADD   X, X, Y
          SUB   Y, X, Y
          MUL   W, X, Y
          DIV   U, X, Y

10.15   PUSH   X
         PUSH   Z
         ADD
         PUSH   W
         PUSH   D
         MUL
         SUB
         POP   X

10.17 Two types of instructions: arithmetic and push/pop.

Chapter 11

11.1

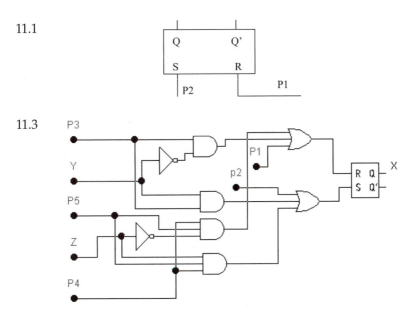

11.3

11.5 In the design we first find all RTL statements with V as the destination flip-flop. We then follow with a design procedure similar to problem 11.3.

11.7

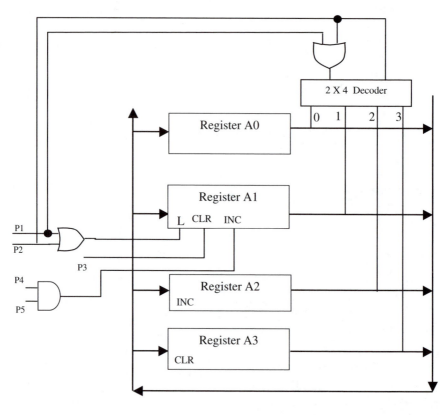

11.9   Bus connections are not shown.

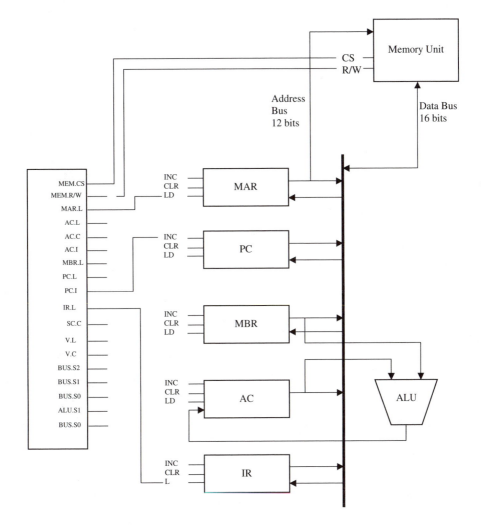

11.13 The connections can be made to the figure given in the solution of problem 11.9 with PC.LD connected to LD of the program counter.

```
11.15          LW     B
               CMP
               INC
               ADD    A
               SKZ
               JMP    ELSE
               SKP
               JMP    ELSE
       IF:     CLA
               ST     A
               JMP    EXIT
       ELSE:   LW     A
               ADD    B
               ST     A
       EXIT:   -
```

Index

A

Abstraction
    levels of, 112, 113
    register level, 114
AC, *see* Accumulator
Accumulator (AC), 393
Accumulator-based CPU, 403, 408
    design of, 441
    memory connection of, 429
Accumulator-based instruction, 398
Adder
    block diagram of, 176
    design of using PAL, 244
    4-bit, block diagram of, 183
    full, 177, 178
        design of, 178, 238
        programming table for, 239
        truth table, 178
    half, 177
    ripple carry, 177
    serial, 327
ADD instruction, 434
Addition, unsigned, 190
Address buses, 369
Addressing
    index, 408
    modes, 408
        common, 405
        memory content used with different,
            409
    register indirect, 409
Adjacency, use of, 134
Algebra, switching, definition of, 38
Alphanumeric information, 27
ALU, *see* Arithmetic logic unit
Analog data, 2
AND array(s), 234
    design of, 250
    manufacture of, 251
    PAL, 245
    programmable, 251
AND CMOS design, 80, 106
AND function, complement of, 101

AND gate(s), 98, 99, 323
    four input, 59
    levels of, 234
    output of, 58
    3-input, 237
AND instruction, 435
AND operation(s)
    associative property of, 58
    bit-wise, 205
AND-OR gates, 123
AND-OR-Invert design, 111
AND-OR-NOT design, 241
Answers to selected problems
    arithmetic logic circuits and
            programmable logic devices,
            454–456
    Boolean algebra, and gate and transistor
            design, 450–451
    Boolean functions, minimization of,
            452–454
    canonical forms and logical completeness,
            451–452
    design of simple AC-based, 469–472
    instruction set architecture, 467–469
    numbers in different bases, 449
    programmable logic devices, 457–460
    registers, counters, and memory
            elements, 465–467
    sequential circuits
        flip-flops and analysis of, 460–462
        state minimization and design of,
            463–464
Arithmetic instructions, 425
Arithmetic logic circuits and programmable
        logic devices, 175–211
    arithmetic circuits using radix
        complement, 190–198
        hardware implementation of signed
            arithmetic, 198
        hardware implementation of
            unsigned arithmetic, 192
        signed number arithmetic in radix
            complement, 193–197